Running QuickBooks® 2014

Premier Editions

Tom Barich
Certified QuickBooks ProAdvisor®
and
Kathy Ivens

CPA911 Publishing, LLC
Jacksonville, FL

Running QuickBooks 2014 Premier Editions

ISBN Number 10-digit: 1-932925-54-6 13-digit: 978-1-932925-54-8

Published by CPA911 Publishing, LLC November 2013

Copyright CPA911 Publishing, LLC

CPA911 is a Registered Trademark of CPA911 Publishing, LLC.

A Note to the Reader

From the Publisher

The QuickBooks Premier editions have features not available in QuickBooks Pro. This book provides explanations and instructions for the features of interest to users of the Premier editions of QuickBooks 2014.

This book does not contain basic instructions for all the features in QuickBooks; instead, it's assumed that you have some knowledge of the software. Covering all the features of the Premier editions, as well as all the information on using QuickBooks basic features, would require a book of over 1300 pages; it just can't be done in one volume.

It's important to remember that this book was published at the time QuickBooks 2014 Premier Editions were released. Intuit issues periodic updates to the software, and those updates may change the way features appear in the software when compared to the discussions in this book.

Acknowledgments

Cover Design: InfoDesign Services (www.infodesigning.com)

Production: InfoDesign Services (www.infodesigning.com)

Indexing: Transcription Conniption (www.transcriptionconniption.com)

The author owes a debt of gratitude to the folks at Intuit, Inc. for responding to questions and bug reports.

The author would also like to thank Brad and Mike at Real World Training for their invaluable assistance.

Tom Barich

Table of Contents

CHAPTER 1:

Getting Started

- Installation
- Chart of accounts
- Multiple currencies
- Opening balances
- Managing company files

In this chapter, we'll go over some of the tips and shortcuts for setting up QuickBooks and your company file. Like most of the discussions in this book, the contents of this chapter assume you're not new to QuickBooks, and you know the basics (a book covering every basic task in QuickBooks and also covering every Premier feature would be well over a thousand pages). If you're new to QuickBooks you'll find that the Help Files are quite good at explaining the basic functions for the software. If you're looking for a comprehensive QuickBooks guide check out our new title "Setting Up and Running QuickBooks 2014: The Accountant's Guide for Business Owners" (http://www.cpa911.com/qb2014_accountants_guide.php).

Installation Tips

If you're installing QuickBooks on a single computer, the installation wizard that starts when you insert the CD is very easy to follow. If you're installing a multi-user version on the network, the process is a little more complex. You can find detailed instructions for installing QuickBooks on a network on the Intuit support site (http://support.quickbooks.intuit.com/support/articles/INF12570).

Therefore, we are not going to provide installation instruction. However, in this section we offer some tips for installing QuickBooks the way IT professionals would. These suggestions make it easier to use, repair, and maintain the software.

Upgrading QuickBooks

If you're upgrading to QuickBooks 2014 from an earlier version, it's not a good idea to install an upgrade over an existing version of the software. Unfortunately, the QuickBooks installation information is somewhat confusing.

When you reach the Choose Your Installation Type screen, it says very clearly that using the Express method will replace the current version. For whatever reason, the information is wrong. If you select the Express method and continue with the installation, it will install Quick-Books 2014 into its own folder (C:\Program Files\Intuit\QuickBooks

2014). You'll see the installation folder on the Ready To Install screen, which is the last screen before the installation begins. If you really want to replace your existing version of QuickBooks (or change the installation location) you have to choose the Custom And Network Options method.

Whichever method you choose, install QuickBooks 2014 into its own folder. When everything is working properly you can remove the older version in the Add/Remove Programs applet (Programs and Features in Windows 7) of the Control Panel.

Opening an Existing Company File

If you replace your previous version with QuickBooks 2014 Premier (installing to the same folder that held your previous version), the first time you launch QuickBooks the software opens the company file that was open when you last closed QuickBooks in the previous version. Then the system begins the process of updating the file to Premier 2014.

If you already have a previous version of QuickBooks, and you installed QuickBooks 2014 in a new folder, select File | Open or Restore Company. Follow the prompts in the wizard, locate the copy of the file you put in the data file folder for 2014 (not the original file from the older version of QuickBooks), open it, and let QuickBooks begin updating it. This is a good way to install QuickBooks, because it lets you learn the new version without permanently updating your company file from the older version. If something goes wrong with QuickBooks 2014, you can continue to work in the older version until you resolve your QuickBooks 2014 problems.

Restoring a Backup File

If you have a backup of your company file that you want to restore in order to update it to QuickBooks 2014, copy that file to the folder you created to hold your QuickBooks 2014 company files.

Choose File | Open Or Restore Company. Select the Restore A Backup Copy option and click Next. Follow the prompts to select the copy of the backup file (in your new QuickBooks 2014 company file folder), and restore it. QuickBooks updates it to 2014 automatically.

Chart of Accounts

The most important step in your company setup is the creation of your chart of accounts. QuickBooks may have created some accounts for you during the initial setup of your company file, but you'll need additional accounts in order to keep books accurately. In this chapter, we'll discuss creating the chart of accounts, as well as the various ways in which you can manipulate the accounts you've created.

It's easier to configure your company file if you create the chart of accounts before you create the other lists you need in QuickBooks. Some of the lists you work with require you to link the list elements you create to accounts. For example, most Items are linked to income accounts.

Designing a Chart of Accounts

If you're designing your own chart of accounts, be sure to do so carefully, because you have to live with the results every time you use QuickBooks. Discuss the design with your accountant, who can help you devise a scheme that works for the types of transactions you have to enter, and the reports you need.

You have several decisions to make about the general format you'll use for your chart of accounts. You need to decide whether to use numbered accounts, and if so, how many digits to use for each account. You should also design a system for the use of subaccounts. Subaccounts make it possible to post transactions in a way that makes it easier to identify the specific categories you're tracking. In addition, you must create a protocol for account naming, and make sure everyone who works with the QuickBooks data files both understands the protocol and applies it.

Using Account Numbers

By default, QuickBooks does not assign numbers to accounts, and you should switch your QuickBooks configuration options to correct that oversight. A chart of accounts with numbers is easier to design, and easier to work with. Numbered accounts also have account names, of course, but you can categorize accounts by number, which makes the chart of accounts easier to work with.

The advantage of using numbers is that you can arrange each section of the chart of accounts by category and subcategory. Within each type of account QuickBooks displays your chart of accounts in numerical order (without numbers, QuickBooks displays each section of your chart of accounts in alphabetical order).

For example, if accounts of the type Expense are arranged numerically instead of alphabetically, you can list related expense accounts contiguously. This means you can export reports to Excel and insert subtotals for related categories, which makes it easier to analyze where you're spending your money.

You can also use subaccounts in a numbered chart of accounts to provide subtotals for expenses or income right on your QuickBooks reports, without the need to export the report to Excel in order to perform calculations.

Numbered accounts are useful in avoiding data entry errors when using a bank account. It's best if your main (most commonly used) bank account is at the top of the drop-down list. If your money market account is named for the bank (AlfaSavings), or even if you name the account Money Market, an alphabetic listing puts that account at the top of the bank account list when your operating account is named OperatingAccount, or it's named for the bank, which might be RiversideBank.

Our experience with clients shows that this became extremely important when companies changed banks. Suppose the people who enter data in your company file have gotten used to selecting the second account on the list (because that's where your general operating account sits in alphabetic order). If your new account is now the third account on a drop-down list, transactions are going to be posted to the wrong account.

By the time everyone notices, figures out, and gets used to, the new bank list, you'll have a lot of research to do, followed by a lot of journal entries. You'll discover this when you try to reconcile your bank accounts. If you use numbered accounts, you can make sure the bank accounts always appear in the most convenient order. Even if your old bank was number

10000, and you want your new bank to use that number, it's a simple task to edit the original bank number to 14990 (moving it to the bottom of the list) and give the new bank the 10000 number to keep it at the top of the list.

Enabling Account Numbers

To switch to a number format for your accounts, you have to change the QuickBooks preferences as follows:

1. Choose Edit | Preferences from the menu bar to open the Preferences dialog.
2. Select the Accounting icon in the left pane.
3. Click the Company Preferences tab.
4. Select the Use Account Numbers check box.

All the accounts included in the chart of accounts you selected during company file setup are automatically switched to numbered accounts. These numbers are built in by QuickBooks and you can change them to match the order of accounts you prefer (see "Editing Accounts" later in this chapter).

When you select the option to use account numbers, the option Show Lowest Subaccount Only becomes accessible (it's grayed out if you haven't opted for account numbers). This option tells QuickBooks to display only the subaccount on transaction windows instead of both the parent account and the subaccount, making it easier to find the account you need in the narrow field of a drop-down list. (Subaccounts are discussed later in this chapter in the section "Using Subaccounts.")

QuickBooks does not automatically number accounts you added manually, so you must edit those accounts to add a number to each account record. If some accounts lack numbers, when you select Show Lowest Subaccount Only, QuickBooks displays an error message that you cannot enable this option until all your accounts have numbers assigned. After you've added account numbers to all accounts, you can return to this Preferences dialog and enable the option.

Designing an Account Number Scheme

After you've converted your chart of accounts to numbered accounts, you must use the numbers intelligently as you create or edit accounts. It's best to assign ranges of numbers to account types.

You should check with your accountant before finalizing the way you use the numbers, but the example presented here is a common approach. This scheme uses five-digit numbers, because that's the default in QuickBooks 2014, and the starting digit represents the beginning of a range:

ProAdvisor NOTE: You can have as many as seven numbers (plus the account name) for each account.

- 1xxxx Assets
- 2xxxx Liabilities
- 3xxxx Equity
- 4xxxx Income
- 5xxxx Expenses (of a specific type)
- 6xxxx Expenses (of a specific type)
- 7xxxx Expenses (of a specific type)
- 8xxxx Expenses (of a specific type)
- 9xxxx Other Income and Expenses

You can, if you wish, have a variety of expense types and reserve the starting number for specific types. Many companies, for example, use 5xxxx for sales expenses (they even separate the payroll postings between the sales people and the rest of the employees), then use 60000 through 79999 for general operating expenses, and 8xxxx for other specific expenses that should appear together in reports (such as taxes).

Some companies that track inventory use 5xxxx for Cost of Goods Sold and begin grouping expenses with 6xxxx. Other inventory-based companies start the Cost of Goods Sold accounts in the 45xxx range (since most companies don't have a large number of income accounts, the number range 40000 to 44999 is sufficient for income).

Some companies use one range of expense accounts, such as 70000 through 79999 for expenses that fall into the "overhead" category. This is useful if you want to track overhead expenses so you can apportion them to appropriate classes or jobs.

Also, think about the breakdown of assets. You might use 10000 through 10999 for cash accounts and 11000 through 11999 for receivables and other current assets, then use 12000 through 12999 for tracking fixed assets such as equipment, furniture, and so on.

Follow the same pattern for liabilities, starting with current liabilities and moving to long term. It's also a good idea to keep all the payroll withholding liabilities together.

Usually, as you create new accounts, you should increase the previous account number by 10, so that if your first bank account is 10000, the next bank account is 10010, and so on. These intervals give you room to create additional accounts that belong in the same general area of your chart of accounts.

Accounts Sort Order

You have to create a numbering scheme that conforms to the QuickBooks account types because QuickBooks sorts your chart of accounts by account type (and uses your account numbers within each account type). If you have contiguous numbers that vary by account type, your reports won't be in the order you expect. QuickBooks uses the following sort order for the chart of accounts:

- Assets:
    - Bank
    - Accounts Receivable
    - Other Current Asset
    - Fixed Asset
    - Other Asset

- Liabilities
  - Accounts Payable
  - Credit Card
  - Other Current Liability
  - Long-Term Liability

- Equity

- Income

- Cost Of Goods Sold

- Expense

- Other Income

- Other Expense

Non-Posting Accounts

Non-posting accounts don't post financial amounts to the general ledger. They are created automatically by QuickBooks when you enable features that use those account types, such as Estimates, Purchase Orders, Sales Orders, etc. You can open the account register of non-posting accounts to see the transactions that fall into the appropriate account category, but you don't have to worry about any amounts impacting your financials (which means they don't affect your tax returns).

Displaying Accounts Alphabetically in Reports

As convenient as it is for you (and your accountant) to have numbered accounts so you can track your finances by category and subcategory, suppose you have to submit financial reports to a bank because that's part of the requirements of your line of credit? Your bankers have certain financial categories they look at first, and it's easier for them if your accounts, especially your expenses, are in alphabetical order.

To produce reports without account numbers, putting each account type list back into alphabetical order, turn off the account number feature by deselecting the option in the Preferences dialog. Print the reports, and then turn the feature on again to restore the numbered order.

Account Naming Protocols

You need to devise protocols for naming accounts, whether you plan to use numbered accounts, or only use account names. When you're posting transactions to the general ledger, the only way to know which account should be used for posting is to have easy-to-understand account names.

Your protocol must be clear so that when everyone follows the rules, the account naming convention is consistent. This is important because without rules it's common to have multiple accounts for the same use. For example, we frequently find expense accounts named Telephone, Tele, and Tel in client systems, and all of those accounts have balances. Users "guess" at account names, and if they don't find the account the way they would have entered the name, they invent a new account (using a name that seems logical to them). Avoid all of those errors by establishing protocols about creating account names, and then make sure everyone searches the account list before applying a transaction.

Here are a few suggested protocols—you can amend them to fit your own situation, or invent different protocols that meet your comfort level. The important thing is to make sure you have absolute rules so you can achieve consistency.

- Avoid apostrophes
- Set the number of characters for abbreviations. For example, if you permit four characters, telephone is abbreviated "tele", a three-character rule produces "tel".
- Decide whether to use the ampersand (&) or a hyphen. For example, is it "Repairs & Maintenance" or "Repairs - Maintenance"? Do you want spaces before and after the ampersand or hyphen?

Creating Accounts

After you've done your homework, made your decisions, designed your protocols, and checked with your accountant, you're ready to create accounts.

Start by pressing Ctrl-A to open the Chart of Accounts list. Then press Ctrl-N (the "N" is for "New") to open the Choose Account Type dialog (see Figure 1-1).

Figure 1-1: Creating an account starts by selecting the type of account.

Select the type of account you want to create. The major (most used) account types are listed on the dialog. Accounts that are less frequently created by users are listed in the drop-down list you can view when you select Other Account Types.

After you select the account type, click Continue to open the Add New Account dialog. The dialog for creating a new account changes its appearance depending on the account type you select, because each account type contains particular fields to hold relevant information. Figure 1-2 shows the New Account dialog for an expense account.

Some accounts have a field labeled Tax Line. The Tax Line field is useful if you're planning to prepare your own business tax return using TurboTax® or if your accountant prepares your taxes using Intuit tax software. Many of the tax lines are filled in automatically when you select your business entity type (Sole Proprietor, LLC, and so on).

ProAdvisor NOTE: *If you choose Other/None as your business entity when you create a new company file, the Tax-Line Mapping field does not appear in the account records. You can enable it by opening the Company Information dialog (Company | My Company | Edit), clicking Report Information, and then making a selection from the Income Tax Form Used field. Using this method, you'll have to manually enter all Tax-Line Mapping information as none is automatically configured.*

Figure 1-2: The only required entries for a new account are a number (if you're using numbers) and a name.

As you finish entering each account, click Save & New to move to another blank Add New Account dialog. By default, QuickBooks uses the same account type as the account you just created, but you can change the account type by selecting another type from the drop-down list at the top of the dialog.

Select Accounts from Examples

If you created your company file in QuickBooks 2014 or updated a company file created in QuickBooks 2008 or later, some account types display a button labeled Select From Examples in the Add New Account dialog.

Clicking the button produces a list of accounts that QuickBooks thinks you might want to consider adding to your chart of accounts. As you can see in Figure 1-3, the list of suggested accounts matches the account type you're creating.

ACCOUNT NAME	DESCRIPTION
Business Licenses and Permits	Business licenses, permits, and other business-related fees
Cash Drawer Payouts	Small expenses paid out in cash from the cash drawer
Cash Over and Short	Cash overages and shortages from operations
Charitable Contributions	Contributions to qualifying charitable organizations
Dues and Subscriptions	Subscriptions and membership dues for civic, service, professional...

Example Accounts: Expense Account

Select an account to add.

You can change the account description later to suit your own business needs.

OK   Cancel

Figure 1-3: QuickBooks suggests accounts.

The accounts that are suggested are those accounts that were available for the industry you selected when you created your company file but were not selected for inclusion in your chart of accounts for one of the following reasons:

- If you used the EasyStep Interview to create your company file, you had an opportunity to select accounts that were not already selected or to deselect accounts that QuickBooks had selected by default. Accounts that remained unselected appear in the Example Accounts list.

- If, during the EasyStep Interview, you selected accounts for which QuickBooks suggests subaccounts, the account appears in the list but is grayed out (because it was selected and does not need to be added to your chart of accounts). Only the subaccounts are listed.

- If you skipped the EasyStep Interview, QuickBooks installed the accounts that were selected by default for the industry you chose during company file setup. Accounts that were not installed at that time appear in the Select From Examples list.

If you add an account to your chart of accounts from this list, that account is removed from the suggested accounts list. If you delete the account from your chart of accounts, it is put back on the suggested accounts list.

If you did not select an industry during company file setup (instead, selected Other/None), the Select From Examples button does not appear.

The following account types do *not* display Select From Examples:

- Account Receivable
- Accounts Payable
- Credit Card
- Long Term Liability
- Equity

When you're finished entering accounts, click Save & Close, and then close the Chart of Accounts list.

Automatically Created Accounts

QuickBooks has some "special" accounts that the software automatically creates. Some of these are added when you create a company file. Others are added when you enable a feature in one of the Preferences dialogs, or when you open a transaction window for a feature you've enabled in one of the Preferences dialogs. Most of these special accounts have a special marker within the programming code that QuickBooks uses to indicate the fact that the account has a special use.

In the following sections we'll explain these special accounts, and offer solutions for the special accounts that might cause problems if you created similar accounts manually.

ProAdvisor TIP: The special marker is visible when you export your chart of accounts to an .IIF file, and you can also create these special accounts, including the data for the hidden marker, when you prepare a chart of accounts in an .IIF file and then import the chart of accounts into a company file. See Appendix B for more information about working with .IIF files.

Special Accounts in All Company Files

The following special accounts are always automatically created when you create a company file.

- Opening Balance Equity
- Retained Earnings

Both of these accounts are equity account types, and aren't accounts you would normally create manually.

In addition, QuickBooks automatically creates the following accounts for tracking payroll (even if you don't enable payroll):

- Payroll Liabilities
- Payroll Expenses

You cannot delete these payroll accounts, but you can hide them (make them inactive) if you don't need them.

Feature Based Special Accounts

The following special accounts are added when you enable the attendant feature in the Preferences dialog:

- Estimates (a non-posting account) when you enable estimates in the Jobs & Estimates Preferences dialog.
- Sales Tax Payable (Other Current Liability account type) when you enable Sales Tax in the Sales Tax Preferences.

ProAdvisor CAUTION: *Don't create a sales tax liability account when you're creating your chart of accounts, because you have no way to link that account to transactions. QuickBooks only uses its own sales tax account, which it creates when you enable the sales tax feature.*

The following accounts are added the first time you open a transaction window, after you enable the attendant feature:

- Sales Orders (Non-Posting account type), which is added the first time you open the Create Sales Orders transaction window.

- Undeposited Funds (Other Current Asset account type), which is added when you open either the Receive Payments transaction window or the Enter Sales Receipts transaction window.

- Purchase Orders (Non-Posting account type), which is added when you open the Create Purchase Orders transaction window.

These are not accounts you'd normally create when you're creating your chart of accounts, so you don't have to worry about duplicates or conflicts with the accounts QuickBooks creates automatically.

The following accounts are added the first time you open a transaction window if you did not previously create the account:

- Accounts Receivable (Accounts Receivable account type), which is added when you open the Create Invoices transaction window, unless you created the account manually.

- Accounts Payable (Accounts Payable account type), which is added when you open the Enter Bills transaction window, unless you created the account manually.

You don't have to fill in the transaction; merely opening the Invoice or Enter Bills window creates the account.

When you open any of the transaction windows mentioned in this list, QuickBooks checks to see if the appropriate account exists in the chart of accounts. If you already created the account, QuickBooks does not add the account automatically.

Accounts Receivable and Accounts Payable do not have special hidden markers, because they're earmarked as unique accounts by their account type. Accounts Receivable is an account type "Accounts Receivable" in QuickBooks, even though it's technically a current asset in standard accounting terms. Accounts Payable is an account type "Accounts Payable" in Quick-Books, even though it's technically a current liability in standard accounting terms.

QuickBooks created these account types to make sure the software links transactions properly. As long as you created these account types, no matter what account name you assigned the accounts, QuickBooks uses the accounts appropriately.

One advantage of this approach is the ability to have multiple A/R and A/P accounts. For example, some professional service businesses prefer to track retainer A/R separately from A/R for hourly fees. Many nonprofit organizations have one A/R account for grants and another for individual pledges. Some companies like to separate A/P for inventory products from A/P for other expenses.

> ***ProAdvisor NOTE***: *If you enable multiple currencies, QuickBooks creates an A/R and A/P account for each currency as soon as you use the currency in a transaction. See the section, "Multiple Currencies" later in this chapter.*

Using Multiple A/R and A/P Accounts

If you create multiple A/R or A/P accounts, you must be careful about posting transactions to the appropriate account. When you create invoices and enter bills, you must remember to select the appropriate A/R or A/P account from the drop-down list at the top of the transaction window.

Each A/R account keeps its own set of invoice/credit memo numbers. When you enter the first invoice number in a transaction linked to one A/R account, all invoices linked to that A/R account will use the next available number.

For the second A/R account, start the invoice numbers with a totally different number scheme, so that customer and aging reports let you determine the A/R link easily. For instance, if you start numbering invoices for one A/R account at 101, start numbering invoices in the other A/R account at 5001.

When you receive payments from customers, you must remember to select the appropriate A/R account at the top of the Receive Payments window. The only invoices that appear when you select a customer are those linked to the selected A/R account.

Similarly, when you pay bills the A/P account selected at the top of the Pay Bills transaction window determines the bills that display.

Inventory Special Accounts

If you enable inventory and purchase orders in the Items & Inventory Preferences dialog, no accounts are added to your chart of accounts. Instead, QuickBooks waits until you create an inventory item to install inventory accounts.

As soon as you open a New Item dialog and select Inventory Part as the item type, QuickBooks automatically creates the following accounts:

- Inventory Asset (Other Current Asset account type)
- Cost of Goods Sold (Cost of Goods Sold account type)

The accounts are created before you fill in any data for the new inventory item, and are automatically entered as the default posting accounts.

Don't Create Your Own Inventory Accounts

If you create your own accounts for Inventory (Other Current Asset type) and Cost of Goods Sold (Cost of Goods Sold types), you'll have duplicate accounts.

Every time you create an inventory part, QuickBooks automatically uses its own accounts as the default accounts for the Inventory Asset account and the COGS account. If you delete the default accounts (which you can do before they have posted transactions) QuickBooks simply recreates them and uses them as the default accounts the next time you create an inventory item.

If you haven't used the accounts you created yourself, delete them. If the manually created accounts have balances (you entered transactions), they can't be deleted, and some users decide they'll continue to use their own accounts by replacing the QuickBooks special accounts when they create inventory items. This is risky because you'll often forget to change the account setup.

Some users make the QuickBooks special inventory accounts inactive, because inactive accounts are hidden in drop-down lists as you use dialogs and transaction windows. Not these inventory accounts! Inactive, hidden, it doesn't matter; the accounts are automatically made the default accounts when you create an inventory part item. (Hiding accounts by making them inactive, and using hidden accounts, are topics discussed later in this chapter.)

It's almost impossible to win this tug-of-war; somebody will eventually link an inventory item to the default QuickBooks special inventory accounts and throw your system out of whack.

If you have your own manual inventory accounts, and they contain postings, merge them into the QuickBooks accounts. Then you can remove the asterisk from the account name and change the account number of the QuickBooks accounts to match your own numbering system. Merging accounts is covered later in this chapter.

Never Enter Opening Account Balances

Some account types have a field for an opening balance. Do *not* enter a balance while you're creating new accounts. These opening balance fields are not part of standard accounting data entry; instead, they're a QuickBooks invention that makes no sense. Your accountant will have to spend a lot of time dealing with the postings that QuickBooks uses to record these opening balances. That time is billable.

The best way to put the account balances into the system is to enter historical transactions and historical totals via a journal entry (see the section "Opening Trial Balance" later in this chapter to learn how to enter your historical information and create opening balances).

The account types that offer an opening balance field (remember, this is the field to ignore and avoid) are the following:

- Asset accounts except Accounts Receivable
- Liability accounts except Accounts Payable
- Equity accounts

ProAdvisor NOTE*: Customers, Vendors, and Inventory Items also have an Opening Balance field available. Never use them. Instead, use transactions to populate the historical data.*

Using Subaccounts

Subaccounts provide a way to post transactions more precisely, because you can pinpoint a subcategory. For example, if you create an expense account for insurance expenses, you may want to have subaccounts for vehicle insurance, liability insurance, equipment insurance, and so on.

When you have subaccounts in your chart of accounts, post transactions ***only to the subaccounts, never to the parent account***. When you create reports, QuickBooks displays the individual totals for the subaccounts, along with the grand total for the parent account.

To create a subaccount, you must first create the parent account. If you're using numbered accounts, when you set up your main (parent) accounts, be sure to leave enough open numbers to be able to fit in all the subaccounts you'll need. If necessary, use more than five digits in your numbering scheme to make sure you have a logical hierarchy for your account structure.

When you view the chart of accounts, subaccounts appear under their parent accounts, and they're indented. When you view a subaccount in the drop-down list of the Account field in a transaction window, it appears with a colon between the parent account and the subaccount.

Because many of the fields in transaction windows are small, you may not be able to see the subaccount names without scrolling through the field. This can be annoying, and it's much easier to work if only the subaccount to which you post transactions is displayed.

That annoyance is cured by enabling the preference Show Lowest Subaccount Only, discussed earlier in this chapter. When you enable that option, you see only the last part of the subaccount name in the transaction window, making it much easier to select the account you need.

Using Subaccounts for Easier Tax Preparation

One clever way to design your parent accounts and subaccounts is to design your chart of accounts around your tax return. This saves your accountant time, and that means you save money.

For example, the tax return you use may have a line into which you enter the total for office expenses. However, for the purpose of analyzing where you spend your money, you prefer to separate office expenses into multiple accounts, such as Computer Supplies, Paper & Other Consumables, and so on. Office Supplies becomes the parent account, and any specific subcategories you care about become the subaccounts.

In fact, to save even more money on accounting services, arrange the order of your income and expense accounts and subaccounts in the order in which they appear on your tax return.

Editing Accounts

If you need to make changes to an account, open the Chart of Accounts window, click the account's listing to select it, and press Ctrl-E. The Edit Account dialog appears, which looks very much like the account dialog you filled out when you created the account.

Adding and Changing Account Numbers

One of the most common reasons to edit an account is to add or change account numbers for existing accounts. After you enable the account number feature, QuickBooks automatically attaches numbers to any existing accounts that came from one of its own predefined chart of accounts, but fails to attach numbers to any accounts you created manually. Therefore, you must add the missing numbers. In addition, if you don't like the numbering scheme that QuickBooks used, you can change the account numbers.

If you want to make wholesale changes in the numbering system QuickBooks used, it's easier to export the chart of accounts to Excel, make your changes with the help of the automated tools in Excel, and then import the changed chart of accounts into your company file, either as an IIF file or as an Excel file. This works as long as you make no changes to anything except the account numbers, because QuickBooks will use the account name to accept the new data properly (they won't appear to be duplicates). You can also use the Add/Edit Multiple List Entries feature, although the automated tools in Excel that let you increment numbers automatically aren't available in the Add/Edit Multiple List Entries window.

Be sure to back up your company file before trying this, in case something goes awry. To learn how to export/import the chart of accounts, see Appendix A (importing Excel files), and Appendix B (importing IIF files).

Editing Optional Account Fields

You can edit any field in the account, except the Account Type, which is limited to certain changes (covered next). For example, you may want to add, remove, or change a description. For bank accounts, you might decide to put the bank account number in the account record, or select the option to have QuickBooks remind you to order checks when you've used a specific check number.

If you want to change the account type, the following restrictions apply:

- You cannot change A/R or A/P accounts to other account types
- You cannot change other account types to be A/R or A/P accounts
- You cannot change the account type of accounts that QuickBooks creates automatically (such as Undeposited Funds).
- You cannot change the account type of an account that has subaccounts. You must make the subaccounts parent accounts (it's easiest to drag them to the left in the Chart of Accounts list window). Change the account type of each account, and then create the subaccounts again (drag them to the right).

Deleting Accounts

To delete an account, select its listing in the Chart of Accounts window, and press Ctrl-D. QuickBooks displays a confirmation message, asking if you're sure you want to delete the account. Click OK to delete the account.

Some accounts cannot be deleted, and after you click OK, QuickBooks displays an error message telling you why you cannot complete the action. Any of the following conditions prevent you from deleting an account:

- The account is linked to an item
- The account has been used in a transaction
- The account has subaccounts

If the problem is a link to an item, find the item that uses this account for posting transactions, and change the posting account. Check all items, because it may be that multiple items are linked to the account. (When you open the Item List window, you can view the posting accounts in the Account column.)

If the problem is that the account has been used in a transaction, you won't be able to delete the account. QuickBooks means this literally, and the fact that the account has a zero balance doesn't make it eligible for deletion. Some users have painstakingly created journal entries to move every transaction out of an account they want to delete, posting the amounts to other accounts. It doesn't work.

If the problem is subaccounts, you must first delete all the subaccounts. If any of the subaccounts fall into the restrictions list (usually they have transactions posted), you can make them parent accounts in order to delete the original parent account. To turn a subaccount into a parent account, either drag its listing to the left in the Chart of Accounts window, or edit the account to remove the 'Subaccount Of' check mark.

An account that was created automatically by QuickBooks can be deleted (as long as it doesn't fall under the restrictions). QuickBooks will not alert you, but if you should use the feature later, it will recreate the account. For example, if QuickBooks created an account for Purchase Orders, you can delete it if you haven't yet created a Purchase Order (that is, you opened a PO transaction form to create the account automatically, but you didn't create and save a transaction). However, the next time you open the PO transaction window, QuickBooks automatically recreates the account.

If you're trying to delete an account because you don't want anyone to post to it, but QuickBooks won't delete the account, you can hide the account by making it inactive. See the next section "Hiding Accounts".

If you're trying to delete an account because transactions were posted to it erroneously, you can merge the account with the account that should have received the postings. See the section "Merging Accounts".

Hiding Accounts

If you don't want anyone to post to an account but you don't want to delete the account (or QuickBooks won't let you delete the account), you can make the account inactive. In the Chart of Accounts window, right-click the account's listing and choose Make Account Inactive from the shortcut menu.

Inactive accounts don't appear in the account drop-down list when you're filling out a transaction window, and therefore can't be selected for posting. By default, they also don't appear in the Chart of Accounts window, which can be confusing. For example, you may have money market bank accounts that you don't want anyone to use during transaction postings. However, if you don't see the account in the Chart of Accounts list window, you won't know its current balance. In fact, you might forget it exists.

To view all your accounts in the Chart of Accounts window, including inactive accounts, select the option Include Inactive at the bottom of the window. A new column appears on the left side of the window with a column heading that's a large black X. Inactive accounts display a large black X in this column. To make an inactive account active, click the black X (it's a toggle).

ProAdvisor TIP: *If the Include Inactive option is grayed out, there are no inactive accounts.*

Using a Hidden Account in Transactions

Sometimes, the bookkeeper or owner wants to prevent other users from posting transactions to a certain account. For example, it's not unusual for equity accounts (such as Draw) to be misused, and it's rather common to see inappropriate postings to Miscellaneous Expenses. It's better if only people with some expertise post transactions to these account types.

You can hide an account (make it inactive), and still use it. When you're entering data in a transaction window, don't use the drop-down list in the Account field (because of course, the account won't appear). Instead, enter the account name or number manually.

QuickBooks displays a message asking if you want to use the account just once, or reactivate the account. Click the option to use the account just once. (You can use the account "just once" as many times as you want to.)

Merging Accounts

Sometimes you have two accounts that should be one. For instance, you may be splitting postings inappropriately, and your accountant suggests that one account would be better. Perhaps there's no reason to post some revenue for consulting work to an account named Income-Consulting, and other revenue to an account named Income-Fees.

Often, you may find that accidentally, two accounts were created for the same category. As discussed earlier in this chapter, it's not uncommon to encounter accounts named Telephone and Tele, with transactions posted to both accounts. Those accounts badly need merging. Accounts must meet the following criteria in order to merge them:

- The accounts must be of the same type
- The accounts cannot have subaccounts
- The accounts must be at the same level (parent or subaccount of the same parent account)

If the accounts aren't at the same level, move one of the accounts to the same level as the other account. After you merge the accounts, you can move the surviving account to a different level. If one or both of the accounts has subaccounts you'll have to delete them or make them parent accounts.

Take the following steps to merge two accounts:

1. Open the Chart of Accounts window.
2. Select (highlight) the account that has the name you *do not* want to use anymore.
3. Press Ctrl-E to open the Edit Account dialog.
4. Change the account name (or number) to precisely match that of the account you want to keep.
5. Click OK.

QuickBooks displays a message telling you that the account number/ name you've entered already exists for another account, and asks if you want to merge the accounts. Click Yes to confirm that you want to merge the two accounts. All the existing transactions from both accounts are merged into the account you chose to keep.

If you're doing some serious housekeeping on your company file, and you find three (or perhaps more) accounts that should be merged into a single account, merge the first two, then merge the surviving account with the third account.

Importing the Chart of Accounts

Importing a chart of accounts is an efficient way to get exactly the chart of accounts you need without going through all the work of entering accounts one at a time. Of course, to import a chart of accounts, you have to have an import file. You can import data into QuickBooks from either of these source file types:

- A spreadsheet with a file extension .xls, xlsx, or .csv (covered in Appendix A).
- A tab-delimited text file, with a file extension .iif (covered in Appendix B).

If you're an accountant, creating import files that you can take to clients provides a valuable service for your clients, and also makes your own work easier—the chart of accounts is configured properly for your tax, planning, and analysis services. Many accountants create import file templates to create a customized chart of accounts for each QuickBooks client.

Multiple Currencies

QuickBooks supports multiple currencies, so if you do business with customers or vendors in other countries you can create transactions in their currencies within QuickBooks, instead of maintaining exchange rate information outside of QuickBooks.

ProAdvisor TIP: *Since you can't change your mind after you turn on multiple currencies, it's a good idea to make a backup of your company file before enabling the option. When you create the backup, change the name of the file from the usual <CompanyFileName>.QBB to <CompanyFileName>-BeforeMulticurrency.QBB. It's also a good idea to copy this backup file to a CD for safekeeping.*

To enable the multicurrency feature, choose Edit | Preferences and click the Multiple Currencies category icon in the left pane. In the Company Preferences tab, select Yes I Use More Than One Currency. When you select this option, QuickBooks displays a message warning you that you cannot undo this action, and suggests you create a backup of your company file before enabling the feature.

After you enable the multiple currency feature and specify your own currency (usually US Dollar), click OK. QuickBooks closes your company file and re-opens it with this feature enabled.

Select the Currencies You Need

QuickBooks provides a long list of currencies you can use, but by default only the commonly used currencies are active (only active currencies appear in the drop-down list when you're assigning a currency to a customer or vendor).

To change the list of active currencies to meet your needs, choose Company | Manage Currency | Currency List to open the Currency List window. If the list displays only active currencies (a short list), select the check box labeled Include Inactive to see the entire list.

To activate an inactive currency, click the X in the left column to remove the X; to make an active currency inactive, click in the left column to place an X in the column.

Tracking Exchange Rates

QuickBooks tracks the exchange rates between foreign currencies and United States Dollars (USD). To update the exchange rate for all your active currencies, make sure you have an active internet connection. Then choose Company | Manage Currency | Download Latest Exchange Rates.

QuickBooks travels to the Internet to get the current rates (you don't see an Internet page; all of this is done in the background). When your active currencies have been updated, QuickBooks displays a success message. The updated exchange rates are displayed in the Currency List.

Linking Customers and Vendors to Currencies

You need to identify the currency of every customer and vendor in your company file. QuickBooks automatically assigns your home currency (usually USD) to all customers and vendors, so you only need to change those that do business in a different currency.

Changing Currency for Existing Customers and Vendors

You can only change the currency specification for existing customers and vendors who have no transactions (and it's unlikely you have many customers or vendors with that status).

It doesn't matter whether the current open balance is 0.00; the existence of any historical transaction prevents you from changing the currency (the Currency field in the customer record is grayed out). For those customers and vendors, you must create a new entity with the new currency (discussed next).

ProAdvisor NOTE: You cannot merge customers or vendors that have different currencies.

To edit the currency of an existing customer or vendor that has no existing transactions, open the appropriate Center, select the customer/vendor, and click the Edit icon (a pencil nub) in the right pane. Select the currency from the drop-down list in the Currency field, and click OK.

Creating Duplicate Customers and Vendors for Multicurrency

To duplicate a customer or vendor that has transactions with a foreign currency specification, create a new entity using the following guidelines:

In the Name field, use the same name as the existing entity, but add text to make the name unique. It's best to add text after the name, so the customer/vendor appears in the right place in drop-down fields in transaction windows.

One way to add text to the existing name is to add the 3-character abbreviation for the customer's currency to create a unique name, such as changing the name Bizcom to Bizcom-EUR (if that company uses the Euro).

ProAdvisor NOTE: *The text in the Name field doesn't appear on transaction documents; instead, QuickBooks uses the data in the Company Name and Address fields (and, for Vendors, there's even a field labeled "Print Name On Check As").*

Managing Currency in Existing Open Transactions

When you create new customers and vendors, you have to manage existing open transactions using the original customer or vendor. You cannot use the new entity to accept payments or create bill payments linked to the original entity.

When the open balance for the original entity becomes zero, you can make the original customer or vendor inactive so the listing doesn't appear in drop-down lists in transaction windows. Use the new (duplicate) entity for all new transactions.

Assigning Currency to New Customers and Vendors

When you create new customers and vendors who do business in another currency, the basic steps are the same as creating any new customer or vendor in QuickBooks. The only difference is the existence of a Currency Field in the New Customer or New Vendor dialog.

By default, QuickBooks inserts US Dollar in the Currency field, but you can choose another currency from the drop-down list (which displays only those currencies you've marked Active).

ProAdvisor NOTE: *If you select a currency other than USD, the Opening Balance field is inaccessible, which is a good thing since you should never use that field when setting up a new customer or vendor.*

Accounts for Multicurrency Transactions

As you create customers and vendors with other currencies QuickBooks adds accounts to your chart of accounts:

- An Accounts Receivable account for each currency
- An Accounts Payable account for each currency

A third new, Other Expense account is created the first time you create a home currency adjustment (Company | Manage Currency | Home Currency Adjustment). The new account is called Exchange Gain Or Loss.

Creating Transactions in Other Currencies

When you open a sales or payment transaction window, QuickBooks automatically takes care of the currency issues by adding fields to the transaction window.

If the customer or vendor currency is USD, you won't see much difference between the transaction window for multicurrency, and the same transaction window before you enabled multicurrency. The only real difference is that the text "USD" appears for "Total" amounts.

If the customer or vendor is configured for another currency, the transaction window changes to provide the information you need, as follows:

- The A/R or A/P account is specific to the currency.
- The amounts in the line items are displayed in the customer/vendor currency.
- There are two totals: one for the transaction currency and one for USD.
- The Exchange Rate field displays the exchange rate used when this transaction was created.

The printed versions of transactions that are sent to customers (invoices, credits, and so on) and vendors (checks) do not display any fields or data related to USD; those fields only appear on the screen for your convenience.

ProAdvisor TIP: *If you use multiple currencies and take advantage of online banking, be sure to set your downloaded transactions viewing mode to Classic Mode (Edit | Preferences | Checking | Company Preferences). This way you'll be able to enter transactions for payees using all currencies and exchange rates. The Express Mode only shows payees using the US Dollar.*

Creating Reports on Multicurrency Transactions

By default, reports on customer and vendor transactions (such as Aging, Sales, Purchases, and other similar reports) are displayed in your home currency (USD). However, you can modify the reports so they display the appropriate currencies.

- For Summary reports, click Customize Report and in the section labeled Display Amounts In, select The Transaction Currency.
- For Detail reports, click Customize Report and select Foreign Amount in the Columns list. You may also want to add the Currency column.

Memorize these reports, using a name that reflects the contents (e.g. A/R Aging with Transaction Currency) so you don't have to customize them each time you create them.

Opening Trial Balance

QuickBooks does not have a feature called "Enter Opening Trial Balance," but since every account register is sorted by date, when you begin entering transactions in QuickBooks, you can follow these rules:

- Enter current transactions using dates on or after first day of your current fiscal year.
- Enter historical transactions using any date prior to the first day of your current fiscal year.

Understanding the Opening Trial Balance

The goal you seek when you enter historical transactions is to build an opening trial balance for the first day of your current fiscal year. A trial balance is a list of all your accounts and their current balances.

However, the report accountants refer to as the *Opening Trial Balance* is a bit different from the trial balance reports you create normally. The opening trial balance is the balance of the general ledger accounts on the first day of the fiscal year (usually the same as the calendar year for small businesses).

On the first day of a fiscal year, you do not have any income or expenses. The previous year's income and expenses have been calculated as a net number by subtracting the total expenses from the total income.

Let's hope the result is a positive number so you have a net profit (a negative number means a loss).

That net number is posted to an equity account (called Retained Earnings), and the income and expense accounts all show zero balances, waiting for your first sales and expense transactions of the year. Therefore, the opening trial balance only has balances for asset, liability, and equity accounts (generally referred to as *balance sheet accounts*).

To get to this point, you need to enter historical information, and QuickBooks will automatically create the opening trial balance accurately for the first day of the current year.

Entering Historical Transactions

To enter historical transactions, follow these guidelines:

- Enter open (unpaid) customer and vendor transactions using QuickBooks transaction windows.

- Use journal entries to record closed sales and expenses totals that contribute to last year's retained earnings figures.

- Use journal entries to record running balance sheet totals for assets, liabilities, and equity (but not Accounts Receivable or Accounts Payable; those are built by entering the open transactions).

Confer with your accountant to check your work and develop your final opening balances, which often requires adjusting the equity accounts (which are affected by the historical transactions you enter) to match your final retained earnings as of last year.

In this section, we're assuming the following:

- You're setting up your QuickBooks company file to track transactions from the first day of your fiscal year, even if you started using QuickBooks later in the year. This gives you all the information you need to create final reports on your business year, making it much easier to file your tax returns.

- You've entered your lists—customers, vendors, and items in addition to the chart of accounts. (See Chapter 2 to learn about creating your lists.)

Entering Current Transactions while Entering Historical Transactions

Because QuickBooks is date sensitive, you can begin using the software for current transactions before you've entered all your historical transactions. To make it easier for your accountant to validate the opening trial balance for your fiscal year, don't enter any current transactions that are dated the first day of the year.

Using a calendar year as an example, that means that even if you had sales or wrote checks on January 1, 2015, enter those transactions with the date January 2, 2015. That leaves January 1, 2015 "pristine" and your opening trial balance on that date reflects only the totals of your historical transactions.

After you're sure your opening trial balance for January 1 is correct, you can edit the January 2 transactions that were really created on January 1 to correct the date (or you can leave the date as January 2).

Entering Open Customer Balances

You have to get all of your open customer balances as of the last day of the year into QuickBooks. (If any of the invoices were paid this year you enter those payments as current transactions; for the purpose of establishing an opening balance, the invoices must be entered as transactions in the previous year). You also have to enter any outstanding credits as of the end of last year.

Creating an Item for Historical Transactions

Since all sales transactions require you to use an item, one efficient way to do this is to create an item specifically for these historical open invoices. You can call the item Historical Sales or something similar and link it to an existing income account. Use a Service or Other Charge item type.

If you remitted sales tax for the last reporting period of last year with a check dated before the end of the year (which means you don't have to track sales tax for historical transactions), make the item nontaxable.

If you haven't yet paid sales taxes for the last reporting period of last year, create two items: HistoricalSalesTaxable and HistoricalSalesNon-Taxable, and mark their tax status appropriately. See the next section "Tracking Historical Sales Tax" for more information on this topic.

For each customer, you can enter the open invoices in either of two ways:

- Enter each individual invoice, using the real date of that invoice. This works well for customers who send payments earmarked for a specific invoice and also permits you to generate an accurate A/R aging report.
- Enter one invoice representing the total outstanding balance, dating it December 31. This is less data entry but only works well if your customers send payments to be applied against a running open balance, and you don't track aging by individual invoice due dates.

Tracking Historical Sales Tax

If you filed and paid all of your previous year sales taxes by the last day of last year, you don't have to worry about sales tax when you enter the historical transactions. However, if you hadn't yet remitted sales taxes for the last period of last year (either the last quarter or the last month, depending on the frequency of your tax reporting), you have to build the tax liability as you enter the transactions.

If you're using actual invoice dates as you enter historical transactions, do not use the taxable item in any transaction that falls in a period for which you already remitted your sale tax payment. For example, if you're a quarterly filer, make all transactions in the first three quarters nontaxable, and create taxable transactions for the last quarter. Then, in the current year, use the QuickBooks sales tax feature (Vendors | Sales Tax) to generate the appropriate report for the quarter and remit the taxes.

If you prefer to enter summarized total transactions, you must create one summary nontaxable transaction for the periods covered by sales tax reports you remitted to the tax authorities last year (use the nontaxable item for those transactions) and another summary taxable transaction for the period yet to be reported (using the taxable item).

Creating Historical Invoices

Use the following guidelines to enter historical transactions still open:

- If you track individual invoices for customers (instead of using a balance forward system), use the original invoice date and invoice number to make it easier to track aging and discuss open balances with the customer.
- In the Item column, select the historical transaction item you created.
- Move directly to the Amount column to enter the total for each invoice (skip the Qty and Description fields).
- Use the Memo field for any notes you think might be important if you have to discuss this invoice with your customer.
- Deselect any check marks in the Print Later or Email Later boxes at the top of the window.

ProAdvisor TIP: *Use the Intuit Service Invoice template for historical transactions because it has fewer fields and columns than other built-in templates.*

Figure 1-4 shows an invoice that uses the non-taxable historical item because the products/services rendered were not taxable, or were taxable but you've already remitted the sales tax to the tax authorities. A similar invoice using the *taxable* historical item is created if the invoice represents a taxable item and the sales tax hadn't been remitted as of the last day of the previous year.

When you enter a transaction that is 90 days before the current date, or 30 days after the current date, QuickBooks issues a warning (which is a nifty idea because it avoids typos that can create some very strange financial reports). Click Yes to confirm you want to use this date.

> **ProAdvisor TIP**: *If you're entering individual historical transactions and you don't want to click Yes after saving each transaction, you can turn off this function in the Company Preferences tab of the Accounting Preferences dialog (choose Edit | Preferences and select the Accounting category in the left pane). Disable the Date Warnings on the Company Preferences tab. Turn the warnings on again after you've completed your historical transactions.*

Figure 1-4: Enter historical customer balances by creating invoices.

Creating Historical Credits

If any of your customers had outstanding credit balances at the end of the year, you must enter them. You can apply them against customer payments or invoices that are entered for the current year.

When you create the credit memo, use the real date from the previous year if you're tracking payments by invoices. Summarize multiple credit memos and use the last day of the year if you're using running balances.

Use the item you created for historical transactions. The same rules about sales tax apply as discussed in the previous section. When you save a credit memo, QuickBooks asks how to handle the transaction (see Figure 1-5). Since this is a prior year credit that will be applied against a current year transaction, select the option Retain As An Available Credit.

Figure 1-5: Save existing credits so you can apply them to current year transactions.

Entering Open Payables

Enter all the vendor bills that were still outstanding as of the last day of the previous year. If multiple bills existed for any vendors, you can enter individual bills, or enter one bill to cover the entire amount.

If you normally pay your bills on a per-invoice basis, it's best to enter each bill individually. This makes recording payments more straightforward and also makes it easier to have conversations with the vendor in the event of a dispute.

Entering Inventory

If you track inventory, enter the quantity and value of each inventory item as of the last day of the year.

Choose Vendors | Inventory Activities | Adjust Quantity/Value On Hand. When the transaction window opens, select Quantity And Total Value from the Adjustment Type drop down list to add the New Value column to the window

---

ProAdvisor CAUTION: *Never fill in the fields labeled On Hand and Total Value that appear in the item record when you create an Inventory Item. Instead, during company file setup, use an Inventory Adjustment transaction window to tell QuickBooks about your inventory quantity and value.*

For each inventory item, enter the appropriate numbers in the New Qty column and the appropriate costs in the New Value column. When you complete this task, you end up with the following:

- The total value of your inventory is posted (as a debit) to your inventory asset account as of the last day of the year.

- The cost per unit of your inventory items has been calculated by QuickBooks. This number is used to post amounts to cost of goods when you enter sales transactions in the current year.

- The inventory adjustment account (selected from the drop-down list in the Adjustment Account field at the top of the window) has been credited with the offsetting total.

The inventory adjustment account requires some discussion with your accountant. If you're adding inventory as an adjustment instead of receiving goods via a purchase order and vendor bill (as is the case in this opening entry), the inventory adjustment account is credited. By default, QuickBooks creates the account as an expense type, but most accountants prefer a cost of goods account type.

Creating the Trial Balance for Last Year

When your historical transactions are posted, you can begin to create a trial balance report as of the last day of the previous year.

Creating Reports on Historical Transactions

Start by viewing the current trial balance, which shows the totals posted for all the historical transactions you entered.

To generate the report, choose Reports | Accountant & Taxes | Trial Balance. When the report opens, set the date range to the previous fiscal year. You probably have balances for the following accounts (depending on the types of historical transactions you entered):

- Accounts Receivable
- Inventory
- Accounts Payable
- Sales Tax Payable
- Income (the account you linked to the item you created for entering historical invoices)
- Expenses (postings from the open vendor bills you entered)

Print this report; you need it as a reference when you create the journal entry to enter balances in all your accounts, because you don't want to enter these totals twice.

You also need to create a balance sheet report as of the end of the year, so you can see the effect of your entries on your balance sheet accounts, including equity accounts.

To generate the report, choose Reports | Company & Financial | Balance Sheet Standard. When the report window opens, select Last Fiscal Year as the date range.

Print the report, because you have to know what's already posted and calculated (creating the net profit or loss in the equity account) when you enter the remaining account totals.

Entering the Remaining Account Totals

The totals for the remaining accounts can be entered as a single journal entry dated the last day of the previous year. Remember not to use the accounts that received postings as a result of your transaction entries (with the exception of thc sales tax liability account, which is discussed in the section "Entering Sales Tax Liabilities Balances").

The goal is to create an opening trial balance for the first day of the current year, which has only balance sheet accounts. The best way to get there is to create a journal entry as of the last day of the previous year that uses all your accounts (including income and expense accounts). Then let QuickBooks perform the calculations that turn the numbers into an opening trial balance on the first day of the current year.

Enter all the totals you calculate from your manual or spreadsheet-based former bookkeeping system. This puts all the income and expense totals into your QuickBooks company file, which makes it easier to create budgets for the current year and also lets you create reports comparing sales and expenses between the current year and last year.

Some of the entries in your journal entry are easy to figure out, but others require some thought. For example, the totals for accounts of the type Other Current Assets (excluding inventory) and Other Assets are usually easy to calculate. Most Current Liabilities and Long Term Liabilities totals are equally straightforward. However, the totals you enter for your bank accounts, fixed assets, and payroll liabilities need special attention and are covered in the following sections.

Entering Opening Bank Account Balances

To enter bank account balances, use the reconciled balance as of the last day of the last fiscal year in the journal entry (most banks generate statements as of the last day of each month for business accounts). Don't include any transactions that hadn't cleared as of the last day of the year.

After you finish and save the opening balances journal entry, use individual transactions to enter the previous unreconciled transactions, which allows you to see those transactions when you reconcile the bank account in QuickBooks.

Entering Fixed Asset Balances

You can enter your current balances for fixed assets in either of the following ways:

- Enter the net amount (the purchase amount less accumulated depreciation).
- Enter the original purchase amount and also enter the accumulated depreciation.

The latter is preferable if you like your accounting system to provide as much detailed information as possible.

Entering Payroll Liabilities Balances

If you ended the year with payroll liabilities still unpaid, enter them in the opening balance journal entry. They'll wash when you enter the transaction that paid them during the current year.

Entering Sales Tax Liabilities Balances

If you have taxable sales for the last reporting period, you have to enter the total sales tax liability for those transactions *not* included in the historical transactions you entered. Paid customer transactions (not open and due as of the end of the year) also contributed to your tax liability, and you have to add that total to the sales tax liability account in order to remit taxes accurately.

Entering Income and Expense Balances

If you're working with calculated totals from the previous year (that you calculated in your old bookkeeping system), you may have to "back out" the amounts you posted when you entered the open receivables and payables.

For example, if you know your calculated sales total from your old system includes the unpaid invoices you entered in QuickBooks, subtract the total of the entered transactions from your year-end total. Do the same for your expense balances, backing out any vendor bills still due.

Entering Equity Account Balances

When you enter equity account balances you have to build in the accumulated equity (retained earnings) for your business. The way you enter equity account balances depends on the way your business is organized. If your business is a proprietorship or partnership, and you track capital in and draws out, you need to enter those individual totals.

If your accountant has prepared an end-of-year trial balance, including final equity balances as of the last day of the year, you can use those figures as a starting point. However, you have to subtract the equity that resulted from the historical transactions you entered. Ask your accountant for help and advice on recalculating that equity.

Creating the Historical Journal Entry

To create the journal entry that populates the account balances as of the last day of the prior year, choose Company | Make General Journal Entries and enter the totals.

Remember to omit the balance sheet accounts you used when you entered your open transactions (except for sales tax liabilities as described earlier). For income and expense accounts, subtract the totals of the historical open transactions you entered from the totals you have from your previous system (assuming those previous totals included open transactions).

Checking the Results

You need to check your work against two standards:

- The closing reports for the previous year, to make sure the numbers match your accountant's numbers, including the numbers used for your tax return.
- The opening trial balance for the current year, which should contain no accounts except balance sheet accounts, and the account balances should match your accountant's numbers.

Creating Reports on the Previous Year

To make sure your previous year numbers are correct (they're the basis of your tax return in addition to being the basis of your starting numbers for the current year), run the standard financial reports and set the date range for each report to the previous year.

- Profit & Loss Standard
- Balance Sheet Standard
- Trial Balance

Check the numbers against your accountant's figures. If they don't match, you can drill down through the reports to find the entries that are causing the problem.

Generating the Trial Balance for the Current Year

Run a trial balance report for the first day of the current year. Only the balance sheet accounts should display on the report; if you see any income or expense accounts, drill down to the offending transaction (which almost certainly has a date entered incorrectly) and correct the transaction.

Managing Company Files

In this section, we'll go over some of the common file manipulations that users perform (or ask us about).

Versions Vs. Editions

In QuickBooks, the version is the year, which is part of the software's name. This book is about QuickBooks 2014, or "version" 2014. The edition is the "flavor" such as Premier Accountant Edition, Premier Contractor Edition, Pro Edition, and so on.

- You can open a company file in the version in which it was last used, or in any later version. You cannot open a company file in a previous version.
- If the version is the same, you can open any company file in any edition of QuickBooks Pro or Premier.

Opening Files in Another Edition

You can open any file in any edition; the files must be of the same version. This means if you're using Pro Edition and your accountant is using Premier Accountant Edition, your file will open properly on your accountant's computer, and when the file is returned to you, it's still Pro Edition, and will open in QuickBooks Pro.

If you're using Pro Edition and somebody asks you to look at or use a company file that was created or last saved in a Premier Edition, the file will load properly and work fine in your Pro edition software. If you're using one of the industry-specific versions of Premier, you can load your file in any other version of Premier.

The bottom line is that all that counts is the version; after that, you can freely open files from any Pro/Premier edition in any other Pro/Premier.

If a company file is used in a Premier edition, and Premier-only functions are employed in the file, when it's opened in Pro Edition you can see the results of those Premier-only functions. For example, if you use the Sales Order feature in a file that's loaded in a Premier edition, when you open the file in Pro you'll see the sales orders. You can even edit them and convert them to invoices. However, you can't create new sales orders, because Pro doesn't support creating sales orders.

Accountant Edition Toggle Feature

The Premier Accountant Edition has a Toggle feature, which lets users switch among all Premier editions and Pro. However, because it's possible to load client files from any edition of QuickBooks into the Premier Accountant Edition, it's not necessary to toggle to the edition the client is using when you need to work on a client's file.

ProAdvisor TIP: *The toggle feature is a good way for accounting professionals, when providing telephone support, to see exactly what the client is seeing in the menus and dialogs.*

The toggle feature works by closing QuickBooks, and then reloading QuickBooks in the edition you selected in the toggle dialog (actually named the Select QuickBooks Industry-Specific Edition dialog). If you have a company file open when you toggle, when QuickBooks opens, that file is still loaded. Note that if you close QuickBooks while another edition is running via the toggle feature, the next time QuickBooks opens it loads Premier Accountant Edition.

Copying and Deleting Company Files

It's a good idea to make a copy of your company file to use as a test file, so you can experiment with transactions, customized reports, and other functions. Working with your own, familiar, customers, vendors, and accounts is an easier way to learn than using the sample files that are provided with the software. Some businesses make multiple test copies, and use them for different purposes, such as testing user permissions. Some of those test copies are later deleted, but they continue to appear in the list of previously used files (where selecting them causes QuickBooks to appear to stall for a while and then, finally, to report that it can't open the file).

Creating a Training File

To create a test/experimental company file from your real company file, you have to make a copy of the file and change the filename. To begin, make sure the file you want to copy isn't in use; either close the file in QuickBooks (use File | Close Company/Logoff if it's currently loaded in QuickBooks), or close QuickBooks. Then take the following steps:

1. In My Computer or Windows Explorer, navigate to the folder that holds the company file.
2. Right-click the .qbw file's listing and choose Copy from the right-click menu.
3. In the My Computer/Windows Explorer window, navigate to a different location on your computer (the Desktop, the C Drive, or a USB flash drive). Right-click and choose Paste.
4. Press F2 to put this file listing in Edit mode.

5. Press the Home key on your keyboard to move the cursor to the beginning of the filename, and enter *Training* at the beginning of the filename. (For example, the file named Mybiz.QBW is renamed TrainingMybiz.QBW.)

6. Press Enter to take the file listing out of Edit mode.

7. Right-click the newly named file's listing and choose Cut from the right-click menu.

8. Return to the file's original folder, right-click, and then choose Paste to put the test file into your regular QuickBooks company file folder.

ProAdvisor NOTE: The File menu in QuickBooks contains a Create Copy command. However, that command is only for making backups, portable files, and accountant's copies. It will not make a complete copy with a different name.

This file can now be opened in QuickBooks. However, you need to make sure you know you're working in the test file instead of the regular file. The title bar on the QuickBooks window displays the name of the company, not the filename.

Choose Company | My Company to open the My Company dialog. Click the Edit button (pencil nub icon) to display the Company Information dialog, and change the company name to Training *<company name>*. Now, there's no confusion about the file you're working in.

Deleting a Company File

You can delete a company file from My Computer or Windows Explorer by selecting the filename and pressing the Delete key.

- Windows does not let you delete a file that's in use, so make sure QuickBooks is closed, or has a different company file loaded.

- QuickBooks loads the last-used company file when it opens, so make sure you did **not** have this file loaded when you closed QuickBooks. If you're not sure, open

QuickBooks and if this file appears, open a different company file or choose File | Close Company/Logoff and then close QuickBooks.

Then delete the following files:

- <Filename>.QBW
- <Filename>.QBW.ND
- <Filename>.QBW.DSN
- <Filename>.QBW.TLG

QuickBooks Won't Open a Missing or Corrupt File

If QuickBooks takes a very long time to load, it could be because it's trying to open a file that is either missing or corrupt.

If you delete a company file, and that file was loaded when you closed QuickBooks, the software displays the No Company Open dialog, which lists the previously used company files (including the file you deleted – see the next section "Managing the Previously Used File List" for more information).

If the last-used file is corrupt, and won't load, QuickBooks may not even open; instead, it gives up with an error message that doesn't clearly describe the problem.

Open QuickBooks Without Opening the Last Used File

To by-pass the "open the last used file" paradigm, press the Ctrl key when you double-click the desktop shortcut to QuickBooks and continue to press the Ctrl key until QuickBooks opens.

QuickBooks displays the No Company Open dialog and you can select the company file you want to open from the list, or by choosing the Open Or Restore option (to open a company file not on the list).

If a file is corrupt and won't open, you can't verify or repair it. In that case, restore the last backup. It's a good idea to configure QuickBooks for multiple backups (e.g. saving the last three backups) so that if the last backup is also corrupt, you can go back another day.

Open QuickBooks Without Loading the Open Windows in a File

Sometimes the company file isn't corrupt, but some component in the file is corrupt. For instance, it's not uncommon to find a memorized report that's corrupt. If that report was open when you closed QuickBooks, the software often has a problem starting.

To open the file without opening the windows that were displayed when you closed the file, access the No Company Open dialog (see the previous section), hold down the Alt key while you select the file, click Open, and continue to hold the Alt key until the file opens.

It's a good idea to change the configuration in the Desktop View section of the Edit | Preferences dialog so that the Don't Save The Desktop option is selected on the My Preferences tab. Even if one of the open components is not damaged, it takes more time for QuickBooks to load a saved desktop than it takes to click a few times to open the windows you need to work with after you're logged on.

Managing the Previously Used File List

As you load multiple company files in QuickBooks, the software maintains a list of previously opened files. Even if you only have one company file, it's possible that you opened one of the sample files that are installed with the software, and that file is in the list.

The Previously Used File List is displayed in two locations: on the File menu when you choose File | Open Previous Company; and in the No Company Open dialog when you close a company file or open QuickBooks while holding the Ctrl key to prevent the last opened file from loading.

If you delete a file or move it to another location, the Previously Used File List doesn't update, and the missing file continues to be listed.

To clean up the Previously Used File List, you must close the company file to display the No Company Open dialog. Click the Edit List link to open the Edit Company List dialog box. Deselect (place a check mark to the left of) each company file you want to remove from the list. Click OK when you're done, and the file names are removed from both the No Company Open dialog and from the Open Previous Company menu.

ProAdvisor TIP: *You can change the number of company files that appear on either the Open Previous Company menu or the No Company Open dialog. Choose File | Open Previous Company | Set Number Of Previous Companies to open the Set Number Of Previous Companies dialog box. Be advised however, that this will not remove company file names from either list. It simply displays the number of previous companies allowed by the number set. If you change it to a smaller number, some of the company names disappear. If you return and change it to a larger number, they reappear.*

CHAPTER 2

Lists and Classes

- Creating lists
- Creating custom fields in lists
- Adding custom fields to templates
- Creating classes

Lists are mini-files within your QuickBooks data file that contain the data you use when you create transactions. For example, the names of your customers and vendors are held in QuickBooks lists. (Database developers usually refer to these files-within-the-file as *tables*.)

ProAdvisor NOTE: *QuickBooks Premier Editions have more fields and types of list entries than QuickBooks Pro, such as Assemblies, the U/M Set List, Item Price Levels, etc.*

Setting Up Your Lists

Most of the fields in the QuickBooks transaction windows require you to make a selection from a drop-down list that displays the entries you've created for the list being used in the field. If the selection you need isn't there, you can create it while you're creating the transaction (which is called *on the fly* data entry). However, that interrupts the process of creating a transaction, which makes you less productive. Take the time to get this basic data into your system when you first start using QuickBooks.

Creating your lists is one of those "which came first, the chicken or the egg" exercises. Some lists have fields for other list items, such as the Customers & Jobs list, where each setup window contains fields for data that's contained in auxiliary lists (Terms, Price Level, Type, and so on).

In this section, we present an overview of the lists, providing some of the things we've learned from clients and accountants about creating and using them in a productive way.

We'll start with the auxiliary lists, which QuickBooks calls the Customer & Vendor Profile Lists. After you create components in these lists, you can choose data from them when you encounter a field for these lists while you create the larger lists.

Customer & Vendor Profile Lists

Some of the Customer & Vendor Profile lists let you filter, sort, and categorize information about your customers, jobs, and vendors. Other lists in this category are for maintaining information that makes it easier to manage transactions.

When you create customers and vendors, you can pre-assign the entries in some of these profile lists as default settings, and the data will appear in transaction windows involving those customers and vendors. The default settings you specify aren't etched in stone; you can change any field's data in any transaction window.

To access these lists choose Lists | Customer & Vendor Profile Lists, which displays a submenu containing the following lists (all of which are covered in this section):

- Sales Rep List
- Customer Type List
- Vendor Type List
- Job Type List
- Terms List
- Customer Message List
- Payment Method List
- Ship Via List
- Vehicle List

Sales Rep List

The Rep field on transaction windows is used to link a sales representative to a customer. You need this information if you pay commissions to sales reps, but even if you don't have a commission structure, it's often helpful to know who the primary contact is for a customer (sometimes referred to as a service rep instead of a sales rep).

When you create a sales rep, you enter the name and initials. The initials become the code for the sales rep, and those initials appear in the Rep field of sales transaction forms.

Creating this list is one of those "chicken or the egg" situations, because in order to add a sales rep, the name must already exist in the Employee, Vendor, or Other Names list.

If the sales rep's name is not already on one of those lists, you can create the entry in the Sales Rep list, and when you press Tab to move to the next field, QuickBooks displays a dialog that lets you add the new rep to your Employee, Vendor, or Other Names list.

Customer Type List

Use the Customer Type list to sort your customers by a type you deem important or convenient when you create reports. For example, you may decide to signify wholesale and retail customers by type.

Types don't work well unless they're similar in category. If you want to use types such as "retail" and "wholesale" to categorize customers, then you can't use "yellow pages" or "local newspaper ad" to track the source of referrals. If you mix categories, you won't be able to sort or filter reports properly to gain useful information. If you really need more than one category of customer type, use custom fields for some of the categories (see "Creating Custom Fields", later in this chapter).

ProAdvisor TIP: *If you insist on mixing categories, you can use subtypes to differentiate them. For example, if you want to track wholesale and retail customers, but broken down by how they were recruited, use Wholesale and Retail as parent types. Then create subtypes such as Wholesale:Yellow Pages, Wholesale:Web Page, Wholesale:Walk-in.*

Vendor Type List

Use this list to classify your vendors by type, so you can create reports sorted by the criteria you establish when you invent your vendor type entries. For example, you may want to create a type for those vendors from whom you buy inventory items to separate them from vendors for whom expenses are part of overhead, or government agencies to whom you remit payments. As with Customer Types, Vendor Types don't work well if you mix categories.

Job Type List

The entries you create for this list help you classify jobs (if you track jobs or projects) so you can create reports sorted by different types of jobs. For example, you may want to have job types to separate fixed fee jobs from time and material jobs. Or, you may want to classify jobs by those you do with in-house personnel and those that involve outside contractors.

Terms List

The word "Terms", of course, refers to payment terms. The terms you create can be linked to both customers and vendors, and you may need additional terms to make sure you've covered all your customer and vendor terms. QuickBooks supports two types of terms:

- Standard terms, which have a due date following a certain amount of time after the invoice date.
- Date driven terms, which are due on a particular day of the month, regardless of the invoice date.

Create a name for the new terms, using a name that makes it easy to understand the terms when you see it on a drop-down list in a transaction window. For example, if you create standard terms of 25 Days, name the entry 25Days. If you create date driven terms where the payment is due on the 15th of the month, name the entry 15thMonth.

To create a new terms item, choose Lists | Customer & Vendor Profile Lists | Terms List, and press Ctrl-N to display the New Terms dialog.

Creating Standard Terms

For standard terms, select Standard, and set the options to match the terms. Net Due is the number of days you allow for payment after the invoice date.

To give customers a discount for early payment, enter the discount percentage and the number of days after the invoice date that the discount is in effect. For example, if you allow 30 days for payment but want to encourage customers to pay early, enter a discount percentage that is in effect for 10 days after the invoice date.

Creating Date Driven Terms

For date driven terms, select Date Driven, and enter the day of the month the invoice payment is due. Then enter the number of days before the due date that invoices are considered to be payable on the following month (remember, it's not fair to insist that invoices be paid on the 10th of the month if you mail them to customers on the 8th of the month).

To give customers a discount for early payment, enter the discount percentage and the day of the month at which the discount period ends. For example, if the standard due date is the 15th of the month, you may want to extend a discount to any customer who pays by the 8th.

ProAdvisor NOTE: *Terms that provide discounts for early payment are commonly used by manufacturers and distributors of products. It's not a common practice to provide discounts for early payment if you sell services. Another incentive for customers to pay their bills on time is to use finance charges when payments are late.*

Customer Message List

This list holds the messages you can print at the bottom of customer transaction forms (invoices, sales receipts, estimates, etc.). The messages can contain up to 101 characters (including spaces and punctuation).

Payment Method List

This list contains the various types of payments you accept from customers. Tracking the payment method for customers helps you resolve disputes because you have a detailed report of every payment you receive.

In addition, specifying the payment method lets you group deposits by the appropriate categories when you use the Make Deposits window. Your bank statement probably displays separate entries for credit card receipts, electronic transfers, and cash/checks. Depositing funds by payment method makes it easier to reconcile the bank account.

Ship Via List

Use this list to specify the way products are shipped when you sell products to customers. The list is pre-populated with the major carriers, as well as the US Postal Service. If you have your own trucks or cars, add self-delivery to your list.

Vehicle List

Use this list for vehicles for which you want to track mileage. Once you've entered a vehicle in the Vehicle List, you can track mileage for that vehicle.

Tracking Vehicle Mileage

To track vehicle mileage, choose Company | Enter Vehicle Mileage. The dialog that appears is easy to fill out and can be extremely useful (see Figure 2-1).

Figure 2-1: You can track mileage for all the vehicles in your
Vehicle List.

If you enter the odometer readings for the beginning and end of the trip, QuickBooks will automatically calculate the miles. Alternatively, you can enter the miles directly into the Total Miles field.

Mileage data can be used for numerous purposes:

- Bill customers for mileage (reimbursement amounts for trips marked Billable are automatically available when you invoice the customer).

- Link trips to customers/jobs without billing the customers, in order to track job costs.
- Track mileage for tax deduction purposes.
- Track mileage for vehicle maintenance purposes.

Customers & Jobs List

In QuickBooks, customers and jobs are handled together, because jobs must be linked to customers. You can create a customer and consider anything and everything you invoice to that customer a single job, or you can have multiple jobs for the same customer. You can link as many jobs to a single customer as you need.

ProAdvisor TIP: *If you are going to track jobs, it's more efficient to create all your customers first, and then create the jobs.*

Customer Name Protocols

You have to develop a set of rules, or protocols, for naming your customers. Some businesses use number codes, some use a combination of letters (using the first few letters of the customer name) and numbers, and some use the actual name. What's important is to have a consistent pattern for creating customer names; otherwise, you run the risk of entering the same customer multiple times. Imagine trying to track receivables under those circumstances!

When you create a customer in QuickBooks, the first field in the New Customer dialog is Customer Name. Don't take the name of that field literally; instead, think of the data you enter in that field as a code rather than a real name. This code is a reference that's linked to all the information you enter in the customer record (company name, primary contact name, address, and so on).

The code doesn't appear on printed transactions (such as invoices or sales receipts); the Customer or Job record has a field for the Company Name, and that's what appears on transactions, not the text in the Name field. You must invent a protocol for the customer name (the code) so you enter every customer in the same manner.

Avoiding punctuation and spaces in codes is a good protocol for codes. This avoids the risk that you'll enter any customer more than once. Consider the following customer codes we've found in client files (each of these represents a single customer entered multiple times):

- O'Neill and Oneill
- Sam's Pizza, Sams Pizza, and SamsPizza
- The Rib Pit, Rib Pit, and RibPit

Incidentally, the last listing in each entry of this list represents the best protocol. Customer names such as SamsPizza and RibPit have a capital letter in the middle of the name to make it easier to read the name. However, if you're typing the name in a list box (it's easier to select a name from a long drop-down list by typing than by scrolling), you don't have to capitalize any letters—data in drop-down lists is not case- sensitive.

If your business has most of its customers in the same industry, you may find that many customers have similar (or identical) names. We had a client who sold supplies to video rental stores, and at least seventy percent of the customer names started with the word "Video". A large number of those stores had identical names, such as Video Palace, Video Stop, Video Hut, and so on. In fact, some customers were individual stores owned by a chain; so all the names were identical (except for the store number). To make it possible for each customer in the system to have a unique customer name, we used telephone numbers (including the area code) after the customer name, such as VideoHut-215-555-9999.

ProAdvisor NOTE: *You can use up to 41 characters in the Customer Name field.*

Importing the Customer List

If you've been keeping a customer list in another software application, you can avoid one-customer-at-a-time data entry by importing the list into

QuickBooks. You have four methods at your disposal for importing the list:

- Use the QuickBooks Setup wizard (covered in Appendix A).
- Import the list directly from an Excel file or a CSV file (covered in Appendix A).
- Use the Add/Edit Multiple List Entries window (covered in Appendix A).
- Import the list from an IIF file (covered in Appendix B).

If you've been using another accounting application, you must export the data from that application to create your import file. This is only possible if your former accounting application is capable of exporting data to one of the following formats:

- Excel file
- CSV (comma separated value) file
- Tab-delimited text file.

All three of these file types can be opened in Excel. If you use another spreadsheet application, you can use a CSV file or a tab-delimited text file (and some spreadsheet software is capable of loading Excel files and converting them to its own document type).

A QuickBooks customer import file can contain all the information you need to fill in all the fields in the customer dialog, such as customer type, sales tax status, and so on. It's unlikely you've kept records in a manner that matches these fields, but you can import whatever information you already have, and later enter additional information by editing the customer records.

If you keep your customer list on paper, or in a software application that can't export to the required file type, you can enter the customer information in a spreadsheet-like table provided in the Add The People

You Do Business With section of the QuickBooks Setup wizard (covered in Appendix A).

Vendor List

Your vendors have to be entered into your QuickBooks system, and it's easier to do it while you're setting up your company rather than during transaction entry.

As with the customer list, the Name field in a vendor record is a code. The vendor record dialog includes fields labeled Company Name, and Print Name On Check As. Use the Name/Code to create vendors for specific payment types when the same vendor exists for a variety of payment types.

For example, if you have multiple phone bills, you can't create a vendor named PhoneCompany, because QuickBooks (like all other software) will issue one check for all the bills you input. The phone company wants a separate check for each phone bill, so the solution is to enter the phone number in the Name field, and then put PhoneCompany into the Company Name and Print Name On Check As fields.

Even more common is a government vendor. If your state has a Department of Revenue, the odds are that several types of payments are made to that vendor, but each payment type requires its own discrete check. Therefore, name the vendor by the payment type, creating a vendor for state corporate taxes, state income tax withholding, sales tax remittances, unemployment tax remittances, and so on. For the feds, you need a separate vendor for 940 and 941 remittances.

Importing the Vendor List

If you've been tracking vendors in Excel, or even in Word, or in another software application, you can import the vendor list into QuickBooks, which saves all that one-customer-at-a-time data entry you'd have to perform in QuickBooks. The methods are the same as those outlined in the earlier section entitled "Importing the Customer List."

Fixed Asset Item List

Use the Fixed Asset Item List to track information about the assets you depreciate. As you can see in Figure 2-2, the dialog for a fixed asset includes fields that allow you to keep rather detailed information.

Figure 2-2: Track depreciable assets in the Fixed Asset Item List.

When to Use the Fixed Asset Item List

Unless you're using Premier Accountant Edition, the Fixed Asset Item List is inert. It doesn't do anything, and isn't used for any type of transaction in QuickBooks.

When you enter a fixed asset in the Fixed Asset Item List, the financial information you enter isn't transferred to your Fixed Asset accounts, even though you must specify an account in the New Item dialog. You have to create separate transactions in your chart of accounts to enter that information into your fixed asset accounts. It doesn't work the other way around, either; the Fixed Asset Item List won't read the information from the fixed asset account you specify.

QuickBooks adds all the fixed assets you keep in this list to the Item drop-down list you see when you're creating a transaction. You have to scroll through all the fixed asset entries as well as your "regular" items to select an item for the transaction.

The Fixed Asset Item List is not any more useful than a list you could keep in Word or Excel. If you design a table in Word, with a column for each category you want to track, or you keep your fixed assets in Excel, you can sort the data to match whatever information you need to see. In fact, entering the data is much easier in Word or Excel, because you don't have to keep clicking OK to open a new blank dialog to enter each asset. Instead, you can just move down the columns and across the rows.

However, the Fixed Asset Item List is useful if you send your file to your accountant to depreciate your assets (assuming your accountant is running the Premier Accountant Edition).

QuickBooks Premier Accountant Edition includes the Fixed Asset Manager (discussed in Chapter 9), a tool that *does* use the information in the Fixed Asset Item List to generate depreciation (refer back to Figure 2-2).

The Fixed Asset Manager automatically performs depreciation transactions, applying depreciation amounts to the appropriate fixed asset accounts. If your accountant uses the Fixed Asset Manager, you can send your company file or an Accountant's Copy file to automate the process of depreciating your assets. Since this may make your accountant's work easier and faster, it may reduce your bill for tax preparation. That trade-off may be worth the annoyances that come with the decision to use the Fixed Asset Item List.

Price Level List

The Price Level List is a nifty way to fine-tune your pricing schemes. You can use price levels to make sure your customers are happy and your bottom line is healthy.

ProAdvisor NOTE: *The Price Level List only appears on the Lists menu if you turned on the Enable Price Levels option in the Sales & Customers section of your Preferences dialog.*

QuickBooks Premier editions offer two types of price levels:

- Fixed percentage price levels (available in QuickBooks Pro and Premier editions)
- Per item price levels (available only in QuickBooks Premier editions)

Fixed Percentage Price Levels

Fixed percentage price levels can be applied to a customer, a job, or an individual sales transaction. The price levels are applied against the standard price of items (as recorded in each item record).

For example, you may want to create a price level that gives your favorite customers an excellent discount. Another common price reduction scheme is a discounted price level for all customers that are nonprofit organizations.

On the other hand, you may want to maintain your item prices for most customers, and increase them by a fixed percentage for certain customers.

ProAdvisor TIP: *You can also apply a price level to an individual sale instead of to a customer's record. This works for estimates, invoices, or sales receipts.*

To create a percentage-based price level, open the Price Level List by choosing Lists | Price Level List from the QuickBooks menu bar. When the Price Level List window opens, follow these steps:

1. Press Ctrl-N to open the New Price Level dialog (see Figure 2-3).

2. Enter a name in the Price Level Name field. Use a name that reflects the algorithm you're using for this price level, such as 10-Off for a ten percent reduction.

3. In the Price Level Type field, select Fixed % from the drop-down list, if it's not already selected.

4. Specify whether the price level is a decrease or increase against an item price.

5. Enter the percentage of increase or decrease. (You don't have to enter the percent sign—QuickBooks will automatically add it.)

6. Click OK.

Figure 2-3: A fixed percentage price level is uncomplicated and easy to create.

Specify Rounding Rules

When you use a percentage-based price level, the resulting price is usually not an even dollar amount. QuickBooks lets you set a rounding algorithm for your price levels.

To select a rounding algorithm, click the arrow to the right of the field labeled Round Up To Nearest, and select the rounding amount to apply to this price level. The choices in the drop-down list provide some rather powerful methods for configuring the price.

As you can see in Figure 2-4, the first seven choices represent commonly used rounding algorithms. You can use the .01 option to round up to the nearest whole amount, avoiding three or four decimal places (e.g. $45.4535 becomes $46.46). You can use the other options to round up to an even amount that represents the pricing scheme you want, such as prices that always end in fifty cents (e.g. $19.50).

Figure 2-4: Your rounding choices are extensive.

Customizing Rounding Rules

You can customize the rounding algorithm, which gives you more precision, and also gives you the ability to use standard rounding rules (which means you can round down when it's appropriate).

To create your own customized rounding scheme, select User Defined from the Rounding drop-down list (it's at the bottom of the list). The dialog adds fields to accommodate your creation of the custom rounding algorithm (see Figure 2-5).

The three fields at the bottom of the dialog provide the specifications you need to create a price when you're applying a fixed percentage price level.

The "nearest" field offers the following three options:

- To Nearest, which rounds to the nearest specified number, which may be higher or lower.
- Up To Nearest, which rounds up to the specified number.
- Down To Nearest, which rounds down to the specified number. The $ field is where you enter the number you want to round to, such as .01, .25, .50, and so on.

Figure 2-5: Create a rounding scheme that provides precisely the price you want to charge.

The Plus-Minus field is where you enter the amount you want to add or subtract after the rounding value has been calculated. For example, if the $ field is .50 and you enter Minus .01, your prices will end in .49.

Using a Fixed Percentage Price Level in Transactions

You can link price levels to customers and jobs, or apply price levels while you're creating sales forms (invoices, sales orders, sales receipts, and credit memos). The method you use produces different results, as follows:

- If you link a price level to customers or jobs, the price level is automatically applied to all items whenever you use that customer or job on a sales form.

- If you apply the price level while you're creating a sales form, the price level is applied against the standard price for the item. If the item is already discounted because of a price level applied to the customer, that discounted price is ignored in favor of the price level you're applying to the sales form.

Linking a Fixed Percentage Price Level to a Customer or Job

To link a price level to a customer or a job, you need to edit the customer or job record to reflect the link. Press Ctrl-J to open the Customers & Jobs list in the Customer Center and take the following actions:

1. Double-click the listing for the customer or job you want to link to a price level, to open the Edit Customer dialog.
2. Move to the Payment Settings tab.
3. Click the arrow in the Price Level field to display a drop-down list of all the price levels you've created.
4. Select the appropriate price level.
5. Click OK.

Repeat this for all the customers and jobs you want to link to a price level. Be aware of the following "rules" governing the application of price levels to customers and jobs:

- If you link a price level to a customer, it does not apply to that customer's jobs. You will only see the price level applied if you create a sales form for the customer (which is hardly ever done when you're tracking jobs).

- If you link a price level to a job, only sales forms related to that specific job reflect the price level.

These rules make it possible to apply different price levels to each of a customer's jobs, if that's your plan. Unfortunately, that's hardly ever the plan (at least it's rare).

QuickBooks didn't think to include a dialog that pops up when you apply a price level to a customer and asks if you want to apply that price level to all of the jobs for that customer.

It would be even nicer if such a dialog box included the selection "apply to future jobs for this customer".

It would be absolutely terrific if the dialog listed all the current jobs, so you could select those that should be configured for this price level, along with the "Apply this to future jobs" option.

Since these helpful tools aren't available, if you have a lot of customers who have many jobs that need price levels applied, there's a workaround in the section, " Applying Price Levels to Customers in Batches" later in this chapter.

Applying a Fixed Percentage Price Level in a Sales Form

You can change the price of an item on a sales form by applying a price level as you create the sales form. This gives you quite a bit of flexibility for passing along discounts (or price hikes) to any customer. Use the following steps to apply a price level to a sales form:

1. Fill out the sales form in the usual way.
2. Click the arrow in the Rate (Price Each) column to display price levels.
3. Select a price level to apply to the item.

This can become complicated, because the price level you're selecting is applied to the recorded price of the item (the price you entered in the item's record when you created the item), which may not be the price displayed on the sales form, because *that* price may be linked to a price level you applied to this customer.

If you linked a price level to the customer, the price that appears on the sales form reflects the application of the price level. Applying another price level at this point may be butting into a rate that has already had a price level applied. The price level you select while you're working in the sales form wins—any amount calculated by a customer-linked price level is overwritten.

For example, the customer may be linked to a price level that caused the item's price to be reduced automatically by 15%. If you select a 10% price level decrease from the drop-down list in the sales form, the customer pays more. While the ability to set a price level in a sales form gives you some flexibility in determining prices for a customer, you need to be careful about undoing a promised discount.

Applying Price Levels to Customers in Batches

If you already had a large number of customers and jobs in your system when you created percentage-based price levels, you have to open each customer record, and each job record, move to the Payment Settings tab, and assign a price level by selecting one from the drop-down list in the Price Level field.

That's a lot of work, and besides, it's so boring! And, you have to do the same thing if you create new price levels that you want to assign to customers to replace existing price levels, or assign to customers for whom you hadn't previously assigned price levels. More time consuming, boring work!

There's an easier way. Use the Add/Edit Multiple List Entries feature.

1. Choose Lists | Add/Edit Multiple List Entries from the menu bar to display the Add/Edit Multiple List Entries window.

2. Choose Customers from the List drop-down list.

3. Click the Customize Columns button to open the Customize Columns dialog.

4. Scroll down the Available Columns pane and highlight the Price Level item.

5. Click the Add button to move it to the Chosen Columns pane. The field is placed at the bottom of the list (which means all the way to the right in the window).

6. Use the Move Up button to move the Price Level field to the left in the window so you can see it without scrolling.

7. Click OK to return to the Add/Edit Multiple List Entries window and locate the Price Level field.

8. Choose the appropriate price level from the Price Level field drop-down list.

Remember that you can use the Copy Down command to add the same price level to multiple fields. See Appendix A for information on the Add/Edit Multiple List Entries feature.

Per Item Price Levels

Available only in QuickBooks Premier editions, per item price levels let you set multiple prices for each item you sell, and then apply the appropriate price level when you're creating a sales form. This paradigm gives you a great deal of flexibility as you try to enhance your business by balancing individual customer activity and competitive prices.

A per item price level can be a fixed amount (an amount different from the standard price you entered when you created the item), or a percentage (higher or lower than the standard price).

To create an item price level, choose Lists | Price Level List to open the Price Level List window. Then, follow these steps:

1. Press Ctrl-N to open the New Price Level dialog.

2. Name the price level, using text that will remind you of the algorithm you're using for the price changes. If you're creating prices that have a fixed rate, use a name like 10$Off, for a percentage use 10%Off.

3. Select Per Item in the Price Level Type field. The dialog displays all the service, inventory, and non-inventory items in your Item List.

Now you can create a fixed price level, or a percentage-based price level, as described in the following sections.

ProAdvisor Sidebar:
Per Item Price Levels and Costs

The per item New Price Level window includes columns for the cost and the price of inventory items, so you can't inadvertently reduce a price to the point that you lose money. There are several problems you can run into if you use the data in the cost column.

Some item types such as Service and Non-Inventory Items may not have costs associated with them. You must be aware of cost, including overhead, when you create reduced prices for these items.

Inventory Item costs may be displayed, but they aren't necessarily accurate. QuickBooks displays the data you entered in the Cost field when you created (or edited) the item. These are not the calculated costs for the inventory item. The data in the Cost field is not used when QuickBooks calculates Cost of Goods Sold. The actual cost of inventory is calculated when you purchase inventory, either through a Receive Items transaction or a direct disbursement (Write Checks). Many users don't bother to enter data in the Cost field, and those items appear in this dialog with a cost of 0.00.

The only way to determine the average cost of an inventory item is to open the item's record and look at the Avg Cost figure at the bottom of the window.

In addition, many users don't fill out the Price field for items, preferring to set the price at the time of sale. You need to be aware of these quirks when setting per-item price levels.

Creating Fixed Rate Per item Price Levels

You can create a specific price as the new price level, and it can be higher or lower than the standard price (depending on the way in which you plan to use price levels).

To set a new price level for any item, click in the Custom Price column of the item's listing, and enter a new price (see Figure 2-6). You can perform this action on as many items as you wish. When you are finished entering the custom prices, click OK.

✓	ITEM	COST	STANDARD PR...	CUSTOM PRICE
	Cabinets:Cabinet Pulls	3.00	9.95	
	Cabinets:Light Pine	1,500.00	2,250.00	1,995.00
	Door Frame	15.00	24.00	
	Hardware	0.00	0.00	
	Hardware:Brass hinges	3.00	9.95	
	Hardware:Doorknobs Std	15.00	30.00	

Figure 2-6: Prices for some items are being reduced for a special sale.

ProAdvisor TIP: *Don't select the items you want to adjust, simply enter the new prices in the Custom Price column. If you check the item(s) QuickBooks assumes you want to apply a percentage discount and will ask you if you want to adjust the items when you click OK.*

Creating Percentage-Based Per Item Price Levels

You can also create price levels for individual items that are based on a percentage of the item's standard price or cost.

Select an item, or multiple items, by clicking in the leftmost column to place a check mark in that column. You can choose the Mark All option to select all the items, and if you want to exclude a few items, click the leftmost column to remove their check marks (the check mark is a toggle).

When all the items for this percentage-based price level are selected, fill in the fields at the bottom of the dialog (the section labeled Adjust Price Of Marked Items To Be) as seen in Figure 2-7.

Figure 2-7: Creating percentage based price levels is a breeze.

Enter the percentage for this price level. You aren't restricted to whole numbers; you can enter 8.5 or 7.25 if you wish. You only have to enter the number—QuickBooks automatically adds the percent sign.

In the next field, select Lower or Higher from the drop-down list. Then select one of the following options from the drop-down list in the next field:

- Standard Price, which applies the percentage to the item's price as established in the item's record. Use this for a price level for which you selected Lower in the previous field.

- Cost, which applies the percentage to the item's cost as established in the item's record. Use this for a price level for which you selected Higher in the previous field.

- Current Custom Price, which applies the percentage to a custom price you create for the item. Check the item, enter the custom price, and apply a percentage adjustment.

Select a rounding algorithm, and then click the Adjust button to have QuickBooks calculate the prices.

Printing Price Level Reports

QuickBooks provides printable reports on price levels, but they're not well thought out, and not well designed, so you have to modify the reports to make them useful. You can create and print a report on a specific price level, or on all the price levels in your system.

Printing a Specific Price Level Scheme

To create a report on a specific price level, right-click the price level's listing in the Price Level List window and choose Price Level Report from the shortcut menu.

The report that opens isn't suitable for printing and sending to customers, nor for your own use if you want to discuss special pricing with a customer. By default the report displays four columns: Item, Description, Preferred Vendor, and the prices for each item in this price level scheme. If you have the Unit of Measure feature enabled a fifth column U/M appears as well.

You need to modify the report so it displays the standard price of each item, in addition to the price for this price level (so you can see the difference). Also, there's no need to include the preferred vendor. Follow these steps to modify the report:

1. Click Customize Report to open the Modify Report dialog with the Display tab in the foreground.
2. In the Columns list, deselect everything except Item, Description, and the price level name.
3. In the Columns list, select Price.
4. Click OK.

If the report displays items that have no prices (the price is set at zero), use the Filters tab in the Modify Report dialog to remove them from the report. Select Price in the Filter list, and filter the criteria so only prices greater than .01 are displayed.

If this price level scheme only applies price levels to one type of item (e.g. inventory items), you can remove the other item types from the report, which usually makes the report much shorter and easier to read.

To restrict the report to the single item type involved in this price level, go to the Filters tab and select Type in the Filter list. In the Type field, select the appropriate item type from the drop-down list.

Unfortunately, there's no way to have the report list only those items with prices that differ in this price level scheme, and eliminate the items that aren't affected.

If you want to send a printed copy of this report to customers, you can hope they'll notice which items are affected, or you can export the report to Excel, tweak it to make it look like a catalog list, and then print it from Excel.

Printing a Report on All Price Levels

It's a good idea to have a list of all price levels in the office, so your sales calls can quote accurate, current prices. QuickBooks doesn't offer such a report, but it's rather easy to build one using the following steps:

1. Choose Reports | List | Item Price List. All of your items appear, along with their recorded standard prices.
2. Click Customize Report.

3. In the Display tab Columns list, deselect the Preferred Vendor listing (you might also remove the Description listing to make the report less crowded).

4. In the Display tab, scroll through the Columns list and select your price levels by name (the listings are at the bottom of the Columns list).

5. In the Filters tab, select Price and then select Greater Than (>=) .01.

6. Click OK to return to the report window, which now displays columns for each of your price levels.

ProAdvisor TIP: *Memorize this report so you don't have to go through all this customization again.*

Billing Rate Level List

The Billing Rate Level list lets you assign a billing rate to a person performing a specific service (the *service provider*). This list is only available in the following Premier Editions:

- Accountant Edition
- Contractor Edition
- Professional Services Edition

After you create billing rate levels, and associate them with service providers, invoicing for services becomes automatic. Every time you create an invoice with billable time, QuickBooks automatically fills in the correct rate for the service, based on the person who performed the work.

To track services for each service provider and associated billing rate level, the service providers must use the QuickBooks Timesheet feature.

Creating a Billing Rate Level

To create a billing rate level, choose Lists | Billing Rate Level List. When the list window opens, press Ctrl-N to open the New Billing Rate Level dialog. You can choose either of the following types of billing rate levels:

- A Fixed Hourly Rate, which is a specific hourly rate assigned to certain service providers.
- Custom Hourly Rate Per Service Item, which is a rate tied to a service, but it differs depending on the rate assigned to the service provider.

Creating a Fixed Hourly Billing Rate

To create a fixed billing rate that you can assign to a service provider, select Fixed Hourly Rate as the rate type. Then, enter a name for this billing rate level, and enter its hourly rate (see Figure 2-8).

Figure 2-8: Establish an hourly billing rate you can link to specific service providers.

After you link this billing rate to service providers, you can automatically invoice customers at this rate for any service performed by those people. Create all the fixed hourly rates you need.

Creating a Custom Hourly Billing Rate

To create a custom hourly rate, enter a name for the rate, and then select Custom Hourly Rate Per Service Item. The dialog changes to display all your service items (see Figure 2-9). Enter the hourly rate for each service that is performed by a person linked to this billing rate.

Figure 2-9: Enter the custom hourly rates for this billing rate.

Creating a Percentage Based Custom Rate

You can also create a custom rate by applying a percentage to the standard rate for a service. For example, you might want to set a rate of 10% more than the standard rate for service providers linked to the rate.

To accomplish this, follow the instructions for creating a custom hourly billing rate in the previous section. However, instead of entering a custom rate, select (check) the services you want to include, and then click Adjust Selected Rates. Configure the adjusted rate for either of the following choices:

- Indicate a percentage by which you want to raise or lower the rate based on the standard rate for the selected services.

- Indicate a percentage by which you want to raise or lower the rate based on the current billing rate level (one that you entered in the dialog before beginning the adjustment).

QuickBooks multiplies the amount by the percentage, and automatically fills in the rate (see Figure 2-10).

Figure 2-10: Automatically adjust a billing level by a percentage to create a custom rate.

Assigning Billing Rate Levels to Service Providers

After you've created billing rate levels, you must assign a level to each service provider. To do this, open the appropriate names list (Vendor, Employee, or Other Names) and select a service provider. Edit the record by selecting a rate from the Billing Rate Level drop-down list. (In the Employee record you must go to the Additional Info tab to find the Billing Rate Level field. In the Vendor record it's on the Payment Settings tab.)

Invoicing with Billing Rate Levels

To prepare invoices that use billing rate levels, you must use the timesheets that each service provider hands in. When you invoice your customers, the Billable Time/Costs dialog appears asking if you want to add the billable time and costs to the invoice. If you choose not to, you can still change your mind and click the Add Time/Costs icon on the invoice to add the costs. You can also apply any customer's percentage price level (usually a discount) to the billing rate invoice items.

You can also take advantage of the Invoice For Time & Expenses feature, found only in the Premier editions. See Chapter 3 for more about it.

Item List

Items are the things that appear on the sales forms you create, so your Item List contains all the goods and services you sell. However, there are other items you need to create because they, too, might appear on a sales form.

For example, sales tax is an item, as is shipping. Less obvious are some of the other items you need to add to sales forms as you sell your goods and services to customers, such as prepayments received, discounts applied, subtotals, and so on.

Understanding Item Types

Before you create the items you need to run your business, you should understand the item types that QuickBooks offers. Following are the names (and explanations) of the item types available when you create items:

Service

A service you sell to a customer. You can create services that are charged by the job or by the hour.

Inventory Part

A product you buy for reselling. This item type isn't available if you haven't enabled inventory tracking in the Items & Inventory category of the Preferences dialog.

Inventory Assembly

An item you build, usually from inventory parts. This item type is only available in QuickBooks Premier and Enterprise Editions. (See Chapter 6 to learn about using inventory assemblies.)

Non-Inventory Part

Use this item type for products that you don't track as inventory. This could be products you sell (without tracking inventory), or, if you do track inventory, the supplies you use (and charge customers for) for boxing and shipping inventory parts (e.g. tape, labels, and so on).

Other Charge

Use this item type for things like shipping charges, or other line items that appear on your invoices. In fact, some people create a separate Other Charge item for each method of shipping.

Subtotal

This item type adds up everything that comes before it on a sales form. You can use it to calculate a subtotal before you subtract any discounts or prepayments.

Group

You can use this item type to enter a group of items (all of which must already exist in your Item List) all at once. For example, you may sell something that is a package of separate items (and each of those items may be available for individual sale). Some service businesses, such as contractors, put individual services into a group in order to avoid lengthy invoices; for instance you may want a group named Demolition that includes carpentry, hauling, cleaning, and other services that are individual items in your Item List.

Discount

Use this item type to give a customer a discount as a line item. When you enter an item of the Discount Type, you can indicate a percentage as the rate. Keep in mind that it only applies to the line (not lines) directly above it.

Payment

Use this item type to add a customer's prepayment to an invoice. QuickBooks automatically calculates the total appropriately.

Sales Tax Item and Sales Tax Group

Use these item types to add sales tax to an invoice. Sales tax gets complicated in some states, and you have to be extremely careful about the way you set up sales tax items. Chapter 8 explains how to set up Sales Tax Items and Sales Tax Groups.

Creating Items

To create an item, open the Item List by choosing Lists | Item List from the menu bar. Then press Ctrl-N to open the New Item dialog.

Select the item type from the Type drop-down list. The item type you select determines the appearance of the New Item dialog, because different item types have different fields.

Creating Subitems

After you've created an item, you can create subitems. For example, for a particular product you can create subitems for different manufacturers. Or, you can create subitems for product sizes, types, colors, or other variations. Not all item types support subitems—look for the Subitem Of field in the New Item dialog.

To create a subitem, use the same steps required to create an item, and then click the Subitem Of option, and select the appropriate parent item from the drop-down list.

Importing the Item List

If you've been keeping your list of items in another software application, or on paper, you can avoid one-item-at-a-time data entry by importing the list into QuickBooks. You have three methods at your disposal for importing the list:

- Use the QuickBooks Setup wizard for service, inventory, and non-inventory types
- Import the list directly from an Excel file or a CSV file.
- Import the list from an IIF file.

If you've been using another application, you must export the data from that application to create your import file. This is only possible if your current application is capable of exporting data to one of the following formats:

- Excel file
- CSV (comma separated value) file
- Tab-delimited text file.

All three of these file types can be opened in Excel. If you use another spreadsheet application, you can use a CSV file or a tab-delimited text file (and some spreadsheet software is capable of loading Excel files and converting them to its own document type).

If you keep your item list on paper, or in a software application that can't export to the required file type, you can enter the information in a spreadsheet and then import the data into QuickBooks. It's usually faster to work in the rows of a spreadsheet document than to move from field to field, one item dialog at a time, in QuickBooks.

A QuickBooks item import file can contain all the information you need to fill out all the fields in the item dialog, but it's unlikely you've kept records in a manner that matches these fields. You can import whatever information you already have, and later enter additional information by editing the item records.

Detailed instructions for creating and importing Excel/CSV files are in Appendix A, and detailed instructions for creating and importing IIF files are in Appendix B. These instructions include all the column headings and keywords you need to import items into your QuickBooks company file.

You can also use the Add/Edit Multiple List Entries feature to add the following item types:

- Service
- Non-inventory part
- Inventory part

Manipulating List Data

You can perform the following actions on the records in your lists:

- Edit the fields in the record (see the ProAdvisor Note below for exceptions).
- Delete the record, providing no transactions are attached to the record.
- Hide the record by making it inactive.
- Merge two records to combine their histories.

ProAdvisor NOTE: *For an item record, you cannot edit the item's type unless the item is a Non-inventory Part or an Other Charge. All other item types are permanently assigned when you create the item, with one exception. You can change an Inventory Part to an Inventory Assembly, but nothing else.*

Using a Hidden List Component in Transactions

Hiding a record means making it inactive, which you can do by right-clicking the listing and choosing Make <List Name> Inactive. To see all the entries in a list, including inactive entries, take the following action:

- For the Customers & Jobs, Vendors, and Employees Lists, select All *<List Name>* from the View drop-down list at the top of the tab.
- For all other lists, select the Include Inactive option at the bottom of the list window.

When you view all entries, the inactive entries have a large X in the left-most column.

When a record is hidden, it doesn't appear in drop-down lists in transaction windows. Usually, you make a record inactive because you don't want anyone to use it, and you can't delete it (because it has been involved in transactions).

However, you may have other reasons to hide entries from users who create transactions, such as:

- A customer has a large overdue balance, and you don't want anyone to sell that customer more products or services, so you hide the customer (which automatically hides all the jobs).
- An item is seasonal, or will be out of stock for a long time (re-activate it when it can be sold again).
- Prevent purchasing goods from a vendor with whom you're having a dispute.

You can hide a record and still use it, which is a feature often used by business owners and bookkeepers who don't want other users to use certain records in transactions (so don't tell other users about this feature).

When you're entering data in a transaction window, don't use the drop-down list in the appropriate field (e.g. Vendor) because of course, the record won't appear in the list. Instead, enter the name manually.

QuickBooks displays a message asking if you want to use the account just once, or reactivate the account. Click the option to use the account just once. (You can use the account "just once" as many times as you want to.)

List Limits

QuickBooks limits the number of entries you can have in a list (except for the Enterprise Solutions Editions). Table 2-1 specifies the number of entries for each list. The entry labeled Names includes the following lists:

- Customers & Jobs
- Vendors
- Other Names
- Employees

However, the limits are a bit more complicated, and more stringent, than the table indicates. It's important to realize the following:

- The combined total of names for all the names lists cannot exceed 14,500.

- Once you have reached 10,000 names in a single name list, you cannot create any new objects for that list.

- Once you have reached 14,500 names in your combined name lists, you can no longer create any new names in any names list.

List	Maximum
Names (each list)	10000
Chart of accounts	10000
Items (excluding payroll items)	14500
Job types	10000
Vendor types	10000
Customer types	10000
Purchase orders	10000
Payroll items	10000
Price Levels	100
Classes	10000
Terms (combined A/R and A/P)	10000
Payment methods	10000
Shipping methods	10000
Customer messages	10000
Memorized reports	14500
Memorized transactions	14500
To Do notes	10000

Table 2-1: Maximum number of entries in lists.

When you reach a list maximum, QuickBooks locks the list(s), and when a list is locked, that's a permanent decision. Deleting objects doesn't free up space for new entries. It's too late.

ProAdvisor TIP: *To view your current list numbers press F2 to open the QuickBooks Product Information Window. The List Information box displays the list totals.*

QuickBooks also imposes a maximum on the number of transactions in a file, but since that number is 2,000,000,000 (yes, two billion), it's unlikely that a small business would exceed that number.

Every individual action you perform is a transaction. Filling out a transaction window is an obvious transaction, but when you edit, delete, or void a transaction, that counts as a transaction. If you reach the maximum number of transactions, your company file is locked and you can't add anything to that file.

Creating Custom Fields In Lists

Custom fields are useful if there's information you want to track, but QuickBooks doesn't provide a field for it. You can add custom fields to the customer, vendor, employee, and item lists.

After you create a custom field, you must populate the field with data in each record that uses the custom field. In addition, you can add the custom field to transaction templates, so you can see the data you entered while you're creating a transaction.

ProAdvisor TIP: *You can customize most QuickBooks reports to include the data in custom fields.*

Custom Fields for Names Lists

You can add a custom field to the any names list except Other Names, which means you can add custom fields to the customer, vendor, and employee lists.

After you create a custom field, you can assign it to multiple names list. For example, an owner whose business participates in a softball league (for businesses in his industry), might add a custom field labeled Team Name to his employee, vendor, and customer lists.

You can create up to fifteen custom fields, but you can only add seven fields to an individual list. A custom field that overlaps lists counts as one field on each list. For example, if you add the same field to all three lists, you can still add six other fields to each list.

To add a custom field to your QuickBooks file that you can apply to a names list, open any employee, vendor, or customer record. It doesn't matter which list you use to create the custom field; after the new field exists you assign it to the names list (or multiple names lists) for which it's intended.

In the record you open, move to the Additional Info tab and click the Define Fields button. Enter names for the custom fields and select the list(s) to which you want to add this field (see Figure 2-11).

Figure 2-11: Create a custom field and assign it to as many names lists as necessary.

Custom Fields for Items

You can add up to five custom fields for items. However, your custom field won't be available for the following item types:

- Subtotals
- Sales tax items
- Sales tax groups

To create a custom field, open any item record that supports custom fields, click Custom Fields, and then click Define fields. If this is the first custom field you're creating for items, QuickBooks displays a message saying that no custom fields currently exist, and telling you to click the Define Fields button to create a custom field.

In the Define Custom Fields for Items dialog, enter the custom field name, and place a check mark in the Use column to place the field in item records (see Figure 2-12).

Figure 2-12: Add custom fields to items for information you need when you create transactions and reports.

After you've created your first custom field for items, when you click the Custom Fields button on an item record, the Custom Fields For *<item name>* dialog opens, displaying the existing custom fields. To create additional fields, click Define Fields.

Entering Data in Custom Fields

Custom fields aren't useful until you populate them with data in the names and/or item records.

To add data to a custom field in a Names list, open the appropriate record (e.g. a customer or vendor name) and move to the Additional Info tab. Enter data that's specific to this record, and continue to enter data in every record that requires information in the custom fields.

To add data to a custom field in the Item List, open the appropriate item and click Custom Fields. Then add data for this item in the custom fields.

The data you enter in custom fields should be consistent from record to record. For example, let's say you're tracking vendor information or item information in a custom field named Co-op Adv (to display the formula for co-op advertising revenue). If the formula is a certain percentage of co-op refunds for a minimum purchase, decide on the format of the text to use for every record. For example, you could enter 10%-20K if the co-op formula is 10% for a minimum purchase of $20,000.00. Don't enter the same type of data in different ways, such as:

- 10-20000
- 10%-20K
- 10-$20K

If your data is inconsistent, it's difficult (if not impossible) to produce reports that provide the information you need about the data in custom fields.

Adding Custom Field Data in Batches

If you have a lot of names or items for which you need to populate custom fields with data, you can make the changes in Excel (after exporting the list as an IIF file and importing the changed file back in QuickBooks) or in the Add/Edit Multiple List Entries window.

Adding Custom Fields to Transaction Forms

Some custom fields should appear in transaction templates, because the data in the field helps you create the transaction more efficiently.

For example, QuickBooks doesn't provide a field in customer records to indicate how the customer wants you to deal with backorders. There's no point in tracking backorders for customers who indicate they want you to ship what's available and forget the rest of the order, or for a customer who wants you to hold shipment until backordered items are available.

Create a custom field named Backorders, and enter data for each customer to indicate how backorders should be handled. Then, customize sales transaction templates to include the customer's backorder data on the screen when you're creating the transaction.

You should be aware of the "rules" that govern the way custom fields are added to transaction windows. (According to the e-mail queries we receive, this rule isn't well known.):

- Custom fields in the Names lists are added to the transaction template as fields in the **heading section**.
- Custom fields in the Item List are added to the transaction template as **columns** in the line item section.

Customizing a template is a two-step process: First, duplicate the built-in template you want to use as the basis of the new template and give it a new name, and second, customize the new template.

Duplicating a Template

Use the following steps to duplicate a built-in template:

1. Choose Lists | Templates to open the Templates list window.
2. Select the listing for the template you want to customize, click the Templates button at the bottom of the list, and choose Duplicate.
3. In the Select Template Type dialog, select the type of template and click OK.
4. The Templates list window displays a listing named Copy Of: <Template>,
5. Double-click that listing to open the Basic Customization dialog.
6. Click Manage Templates and in the right pane of the Manage Templates dialog, change the name of the template. Use a name that describes your customization—for example InvoiceWithBackorderInfo.
7. Click OK to return to the Basic Customization dialog.

In this dialog you can make minor changes to the template, such as changing fonts, colors, the company information that prints on the transaction document, and so on.

However, in this case you want to make major changes to the template, to add fields or columns to the document. The following section, Customizing the Template, covers those tasks.

Customizing the Template

With your new template displayed in the Basic Customization dialog, click the Additional Customization button at the bottom of the dialog. This action opens the Additional Customization dialog seen in Figure 2-13.

Figure 2-13: Customize the template to make sure all the information you require is included.

On the Header tab you can include or exclude fields for the on-screen version, the printed version, or both. For example, if you've created a custom field for backorder data (refer back to Figure 2-13), you'll only need it to appear on the screen as you prepare the invoice, and not on the printed document you send.

As you begin making changes QuickBooks may display a message about using the Layout Designer to make sure all the elements you're changing fit properly in the template. Most of the changes you make don't require a complete overhaul of the layout, so you can select the option to stop displaying the message.

Keep an eye on the preview panel in the right pane, or click Print Preview to see if changes you're making (for the printed copy) cause fields or columns to overlap. If so, you can use the Layout Designer to move fields and columns. The Layout Designer is not difficult to use, so we're not covering it here – the QuickBooks Help Files provide good assistance.

Move to the Columns tab (see Figure 2-14) to see if there are any columns you want to select or deselect. The custom fields you created for items are included in the list. You can also change the order in which columns appear by changing the number in the Order list.

Figure 2-14: The custom field named Bin can be added to the template.

Click OK when you finish customizing fields and columns, and then click OK in the Basic Customization dialog to save the new template. Now you can select it from the Template field when you create transactions.

Classes

Classes let you group transactions to match the way you want to track and report your business activities. You can use classes to "classify" your business by some pattern, such as divisions, branches, or type of activity.

The ability to classify your business means you can produce P & L reports by class, so you can see how each department, division, or location is doing. You can also see the class totals for each class in your Balance Sheet.

To use classes, you must enable the feature, which is listed in the Accounting category of the Preferences dialog. Once classes are enabled, QuickBooks adds a Class field to your transaction windows. For each transaction, you can assign one of the classes you create.

Classes only work well if you use them consistently, but it's common for users to skip the Class field in transactions. QuickBooks offers a feature to help everyone remember to assign a class to a transaction. You can enable that feature by selecting the option Prompt To Assign Classes, which is available in the same Preferences dialog you use to enable classes (the Company Preferences tab of the Accounting category).

When you enable this feature, any time a user tries to save or close a transaction without assigning classes, QuickBooks displays a reminder message about assigning a class. However, the message is merely a reminder, and QuickBooks will let the user continue to save the transaction without class assignments. You must train users about the importance of assigning classes, or you won't get the reports you want.

When you create your classes, include the following two classes in addition to the classes you create for departments, division, locations, etc..

- Other, which users can select if they're not sure which class a transaction belongs to. Later, you can create a report on transactions linked to the Other class, and drill down through each transaction to apply the appropriate class.
- Administration (or Overhead), which you can use for posting expenses that aren't applicable to a specific class

you created. Use the totals in this class to allocate that overhead to class expenses (via a journal entry).

Creating a Class

To create a class choose Lists | Class List to open the Class List. Press Ctrl-N to open a New Class dialog (see Figure 2-15), and enter the name of the class in the Class Name field.

Figure 2-15: Creating a class is one of the easiest tasks in QuickBooks.

Using Subclasses

Classes work best for a single purpose, such as separating your business into locations or by type of business (wholesale and retail). If you need further classifications, you can use subclasses.

Create the broad classes you need, and then create subclasses for those classes that need additional classification. For example, if you create classes for locations, you might want to separate the classification of transactions between wholesale and retail for each location, or between sales and service for each location.

Class Reports

To generate a report on the Profit & Loss for each class choose Reports | Company & Financial | Profit & Loss By Class. To generate a report on class totals on the Balance Sheet choose Reports | Company & Financial | Balance Sheet By Class. The reports display columns for each class.

The Unclassified column (if it exists in the report) contains all the totals for transactions in which the user failed to enter a class. You can drill down into those transactions to add the appropriate class.

CHAPTER 3

Premier Sales Features

- Easier invoicing for time and expenses

- Internal costs reimbursements

- Sales orders

- Backorders

- Creating transactions automatically

The QuickBooks Premier editions have features that enhance the functions available to you for sales transactions. These features aren't available in QuickBooks Pro, and in this chapter we'll discuss the additional power you get in your Premier edition.

Easier Invoicing for Time and Expenses

In the Premier editions you can create customer invoices for time and reimbursable expenses from a single window (named Invoice For Time & Expenses) that displays all the charges waiting to be invoiced to customers. This means you can invoice customers for time and expenses in two ways:

- You can use the Invoice For Time & Expenses window to create invoices for these charges quickly.
- You can use the standard QuickBooks Add Time/ Costs feature to invoice customers for these charges when you're creating a regular invoice for items and services.

ProAdvisor TIP: *You can also add "regular" charges for products and services to any invoice you create from the list of time and expenses.*

The advantage of the Invoice For Time & Expenses window is that when you're creating invoices, the list eliminates the need to wait until you're preparing an invoice for a customer to learn whether there are reimbursable costs that need to be invoiced.

Enabling the Invoice for Time & Expenses Feature

You have to enable this feature in the Time & Expenses category of the Preferences dialog. Select the Company Preferences tab (see Figure 3-1) and check the option labeled Create Invoices From A List Of Time And Expenses.

Note that this feature is independent of the other options on this dialog. Even if you don't track time, or don't treat reimbursed expenses as income (instead, you post reimbursed expenses back to the expense account that received the original posting), you can enable this feature.

Figure 3-1: Enable this easy-to-use list for invoicing expenses to customers.

Opening the Invoice for Time & Expenses Window

When this preference is enabled, QuickBooks adds the command Invoice For Time & Expenses to the Customers menu. Select that command to open the Invoice For Time & Expenses window.

Changing the Columns in the Invoice for Time & Expenses Window

You can control the columns that appear in the window. Right-click anywhere in the listings part of the window to see the available columns

(Time, Expenses, Mileage, and Items), and select or deselect the columns you want to view (see Figure 3-2).

Figure 3-2: View the list of customers who have reimbursable charges waiting to be invoiced.

Choosing the Date Range for Time & Expenses

You can select a date range for viewing unbilled expenses by filling in the From and To fields, but it's hard to think of a good reason to enter data in the From field. If you do, and if there are unbilled reimbursable expenses before the date you enter in the From field, the system omits them. In the To field, enter the date you'll be using for invoices. From the Template field select the invoice template you wish to use.

How the Invoice for Time & Expenses Window Calculates Amounts

The list of time and expenses found here is a convenience; a way to view the list of customers for whom you assigned expenses that haven't yet been added to invoices for those customers. The amounts that appear in this list may not be the amounts you'll add to their invoices. In fact, the amounts you see on the list may confuse you.

For example, in Figure 3-2, the customer Barley, Rene displays zero in every category. Obviously, some expense or other has been linked to this customer or else the customer wouldn't appear on the list. What's going on?

To understand the totals you see, you have to understand the process that builds the list. This process varies according to the type of reimbursable charge.

For Expenses and Items, QuickBooks uses the following process:

1. Checks transactions (usually Vendor bills or direct checks) to see if a customer or job is linked to the transaction.
2. If a customer or job is linked, checks the status of the Billable field for the transaction.
3. If the Billable field is marked, uses the amount in the calculation for this customer.

For Time charges, the following process occurs:

1. Checks timesheets to see if a customer or job is entered on a timesheet charge.
2. If so, checks the status of the Billable field for the charge.
3. If marked Billable, checks the price of the Service item using the data in the item's record in the Item List.
4. Multiplies the number of hours by the price that exists in the item's record and use the amount in the calculation for this customer.

For Mileage charges, the following process occurs:

1. Checks transactions entered in the Enter Vehicle Mileage transaction form to see if a customer or job is entered on the form.
2. If so, checks the status of the Billable field for the charge.

3. If marked Billable, checks the price of the mileage item in the mileage item's record in the Item List.

4. Multiplies the number of miles by the price that exists in the item's record and use the amount in the calculation for this customer.

The problem, or potential problem, occurs in time or mileage charges you've posted as billable to a customer. If the service item or mileage item doesn't have a price in its item record, the price is considered to be zero. If the timesheet or the vehicle mileage transaction form records a quantity of X, the calculation is "X multiplied by 0", which is, of course, zero.

When you select the listing in order to create an invoice, click the Add/Time Costs in the transaction window. Look in the Mileage and Time tabs to see the reimbursable costs that are linked to the customer. Then enter the amount you want to use for the invoice.

ProAdvisor TIP: *The best way to set up items (to use this list efficiently and to make it easier to track job costing) is to configure items with both cost and price information. A price field is always available in an item record. Item dialogs for many item types include an option that says the item is used in assemblies, or is subcontracted, or purchased for a customer (the text differs depending on the type of item). Selecting that option adds fields to the dialog where you can enter costs and select the expense account.*

Creating Invoices from the Invoice for Time & Expenses Window

You have two methods for creating an invoice from the Invoice For Time & Expenses window:

- Automatically create the invoice using the data displayed for the customer.

- Select the option labeled Let Me Select Specific Billables For This Customer:Job

The latter method lets you enter a different rate for expenses (necessary if the displayed expenses are zero), and also lets you choose specific expenses for the invoice you're preparing (leaving the remaining expenses for a later invoice).

Creating Invoices Automatically

To create an invoice automatically, place a check mark to the left of the Customer:Job for which you want to create an invoice and click Create Invoice. QuickBooks opens the Create Invoices transaction window with the customer or job, and the invoice data already entered.

You can add other items (services or products) to the invoice. Then click Save & Close to return to the Invoice For Time & Expenses list.

Creating Batch Invoices

The ability to create multiple invoices at once is another handy feature you'll find here. Simply place a check mark next to each Customer:Job that you want to invoice and click Next Step (formerly Create Invoice). This opens the Batch Invoice For Time & Expenses window seen in Figure 3-3.

Figure 3-3: Creating batch invoices save a lot of time.

You can change the settings for how billables are transferred by clicking the Edit Options button. If you want to take a look at the billables before creating the invoices click the Review Billables button. When you're satisfied everything is correct, click Create Invoice (or Next Step) to generate the invoice(s) for the selected Customer:Job(s).

Modifying Billables

When creating a single invoice you can review the billables by selecting the option labeled Let Me Select Specific Billables For This Customer:Job. When you click the Create Invoice button, a Create Invoices transaction window opens, along with the Choose Billable Time And Costs dialog (see Figure 3-4).

Figure 3-4: Select the reimbursable costs you want to add to the invoice.

This is the same dialog you see when you're creating invoices and click the Add Time/Costs button on the transaction form toolbar. You can select the costs you want to include on the invoice and click OK to return to the Invoice transaction form. If the cost in the Add Time/Costs window is 0.00, select it and after it's transferred to the Invoice form you can enter the amount.

In addition to the billable expenses, you can add services and products to the invoice before saving it.

Internal Costs Reimbursements

This function isn't a built-in function in QuickBooks Premier editions, but it's a clever way to track internal costs and add those costs to invoices.

Some of the office work you do for customers generates internal costs, such as the use of a copy machine, expenses for special mailings, messenger or delivery services by employees, charges for the use of special equipment, or any other work involving equipment or time that has a real cost.

Many businesses add an "overhead" charge or a "handling" charge to their invoices, based on a calculated average cost. It's possible, however, to track these costs more accurately, and add specific reimbursement charges to customer invoices.

Setting Up Internal Cost Tracking

Passing regular vendor costs to customers is easy; you just mark the vendor's cost as billable to a specific customer. However, when you want to invoice customers for reimbursement of internal costs, there's no check to a vendor. The cure is a "fake" vendor, which in turn requires a "fake" bank account (because you can't write checks to your fake vendor from your real bank account).

- Create a vendor named InternalCosts.
- Create a bank account named Internal Costs Clearing Account. The bank account will always have a zero balance, so it won't affect your balance sheet.
- Create Items for invoicing internal costs (usually an Other Charge item).

The item you create can be generic, named Costs, or you can create a parent item named Costs and use subitems for specific costs (such as color copies, special postage costs, etc.).

Link the item to Other Expenses, or create another expense account specifically for each item. The expense account won't ever have a balance, so it won't affect your P & L.

You can set a price for those items that have known prices, such as .03 for black & white copies and .13 for color copies. Some costs can't be priced until you create the transaction, such as the cost of using an employee to deliver something or run another type of errand.

Creating Reimbursable Charges for Internal Costs

To create a reimbursable charge, open the Write Checks window (see Figure 3-5) and take the following steps:

1. Select the fake bank account you created for internal costs.

2. Ignore (or remove) the check number; this account is never reconciled.

3. Select the Internal Costs vendor.

4. Use the Items tab, not the Expenses tab.

5. Enter a reimbursable cost item and an amount, select the customer or job, and make sure the Billable column has a check mark.

6. On the next line, enter the same item and enter a negative amount equal to the amount of the reimbursable cost. Do not enter a customer or job on this line.

7. Repeat for each item you need to include on customer invoices.

Now these costs are in your system and can be used in invoices. All of the costs you enter in this manner appear on the Invoice For Time & Expenses window (discussed in the previous section), and on the Items tab of the Choose Billable Time And Costs dialog you see when you're creating an invoice for a customer with unbilled costs.

Figure 3-5: A zero-based check to a fake vendor on a fake bank account creates reimbursable charges for internal costs.

Internal Costs Job Costing

If you want to use internal costs for job costing, without invoicing customers for reimbursement, use the steps described in the previous section, but deselect the check mark in the Billable column of the check. Use the report named Profit & Loss By Job to see your job costs.

Sales Orders

The QuickBooks Premier Editions include support for sales orders, and that makes life a lot easier for you if you sell products. Inherent in sales orders is the ability to track backorders – a sales order that has items waiting to be shipped and invoiced is, in effect, a backorder.

Without the additional features in QuickBooks Premier editions, you have to use complicated workarounds to track these functions.

ProAdvisor NOTE: *Sales orders are most useful for inventory items.*

When you create a sales order, no financial accounts are affected. The transaction itself is posted to the Sales Order account in your chart of accounts, which is a non-posting account. You can run a QuickReport to view or manipulate the sales orders you've created. Highlight the account (non-posting accounts are listed at the bottom of the chart of accounts) and press Ctrl-Q. Double-click a sales order on the report to open the original transaction window.

The inventory items included in a sales order are marked to indicate the fact that they're reserved on a sales order, and the appropriate calculations are made to Quantity Available reports. However, no financial postings are made to income, COGS, or the inventory asset accounts.

Enabling Sales Orders

To use sales orders, you must enable the feature by choosing Edit | Preferences and selecting the Sales & Customers category. In the Company Preferences tab, make sure the option Enable Sales Orders is selected. You can also enable the following additional sales order options:

- Warn About Duplicate Sales Order Numbers. Sales orders have their own self-incrementing number system (unconnected to invoice numbering). It's a good idea to select this option to keep your sales order records accurate.

- Don't Print Items With Zero Amounts When Converting To Invoice. Selecting this option removes any line item that has a zero amount in the Ordered column or in the Rate column from the printed version of the sales order (or the invoice created from the sales order). The onscreen copy of the sales order still shows all the lines.

Enabling Warnings about Inventory Stock Status

All editions of QuickBooks offer the option to warn you that the Quantity On Hand (QOH) is insufficient to ship the product you're selling, when you're creating an invoice.

In the Premier editions, you can enable warnings that are more precise. You can tell QuickBooks to examine additional data when determining whether you have sufficient inventory to turn a sales order into an invoice.

All of the options for enabling warnings about inventory stock status are in the Company Preferences tab of the Items & Inventory Preferences dialog (see Figure 3-6), which you reach by choosing Edit | Preferences.

Figure 3-6: You can specify how QuickBooks reports stock status when you sell inventory items.

Quantity on Hand Vs. Quantity Available

The options referring to calculating and reporting quantities while you're creating sales transactions are actually giving you a choice between tracking Quantity on Hand or Quantity Available.

Quantity on Hand (QOH) is the number of units in the warehouse (or the garage, or wherever you store your inventory). It's a "shelf count".

Quantity Available is a more precise figure; it's the number of those units on the shelves that are available for you to sell. This is where the option entitled When Calculating Quantity Available For My Inventory, Deduct: comes in. It can take into account both pending builds and sales orders.

If you select the option to be warned about the quantity available, QuickBooks deducts all the units of stock that are currently on sales orders that haven't yet been turned into invoices. The resulting number is the amount of stock available for you to enter in a sales order. (When sales orders are turned into invoices, the inventory comes off the shelves, which changes the QOH.)

If you don't select that option, QuickBooks doesn't deduct the number of units currently promised on sales orders, and therefore the quantity available isn't accurate.

If anyone else converts a sales order with the same product into an invoice before you do, and packs and ships the stock, you'll be surprised, because the 10 units of widgets you thought you could sell a customer are not available. That's because you didn't know about those sales orders that were entered before you created your sales order.

Don't get too excited about this feature-unfortunately the warning doesn't appear when you're entering a sales order (which is, of course, when you'd like to know these things). The warning appears when you convert the sales order to an invoice. Well, that's not entirely true. In several of the Premier editions the warning is displayed when you create the sales order. Those include the Accountant Edition (see Chapter 9), Manufacturing & Wholesale Edition (see Chapter 11), and Retail Edition (see Chapter 14)

Creating Sales Orders

After you enable sales orders in the Preferences dialog, a Sales Order icon appears on the Home page, and the Create Sales Orders command appears on the Customer menu. Use either access point to open a blank Create Sales Orders window, which looks very much like an invoice window (see Figure 3-7). Fill in the heading and line item sections, and save the sales order.

Figure 3-7: The Sales Order transaction form is similar to an invoice.

Sales Order Templates

The first time you open the sales order transaction window, the Custom Sales Order template is selected by default. QuickBooks Premier Industry Editions provide several templates for sales orders (the plain Premier Edition offers only the Custom Sales Order template). You can select the template you prefer from the drop-down list in the Templates field.

Sales Order With Rep adds the Rep field to the Custom Sales Order template. The sales rep for the customer is automatically filled in, as long as you entered the sales rep in the customer's record. You can change the sales rep (frequently the person creating the sales order inserts his or her own name in that field), and when you save the sales order, QuickBooks displays a dialog that asks if you want to change the sales rep on the customer's record to match the new selection. Select Yes or No, depending on the circumstances and your policies about sales reps and commissions.

Work Order is almost the same as the Custom Sales Order, but the transaction title is Work Order instead of Sales Order. Also, the Rate column is removed and the Customer Message field is replaced with a Notes field. Use this template when you're creating a custom-built product.

Standard Work Order adds the following fields to the Work Order template: Terms, Rep, and Ship Date.

ProAdvisor NOTE: *QuickBooks also offers a Pick List and a Packing Slip in the Template drop-down list. In some Premier Editions you'll find Layaway and Retail Sales Order templates as well.*

Turning Sales Orders into Invoices

Businesses have a variety of standards and protocols upon which they base the decision to turn a sales order into an invoice. Some businesses require a sales person to obtain a manager's approval to verify the customer's credit status, or to approve a price change (usually when a discount is involved). Some businesses merely wait until the items on a sales order are picked and packed.

Regardless of the protocols you use, eventually you turn a sales order into an invoice, and you have two methods for accomplishing this task:

- Open a blank Create Invoices window, and load the sales order into the form.
- Open the original sales order, and convert it to an invoice with a click of the mouse.

Create an Invoice by Selecting a Sales Order

To create an invoice by loading an existing sales order into the Invoice, press Ctrl-I to open a blank Create Invoices window.

When you select the customer or job in an Invoice template, Quick-Books opens the Available Sales Orders dialog seen in Figure 3-8, which lists all the current open sales orders. (If no sales orders exist for the selected customer or job, the dialog doesn't appear.)

Figure 3-8: QuickBooks automatically displays all the open sales orders for the selected customer or job.

Select the appropriate sales order(s), and click OK. See "Creating the Invoice", later in this section to learn how to move through the rest of the processes.

Converting a Sales Order to an Invoice

You can open the original sales order to create the invoice. You have two quick ways to find the original sales order:

- Select the customer or job from the Customers & Jobs tab in the Customer Center, and select the sales order in the right pane. (If the right pane displays a long list of transactions, filter the list by selecting Sales Orders from the drop-down list in the Show field.)
- Choose Reports | Sales | Open Sales Orders By Customer.

Double-click the listing for the sales order you need, which opens the original transaction window. Then click the button labeled Create Invoice at the top of the sales order to turn the sales order into an invoice.

Creating the Invoice

Whether you start from the Create Invoices window or the Sales Order window, creating an invoice from a sales order works the same way.

QuickBooks displays the Create Invoice Based On Sales Order(s) dialog (see Figure 3-9), so you can decide whether to create an invoice for the entire sales order, or create an invoice for only specific items on the sales order.

Figure 3-9: Select the appropriate option for filling the sales order.

The latter option exists in case some items aren't available (in which case they stay open on the sales order, creating a virtual backorder).

ProAdvisor TIP: *Select Create Invoice For Selected Items, even if you want to invoice the entire sales order. If you elect to create the invoice for all items, QuickBooks does warn you about insufficient on hand quantities, but doesn't bother to inform you which items are affected. Selecting Create Invoices For Selected Items displays the Specify Invoice Quantities For Items On Sales Order(s) dialog which gives you on hand quantities for all items on the sales order.*

If there's not enough stock to fill this sales order, you'll encounter some problems after you select the option to create an invoice for the entire sales order.

However, we'll go over both scenarios, and we'll show you what happens if you opt to fill the entire sales order and then find out you don't have enough stock.

ProAdvisor NOTE: *If the sales order includes only one product, it doesn't matter which option you select.*

Invoicing the Entire Sales Order

If you selected the option to invoice the entire sales order, and you have enough stock to fill the order, the Create Invoices window opens with everything filled in from the sales order. QuickBooks automatically uses the Custom S.O. Invoice template, because it is configured to display columns that can hold the information from the sales order.

Add the shipping costs if you charge customers for shipping. Add other items to the invoice, such as service items, or any additional products the customer has ordered. Then print and send the invoice as you usually do.

Managing Insufficient Quantities

If any items on the sales order don't have a sufficient QOH, the warning message seen in Figure 3-10 appears. Unfortunately, the warning message doesn't tell you which item is in short supply.

Figure 3-10: Uh oh

Click OK to clear the warning message and the invoice appears, automatically filled in with all the items that were on the sales order. However, you still have no indication about which item lacked sufficient QOH to ship this order. (Unless you're running Premier Accountant, Manufacturing and Wholesale, or Retail editions, each of which has a Current Availability icon in the Invoiced column. Clicking the icon displays the Currently Available dialog which provides QOH and Quantity Available information.) There are several methods for solving this mystery:

- Run the Item Listing report (Reports | List | Item Listing) which shows the QOH for all items except

Fixed Asset items. You can then sort by QOH to quickly identify those items either out of stock or low. You could run the Inventory Stock Status By Item report, but since you can't change the sort criteria it's not as useful.

- If you think the inventory records are wrong, or you know you have sufficient quantity to ship because the order has been picked, create an Inventory Adjustment to correct the quantity and then return to the invoice.

- If you don't use pick slips, or you don't pick and pack an order until it's invoiced, you can walk into the warehouse and count the QOH for each item on the invoice. If sufficient inventory exists, create an Inventory Adjustment to correct the quantity and then return to the invoice.

If sufficient stock isn't available, adjust the quantity in the Invoiced column. Repeat for each item in the invoice that has insufficient quantities.

ProAdvisor CAUTION: *Never sell an inventory item into negative quantity – it wreaks havoc with the amount posted to Costs of Goods Sold.*

When you change the number in the Invoiced column, the invoice changes depending on the Premier edition you're using:

- In the Accountant, Manufacturing & Wholesale, and Retail Premier editions, QuickBooks automatically enters the difference between the Ordered and Invoiced columns in the Backordered column. You don't have to look up the current stock status. If you don't see the Backordered column open the template in the Advanced Customization dialog, move to the Prog Cols tab, and add the field to the form.

- In all other Premier editions, no Backorder calculation is available. Instead, the original sales order is saved and displays the number of units you invoiced.

When you open the original sales order (see Figure 3-11), the products that appeared on the invoice are marked closed (a check mark appears in the CLSD column). The products that had insufficient quantity to ship are not closed, and the sales order displays the original number of units ordered as well the number of units Invoiced (and, we can assume, shipped).

Figure 3-11: The sales order now shows the number of products that are included on the invoice.

The sales order remains open, and when you receive the products you can invoice the remainder of the order. Note that the sales order in Figure 3-11 contains a Backordered column, which means that it was generated in one of the three Premier editions that supports backorders.

Invoicing Selected Items

If you chose the option Create Invoice For Selected Items, clicking OK opens the Specify Invoice Quantities For Items On Sales Order dialog.

The information available with this option for creating the invoice makes it much easier to prepare the invoice properly.

The QOH for each item is displayed, but you can't trust the numbers on this dialog unless you select the option to show the quantity available instead of the quantity on hand. The QOH does not take existing sales orders into consideration.

Selecting the option Show Quantity Available Instead Of Quantity On Hand often reveals the fact that the items on hand are already linked to one or more sales orders (see Figure 3-12).

If necessary, adjust the number of units in the To Invoice column of the dialog. The sales order is loaded in the Create Invoices transaction window, using the numbers you adjusted (the units to invoice).

Earlier in this chapter, we told you how to set your preferences to warn about the available quantity instead of the QOH, but that preference only applies when you're creating an invoice. The Specify Invoice Quantities For Items On Sales Order dialog obviously doesn't look up that preference. Therefore, you have to select the option Show Quantity Available... to match the preferences you set.

When the quantity that's available is less than the QOH, it means the item is on a sales order (including the sales order you're currently converting to an invoice), or on multiple sales orders. The items are still on the shelf, they're just promised.

In many companies, this kicks off any of several amusing scenarios involving sprint races and arguments. If the other sales orders aren't yet ready for invoicing, you win. But before you can claim your prize (the right to create an invoice), you have to prevent other people from doing the same thing. Someone may be ready to invoice a sales order that contains the same item. Here's how to win for real:

1. Run, don't walk, to the warehouse, and gather up the quantity you need of the items that are in short supply.

2. Take the items to the shipping desk and mark them with the invoice number you're preparing. (It doesn't hurt to

add a threatening note about the consequences to anybody who thinks about appropriating these items to create an invoice from one of the other sales orders.)

3. If you think Step 2 won't work, bring the items back to your desk and hide them until you finish your invoice, and then take them to the shipping desk and stay there to supervise the packing process.

Specify Invoice Quantities for Items on Sales Order(s)							✕
Invoice for: Balak, Mike:Utility Shed					OK		
For each item below, specify the quantity you will ship on this invoice.					Cancel		
☑ Show quantity available instead of quantity on hand					Help		
ITEM	DATE	S.O. NO.	AVAILABLE	ORDERED	PREV. INV...	TO INVOICE	U/M
Gadget	12/15/20...	7005	-6	4	0	0	
Cabinets:Light Pine	12/15/20...	7005	-1	2	0	2	

Figure 3-12: There's not sufficient quantity available to fill this order.

If multiple users are working on multiple computers on the network, turning sales orders into invoices, it's more difficult to declare yourself the winner. Somebody else may have already confiscated the items, or several of you may arrive in the warehouse at the same time.

Instead of a tug-of-war, you need to set shipping priorities. I've seen these discussions turn into real arguments, although there's usually an executive who declares the winner. Here's the priority list many companies use:

- The first priority is a customer who doesn't accept backorders, and wants you to ship and invoice only what's in stock.

- The second priority is a "best customer"-a customer it's important to keep happy (of course, a "best customer" is usually defined by the amount of money the customer spends with your company).

- The third priority is whatever argument the best debater in the group presents. This usually involves listening to phrases such as "this is the first order from a new customer", or "we've done this to this customer three times already".

If you can't ship all the items, you have to change the numbers in the Specify Invoice Quantities For Items On Sales Order(s) dialog. In the To Invoice column, enter the quantity you want to invoice. Then click OK.

If an item isn't available, and you entered zero for the amount to invoice, QuickBooks issues a warning message about handling zero amount items (see Figure 3-13).

Figure 3-13: QuickBooks warns you not to delete items from the invoice.

The warning is important, because if you delete the zero amount line items, you won't be able to track backorders. (You can tell QuickBooks to avoid printing zero items by setting that preference in the Sales & Customers category of the Preferences dialog in the Company Preferences tab.)

It's helpful to print zero amount line items. After all, the customer certainly remembers the original order, and you're showing the customer that you, too, remember the items in the original order. However, if you choose not to print the zero-based lines, they remain on the on-screen version so you can track the items for backorders. If you're shipping and invoicing fewer than the number of items on the sales order (but not zero), that also qualifies as a backorder.

ProAdvisor TIP: *If you know this customer won't accept backorders, and has issued instructions to ship whatever is available, it's OK to delete the zero-based lines. You won't be tracking backorders for this customer.*

Save the invoice, print it, and ship the goods that are in stock. If the invoice matches the sales order (meaning everything on the sales order was shipped), the original sales order is marked Invoiced In Full when you view it. All you have to do is wait for the customer's check to arrive.

If the invoice didn't match the sales order, the unshipped goods remain on the sales order. When the products arrive, open the sales order, click the Create Invoice button, and start the process again to get the remaining items to the customer.

When you save the invoice, only the amounts on the invoice are posted to the Accounts Receivable, Income, Inventory, and Cost of Goods accounts. The amounts for backordered items are not posted to the general ledger.

Managing Backorders

When you aren't able to ship and invoice all the items in a sales order, the sales order becomes a virtual backorder, even if you're not using one of the Premier editions that tracks backorders, because the sales order maintains information about the items that were not invoiced.

Tracking Receipt of Goods

Unfortunately, as new products arrive in your warehouse, QuickBooks does not assign the products to existing unfilled sales orders (backorders) automatically. Instead, you must manually track incoming goods against the backorders in your system.

You can track incoming goods within QuickBooks, or outside of QuickBooks. In this section, we'll go over some of the techniques that are working well for our clients.

Using Stock Status Reports

You can track the status of items by viewing a stock status report, and comparing the contents to the backorders you're tracking. Get into the habit of printing your backorders, which you can do by calling up a sales order after its partially filled linked invoice has been created, and clicking the Print button.

To see a stock status report, choose Reports | Inventory | Inventory Stock Status By Item. The report that opens lists every item in inventory, along with its current status (on hand, on purchase order, on sales order).

The usefulness of this report varies, depending on the number of items you stock, and the number of backorders you're tracking. If your company has a limited number of items, it's not terribly difficult to go through the report to find the items you're looking for in order to fill your backorders. However, if you have a lot of items, or many backorders (or both), it's more efficient to design reports that give you what you need quickly.

Creating Customized Stock Status Reports

If you create customized stock status reports for backorders, you can check each customer's backorder quickly, which is handy if the customer calls and asks when you expect to ship the remaining products.

To do this, you need to customize the report on a per-customer basis, or on a per backorder basis. Either way, start by choosing Reports | Inventory | Inventory Stock Status By Item.

Customizing the Display of a Stock Status Report

When the report opens, make it easier to read by eliminating columns that don't provide information you need. You cannot use the Customize Report feature to remove columns on this particular report, but you can close up the columns so you don't have to scroll through the report.

Use the diamond-shaped marker to the right of any column you don't need, dragging it to the left until the column disappears. The following columns can safely disappear for the purpose of tracking backorders:

- Pref Vendor
- Reorder Pt
- Order
- Sales/Week

Customizing the Content of a Stock Status Report

To customize the report for customers or backorders, click Customize Report, and make the following customizations:

1. In the Filters tab, select Item from the Current Filter Choices list on the right.

2. In the Item field, click the arrow and scroll to the top of the list, and choose Multiple Items to open the Select Item dialog.

3. Select Manual, and then choose the appropriate items:
   - For a customer report, select all the items a single customer is waiting for (all the customer's backorders).
   - For a backorder report, select all the item(s) attached to a particular backorder.

4. Click OK to return to the Filters tab, then click OK again to return to report window.

The report displays only those items you selected, and you can use it to compare stock status against existing backorders.

Checking Receipt of Goods Manually

It's always a good idea to keep an eye on the items you're waiting for by tracking what comes in. This works well if you enlist the help of the warehouse personnel who receive goods. In fact, it's a good idea to establish a policy that receiving personnel must check backorder lists.

Print a list of the products you're awaiting to fill backorders by choosing Reports | Sales | Open Sales Orders By Item. The report displays each item on a backorder, along with the customer's name, the sales order number, the quantity on the backorder, and the quantity already invoiced (see Figure 3-14).

ProAdvisor NOTE: *The Open Sales Orders By Item report shown in Figure 3-14 contains a Backordered field in all Premier editions, not just those that support backorders.*

Figure 3-14: Print a report of items that are on backorder so the warehouse knows what to look for.

The quantity you need is the difference between the quantity ordered and the quantity invoiced. Hang the list in the receiving area, and write your name and telephone extension on the document so you can receive a call when the goods arrive.

If you need to order goods from vendors to fill backorders, have the order delivered directly to the person who's tracking the backorders for these items (maybe that's you). If you use purchase orders, make sure the shipping address has your name on it. If you order by telephone, or over the Internet, be sure to indicate the shipment is to be directed to the person who's tracking the backorders for these items.

Even if you have shipments sent to your attention, or to the attention of the person who's tracking backorders, you cannot immediately fill the backorders. You must first use the Receive Items procedures to record the fact that the items came in. Then you can create invoices from the backorders to ship the items to customers. No shortcuts, please, it really messes up the accounting records.

Creating Transactions Automatically

In QuickBooks Premier editions, you can automatically create transactions from transactions, which is rather nifty. I've already explained how to create an invoice automatically from a Sales Order.

You can perform the same one-click transformation for other transactions by clicking the appropriate button on the transaction window toolbar.

- Create a Purchase Order from a Sales Order
- Create an Invoice from an Estimate
- Create a Sales Order from an Estimate
- Create a Purchase Order from an Estimate
- Create a Sales Order from a Quote
- Create an Invoice from a Quote
- Create a Purchase Order from a Quote
- Create an Invoice from a Proposal
- Create a Sales Order from a Proposal
- Create a Purchase Order from a Proposal
- Create an Invoice from a Work Order
- Create a Purchase Order from a Work Order

ProAdvisor NOTE: *Quotes, Proposals, and Work Orders are transaction templates that are built into some of the industry-specific versions of QuickBooks. All of them are customized versions of estimates or sales orders.*

Automatic Purchase Orders From Sales Orders

One of the most useful of the QuickBooks automated transaction features is the ability to turn a sales order into a purchase order automatically. When you're creating a sales order that includes an item you know you're out of, a mouse click creates a purchase order.

ProAdvisor TIP: *This is also a useful feature for items you don't keep in stock, and purchase only when a customer orders.*

Fill in the sales order, and then click the Create Purchase Order button on the Sales Order toolbar. QuickBooks displays the Create Purchase Order Based On The Sales Transaction dialog, seen in Figure 3-15. (The word "allowed" appears in the dialog because items that are percentage based can't be transferred to a purchase item automatically.)

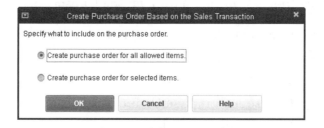

Figure 3-15: Select the appropriate option for purchasing the item(s) on this sales order.

Create a PO for All Items on the SO

The option to create a purchase order for all allowed items only works if all the items on the sales order are purchased from the same vendor or if the sales order contains only one item.

Selecting this option opens a Create Purchase Orders window with the line items pre-filled. If the items have a Preferred Vendor entry in the item record, the vendor's name is also filled in automatically.

Create a PO for Selected Items on the SO

Most of the time, the option to create a purchase order for selected items works best. Selecting that option opens the dialog seen in Figure 3-16, where you can select the item(s) you want to purchase.

Select each item you need to purchase by clicking in the leftmost column to place a check mark in the column. QuickBooks displays the current QOH, and automatically fills in the quantity to order, using the quantity entered in the sales order. You can change the value of the Qty column if you want to order more than needed for this sales order.

Figure 3-16: Select the items you need to purchase to complete this sale.

When you click OK, QuickBooks opens a Create Purchase Orders window with the product information filled in (see Figure 3-17).

Figure 3-17: The customer's missing merchandise is automatically ordered, and linked to the customer.

Delete the customer or job name from the Customer column. The fact that the customer name (or job) is automatically inserted in the line item makes the transactions involved in the future very complicated. (The following paragraphs explain what happens if you don't delete the customer or job name from the Customer column.)

If the customer or job is linked to the purchase order, when you receive the goods, and the bill for the goods, the fact that a customer or job name is on the transaction automatically makes this a reimbursable expense. You already have a sales order waiting to become an invoice, so you don't want to create another, new, charge for this customer.

When you turn the sales order into an invoice, QuickBooks automatically enters the products in the sales order into the invoice. QuickBooks also automatically displays a message reminding you that this customer has outstanding billable time or costs.

When you click the Time/Costs button at the top of the invoice window, you see the purchase you linked to this customer as a reimbursable expense. If you don't transfer the amount to the invoice, you'll see the message about outstanding billable time or costs every time you create an invoice for this customer or job.

Using both the automatic conversion of a sales order to an invoice and the reimbursable costs creates two item lines.

- If you delete the item line that's connected to the reimbursable costs, the costs go back to their "uncollected" status and you will see a reminder to include them in invoices forever.

- If you delete the item line that was transferred from the sales order (and correct the amounts for the reimbursable expense line that remains on the invoice), the inventory isn't decremented and no postings are made to the COG account. The reimbursable expense isn't an inventory item.

So, remove the customer name, and save the purchase order. You're returned to the sales order, and you can save the sales order.

ProAdvisor NOTE: *QuickBooks enters the sales order number in the memo field of the purchase order to indicate it was created automatically, and to remind you which sales order is awaiting these products.*

Automatic Sales Orders from Estimates

If you create an estimate (or a proposal or quote) for a customer, after the customer approves your estimate you can create a sales order automatically. Then, from the sales order, you can automatically create purchase orders and invoices.

Click the Create Sales Order button on the Create Estimates transaction window ribbon bar. QuickBooks displays a message telling you it has transferred the items on the estimate to a sales order (see Figure 3-18). Click OK to open the sales order transaction window, where you can add items, change the shipping address, and make any other needed changes.

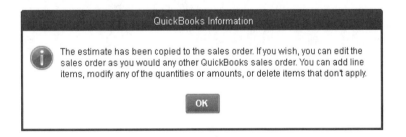

Figure 3-18: QuickBooks does most of the work for you:

Save the sales order, automatically create a purchase order for any needed inventory items, and when you're ready to invoice the customer, that's automatic, too.

ProAdvisor TIP: *You can also create a purchase order automatically from an estimate.*

CHAPTER 4

Premier-Only Accounting Functions

- Advanced functions for journal entries

- Additional bank reconciliation features

The QuickBooks Premier editions include features that provide efficiency, power, and added value to your accounting tasks. These features, which are unique to the Premier editions, are the subject of this chapter.

Some of these features are only available in certain Premier editions, and we'll note those restrictions when discussing those features.

Journal Entries

Journal entries provide a quick and efficient way to create transactions directly in the general ledger (such as depreciation entries), and to fine tune existing account balances (for job costing, class assignments, or allocation across classes). The Premier editions offer some nifty features that add convenience and power when you're creating journal entries.

If you're tracking classes, you can use a journal entry to post existing transactions to a class. All you have to do is journalize the appropriate totals by moving amounts in and out of the original accounts, and adding the class information to each line of the JE. This is a great way to allocate overhead expenses to the divisions, departments, or programs (in nonprofit organizations) for which you established classes.

Similarly, journal entries provide a way to add job costs to existing account totals; merely create a JE that applies a customer or job against existing postings.

Entering a single JE transaction to include class or job information to multiple previous postings is faster than editing each original transaction to add the class or job.

However, we frequently hear from business owners and accountants about JEs created for job costing that don't seem to work. The job costing reports don't reflect the information that was entered in the JE.

Fine-tuning your account balances with JEs can be a trip down a rabbit hole if you don't understand the way QuickBooks stores information contained in JEs (see the section " JE Source and Target: Solving the Mystery ").

> **ProAdvisor NOTE**: *We use the term journal entry, and abbreviate it JE, out of habit. QuickBooks calls this transaction type a General Journal Entry, and uses the abbreviation GJE.*

Adding a JE Icon to the Icon Bar or Favorites Menu

If you use journal entries frequently, add an icon to the icon bar, using the following steps:

1. Choose Company | Make General Journal Entries to open a blank GJE window.
2. On the QuickBooks menu bar choose View | Add "Make General Journal Entries" To Icon Bar.
3. In the Add Window To Icon Bar dialog you can change the default Label or Description text, and also change the default graphic for the icon.
4. Click OK to place the icon on your icon bar.

The text in the Label field represents the text that displays under the icon on the icon bar. The text in the Description field is the text you see when you hover your mouse over the icon (also called a *tooltip*).

If you prefer to use the Favorites menu instead of the icon bar, use the following steps:

1. If the Favorites menu isn't on the Menu Bar, add it by choosing View | Favorites Menu.
2. When the Favorites menu appears, choose Favorites | Customize Favorites, which opens the Customize Your Menus dialog.
3. In the left pane (labeled Available Menu Items), select Make General Journal Entries.
4. Click Add to move your selection to the right pane (labeled Chosen Menu Items).
5. Click OK to add this command to your Favorites menu.

AutoFill Memos in Journal Entries

In QuickBooks Pro, the text you enter in the memo field of any line in a journal entry stays with that entry line. This means you see your comments when you open the register for the account that entry line posted to.

For example, if you are entering a journal entry for a correction your accountant told you to make, you could enter the comment "Bob's Memo-5/4/17" (assuming your accountant's name is Bob).

Most people enter memo text only in the first line of the journal entry. Later, if they view the register of one of the accounts involved in the JE (the accounts below the first line) there's no text in the memo field. You don't see any explanation for the transaction unless you open the original transaction. To avoid that problem, some users enter (or copy and paste) the text in the memo field manually, on each line of the General Journal Entry. That's extra work!

QuickBooks Premier editions offer a clever feature called AutoFill Memo In General Journal Entry. This means that the text you enter in the Memo field on the first line of the transaction is automatically entered on all lines of the transaction. When you view the register of any account involved in the journal entry, the memo text is available to help you remember or understand the reason for the transaction.

This feature is enabled by default in the Preferences dialog, on the My Preferences tab of the Accounting section. If your memo text isn't repeated on the second line of your JE, somebody disabled the feature. Choose Edit | Preferences, select the Accounting section of the Preferences dialog, and enable it.

ProAdvisor TIP *(FOR ACCOUNTANTS)*: *For your clients who aren't using one of the QuickBooks Premier Editions, you might want to pass along the suggestion to copy and paste memo text to every line of a JE. This means you'll know the reason for the JE when you see it in an account register. Without the memo, you have to open the original transaction to see the memo that appeared only on the first line.*

Auto Reversing Journal Entries

Auto reversing journal entries, which are only available in Premier and Enterprise editions, are very handy. To create an auto reversing journal entry, open the Make General Journal Entries window by choosing Company | Make General Journal Entries.

To create a reversing journal entry follow these steps:

1. Enter the data for the journal entry.
2. Click the Reverse icon (instead of clicking Save & Close, or Save & New).
3. The Make General Journal Entries window displays the reversing entry (don't worry, the original entry was saved, click Previous to see it if you don't believe it).
4. Click Save & Close if you're finished with the GJE window; click Save & New to enter another journal entry.

The Reversing Entry is automatically dated the first day of the following month, but you can change the date. If you're using automatic numbering for GJE transactions, the reversing entry number has the format *xxx*R, where *xxx* is the number of the original journal entry.

Adjusting Journal Entries

Available only in QuickBooks Premier Accountant Edition, this feature lets you specify a journal entry as "Adjusting". The GJE window includes a check box labeled Adjusting Entry, which is enabled by default.

The way QuickBooks reports on adjusting entries, compared to journal entries that aren't designated "adjusting", is inconsistent. After you create an adjusting entry, when you view the registers of the affected accounts, the transaction type is GENJRNL. That's the same transaction type that QuickBooks records for a journal entry that's not configured as an adjusting entry.

QuickBooks has a built-in report of adjusting entries that you can see by choosing Reports | Accountant & Taxes | Adjusting Journal Entries. This report, like the feature, is only available in Premier Accountant Edition. Also available in Premier Accountant is the Show List Of Entries feature. Click the Show List button on the Main tab to see a list of GJEs to which you can apply a date filter.

Discussing adjusting entries always makes us want to ask, "What's the difference between an adjusting entry and any other type of journal entry; aren't all JEs adjustments?" So, we literally asked the question of our own accounting firm, and the answers we received indicate that the difference is subtle, but apparently understood by all accountants. One of the accountants replied, "It's really a distinction without a difference; an adjusting journal entry is posted to correct or update an account in the general ledger." Another accountant added, "Often when referring to an adjusting entry, the term is used in the sense of preparing a financial statement and not as a permanent entry; it's often reversed the next day".

Send GJEs

A useful feature for accountants has been added to the Premier Accountant Edition (and only the Accountant Edition) called Send GJEs. The concept is fairly straightforward. Much of the work done in client files is journal entries. This feature allows accountants to create journal entries in their copies of clients' files while the clients are still working in theirs. The accountant then sends the new journal entries to the client for import. There's no need for an Accountant's Copy with its inherent restrictions.

Using the feature is also quite simple. You have two ways to access the Send General Journal Entries window:

- Use the Make General Journal Entries command (Accountant | Make General Journal Entries), when you need to create a new GJE to send to the client. After you create the GJE(s) click the Send GJEs command to open the Send General Journal Entries window (see Figure 4-1).

- If you want to send existing journal entries, go directly to the Send General Journal Entries window by choosing Accountant | Send General Journal Entries.

Figure 4-1: Choose the existing JEs to send

Once you're in the Send General Journal Entries window it's a simple mater of locating the appropriate journal entries, checking them off, and either e-mailing them as attachments or saving them as files to be sent later. When the client receives the file all she has to do is import it.

ProAdvisor TIP: *If your client is savvy enough to make decisions about which journal entries to import, you can check the Allow Recipient To Select Which GJEs To Post To File option. It is not checked by default, which means the client will be forced to import all or none unless you enable the option.*

When the client receives the file, all she has to do is save it to her hard drive. Then, from within QuickBooks, select File | Utilities | Import | General Journal Entries to locate the file, and open it in the Add General Journal Entries To Your File window. From there she can review and add the GJE(s).

History and Reports in the GJE Window

In the Premier Accountant edition, the Make General Journal Entries transaction window displays existing (prior) JE transactions. Each time you open the GJE window, you can quickly check the existing journal entries. This means you won't re-enter a journal entry you already made, which is an occasional problem during end-of-period activities.

ProAdvisor NOTE: *If you don't see the list, click the Show List icon on the Main tab.*

By default, the list includes all the journal entries created in the last month, but you can change the time period. Click the arrow to the right of the List Of Selected General Journal Entries text box to select a different time interval for displaying journal entries. All journal entries that match the date range are displayed.

When the previous entries are displayed, the number of lines that appear in the GJE transaction window is reduced. If you have a long journal entry to record, click the Hide List icon to reveal a full GJE transaction window. The icon label changes to Show List so you can bring back the list with a click of the mouse.

When you close the GJE window, QuickBooks remembers its state (whether the list of previous journal entries is displayed, and if so, which time interval is selected), and the next time you open the window you see that same state.

Viewing and Editing Existing Journal Entries

The journal entries in the history list display the first line of the JE. To see the contents, click the appropriate item in the history list. The contents of that JE are loaded into the GJE transaction window, and the transaction becomes the current transaction. You can edit the JE, making changes to any part of the transaction, and selecting/deselecting the Adjusting Entry designation.

Quick Reports from the GJE Window

The GJE window in the Premier Accountant Edition also has a Reports tab at the top of the transaction window. Click the tab to view the available reports. You'll find a Transaction History and a Transaction Journal report, along with a drop down menu of Entries Entered reports:

- Today
- Last Month
- Last Fiscal Quarter
- This Fiscal Year To Date
- All Entries

When you open one of these reports, the report is collapsed, which means a total is displayed for each account used in each JE. Click the button labeled Expand to display each posting to any account that has multiple postings in the JE. (The button changes its name to Collapse)

Allocating Overhead Expenses to Jobs

Real job costing includes the allocation of overhead and other expenses not specifically incurred for a job. These allocations are made in addition to the job costing entries you make during transaction data entry (when you enter an expense and then link all or part of it to a job).

When you link expenses to a job (if you select the option to bill the customer/job), the expense is available when you invoice the customer/job. If you deselect the option to bill for reimbursement, the amount you linked to the customer/job is saved and you can create reports that display your costs for each customer/job.

If you use timesheets to track employee and subcontractor time, you can either invoice customers for that time, or merely link that expense to jobs for the purpose of job costing. If you track mileage, you can accomplish the same thing for the cost of travel.

Overhead expenses usually have to be managed separately. It's often the case that overhead expenses contribute to the cost of a job, and you can use JEs to allocate those expenses to jobs. This is the only way to see the real cost of a job, and that information makes it easier to bid properly on future jobs. Some of the overhead expenses commonly used in job cost allocation include:

- Staff payroll, including employer tax and benefit expenses (if you're not already assigning specific employees' time and/or payroll items to jobs).

- Office supplies, including consumables such as paper, printer cartridges and toner.

- Utility bills. (Long distance charges should be specifically applied to the job when you pay the telephone bill.)

- Vehicle overhead expenses (if you're not using the QuickBooks mileage tracking feature).

You need to spend some time thinking about the staff, consumables, and other expenses that were connected to a particular job in order to come up with a figure. For short-term jobs, most businesses allocate overhead after the job is complete. For long-term jobs, you can allocate monthly to keep an eye on the totals. A job allocation JE is quite simple:

- Credit the original expense for the amount you're allocating to a job (or multiple jobs).

- Debit the original expense for the same amount, and select the appropriate job(s), deselecting the option to bill the customer.

The allocated data appears in your job reports (but sometimes it doesn't – see the next section on JE source and target, which explains why some job costs get "lost").

JE Source and Target: Solving the Mystery

One common use of a JE is to allocate an expense across jobs to track job costs. It's easy, you debit the same expense account multiple times in order to select a customer or job for each applicable portion of the expense, and credit the original expense total so the general ledger totals aren't changed. You can do the same type of JE to allocate costs (usually overhead) across classes. Table 4-1 is a representation of a JE designed to track job costs.

Account	Debit	Credit	Memo	Name
Shipping		200.00	Allocation	
Shipping	100.00		Allocation	Cust:Job #1
Shipping	50.00		Allocation	Cust:Job #2
Shipping	50.00		Allocation	Cust:Job #3

Table 4-1: Allocate expenses to track the cost of jobs.

After performing this task, it's a common complaint that the job costing reports don't show the expenses that were allocated in the journal entry. If you run an Unbilled Costs By Job report, some or all of the data in your JEs doesn't appear. If you marked the amount as billable in the JE, the billable costs show up when you invoice the customer, they just don't show up in reports.

Often, when you create a JE that moves expenses from one customer to another, the wrong customer receives the cost posting.

What's going on? The answer is that all transactions in QuickBooks have a source and a target, and if you don't get them right, you end up with unexpected results.

The source is the account where the transaction originates, and the target is the account where it is completed. When you write a check to a vendor, the bank account is the source (it's where the money starts) and the expense account is the target (it's where the money ends up).

If you attach additional information to the check, it travels with its source or target counterpart. For example, assigning a customer to the line that contains an expense account (for job costing) links the customer information and the amount to the target (because a line item, in which this data exists, is part of the target).

For JEs that perform job costing allocations there are two important facts to remember:

- QuickBooks assigns job costing or other information when it's part of the target, and ignores it when it's part of the source.
- The first line of a JE is the source and all other lines are targets.

This means that if you're moving job costing information from one customer to another or from one job to another for the same customer, you will almost certainly end up with one or more incorrect postings.

Creating JEs With No Source Accounts

We've learned that to play it safe, the best way to create a JE that's connected to job costing is to make every line in the transaction part of the target. Remembering that only the first line is the source, the solution is to avoid using the first line for anything "real".

In the first line of a JE, enter only a memo. Starting with the second line, enter real information. Because everything is a target, everything posts appropriately, and you can create reports that show your activities.

If you've already encountered the source/target problem, you don't have to void and re-enter all the journal entries that had a source/target mix up. Just edit the journal entry to change the source line, as follows:

1. Open the JE transaction and click anywhere in the first line to select that line.
2. Press Ctrl-Ins (or Ctrl-Insert, depending on the label your keyboard uses) to insert a blank line above the current first line.
3. Enter text in the Memo field to create a source line.
4. Close the Make General Journal Entries transaction window.
5. QuickBooks displays a message that you've changed the transaction and asks if you want to save it.
6. Click Yes.

Everything posts correctly. If you notice that QuickBooks has lost track of the automatic numbering feature for JEs just re-enter the JE number to kick-start automatic numbering again. This was a problem in the past, but appears to be cleared up now.

Allocating Overhead Expenses to Classes

If you're already tracking divisions or departments of your business with classes, you can post overhead expenses to classes with a journal entry.

This works best if you create a generic class for overhead, or general expenses, and then move expense totals out of that class into your departmental classes. Common names for the generic class include Other, Administration, General and other generic terms that represent general office expenses.

During transaction data entry (entering bills or writing checks) always post expenses to a class, either the class specifically tied to the expense, or your generic glass. Then you can journalize the appropriate portions of overhead and general expenses. To do so:

- Credit the original expense for the amount you're allocating to classes, and link that line in the JE to the generic class.
- Debit the same expense the appropriate amount for each class, linking each line in the JE to the appropriate class.

Auto-calculating by Percentage

QuickBooks has a nifty function you can use to automate some allocations that would require the use of a calculator. For example, if you're splitting an expense unevenly—perhaps 66% to one class and 34% to another class, you can do the math right in the JE, as follows:

1. Enter the Memo text in the first line.
2. In the next line, enter a credit for the expense account you're allocating.
3. In the next line (which automatically displays an equal amount in the Debit column), enter the same expense account.

4. Tab to the Debit column and enter an asterisk (*) to open the QuickBooks calculator.

5. Enter the percentage in decimal form, as seen in Figure 4-2.

6. Press Tab to have QuickBooks perform the calculation against the number that was originally in the column. The new amount appears in the Debit column.

7. The next line contains the correct amount for the debit to the expense in the next row.

Figure 4-2: Let QuickBooks do the arithmetic.

You can also use this function to split an allocation across three classes:

1. In the Debit column of the JE line for the first class, enter *.33.

2. In the Debit column of the next JE row, enter *.50 (half the amount that appeared after calculating the previous row).

3. The last JE row is automatically calculated correctly.

For more than three classes, this gets a bit complicated, and you'll probably need a calculator to figure out the formula.

Previous Bank Reconciliation Reports

All of the Premier editions automatically save bank reconciliation reports, even if you don't print or display the reports when you finish reconciling your bank account.

Without this feature, the only way to see previous bank reconciliation reports is to remember to print a report every time you reconcile a bank account. When you need a previous report, go to your filing cabinet for hard copies, or the folder in which you store PDF versions. That's what users of QuickBooks Pro have to do, because they only have access to the last reconciliation report. Luckily for you, QuickBooks Premier editions store multiple reconciliation reports.

You may want to see a previous reconciliation report before you begin the next reconciliation process, or you might find you need to look at a previous report when you're in the middle of reconciling the current month, and you run into a problem.

In addition, at the end of your fiscal year, most accountants want to see the reconciliation report for the last fiscal month. If you don't meet with your accountant until several months after your fiscal year end, the ability to print the right reconciliation report is very handy.

Choose Reports | Banking | Previous Reconciliation to open the Select Previous Reconciliation Report dialog. If you have more than one bank account, select the appropriate account from the drop-down list in the Account field. Then select the report you want to see by choosing its statement ending date.

Choosing the Type of Reconciliation Report

You have a variety of choices for the type and format of the reconciliation report for the statement period you select. The Type Of Report section at the top of the dialog has three options: Summary, Detail, and Both.

- Select Summary to see the totals for transactions that were cleared and not cleared at the time of the reconciliation. The report also lists the totals for new transactions (transactions entered after the reconciliation). Totals are by type, so there is one total for inflow (deposits), and another total for outflow (payments).

- Select Detail to see each transaction that was cleared or not cleared in a previous reconciliation, and also see each new transaction since that reconciliation.

- Select Both to open both reports (not one report with both sets of listings).

After you select the type of report, select the type of content you want in the report.

Selecting the option Transactions Cleared At The Time Of Reconciliation (Report Is Displayed As A PDF File), results in a Portable Document Format (PDF) file.

To view a PDF file, you must have Adobe Acrobat Reader installed on your computer. If you don't, when you select this report, QuickBooks opens a dialog with a link to the Adobe website, where you can download Acrobat Reader (it's free).

PDF files are graphical and let you view and print information. You cannot drill down to see details since this report is not directly linked to your QuickBooks data. However, the report gives you an accurate picture of the last reconciliation. (If you printed a reconciliation report the last time you reconciled the account, the PDF file matches your printout.)

Selecting the option Transactions Cleared Plus Any Changes Made To Those Transactions Since The Reconciliation opens a standard Quick-Books report window.

Unfortunately, this report is neither useful nor accurate if you need to see a report on the reconciliation for the date you selected. This is not really a reconciliation report. It's merely a report on the current state of the account register, and it displays the account's transactions sorted by the following categories:

- Cleared
- Uncleared
- New

If you, or someone else, changed a cleared transaction, this report shows the new information, not the information that existed at the time you reconciled the account. If you're viewing the previous reconciliation to try to determine whether any changes were made to cleared transactions, this report fools you—it's dangerous to rely on its contents.

If you need to see an accurate, trustworthy, previous reconciliation report in order to track down discrepancies, either use the PDF file or make sure you print and file a detailed reconciliation report every month when you reconcile your bank account.

Resolving Reconciliation Problems

Often, the reason you open a previous reconciliation report is to investigate problems in the current reconciliation. Usually this means the Begin Reconciliation dialog displays a beginning balance that differs from the opening balance shown on your bank statement.

Click the Locate Discrepancies button on the Begin Reconciliation dialog to open the Locate Discrepancies dialog (see Figure 4-3). You have access to your previous reconciliation reports in this dialog, as well as a discrepancy report that may help you locate the reason for the difference between the beginning balances.

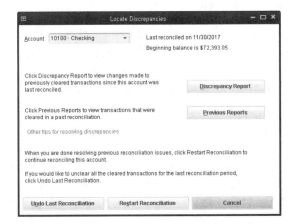

Figure 4-3: Use the tools in the Locate Discrepancies dialog to troubleshoot reconciliation problems.

If the previous reconciliation reports don't provide the answer to your problem, choose Discrepancy Report. This report displays information about transactions that were changed after they were cleared during reconciliation. This report should be empty—if it displays any transactions, somebody manipulated a cleared transaction—that's a no no.

The reconciled amount is the amount of the transaction as it was when you cleared it during reconciliation. If that amount is a positive number, the transaction was a deposit; a negative number indicates a disbursement (usually a check).

The Type Of Change column provides a clue about the action you must take to correct the unmatched beginning balances:

- Uncleared means you removed the check mark in the Cleared column of the register (and you persisted in this action even though QuickBooks issued a stern warning about the dangers).

- Deleted means you deleted the transaction.

- Amount is the original amount, which means you changed the amount of the transaction. Check the Reconciled amount and the amount in the Effect Of Change amount, and do the math; the difference is the amount of the change.

Unfortunately, QuickBooks doesn't offer a Type Of Change named "Void," so a voided transaction is merely marked as changed. A transaction with a changed amount equal and opposite of the original amount is usually a check that was voided after it was cleared.

ProAdvisor NOTE: *When you alter a cleared transaction QuickBooks displays a message warning you that the transaction has cleared the bank and should not be changed. Some users don't take this warning seriously (or don't understand what "cleared" means) and keep going. That attitude baffles their accountants.*

To resolve the problem, open the transaction by double-clicking its listing and restore it to its original state. This is safe because you can't justify changing a transaction after it was cleared — a transaction that cleared was not supposed to be changed, voided, deleted, or uncleared; once cleared, it must remain what it was forever. When the transaction is returned to its original state it disappears from the Discrepancy Report.

If you don't see the problem immediately, try comparing previous reconciliation reports to the account register. Any transaction that is listed in a reconciliation report should also be in the register, with the same amount.

- If a transaction is there, but marked VOID, re-enter it, using the data in the reconciliation report. That transaction wasn't void when you performed the last reconciliation, it had cleared. Therefore, it can't possibly meet any of the criteria for voiding a transaction.

- If a transaction appears in the reconciliation report, but is not in the register, it was deleted. Re-enter it, using the data in the reconciliation report.

- Check the amounts on the check reconciliation report against the data in the register to see if any amount was changed after the account was reconciled. If so, restore the original amount.

Reconciliation Vs. Downloading Transactions

Many users don't understand the difference between downloading transactions from their bank account and reconciling the bank account.

If your bank supports QuickBooks transaction downloads, you can import the transactions into your bank register via the Online Banking feature.

You cannot import a monthly bank statement; instead you must use the Reconcile command on the Banking menu to reconcile the account manually, using the data in the statement.

Most banks let you download your monthly statement instead of waiting for it to arrive in the mail, but the statement is downloaded as a document that you print in order to reconcile the bank account. There isn't any automated process to reconcile the bank register with the statement.

CHAPTER 5

Reporting and Planning Tools

- Balance sheet sorted by class
- Exporting and importing report templates
- Closing date exception report
- Planning and forecasting tools

The QuickBooks Premier editions contain report features that aren't available in QuickBooks Pro. In this chapter, we'll go over some of the advanced reporting capabilities you have available in your Premier edition. In addition, we'll explain the two planning tools available in the Premier editions that are not available in QuickBooks Pro.

Balance Sheet by Class

This report, which is not available in QuickBooks Pro, is a balance sheet report that sorts and totals by class. Choose Reports | Company & Financial | Balance Sheet By Class to see the report.

Transactions for balance sheet accounts (asset, liability, and equity) that have class links are reported by class, with a column for each class. Each account also displays a total for all classes (the same total you see in the standard balance sheet report).

The report displays a column titled Unclassified for transactions that don't contain a link to a class. Drill down to open those transactions and add a class to move the transaction total into the appropriate class column.

ProAdvisor TIP: *There are a number of things that can adversely affect this report. Therefore, it's advisable to read the guidelines in the help file. The first time you run this report a dialog box appears informing you that you may have to enter transactions in a specific way. Click the link entitled "Please take a moment to review guidelines for this report".*

Exporting Reports as Templates

The ability to customize reports is one of the most popular features in QuickBooks. You can change the layout, filter the content, and modify the sort order of reports. This means you can get exactly the information you want, without wading through information you don't care about.

Adding to the power inherent in report customization is the ability to memorize a customized report. The memorization is intelligent, ignoring the actual data, and retaining only the customized settings for layout, filters, and sort order. When a previously memorized report is opened, the data that appears is fetched from transactions, and is therefore current and correct.

QuickBooks Premier editions add a third layer of power to reports, by providing the ability to export templates of customized, memorized, reports. Here's how it works:

- Only QuickBooks Premier editions can export report templates.
- All QuickBooks editions can import report templates.

You can export a report template when you want to move a customized report to another company file on your own system. If you're an accountant, you can provide exported report templates to your clients to make sure you get exactly the reports you need.

Customizing Reports

A template is an exported copy of a memorized report, and it's assumed the report has been customized. However, the type and scope of the customizations you can apply are limited, because the report must be able to work with another company file.

When you click the Customize Report button in a report window, the tabs in the Modify Report dialog offer a wide range of customization options. The following sections describe the modifications you must *avoid* to ensure the customization includes no company specific data.

Selecting Generic Display Options

When you modify a report, the Display tab of some reports has a Columns list. You can add or remove any of the columns in the list. Generally, summary reports don't offer this list, but detail reports do.

You can customize the report by adding or removing columns, but you must be careful to avoid using any custom fields you created (see Figure 5-1). Those fields probably don't exist in other company files. QuickBooks won't balk when you attempt to export a memorized report with custom fields unique to your company file. However, when you import and use the report in another company file, you'll find that it exchanges incoming custom fields for existing custom fields, which may cause a bit of confusion.

> **ProAdvisor TIP**: *Deselect the column labeled "left margin" (which is automatically selected), because removing that column makes it easier to fit more information on a printed page, and lessens the amount of horizontal scrolling required when you display reports on the screen.*

Figure 5-1: Don't select columns for custom fields you created.

Selecting Generic Filters

You cannot include filters that are unique to the company file that's open when you customize the report. Instead, as you choose the filters, you must be careful to select filters that work anywhere, anytime, for any QuickBooks company file.

For example, if you're filtering for accounts, you cannot select specific accounts unique to your company file. Instead, you must select account types (Income, Expense, etc.). Even then you may run into problems if a unique account is included in the group.

Most of the filters offer universal choices that allow you to customize the report to obtain the data you need. Some filters don't have lists; instead, they have simple options such as Open or Closed. You can't get into trouble with those filters, because they offer no opportunity to use data that's specific to the company file.

Memorizing Reports

After you create the customized report, you can memorize it by clicking the Memorize button on the report window.

However, before you memorize the report, go to the Header/Footer tab of the Customize Report dialog and change the text in the field labeled Report Title. Enter a name for the report that matches its content. It can be disconcerting to open a report that you believe tells you about sales of specific services on Tuesdays if the title you see on the report window says Sales By Customer.

By default, when you memorize a report, QuickBooks names the file to match the text in the Report Title field, and most of the time that's fine. However, if the title is very long, you may want to shorten the filename. Be sure to create a name that makes the report's content clear to everyone. Names that are meaningful to you (because you knew what you wanted to accomplish with your customizations) may not work for other people. For example, the name "OpBillNoAge" may signify to you that the report displays all open vendor bills, but doesn't display the aging; instead, the report displays the date of each bill. If you're planning to export the report, a name such as OpenBillsWithBillDateOnly", or "OpenBills-NoAging" might be a better title/filename.

If the report is going to someone outside your company you should remove the check mark from the Company Name option as well.

Exporting a Template

QuickBooks creates templates for export by saving the report in its own proprietary format, which has a file extension .QBR. To export a memorized report as a template that can be imported into another QuickBooks company file, use the following steps:

1. Choose Reports | Memorized Reports | Memorized Report List.
2. In the Memorized Report List, select the report to export.
3. Click the Memorized Report button at the bottom of the window to display the command list.
4. Select Export Template to open the Specify Filename For Export dialog (which looks like a Save File dialog).
5. Accept the default name for the template (which is the name of the report), or enter a different name.
6. Click Save.

Only the settings are saved in the template, not the data that appeared in the customized report. The data, of course, was specific to the QuickBooks company file that was open when you created the report.

By default, QuickBooks saves the template in the folder in which you installed QuickBooks. It's a good idea to create a different folder for your templates so you can find them easily (the QuickBooks folder is crowded). The best place to save your exported templates is in a subfolder named MyQBReportTemplates that you create under your My Documents folder, or under the folder in which you're storing QuickBooks company files (e.g. C:\QB2014 Company Files\ MyQBReportTemplates).

If the applied filter(s) include unique accounts, QuickBooks may balk and refuse to export the memorized report.

Sending a Template

If you're sending your report template to someone else (instead of importing into another company file on your own system), the easiest way to deliver the file is as an attachment to an e-mail message. Report templates (files with the extension .QBR) use very few bytes. You could also burn a CD and mail it. Don't forget to send the recipient instructions for importing the template (covered next).

Importing a Report Template

Importing a report template actually does nothing more than convert the template file into a memorized report. The report is added to the

Memorized Report List of the company file that's open during the import process. To import a template, use the following steps:

1. Choose Reports | Memorized Reports | Memorized Report List.
2. Click the Memorized Report button at the bottom of the window, and select Import Template.
3. Navigate to the drive or folder that contains the template file, and double-click its listing.
4. In the Memorize Report dialog, enter a name for the report, or accept the displayed name (which is the name used by the person who exported the template).

The report is now available in the Memorized Report List.

Creating Groups of Memorized Reports

Memorized report groups are very handy because they make it easy to find the right report when you need it. Create your groups to match the type of memorized reports you amass. Here's how to create a memorized report group:

1. Choose Reports | Memorized Reports | Memorized Report List, to open the Memorized Report List.
2. Click the Memorized Report button at the bottom of the window, and select New Group.
3. In the New Memorized Report Group dialog, enter a name for the group, and click OK.

If you have existing memorized reports that you want to move into the new group, use the following steps:

1. In the Memorized Report List window, select the report you want to move into a group.
2. Press Ctrl-E to edit the report listing.
3. Check the Save In Memorized Report Group option.
4. Select the appropriate group from the drop-down list.

5. Click OK.

To add a new memorized report into an existing group, when you finish customizing the report, click Memorize. In the Memorize Report dialog, select the Save In Memorized Report Group check box, and then select the appropriate group from the drop-down list.

ProAdvisor TIP: *You can import and export entire memorized report groups using the same procedures outlined earlier for importing and exporting memorized reports. Simply select a memorized report group name instead of an individual memorized report.*

Closing Date Exception Report

The Closing Date Exception report, available only in QuickBooks Premier editions, tells you whether transactions dated before the closing date were modified or created. To understand the importance of the Closing Date Exception report, you have to understand what closing the books means in QuickBooks.

QuickBooks doesn't "close" the books the way many other accounting software applications do. Those applications close a period (month or year) as a definitive action that can't be undone. Once closed, a period is locked, and no transactions in that period can be added, removed, or changed.

The biggest benefit to a closing process that's a true lock-down is that all the reports and tax forms that were produced about the locked period remain accurate and valid forever, because there's no chance that anything can change.

Another benefit is the fact that someone bent on illegal activities (such as embezzling) cannot get into a prior period to hide an illegal transaction. This is a temptation that is based on the usually correct assumption that business owners (and even accountants) rarely look closely at prior period transactions.

On the other hand, a real closing procedure can be a frazzling experience, because you can't close the books until you're sure you've recorded everything that needs to be entered. Many companies with accounting departments fall behind on the day-to-day work for a few days each month, because they're closing the previous month (they're not using QuickBooks).

The same thing happens, with even more intensity, every January or February, when it's time to close the year. Even with all that effort and pressure, it's not unusual to hear "uh oh" after the books are closed. The bookkeeper, controller, or accountant has found a transaction that should have been recorded in the prior year. It's too late!

ProAdvisor TIP: *Don't set a closing date until you have entered any year-end adjustments from your accountant, and your accountant has finished preparing your taxes.*

QuickBooks Closing Date Procedures

When you close a year in QuickBooks, the lock you put into place isn't impenetrable. It's a combination lock (remember the lock on your high school locker?) and anyone who knows, or can guess, the combination can enter.

ProAdvisor TIP: *If you wish, you can use the QuickBooks closing process every month to close the previous month.*

Setting a Closing Date

In QuickBooks, you close a year by setting a closing date in the Accounting category of the Preferences dialog.

Choose Edit | Preferences, select the Accounting category in the left pane, move to the Company Preferences tab, and click Set Date/Password. Only the Admin user can gain access to this dialog.

ProAdvisor TIP: *To get to this Preferences dialog quickly, choose Company | Set Closing Date.*

Enter the date that signifies the end of the period in which users shouldn't change or add transactions, which is usually the last day of your fiscal year (see Figure 5-2).

Figure 5-2: Enter your closing date to specify that all transactions on or before this date are closed.

In addition to entering the date, you should specify a password to allow users (including yourself) to add or modify transactions on or before the closing date. The password is not required, but if it's omitted, any user can continue to record, edit, void, or delete transactions in the previous year.

If you don't create a password, when a user creates, modifies or deletes a transaction that carries a date falling in the closed period, QuickBooks issues the warning seen in Figure 5-3.

If you specified a password when you set your closing date, Quick-Books asks the user for that password (see Figure 5-4). If the user enters the correct password, QuickBooks permits the user to add, remove, or modify transactions in the prior year.

Figure 5-3: Clicking Yes lets any user add, remove, or change a transaction in a closed period.

QuickBooks   ✕

This modification will affect transactions from closed periods and could also affect previous financial reports.

You must enter the "closing date" password to make this change.

Password: [＿＿＿＿＿＿＿]

[OK]   [Cancel]

Figure 5-4: Anyone who knows the password can change the balances on which you based your tax return.

Forgotten Closing Date Passwords

If you forget your password for the closing date, just delete the current password and enter a new one. You don't have to know the current password to make changes. However, only the QuickBooks Admin and an External Accountant user can change the password.

If you have to change something in a closed period, make sure the change doesn't affect account totals. Those totals were used in a tax return, and your accountant may be tracking year-end totals to make sure your beginning balances for the current year match those closing balances. The only appropriate changes are to the text in memos, or other non-financial entries.

Locking Users Out of the Prior Period

You can keep users out of the prior period by setting user permissions appropriately. This means that even if a user has discovered the password for entering prior period transactions, he or she can't perform the task.

Even if you want to give a user full access to all the accounting functions, QuickBooks provides a way to stop that user from creating, changing, or deleting transactions in the closed period. When you set up (or edit) the user, choose the option to give permissions for selected areas. Give all the permissions you want this user to have, but in the last permissions window (see Figure 5-5), select No as the answer to the question about working in a closed period.

Figure 5-5: An ounce of prevention is worth a pound of cure.

Users with this permission denied can't work with a transaction that's dated on or before the closing date. When they try to save the transaction, QuickBooks stops the action with the message seen in Figure 5-6.

ProAdvisor NOTE: *You can re-open your books after you've closed them. Just delete the Closing Date and click OK.*

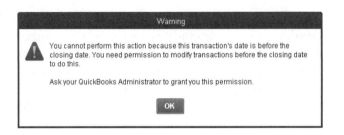

Figure 5-6: Even if this user has learned the password, the closing date is absolute.

Sometimes Password Protection Doesn't Work

If a password is linked to the closing date, only users who know the password can work in the previous year. Unfortunately, this paradigm frequently fails when a business owner trusts a user enough to give that person the password, and the trust is misplaced.

Sadly, in a number of those cases, the nefarious user turns out to be a family member. (Business owners tend to entrust passwords to members of their family who work in the business, and that's not always a wise decision.)

In some instances, illegal activities in a closed period are eventually traced to employees who hadn't been given the password. The problem - , the closing date password was easily available—a note in an unlocked drawer, an easy-to-guess password (the owner's birth date, nickname, dog's name, or another easy logical conclusion), and even notes affixed to monitors.

Then there are the orders that are shipped with a date previous to the closing date, and the neer-do-well employee happily enjoys the ill-gotten goods that are delivered. The shipment is usually sent to an accomplice by creating a new customer for the transaction or by using a new Ship To address for an existing customer. The shipment doesn't appear on reports that are generated as a matter of course, because the transaction doesn't fall in the date range of a current year's report. Eventually, the accountant, or a sharp bookkeeper, may notice the problem, and the hunt for a solution. Sometimes (but not always) he or she uncovers the crime.

Other problems include inventory adjustments (to cover pilfering), and even the deletion of a check made out to cash that somehow made it through the reconciliation process without raising questions. However, to ensure long-term secrecy, the check was deleted *after* the books were closed. Because the changed balances don't show up on current reports, they frequently escape notice. If they *are* noticed, they're often difficult to track.

Sometimes, discovery occurs because of a disparity between the closing balances of the year-end reports, and the opening balances of current reports. Another clue is an out-of-sequence number, or a missing number. For example, if the first invoice in the current year is number 501, and you find that Invoice 506 is dated in the prior year, be suspicious.

If the transaction has been deleted (a missing transaction number), detection can be quite difficult. If the transaction wasn't deleted, it's easy to find the problem if the customer name attached to the transaction isn't familiar. However, a smart embezzler merges that customer into an existing customer, making the investigation more difficult.

Lest you think we dwell only on the darkest side of the world, let us hasten to tell you that the majority of incidents that involve messing around with transactions in the closed period aren't nefarious.

Innocent changes to transactions are frequently made by users who are honestly trying to correct a problem. These users think it's faster and more efficient to change a transaction that was entered erroneously last December than it is to create a journal entry in January to correct balances. For perfectly harmless reasons, users delete or void transactions in the previous year, or add transactions by dating them in the previous year.

Changes to previous periods drive accountants crazy, because the notion that a closing balance must equal the next opening balance is a basic rule of accounting. Incorrect opening balances can also affect your tax returns. And, of course, unexplained changes between a closing balance in one year and the opening balance in the next year can present difficult challenges if you're undergoing an audit.

Generating the Closing Date Exception Report

To view the Closing Date Exception Report, choose Reports | Accountant & Taxes | Closing Date Exception Report. The report lists all transactions that were added or changed to the closed year after the closing date was set. Figure 5-7 is an example of the report.

Figure 5-7: A user wrote a check made out to Cash in the closed period, and then deleted it.

(Only users with permission to view sensitive accounting reports can open this report.)

Interpreting the Closing Date Exception Report

It's important to understand how to read and interpret the Closing Date Exception Report, which can be confusing.

The top of the report contains the Closing Date History. If the closing date was set, then removed (the books were re-opened), and then the closing date was set again, the report shows that fact. (This part of the report isn't displayed in Figure 5-7.)

The section below the closing date information displays the details of each exception (change). A description of the type of transaction appears above each entry.

The columns display additional information about each transaction, and the important data is the following:

- Entered/Last Modified date is the date on which the transaction was changed (or entered, if the transaction is new). This date is *after* the closing date, or the entry wouldn't exist in this report.

- Last Modified By is the name of the user who performed the task. If you're not using logins, you know what was changed (which is the important financial information) but you won't know for sure who did it.

- State is the current state of this transaction (significant if there were multiple actions on a transaction).

- The Date column displays the date used for the transaction.

- The columns on the right display the financial information (posting accounts, amount)

ProAdvisor TIP: *User logins don't work unless you enforce security rules. To make sure users bent on nefarious actions can't gain entry via another user's login, insist that all users close the company file when they leave their desks, even if they're only going to be gone for a short while. Many a Closing Date Exception report displays Admin as the user, when in fact, it was someone else. In those cases the Admin user tends to keep QuickBooks open all day, often leaving the room with the QuickBooks file open to all who wander in.*

Forecasting

The Premier editions provide a forecasting tool. You can create a forecast to help you predict your future revenue and cash flow, and then use the data in the forecast to create "what if" scenarios that help you plan and control the growth of your business.

A good forecast doesn't have to be terribly complicated; it just has to provide the information you need to plan for survival, or for expansion (depending on the current state of your business and your reason for creating the forecast).

The forecasting tool in QuickBooks works on a one-year basis, which is the common duration for a forecast. The forecast is based on income and expense accounts, although you can further narrow it by focusing on a customer or a class.

When you create a forecast, you're bound to notice that the user interface, as well as the processes, is very similar to the QuickBooks budget feature. In fact, everything about a forecast smells a lot like a budget.

While an official set of definitions that spells out the differences between a forecast and a budget seems nonexistent, most accountants think of these two documents as entirely different from each other. Of course, if you ask an accountant, "What's the difference?" you get a rather broad answer. Our own accountant says that in his mind, a forecast is a set of projections you make based on both history and any logical assumptions you care to make about the future, while a budget is based on the "knowns", and excludes assumptions.

Creating a Forecast

To create a forecast, choose Company | Planning & Budgeting | Set Up Forecast. If this is the first forecast you're creating, you see the Create New Forecast window. If this is not the first forecast you're creating, the last forecast you created opens. Click Create New Forecast if you want to create a new forecast.

Enter the year for this forecast. By default, QuickBooks fills in the forecast year field with next year, but if it's early in the current year, you may prefer to create a forecast for this year. Click Next.

Setting the Criteria for a Forecast

In the next window, you can select the criteria for this forecast. The criteria for accounts are set in stone; you must use Profit & Loss accounts for your forecast. However, you can set additional criteria, such as basing the forecast on a customer, a job, or a class. In this discussion, we're going to assume you aren't setting additional criteria.

Choosing the Method for Obtaining Data

In the next window, specify how you want to create your forecast, and click Finish.

- Create Forecast From Scratch means you enter data manually.

- Create Forecast From Previous Year's Actual Data means QuickBooks transfers monthly data from the prior year to the forecast window.

Of course, if you just started using QuickBooks, you have no data for last year, so you'll have to enter the data manually. In this discussion, we'll create a forecast from scratch for the current year (a common approach as long as it's not late in the year).

Entering Data Manually

If you choose manual data entry, the Set Up Forecast window has no data (see Figure 5-8).

It's a good idea to print a Profit & Loss report to get an idea of the actual numbers. If you're creating a forecast because you're expecting to change the way you do business, the existing numbers may not be the figures you want to insert in your forecast. For example, perhaps you're about to offer a new, specialized service, or enlarge your product offerings. Or, maybe you're planning on hiring more employees. Use the numbers in the Profit & Loss report as a base; and as you enter data in the Forecast window, enlarge or reduce the amounts to match what you think your plan will produce.

Figure 5-8: Enter the data you need to create a forecast.

Data Entry Shortcuts

To save you time (and extraordinary levels of boredom), QuickBooks provides some shortcuts for entering forecast figures. You can use these tools if you're entering your data manually, or if you're changing existing data to create a new scenario.

Copy a Number across the Months

To copy a monthly figure from the current month (the month where your cursor is) to all the following months, enter the figure and click Copy Across. The numbers are copied to all months to the right.

This is handier than it seems. It's obvious that if you enter your rent in the first month, and choose Copy Across, you've saved a lot of manual data entry. However, if your rent is raised in June, you can increase the rent figure from June to December by selecting June, entering the new figure, and clicking Copy Across.

The Copy Across button is also the quick way to clear a row. Delete the data in the first month and click Copy Across to make the entire row blank (the Clear button clears the entire page).

Automatically Increase or Decrease Monthly Figures

You may want to raise an income account by an amount or a percentage starting in a certain month, because you expect to offer new products and services, or increase your customer base.

On the other hand, you may want to raise an expense account because you're expecting to spend more on supplies, personnel, or other costs as the year proceeds.

Select the first month that needs the adjustment and click Adjust Row Amounts to open the Adjust Row Amounts dialog seen in Figure 5-9.

Figure 5-9: Automatically increase or decrease amounts across the months.

Choose 1st Month or Currently Selected Month as the starting point for the calculations. You can choose 1st Month no matter where your cursor is on the account's row. You must click in the column for the appropriate month if you want to choose Currently Selected Month.

- To increase or decrease the selected month, and all the months following, by a specific amount, enter the amount.

- To increase or decrease the selected month and all the months following, by a percentage, enter the percentage rate and the percentage sign.

Compounding Automatic Changes

If you select Currently Selected Month, the Adjust Row Amounts dialog adds an additional option named Enable Compounding. When you enable compounding, the calculations for each month are increased or decreased based on a formula starting with the currently selected month and taking into consideration the resulting change in the previous month.

ProAdvisor TIP: *Although the Enable Compounding option appears only when you select Currently Selected Month, if your cursor is in the first month and you select the Currently Selected Month option, you can use compounding for the entire year.*

For example, if you entered $1000.00 in the current month and indicated a $100.00 increase, the results differ from amounts that are not being compounded, as seen in Table 5-1.

Compounding Enabled?	Current Month Original Figure	Current Month New Figure	Next Month	Next Month	Next Month
Yes	1000.00	1000.00	1100.00	1200.00	1300.00
No	1000.00	1100.00	1100.00	1100.00	1100.00

Table 5-1: Compounded vs. non-compounded changes.

Forecast Window Buttons

The Set Up Forecast window has the following additional buttons:

- Clear deletes all figures in the forecast window—you cannot use this button to clear a row or column.

- Save saves the current figures and leaves the window open so you can continue to work.
- OK saves the current figures and closes the window.
- Cancel closes the window without any offer to record the figures.
- Create New Forecast starts the whole process again.

If you've entered any data, QuickBooks asks if you want to record your data before closing the window. If you record your data (or have previously recorded your data with the Save button), when you start again the forecast window opens with the saved data. To create a new forecast click the Create New Forecast button.

No Delete button exists in the forecast window. To delete a forecast, load it in the forecast window, and choose Edit | Delete Forecast.

Editing the Forecast

After you save the forecast, you can modify it as needed. To make changes, choose Company | Planning & Budgeting | Set Up Forecast.

If you only created one forecast, it opens in the Set Up Forecast window. If you've created multiple forecasts (for customers, jobs, or classes), select the forecast you want to modify from the drop-down list in the Forecast field (at the top of the window).

Use the instructions in the previous section to change the data, and then save the forecast.

Creating Reports on Forecasts

You can view your forecast, or compare its data to real figures, by choosing Reports | Budgets & Forecasts, and then selecting either Forecast Overview or Forecast vs. Actual. Selecting either report launches the Forecast Report wizard.

Forecast Overview Report

To view the forecast, select it from the drop-down list in the first wizard window, and click Next. (If you only created one forecast, you don't have any choices, of course.)

In the next wizard window, select the layout for the report. If the forecast you're viewing is a Profit & Loss Accounts forecast, your only choice is Account By Month, which is the spreadsheet-type layout you used when you created the forecast.

If the forecast you're viewing is a Customer:Job or Class forecast, choose Account By Customer:Job, or Customer:Job By Month (substitute Class for Customer:Job if you created class forecasts).

The name of the layout choice holds the description: the first word in the choice represents the rows, and the word after the word "by" represents the columns.

Forecast vs. Actual

This report lets you see how the forecast matches up against actual figures. The wizard offers the same display options as described for the Overview Report. The report displays the forecast, the actuals, the difference between them in dollars, and the difference in percentage.

Business Planner

Business Planner is a robust application that walks you through the process of creating a comprehensive business plan, which is a detailed prediction of your company's future. The tool's user interface is wizard-like, and it works very much like the EasyStep Interview you can use to set up a QuickBooks company file. A series of sections, each of which has multiple windows to go through, cover the categories involved in building a plan.

> **ProAdvisor NOTE***: The business plan you produce is based on the format recommended by the U.S. Small Business Administration for loan applications or a bank line of credit.*

Creating a comprehensive business plan isn't a cakewalk, and you should be prepared to devote quite a bit of time to complete yours, if you want a truly comprehensive plan. You can create a business plan for your own business, or, if you're an accounting professional, for a client's business. One thing to note is that the Business Planner must be opened by the QuickBooks Admin before it can be accessed by another user.

Launch the Business Planner by choosing Company | Planning & Budgeting | Use Business Plan Tool. After you select Agree to accept the licensing terms, the program opens the Welcome screen that explains the processes involved in creating the business plan (see Figure 5-10). Click Next to move through the windows that follow.

Figure 5-10: The Business Planner window has tabs for each section of the process.

Every time you close the Business Planner, QuickBooks automatically saves it in the folder in which your company file is stored, with the filename *<CompanyFileName>*.BPW. This means that each time you open the Business Planner, the information you've already entered remains, and you're taken to the last window you were using. To make changes to any information you entered earlier, click Previous to return to the appropriate window. You can take your time creating your plan without worrying about starting from scratch every time you open the software.

Entering Company Information

The first set of wizard windows is part of the Company Section, where you enter basic information about your business. Depending on the information you enter in each window, the questions in the ensuing windows differ. The following sections offer some guidelines to help you understand the questions you may see, and the information you're asked to enter.

General Company Information Section

A series of wizard windows appears, and you click Next to move through the windows. The data you enter in this section of the wizard appears on the cover of your printed plan, so enter information with that in mind.

For the company name, enter the name you do business as (if your business has both a legal name and a DBA name).

For the company contact information, enter the name, title, and telephone number of the person who will be the contact for the recipient of your plan. For example, if you're planning to give the business plan to a bank, use the name of the person who has the answers to any questions the bank's officers may ask. On the other hand, you may want to list the person who has the best relationship with the bank's officers.

Income Tax Information

Enter the income tax form you use. Only C Corporations (and some LLCs) pay taxes (using Form 1120), so if your business is organized as any other type of entity, no company tax information is calculated. Businesses other than C Corps (and LLCs that report as corporations) pay no income taxes; instead, profits or losses are transferred to your personal tax return.

> **ProAdvisor TIP**: *We've found that many small business owners have a problem finding the appropriate tax form if they're operating as a proprietorship. They look for Schedule C, which isn't listed in the drop-down list of tax forms. Instead, select Tax Form 1040, which is where proprietors file their business income. Schedule C is merely an attachment to that form.*

If your company files Tax Form 1120 (a C corp), the business planner calculates your estimated tax payments. After you select Tax Form 1120, and click Next, you're asked to estimate your corporate tax rate. Remember that you probably have a combined tax rate, because you have to consider both federal and state corporate taxes. For your convenience, the wizard displays a federal tax table you can consult.

Incidentally, even if you remit your estimated corporate taxes quarterly, the business planner calculates the payments on a monthly basis, using the profits for that month. If a month shows a loss, the planner carries over the loss to the next month in order to calculate income taxes.

If your business uses any other tax form, the software doesn't factor in business income tax payments. When you click next, the wizard asks you to fill in the estimated monthly amount for owner distributions.

> **ProAdvisor TIP**: *If your company is an S Corporation, owner distributions don't include salaries paid to the owners (the salaries are expenses).*

Customer Credit Information

In the next window, enter the approximate percentage of your sales that are credit-based. If you don't extend credit to your customers, enter zero, and you won't see the ensuing windows that deal with receivables.

Except for over-the-counter retail sales businesses, most businesses provide credit to their customers. Using agreed upon terms of credit, you send invoices, which means you probably have current (or even overdue) receivables.

ProAdvisor NOTE: *Credit card sales are cash sales, and accepting credit cards from customers is not the same as extending credit.*

If you entered any figure except zero for the question about the percentage of sales that involve credit, the next window asks about terms. Select the payment terms you offer customers from the drop-down list. If you offer multiple terms, enter the terms you apply most frequently.

The drop-down list doesn't offer any terms that imply discounts for timely payment (e.g. 2%10 Net 30), because the business planner doesn't factor in those discounts. The terms drop-down list includes the common terms: Less than 30, Net 30, Net 60, Net 90, Net 120.

In the next window, enter the percentage of your credit sales that you think could qualify as bad debt. Bad debt means money owed to you that you're fairly sure you'll never collect.

Business Plan Start Date

Enter the start date for the business plan, which doesn't necessarily have to coincide with the start date of your fiscal year. By default, the selection is the first month of your next fiscal year.

Enter a start date that seems appropriate for the purpose of your business plan, and for the recipient of your business plan documentation.

For example, you may have a specific project in mind (physical office expansion, product line expansion, and so on), for which you're presenting the business plan to banks or investors. Use a business plan start date that matches, or comes close to, the date on which you plan to begin this new financial project.

Income Projection

In the Income section, you face several chores. You must set up income categories (you can have up to twenty), and project the income for each category for the next five years.

You can enter the data manually, or use the Projection Wizard, which pulls data from your QuickBooks company file. The Projection Wizard saves you a lot of work, and you can always change any of the figures that are automatically entered if you want to create "what if" scenarios.

However, if you've just started using QuickBooks, you won't have sufficient data in your company file to extract anything meaningful, so you must enter the information manually.

Even if you have sufficient data in your QuickBooks company file, you may prefer to enter the income information manually, especially if you're about to embark on a new product or service, or you've just found a new customer base. In that case, you probably want to project income that reflects your new, expanded, business expectations.

In the following sections, we'll cover both scenarios starting with the Projection Wizard, and then explain how to enter projections manually.

Using the Projection Wizard

Open the Projection Wizard by clicking the Projection Wizard icon, which appears on the right side of the icon bar located at the top of the income category table.

The Projection Wizard opens with an introductory window. Click Next to begin the real work. Enter the beginning date for your business plan. By default, the wizard enters the month and year you earlier specified as the beginning of your business plan, but you can change that date.

Choose the Projection Basis

When you click Next, the wizard examines the company data, and then asks how to proceed (see Figure 5-11). The method you choose depends on the amount of data in your QuickBooks company file, and the financial differences among the months of data. The Business Planner uses monthly data to project a percentage of increase (or decrease).

If you select the option I Want To Project Manually, the wizard closes and you're returned to the Business Planner (manual data entry is discussed in the next section).

Figure 5-11: Select the method you want to use to project future income.

If you select the option Use The Last 12 Months Of History, the algorithm is rather complicated, and is adjusted to take into consideration the current month, and the interval between your first month and the current month. The algorithm also attaches more weight to recent months than it does to earlier months.

If your recent months have shown a substantial upturn or downturn in performance, and the cause of that inconsistency isn't permanent, those monthly figures might influence the projections, and make them less reliable. In that case, tell the wizard to Compute A Monthly Average From Last 12 Months.

Apply a Growth Factor

When you click Next, you're offered the opportunity to apply a yearly growth factor (see Figure 5-12). Select a number from the drop-down list, or enter a number directly into the field. The number is interpreted as a percentage.

Figure 5-12: Apply the annual growth to be considered in your projection.

Select the Income Categories to Project

Click Next to see a list of the income accounts the wizard found in your chart of accounts. Each account is pre-selected for inclusion in the wizard's calculations.

You can deselect any income account you don't want to use by clicking the check box to remove the check mark. For example, it's common to exclude an interest income account, or a miscellaneous income account that doesn't reflect ongoing revenue. Click Finish to start the calculations.

ProAdvisor NOTE: *The wizard only selects active accounts. If you've made an account inactive and you want to use it for your projection, close the Projection Wizard and activate that account.*

View the Results

The wizard performs its calculations and fills in the monthly figures for a 60-month projection.

You may see an informational message first, telling you that the wizard used a percentage of gross revenue to calculate cost of goods. The message also explains that you can change the wizard's mathematical assumptions by editing the properties of any income category (see the section "Editing the Properties Behind the Data").

Editing the Wizard's Data

You can edit the data the wizard automatically inserts. It's important to note that the wizard automatically adjusts income figures by subtracting a percentage of the gross to cover cost of goods. You can clean up those numbers, either because the wizard's percentage for cost of goods is radically different from your real costs, or because you don't have any cost of goods deductions since you only sell services.

To change the contents of a cell, select it. Then enter a number to replace the existing number. If you want to change the number by a specific percentage, after you select the cell, press Ctrl-F (or click the Functions icon on the icon bar) to open the Functions dialog for the cell, seen in Figure 5-13. Then specify the percentage by which you want to raise or lower the figure.

Figure 5-13: Use the Functions dialog to change the value of a cell by a percentage.

You can also edit the calculation basis for an entire row by clicking the row heading (the title on the left edge of the row) to select the entire row. Then press Ctrl-F (or click the Functions icon on the icon bar). The same Functions dialog appears, but its impact is on the row instead of a single cell.

Here are the guidelines for using the Functions dialog for a row:

- Select Annual Growth, and then enter a percentage figure, to change the annual growth projection you'd previously entered for the selected row. This is a good way to project your company's future income by revenue type, instead of using a single percentage for the entire business.

- Select Raise or Lower, and then enter a percentage, to change all the figures in the row by that percentage.

- Select Repeat to copy the contents of the first cell in the row to all the other cells in the row.

Editing the Properties Behind the Data

You can change the basic properties of a row (an income account), including its title, and the way Business Planner calculates Cost of Sales. Double-click a row heading to open its Properties dialog, seen in Figure 5-14.

Figure 5-14: Changing the properties for an income category changes the way the data is calculated.

If the selected income category has labor or other costs in addition to, or instead of, standard cost of goods, adjust the data in the dialog to gain a more realistic projection. If no costs of goods are involved for this type of income, change all the fields to zero.

Entering Income Data Manually

If you opt to skip the Projection Wizard, or if the wizard tells you there isn't enough data in your company file to proceed, you can enter the numbers for your income manually. Click Next, and then click Finish in the next wizard window to close the Projection Wizard. The bottom of the program window resembles a blank spreadsheet, with rows for categories and columns for months.

Double-click the row header for the first category to open its Properties dialog (refer back to Figure 5-14), and enter the title (an income category). If the category involves a product, also enter the information for costs of goods (in percentages). If the category is a service, you can omit the cost of goods figures.

After you set up all your categories, you can begin entering figures. Move horizontally through the months by pressing the Tab key. If you want to fine tune your figures by raising or lowering amounts by a percentage, click the Functions icon to perform the task.

Expenses Projection

Entering expenses data is similar to entering data for income. The Projection Wizard is available for finding expense account names and amounts in your company file, or you can choose to design the expenses section manually. Move to the Expenses tab of the Business Planner

Using the Wizard for Expenses

You can click the Projection Wizard icon to automate your expenses projections, which involves almost exactly the same steps involved in using the wizard for projecting income. Click Next to move through the windows.

As with income projections, you can apply an annual growth percentage to the expense data in your business plan.

The Projection Wizard selects and displays the expense accounts it will use for the projection, selecting both parent accounts and subaccounts. The Projection Wizard usually skips the following expenses:

- Interest
- Depreciation
- Amortization
- Bad debt expenses

If any of those expenses are checked, uncheck them. Business Planner automatically calculates the appropriate amounts for the expense types it skips, using information from answers you provide as you go.

You can manipulate the data the Projection Wizard enters. Use the instructions in the previous section on Income Projections to define expense categories, enter financial data, and set the calculation methods.

Entering Expenses Manually

As with the income section, you can enter the numbers for your expenses manually, and use that data for your projections.

Double-click the row header for the first category to open its Properties dialog and enter the title (an expense category). After you set up all your categories, you can begin entering figures. Move horizontally through the months by pressing the Tab key. If you want to fine tune your figures by raising or lowering amounts by a percentage, click the Functions icon to use the utilities it offers.

Interview Section

The next part of the Business Planner is the Interview section. Most of the information you enter in this section is connected to your balance sheet accounts (assets, liabilities, and equity).

Assets

The wizard displays the current balances in your asset accounts, including cash, fixed assets, accumulated depreciation for fixed assets, accounts receivable, and any other asset accounts. These balances are taken from your company file.

The current balances are considered opening balances for the business plan. If you expect significant changes in any of these accounts before the first day of your business plan, make an adjustment to the appropriate account(s) in the Balance column.

Minimum Bank Balances

The next window asks for the minimum bank balance your company must have available at all times. (The window also displays the current balance in each of your bank accounts.) Enter an amount that represents the total cash on hand you believe to be a minimum for sustaining your business.

To define the minimum balance, you must consider your monthly expenses, the number of times you have unexpected expenses (and their average amounts), and any other bank balance considerations you must meet. There are no rules or percentages for you to follow, this is a figure that is closely related to your type of business, and the way you do business. Ask your accountant for advice if you're having difficulty ascertaining a number.

Inventory

The next window asks if you maintain inventory, and if you answer affirmatively, the ensuing windows ask for information related to inventory issues, including the following:

- Inventory related accounts (assets, cost of goods sold, and expenses).

- Terms you have with vendors of inventory items. Only net terms are offered in the drop-down list. The Business Planner ignores discounts for timely payment.

- Inventory levels. Specify fixed or variable. Companies with fixed levels usually have regular, predictable, sales of products (especially common with retail businesses). Companies with variable levels usually have irregular sales, and commonly respond to special orders, seasonal sales, or other variable patterns.

- Inventory values. If you select a fixed inventory level, you need to specify the amount of inventory you maintain, in dollars. If you select a variable inventory level, you must specify the number of days of inventory you like to keep on hand.

Fixed and Other Assets

The next window asks for the estimated amortization for any Other Asset accounts you currently have. After that you're asked to enter the estimated depreciation for existing Fixed Asset accounts.

New Asset Purchases

The Business Planner needs to know whether you plan to purchase additional assets at the beginning of the business plan projection. The assets can be anything except inventory, such as the following:

- Land
- Buildings
- Building improvements
- Equipment (business, manufacturing, vehicles, furniture, fixtures, etc.)
- Start-up costs

If you select No, the Business Planner moves on to the next category (Liabilities). If you select Yes, you have additional information to enter. Start by providing information about the category and cost of your upcoming asset purchase.

The Business Planner asks if you'll be financing any of the asset purchases. If you respond in the affirmative, enter the loan information. Specify whether the loan is a standard loan (fixed monthly payments covering interest and principal), or a one-pay loan (interest only, with a single payment for principal at the end of the loan). The Business Planner can calculate the monthly payment, term, interest rate, or total amount of the loan, as long as you enter data in three of those four categories. You must move your cursor into the field to be calculated to enable the Calculate <selected field> button.

Liabilities

The next part of the Interview section is about your company's liabilities. The Business Planner displays the liability accounts it finds in your chart of accounts, along with the current balance for each of those accounts.

Set Beginning Balances for Liability Accounts

The Business Planner needs to establish beginning balances for the five years of the projection. You can change the amount of any displayed balance to reflect a more accurate amount for projecting your company's financial position.

Enter Line of Credit Information

All of the accounts of the type Credit Card are displayed, along with their current balances. In addition, the Business Planner displays the names of your accounts of the type Current Liability, and asks if any of these accounts are line of credit accounts.

The current balances of the accounts you select as line of credit accounts are added to the total balances of your credit cards, and the grand total is treated as your current line of credit obligation.

In the next window, enter the total credit limit for the aggregate line of credit accounts. If you don't know the limit for any credit card, try to find a copy of a bill—the limit is displayed on every statement you receive. In the next window, enter the average interest rate for all your line of credit accounts.

Long Term Loans

In the Long Term Loans section, the Business Planner displays the name and current balance of all the accounts in your chart of accounts that are of the type Long Term Liabilities.

Enter the description, type of loan, APR, interest rate, and other financial information for each long-term loan. Here again, if you enter data in three of the financial fields, the Business Planner will calculate the fourth.

Investing in Your Business

As you entered data in each of the Business Planner windows, the software performed calculations in the background. The calculations took into consideration your income, the status of your receivables, your debt, and other financial factors. The results of the calculations are displayed in the next window.

If no additional capital is deemed to be required to meet your financial goals and obligations, you're asked if you'd like to invest capital anyway. If you're planning to infuse your business with capital, enter the amount; otherwise leave the amount at zero, and click Next.

However, as a result of the calculations, you may be advised to provide additional capital to meet your monthly expenses over the course of the three years of the projection. For example, if you'd indicated you were planning to purchase an automobile, and didn't indicate an auto loan, you're probably going to be short of cash. Or, perhaps you entered a figure for a minimum bank balance that is larger than your current capital can handle.

The Business Planner displays the amount you need to invest to cover the shortage. Enter the amount you're planning to put towards the shortage, and click Next. If you didn't enter an amount sufficient to cover the shortage, the next window asks about the loans you're planning to cover your shortage.

The next two windows ask about financial transactions you may be considering during the three years of the projection. Enter the amounts for any additional assets you think you may purchase, and the amounts of any loans you think you may incur.

Writing Your Business Plan

Now that all the information about your company's finances has been recorded in the Business Planner, you can begin writing your business plan.

Business plans include detailed written sections that cover a wide range of topics. You must explain the figures, your plans for growth, your marketing goals, and so on. The terminology you use should be chosen with the reader in mind (a bank, a venture capitalist, a potential partner, etc.).

As seen in Figure 5-15, the Business Planner provides assistance by displaying the components of the written plan in the left pane. Expand each section by clicking the plus sign, which reveals the subsections. Move through the components by clicking Next.

ProAdvisor TIP: *Click the Example tab to see sample text for each component.*

The writing area offers standard formatting tools so you can make the written plan look professional. In addition, the icon bar has icons for inserting data and graphs (linked to the data) from the Income and Expenses sections you completed in the Business Planner.

Figure 5-15: Step through each section in the left pane to complete the written plan.

ProAdvisor TIP: *Click the Print Topic Guide button above the writing area to print helpful guidelines about the current topic, or all topics. You can opt to include the sample text in your printout.*

You may find that some of the subsections in the left pane are irrelevant to your business; if so, just skip them. You can rename or delete the section titles you're using in your plan. If you find you need additional sections you can add them. To perform any of these actions select a topic, right click, and make the appropriate selection from the menu that appears.

There's no hard and fast rule that you have to write your plan using the order in which the categories are presented in the left pane. You're perfectly free to organize your writing in a way that makes sense for your company. Add new topics, change the name of existing topics, or just plain delete topics you don't need. Highlight a topic and right click it to view a menu of choices.

Previewing Your Business Plan

To see a preview of the layout of your plan, choose File | Preview Business Plan from the Business Planner menu bar. The Preview Business Plan window displays a summary of your plan's contents (see Figure 5-16). Notice that the financial projections have been placed in the appendixes for the reader's reference.

Figure 5-16: Check the Table of Contents carefully.

Customize the Plan Contents

You may want to customize the contents for a particular recipient—
different types of recipients need different information. You can deselect
parts of the plan before you preview and print it. Deselecting a component
does not remove it, or its contents, from your business plan; it merely
omits the component from the preview document and the printed
document you produce at this time.

- To remove an entire section from the preview/printed
  document, remove the check mark from the section title.

- To exclude specific topics, remove the check mark from
  the appropriate topic title.

- Deselect an Appendix document by removing the check
  mark from the listing.

- Deselect any unnecessary additional documents you
  added to your plan.

After you select and deselect content, click Preview to preview the
plan in its current state.

ProAdvisor NOTE*: It's best to preview the entire plan to make
sure it contains no mistakes before you customize it for any
particular recipient.*

Viewing and Printing the Business Plan

To view the status of your plan, click the Review Plan button. It displays a list of all the selected topics and indicates which have content and
which do not. To print a hard copy of this status report to your default
Windows printer, click the Print Review button.

To view (and print if you wish) the actual plan, click the Preview button. The Business Planner takes a minute to build and format the plan
and presents a preview window containing all the elements selected in the
Preview Business Plan windows (refer back to Figure 5-16). From here
you can view the plan, print it, export it to Word or Excel, or save it as a
PDF file.

Use the Next and Previous buttons on the toolbar to move through the pages of the plan. The box in the upper right corner indicates the current page being viewed, as well as the total number of pages. Click Zoom to zoom in on the currently displayed page so you can see the contents clearly.

To print the plan as previewed, click the Print icon on the icon bar. Specify the number of copies to print, and select the page range:

- All
- Current Page
- Pages From X to Y (substitute starting and ending page numbers for X and Y)

Click OK to begin printing your plan. If you have multiple printers, and the selected printer isn't the one you want to use, close the Preview window and return to the main QuickBooks Business Planner window. Select File | Plan Format from the Business Planner menu bar to open the Plan Format dialog. From the Compose To Printer drop-down list choose the desired printer.

Save the Business Plan as a PDF File

You can save the plan as a PDF file instead of printing it if you want to send it to the recipient via e-mail, or on a CD. To accomplish this, click the Save icon on the icon bar.

In the Save Plan As PDF dialog, name the document, and save it in any folder you choose. By default, the Save As PDF dialog selects the folder in which your company file is stored, but you can change the folder.

Export the Business Plan

Click Export to send the file to your word processor. If you have Microsoft Excel installed on your computer, the Export dialog includes an option to export the financial projections (your appendices) to a Microsoft Excel spreadsheet.

The text part of your business plan is loaded in Word, and you can format, edit, and otherwise manipulate the document as you wish. The file is exported to Word as an RTF (Rich Text Format) file, which means it can be opened in any word processor without changing the formatting or graphics. To save the document, choose File | Save As from the Word menu bar and choose Microsoft Word Document as the File Type, and specify a location and filename.

The non-text part of the plan (the spreadsheet-type information about accounts and amounts and the projections) is loaded in Excel, with a separate worksheet for each year's income and expense projection.

The Word document does not contain the information that was exported to Excel; instead, the document contains links to the Excel document. Clicking a link opens Excel with the linked worksheet displayed.

If you print the business plan from the Word and Excel files, it doesn't have the same layout as printing the plan from the Business Plan Tool. You must collate the pages manually, and the Table of Contents in the Word Document won't be accurate.

Backing Up the Business Plan

QuickBooks backs up your business plan file as part of the standard QuickBooks backup process. However, if you have to restore your company file, the business plan file (with the extension .BPW) is not restored directly to the folder you choose to restore your file. Instead, the .BPW file, in addition to other restored auxiliary files, resides in a folder named Miscellaneous Files, which is a subfolder of a folder named Restored_<*CompanyFileName*>_Files. This folder structure is created by QuickBooks when you restore a company file backup. Copy the .BPW file from the Miscellaneous Files subfolder to the parent folder in which your restored company file resides.

You can make a separate backup of your business plan while you're working in the Business Plan Tool by choosing choose File | Back Up on the Business Planner window. In the Back Up dialog, choose a location for the backup file. Then, if something happens to your business plan file you can restore the business plan file from within the tool. Choose File | Restore on the QuickBooks Business Planner window and locate the backup file. Select the file's listing and click Open, then follow the prompts to restore your plan.

CHAPTER 6

Inventory Tips

- Understanding inventory

- Tracking the cost of inventory

- Units of measure

- Assemblies

- Managing damaged items

- Tracking purchase order prepayments

- Taking inventory on the road

- New improved inventory features

By definition, inventory is a product that you buy or make for the express purpose of selling it. If you buy products to use in the course of business, that's not inventory.

We often find QuickBooks users struggling with the complications of inventory needlessly. Chief among them are contractors who buy pipes, wood, and other construction products that they use in the course of business. This isn't inventory, and they should be using non-inventory items for these purchases.

QuickBooks provides a rather rudimentary inventory feature, and you may find that it just doesn't work for your business. You can purchase a QuickBooks add-on that's designed to provide more inventory functions by looking in the Intuit Marketplace for software that's been tested to make sure it works properly with QuickBooks (http://marketplace.intuit.com/).

Understanding Inventory

Inventory is a complicated system. The financial processes involved in maintaining inventory include tracking inventory costs, additional costs added to inventory items, the total value of your inventory asset, and other financial processes. In addition, you have to understand how to keep track of the inventory items you move in and out of your company. The following sections provide an overview of the way inventory works in QuickBooks.

Cost of Goods Sold

All accounting software, accountants, bookkeepers, and knowledgeable users understand what Costs of Goods Sold (usually abbreviated COGS) means, but unfortunately many users don't understand the term and don't consult a professional when they set up their QuickBooks company files.

The word "Sold" is the clue to understanding the way COGS works in accounting. You post the expense/cost of an inventory item when you *sell* the inventory item. You do not incur an expense when you purchase the inventory item (it's not called Cost of Goods Bought).

When you purchase inventory items, either for re-sale or for use in manufacturing, the following posting takes place:

- Your Inventory Asset Account is debited (increased) by the amount you spent.

- Your bank account is credited (decreased) by the amount you spent. If you entered a vendor bill instead of writing a check, the first credit is to Accounts Payable, then, when you pay the bill, A/P is debited and your bank account is credited – in the end, the money comes out of your bank to pay your supplier.

Notice that nothing posts to an expense account, so nothing shows up on your Profit & Loss reports, and no expenses are posted to reduce your profit. Instead, the expense is posted to the COGS account when you sell the inventory item.

ProAdvisor NOTE*: Some accountants advise users to post the expense of buying non-inventory items to COGS, and this is an acceptable method in some cases. However, in this chapter we're only discussing inventory.*

Inventory Adjustment Accounts

Occasionally, you need to adjust your inventory quantity, or the value of the existing quantity. QuickBooks provides a transaction window for this function; it's called Adjust Quantity/Value On Hand and it's available on the menu you see when you choose Vendors | Inventory Activities.

This transaction window is referenced several times in this chapter, and when you see a Figure in this chapter you'll see that most of the time the Adjustment Account is a Cost of Goods Sold account. This is not something QuickBooks tolerates without a complaint.

When you select an account of the type Cost of Goods Sold as the adjusting account, QuickBooks displays a message telling you it expected an expense or income account (see Figure 6-1).

Figure 6-1: QuickBooks objects to using any account type except
Income or Expense for inventory adjustments.

You can select the option Do Not Display This Message In The Future before you click OK so you're not bothered with this message in the future. However, you should understand what's going on so you can make a decision about the way you configure inventory adjustments.

Some accountants use an expense account whether the adjustment is an increase or a decrease, and the account tracks the net changes. Other accountants prefer to create a COGS account named Inventory Adjustments, and use that account whether the adjustment is an increase or a decrease. We've yet to meet an accountant who agrees that an income account is an appropriate inventory adjustment account. Accountants tell us that using an income account is wrong because increasing the quantity of inventory items doesn't result in increased income. (And, if you post this as income, it could increase your tax liability.)

There are circumstances under which accounts other than inventory adjustment accounts are appropriate when you adjust inventory quantities:

- If you send a sample to a potential customer that's a marketing device; use the Marketing or Advertising expense account for the adjustment.

- If you send inventory to a charitable organization use the Charitable Gifts expense account for the adjustment.

Using the Inventory Center

The Inventory Center, available in all Premier editions, is similar in layout to the Customer and Vendor Centers (see Figure 6-2). It is comprised of a left pane containing the list of inventory and assembly items, and two right panes. The top right pane displays the basic data from the item record selected in the left pane. The bottom right pane displays a listing of transactions in which the item selected in the left pane has been used.

Figure 6-2: The Inventory Center provides one-stop shopping for inventory activities.

Inventory Center Components

As you can see, the Inventory Center has a variety of components, each with its own function. To begin with, it has a toolbar that provides quick access to basic commands such as creating new items and transactions as well as buttons for printing and exporting to Excel.

Item List Pane

The Item List pane on the left provides easy access to all inventory and assembly items. Select an item in the list and you can view its record details as well as transaction information on the right. Here are some of the features associated with the left pane:

- Item Categories. Click the Active Inventory, Assembly button to display a drop-down list of item categories by which you can filter the left pane list. In addition to basic preset filters, you can create your own custom filters which allow you to search custom fields and notes.

- Item Search. In the search box enter the text you want to locate in an item record. For example, enter *hinge* to locate all the records for hinge items.

- Right-Click Menu. Right-click any row in the left pane to display a context menu of related commands. You can create, edit, and make inactive items using these commands. You can check availability, create transactions, and do a lot more.

- Customize Columns. Using this command found on the right-click context menu, you can add, remove, and reposition columns in the left pane.

While you can use the Edit icon in the right pane to open an item record, double-clicking a listing in the left pane will do the same thing.

Inventory Information Pane

This pane is located in the top, right portion of the Inventory Center. When an item is selected in the left pane, the basic information from the item record is displayed. It enables you to quickly review item details without having to open the item record. There are a few other features to be aware of:

- Attach Icon (paperclip). If you want to keep documentation associated with the item close at hand, click the Attach icon to open the Attachments dialog. Here, you can add files from your computer, scan documents from your scanner, or grab files from the Doc Center to attach to the item. For example, you could attach a photo of the item, a spec sheet, or some other related document.

- Edit Icon (pencil nub). Click the Edit icon to open the item record for reviewing or editing.

- Reports. For quick access to common, inventory related reports, click one of the links in the Reports section.

Transaction/Notes Pane

The bottom, right portion of the Inventory Center is reserved for a listing of transactions and notes. The pane has two tabs, Transactions and Notes.

Transactions

Here you'll find a listing of all transactions (invoices, sales receipts, POs, estimates, bills, check, etc.) in which the item or assembly has been included. Double-click a transaction to open it and view the contents.

To filter the list, use one of the filter fields at the top of the pane. The Show field offers a drop-down list of transaction types. The Filter By drop-down list does not offer any choices except All. The Date drop-down list contains the usual date range options found in most Date drop-down lists in QuickBooks.

Right click in the list to view a context menu of commands that includes, among other things, the ability to customize the columns in the list.

Below the list you'll find two buttons, Manage Transactions and Run Reports. The Manage Transactions drop-down list provides commands to create new transactions and edit existing transactions. The Run Reports drop-down list offers to create a report of the existing list of transactions.

Notes

In the event that you want to make a notation about an inventory or assembly item, this is the place to do it. Perhaps, there's a supply problem at the factory, or an upcoming change in price or design. Click the Notes tab, right-click in the list, and choose Add New to create a new note. The Notepad opens, in which you can record a note, add a timestamp, and even access the QuickBooks To Do feature to add a new To Do.

About the only thing you can do in this tab is create, edit, or delete notes related to inventory or assembly items.

Creating an Inventory Item Properly

It's important to understand the fields in the inventory item record (see Figure 6-3).

Figure 6-3: It's important to fill in data fields properly when you configure an inventory item.

Item Name/Number (required)

This one needs no explanation other than using common sense when assigning the item a name.

ProAdvisor TIP: *If you have a lot of inventory items that can be divided into groups it's a good idea to take advantage of subitems. For example, if you run an electronics store and sell television sets you'll probably want to create a parent item called Televisions and a whole bunch of subitems for either sizes or brands. You could even go so far as to create brand subitems and then size sub-subitems (e.g. Televisions:Sony:32inch), or vice versa.*

Manufacturer's Part Number (optional)

Enter the number your vendor uses for this item. QuickBooks will automatically enter this data on purchase orders if you customize a PO template to display this field.

Description on Purchase Transactions (optional)

Enter the text that should appear in the Description field when you create a transaction for purchasing this item.

Description on Sales Transactions (optional)

Enter the text that should appear in the Description field when you create an invoice or a sales receipt. QuickBooks automatically copies the text in the Description On Purchase Transactions into this field, but you can edit the text if the description your customers see should differ.

Cost (optional)

The Cost field is not used for tracking financial data. QuickBooks does not use the data in this field to calculate the value of your inventory or the Cost of Goods Sold; it's irrelevant to the calculation of profit or loss. It's a "text" field that exists only to remind you of the cost of the item at the time you're creating a Purchase Order.

QuickBooks calculates the cost of inventory when you actually purchase an item, either by entering a vendor bill or a direct check to a vendor.

When you create a purchase transaction and enter a cost that's different from the text in the Cost field, QuickBooks asks if you want to update the Cost field. Your choice about updating the field has no effect on your financial records, because the data in this field isn't used in any calculations.

COGS Account (required)

Enter the COGS account that's used when you sell the item.

Preferred Vendor (optional)

This field is useful if you always buy this item from the same vendor. You can enter the item in the Item column in a purchase transaction (PO, direct check, or Vendor Bill) without filling out the top of the transaction window and QuickBooks will automatically fill out the vendor information in the header section of the transaction window.

Sales Price (optional)

Use this field to enter the selling price of the item in a sales transaction window. You can change this amount while you're creating the transaction.

Tax Code (required if Sales Tax is enabled)

If you enabled Sales Tax, you must indicate whether the item is taxable or not. If you haven't enabled Sales Tax, the field doesn't appear.

Income Account (required)

Enter the Income account to which sales of the item are posted.

Asset Account (required)

Enter the inventory asset account to which purchases and sales are posted.

Reorder Point (optional)

Use this field to enter the minimum quantity you want to maintain for this item. When the QOH is down to this number QuickBooks issues a reminder to order more. You must configure this reminder in the Reminder section of the Preferences dialog (Edit | Preferences | Reminders).

On Hand and Total Value (Do Not Use)

These fields at the bottom of the window seem convenient, but filling them in can cause problems for your accountant. When you use these fields, QuickBooks posts the total value to your Inventory Asset Account, and posts the other side of the transaction to the Opening Balance Equity account.

A balance in the Opening Balance Equity account is a problem, because it doesn't tell your accountant (or you) the source. Was it a purchase from your supplier? If so, when? This year? Last year? Is there an open A/P balance for that supplier? If so, is it connected to this amount in total or in part?

Skip these fields and enter transactions to bring in your inventory; if the transactions you enter are from a previous year QuickBooks will use them in the calculation of your closing balances for the previous year. See Chapter 1 to learn about the effect of previous year transactions on your opening trial balance in QuickBooks.

QuickBooks Average Costing

QuickBooks supports only average costing for inventory. There are a number of methods for costing inventory, but if you use QuickBooks you're limited to average costing. Some third party programs provide a way to use First In First Out (FIFO) or Last In First Out (LIFO) as the inventory costing method with QuickBooks.

In QuickBooks, the average cost of an inventory item reflects the total history of that item since the last time that it had a quantity of zero. This is not necessarily the way you need (or want) to track average costing, so you must work with your accountant to come up with the correct figures for your tax return.

The average cost that QuickBooks uses is calculated when you receive inventory, and that average cost is displayed at the bottom of the item record (you can't change it). The amount you enter in the Cost field is never used for calculating the cost/value of your inventory items.

You must be aware of the following QuickBooks "quirks" in computing average cost when you analyze your business financials, and when you prepare tax returns. (The word "quirks" is my word, and it doesn't mean that there's anything illegal or unacceptable in the way QuickBooks manages average costing.)

Average Cost is not Calculated for a Fiscal Period

Calculations include the entire history of the item since the last time the quantity was at or below zero; there are no "period" (annual) calculations.

Selling All Items in Stock Erases Average Cost History

When you sell items to the point of having zero quantity, QuickBooks starts over. For example, if you've been buying a widget for years for $12.00, you've maintained an average cost of $12.00. If your quantity goes to zero and your supplier charges $14.00/widget for the next order, your average cost changes to $14.00, which is going to affect your P & L and Balance Sheet for the year. Unfortunately this number is used to post COGS and inventory asset values (most 4th graders could understand the math needed to provide an accurate average cost).

Selling Stock That's Not Available Creates Serious Problems

If you sell into negative quantity, QuickBooks gets confused. Later, if you receive more widgets, QuickBooks "catches up", but the numbers may not be acceptable to you or your accountant.

Unlike other accounting software, QuickBooks permits users to sell into negative quantity. The only way to avoid the mess this creates is to impose your own controls on user actions.

- Never sell into negative quantities.
- If you know that the QuickBooks Quantity On Hand is wrong (you've counted the stock and you know you have enough to sell the quantity ordered by the customer), do an inventory adjustment before you create the sales transaction.
- If you know that new stock is arriving tomorrow, don't create the sales transaction until the receipt of the goods has been recorded in QuickBooks.

Tracking the Real Cost of Inventory

Inventory tracking isn't always as simple as "buy it, mark it up, and sell it". There are often additional costs attached to bringing inventory into your warehouse, or to create a finished product, and you need to take those costs into consideration.

Inbound Shipping Costs

If you pay for inbound shipping, the cost of shipping can legitimately be included in the cost of an item. For example, if you created a PO for 100 widgets at $10.00/widget, your PO has a total value of $1000.00.

When you receive the items into QuickBooks, if the vendor bill includes a shipping charge of $20.00, you receive 100 widgets for $1020.00, resulting in a per-item cost of $10.20. If the vendor bill for shipping costs arrives later, you can do an inventory value adjustment as follows:

1. In the Adjust Quantity/Value On Hand transaction window, select Total Value from the Adjustment Type drop-down list.
2. Select the item in the Item column.
3. Use a calculator to add the shipping cost to the Total Value of the item and enter the total in the New Value column.

Work in Process Inventory

It's possible to set up a QuickBooks system to track Work in Process (WIP) and then transfer finished goods to inventory, but you have to do it manually because QuickBooks has no built in "WIP to Inventory" process. That's understandable, because QuickBooks is designed for use by businesses that have very simple inventory management needs.

WIP inventory is needed when a finished product is the result of multiple processes such as subcontracted services and/or non-inventory products.

This book is an example of an inventory item that requires WIP tracking. It's created (manufactured) from a variety of services and products; it's not purchased or assembled from existing inventory items.

In the case of this book, the manuscript for each chapter is sent to editors, the edited manuscripts are sent to a production facility that transforms the documents into special files that the printer requires, an artist creates the cover, the printer prints, collates, and binds the book, and then ships cartons of books to our warehouse. Every company involved in these processes submits a bill for each task.

ProAdvisor CAUTION: *WIP processes are difficult in QuickBooks if your business has more than a few inventory products that are tracked this way. In that case, buy a separate software application to track these manufacturing steps. Check the QuickBooks Marketplace Solutions web pages to find a QuickBooks add-on that will work for you.*

Tracking WIP Transactions

To track WIP, create an account of the type Other Current Asset, and name it Work in Process or WIP. Products or services purchased to create inventory items are posted to this WIP account.

Don't use POs for products and services for WIP to avoid having to create an item. (Items need expense and income accounts, which makes tracking WIP more complicated.) Use the Memo field on each transaction to note the product for which you're making the purchase.

ProAdvisor TIP: *If any of the companies involved in creating your product require a PO, you can generate a PO in your word processor. Or, create the PO in QuickBooks but don't receive items against it; in fact, you can void or delete it after you send it.*

Moving Finished Products into Inventory

When the payments for the parts and services have been entered in QuickBooks, and you're ready to move a product into inventory, create a report to determine the cost of inventory, and then perform an inventory adjustment to add the product to your inventory at the right cost.

To gather the information you need about the total cost of parts and services for an inventory product, customize a report to eliminate transactions not included in your WIP system.

Choose Reports | Vendors & Payables | Vendor Balance Detail, and click Customize Report. Make the following changes:

- In the Display tab, select (place a check mark next to) Memo in the Columns list.
- In the Filters tab, select Account in the Choose Filter list, and then select the WIP account.
- In the Filters tab, select Transaction Type in the Choose Filter list, select Multiple Transaction Types, and then select Bill and Check. (The transaction types Bill and Check cover vendor bills you entered and checks written as direct disbursements.)

The resulting report displays the total cost of an inventory product. With the total cost known, move the items into inventory by choosing Vendors | Inventory Activities | Adjust Quantity/Value On Hand. In the Adjust Quantity/Value On Hand dialog take the following actions:

1. Select the option Quantity And Total Value from the Adjustment Type field.
2. In the Adjustment Account field, enter the WIP account.
3. Select the item you're bringing into inventory.
4. In the New Quantity column enter the number of units you're transferring to inventory.
5. In the New Value column enter the total cost of the item (the total of all postings for this item in the WIP account).

Cost of Improving Inventory

Some businesses buy items and improve them, and need to track the cost of the improvements as part of the cost of the item. Most of the inquiries we receive about accomplishing this are from antique dealers (including antique car businesses), but the problem exists for anyone who purchases an item, improves it, and then sells it. There are several ways to do this, but the following method is both easy and efficient. (We're assuming the basic inventory item exists in your QuickBooks system and you've received one or more into inventory.)

Create an Other Current Asset account named Inventory Improvements to track the additional costs. When you pay for the improvements, post the expense to the Inventory Improvements account you created. Put the name of the inventory item in the Memo field so you can link your improvements to the right inventory item.

When the inventory item is totally "improved", adjust the value using the following steps:

1. Choose Vendors | Inventory Activities | Adjust Quantity/ Value On Hand.
2. Select Total Value as the Adjustment Type.
3. In the Adjustment Account field, select the Inventory Improvements account.
4. In the New Value column, enter the total of the current value plus the additional expense(s); you'll probably need a calculator to do this.

This action credits the Inventory Improvements account, washing the debit you posted when you paid for the improvements, and debits your Inventory Asset Account to reflect the higher value of your inventory. The new value is also used in the calculations Quick-Books uses to determine the average cost of the item when posting COGS.

Units of Measure

A unit of measure (U/M) is a way to establish specific information about the basis on which you buy and sell quantities of goods and products. For example, if you sell an inventory item named Chocolate Syrup you can specify the U/M as a bottle, a 6-pack, or a 24-bottle case. You can also use a U/M for the services you sell – perhaps you want to provide services in units of hours or days.

U/Ms are attached to items and each item has its own U/M. Quick-Books provides two ways to track and assign U/Ms:

- Single U/M per item, in which you can assign one U/M to an item.
- Multiple U/M per item, in which you can create a base U/M and then devise multiple conversions of that base U/M to permit sales of different quantities.

Not all Premier editions support U/Ms and some provide only a Single U/M per item. Table 6-1 displays the type of U/M supported by each Premier edition.

Edition	U/M Supported
Premier (not industry specific)	Single U/M only
Professional Services	Single U/M only
Nonprofit	Single U/M only
Accountant	Both Multiple and Single U/M
Contractor	Both Multiple and Single U/M
Manufacturing & Wholesale	Both Multiple and Single U/M
Retail	No U/M available

Table 6-1: Support for Units of Measure for Premier editions.

Businesses that sell inventory items obviously have the greatest need for the U/M feature. Before QuickBooks introduced this feature, selling inventory that you buy in large lots (perhaps a skid of 10 cases), but sell in smaller units such as single cases and single items, required the establishment of Group items. That solution is often clumsy and onerous because a group isn't automatically linked to an item, and has to be created and sold as a discrete item. U/Ms can automate the "buy it one way and sell it another way" function. (If you've already created group items you can assign them U/M functions, which is very handy.)

Enabling Units of Measure

To enable U/Ms, choose Edit | Preferences and select the Items & Inventory category in the left pane. Move to the Company Preferences tab and click the Enable button. In the Unit Of Measure dialog (see Figure 6-4), select the U/M method you want to use. (Depending on your Premier edition, the Multiple U/M option may be grayed out and inaccessible.)

Figure 6-4: Choose the U/M you need for the products and services you sell.

Click Finish to return to the Preferences dialog, and then click OK. QuickBooks adds the U/M field to all the following item types so you can begin establishing U/Ms:

- Inventory Part
- Inventory Assembly
- Non-inventory Part
- Service

ProAdvisor NOTE: *If your company file is opened in a Premier edition that supports U/Ms not supported in your version, those U/Ms can be created. They will be available for use when you reopen the company file in your Premier edition. You just won't be able to create any new U/Ms of that type.*

Creating a Single Unit of Measure

If you enabled Single U/Ms, you can create one measurement type for each item. Open the Item List and double-click the item for which you want to create a single U/M.

ProAdvisor: *It doesn't matter which item you select to create a U/M. The U/M you create is available to all items that can be sold by that U/M (the same way custom fields work). You need to create sufficient U/Ms to cover all the scenarios for all the items you want to buy and sell by U/M.*

In the U/M Set field, select <Add New> from the drop-down list to open the Unit Of Measure wizard.

Select the type of measurement appropriate to this item, and click Next to select the U/M you want to use when you sell this item. The options offered depend on the type of measurement you created in the first wizard window.

The choice you make depends on the way you usually buy, store, and sell the item. If you purchase product by the case and each case contains 48 individual units that you sell one at a time, it makes sense to create a base U/M of Each.

However, suppose the product comes in a case of 48 that contains four wrapped cartons of 12 units each? Creating a U/M of Dozen makes sense. Creating a U/M of Each would mean that every case would need to be opened, and then every 12-pack carton would need to be opened, in order to store individual items. In addition, each individual item would have to be picked and packed for each sale. If customers are buying a dozen-pack, why not just offer a U/M of Dozen?

If the choices available on the Unit of Measure dialog don't include a measurement unit that fits neatly with the way you buy, store, and sell this item, click Other, and then click Next. In this window (see Figure 6-5) create your own U/M. Give the U/M a name and an abbreviation. The abbreviation is what appears on forms and reports, so make sure the text you use clearly defines the U/M.

Figure 6-5: Create your own U/M if the system doesn't provide what you need.

For service items, it's common to create U/Ms based on time, because services are usually sold by the hour or by the day. Some professional services are sold in blocks of minutes, because the company has a "minimum time" rule for billing clients. For example, some professionals have a minimum 10-minute or 12-minute time block. In that case you can create a U/M for that minimum unit.

If you use timesheets and specify customers and jobs on the timesheets, and those customers are invoiced for the time, you can create a U/M for hours because that's how most timesheets are filled out by workers. However, if the service item is already configured in your Item List at an hourly price, and you're already selling the service in multiples of that price, you don't really need a U/M.

The unit of measure you create becomes available for every item that can be sold via a U/M. It's probable that not all items are ablc to use this U/M, so you must repeat this process to create additional U/Ms until you've designed sufficient variations to cover all the items and item types you want to sell by U/M. If you create U/Ms that are fairly generic, you probably only have to create a handful of U/Ms.

Assigning a Single Unit of Measure to Items

After you've created the Single U/Ms you need, you can assign a U/M to every item that you want to sell by U/M. For a Single U/M, each item can only be linked to one U/M (that's why it's called a Single U/M). If you want to be able to sell an item from a choice of U/Ms you must use the Multiple U/M feature (covered later in this chapter).

Open each item and select the appropriate U/M from the drop-down list. If you find an item for which you haven't created an appropriate U/M, select <Add New> and create the U/M you need.

Not all services and products need a U/M. If you've assigned a cost/ rate to a service or a product that is sold in multiples of that rate, you don't have to encumber that item with a U/M.

If you have a service that you sell as a discrete task, for a specific amount, there's no point in assigning a U/M. For example, if you charge a flat fee for installation of a product you sell, there's no point in assigning a U/M. No customer would be asked to pay for two installations for a single product, nor for half an installation of that product.

Selling an Item with a Single Unit of Measure

When you create a sales transaction and select an Item that has been assigned a single U/M, the U/M automatically appears on the line in which you've selected the item (see Figure 6-6).

Figure 6-6: This item can only be sold in the quantity indicated by the U/M linked to it.

The U/M linked to the item is permanent; you cannot switch between it and any other U/M because this is a single U/M. You cannot remove it from the sales transaction form and substitute the basic individual unit you were using for this item before you linked a single U/M to the item. The U/M column is not accessible.

Creating Multiple Units of Measure

To create a Multiple U/M, be sure you've enabled Multiple U/M Per Item in the Items & Inventory category of the Preferences dialog (remember,

Multiple U/M is not available in all editions). Then open an item from the Item List, and select <Add New> from the drop-down list in the U/M field.

In the Select A Unit Of Measure Type window, choose the type of measurement you're setting up. For this example, we've used Count, because it's so common.

Click Next to specify the base unit of measure for this U/M. The options on this window change, depending on the choice you made for the type of measurement in the previous window. Figure 6-7 shows the base unit window choices for the measurement type Count.

Figure 6-7: Your base unit is the smallest unit you track.

The base unit you select must be the smallest unit you track. It doesn't matter how you buy the product, what matters is the smallest unit of the product you're willing to sell. For example, if you buy widgets in skids of 10 cases, and each case contains 100 boxes of 10 widgets/box, and you're unwilling to unpack a box to sell less than 10 widgets at a time, your base unit is a box of 10. If the option you need isn't available in the window, click Other and create the base unit you need (BoxOf10).

Click Next to build multiple U/Ms in the Add Related Units window seen in Figure 6-8.

Figure 6-8: Add the units you can sell from your base unit.

Put a check mark next to each unit you track, either for purchases or for sales, and indicate the number of "base units" (from the previous window) in each of these related units. Check only those units you store and sell, skipping those you won't use.

Be sure to check the unit you use to purchase the item, even if you don't usually sell that unit. If the unit isn't available, e.g. you buy a skid or half skid, add it to the list and make sure it has a check mark. (You enter the purchase unit in the next window.)

Click Next to select your default units of measure, as seen in Figure 6-9. Notice that the operative word is "default" – the unit of measure that will appear automatically in a purchase order or a sales transaction. When you are filling out the form, you can choose another unit from the drop-down list that contains all your added units for this U/M.

The default Shipping U/M is optional. Entering a value determines what appears automatically on pick lists, regardless of the U/M unit on the transaction form. Don't create a Shipping U/M that's larger than the smallest unit you'll sell. For example, if the smallest unit you offer is "pair", the Shipping U/M can be "pair" or "each" (depending on the way the unit is packaged). However, if you sell "each", you can't pick "pair" as the Shipping U/M.

Figure 6-9: Save time when creating transactions by populating the transaction window with a default U/M.

Click Next, and give your Multiple U/M a name. QuickBooks provides a default name, but you can change it to text that you know everyone will recognize as a description for this U/M. Remember that this U/M will be available for linking to multiple items, so the name has to make sense to anyone setting up U/Ms for any item.

Click Finish and then repeat these steps to create all the other Multiple U/Ms you need. QuickBooks creates a list of the U/M sets you create on the Lists menu.

Changing or Removing the U/M for an Item

If you find that the U/M you linked to an item isn't working well, you can change the U/M function for that item. Open the item and go to the U/M field to make your changes:

- Select a different U/M for the item from the drop-down list.

- Create a new U/M that's suitable for this item by choosing <Add New> from the drop-down list.

- Highlight the current U/M and then press the Delete key to make the field blank, removing U/Ms from the item.

If you remove the U/M from the item, QuickBooks displays a message telling you that your action won't affect any transactions that were already completed using the U/M, but future transactions won't have a U/M filled out for this item. Since that's an intelligent approach, click Yes to confirm the removal.

Managing Units of Measure

If you're using Multiple U/Ms, over the course of time, you'll need to manage the U/Ms you create. This section provides an overview of the available functions. All of the functions discussed in this section are available only for Multiple U/Ms.

Editing Units of Measure

You can change the configuration of a U/M by editing it. Open the item, select the U/M to edit, and then click the Edit button next to the U/M Set field in the item record.

You can also edit a U/M by double-clicking its listing in the U/M Set List, which you open from the Lists menu. The changes you make are applied to all the items that are linked to this U/M. However, past transactions are not changed to match your edits.

Removing Units of Measure

QuickBooks provides no way to delete a U/M, but you can make a U/M inactive if it isn't working properly, or is no longer needed. When you make a U/M inactive, it no longer appears in drop-down lists on transaction forms or in item records. To accomplish this, right-click the U/M listing in the U/M Set List and choose Make U/M Set Inactive.

Creating Reports on Units of Measure

QuickBooks offers three reports on your Units of Measure, all of which are available from the Lists submenu of the Reports menu:

- Unit Of Measure Set Listing, which lists the U/Ms with their Base and default U/Ms for purchasing and selling.
- Unit Of Measure Sets With Related Units, which lists each U/M along with all of the related units you configured.
- Items With Units Of Measure, which lists all the items that can accept U/M links and displays the U/M information for those items that have links.

All of these reports display only active U/Ms and active items, so if you're searching for something that appears to be missing, modify the report by going to the Filters tab, selecting the filter named Active Status, and then specifying All.

Inventory Assemblies

Assemblies are products you create using existing items. In the following sections we'll go over the tasks involved in managing assemblies. It's important to understand that the process of managing assemblies has three distinct parts:

1. Create the assembly. This is a design action. You are creating a Bill of Materials (BOM) for an assembled

item. Nothing you do in this step affects the quantity of inventory items or the value of your inventory.

2. Build the assembly. This action moves an assembly item into your warehouse (We use the term warehouse generically, even virtually). The components in the BOM are taken out of inventory, and the new assembly inventory item is added to inventory.

   While this creates changes in quantity, the value of your inventory doesn't change because the value of the assembly is equal to the value of the components (the value is the average cost of each item at the time you build the assembly).

3. Sell the assembly. This action reduces the quantity of the assembly item in your warehouse, and posts the appropriate amounts to the Inventory Asset and COGS accounts.

Creating an Assembly

An assembly is an inventory item, and you start by adding it to your Item List. Choose Lists | Item List to open the Item List window, and then press Ctrl-N to open the New Item dialog.

Select Inventory Assembly as the type of item, and the New Item dialog displays all the fields you need to create an assembly (see Figure 6-10).

The Cost field in the middle of the dialog is optional. The data you enter in this field does not affect the postings to your COGS and inventory asset accounts. Instead, QuickBooks posts the total average cost of the items in the Bill of Materials list.

In the Bill of Materials section, select the inventory items required to build this assembly, and the quantity required for each component. (You can also use items other than inventory parts; see "Using Non-Inventory Parts in an Assembly", later in this section.)

The Sales Price field must be filled in manually. In order to determine a price, you have to know the real value of each component (not necessarily the total cost displayed for the BOM). See the section "Understanding the Cost of an Assembly", later in this chapter, for more information.

Figure 6-10: The New Item dialog holds all the information you need for assemblies.

ProAdvisor NOTE: *The New Item dialog for an assembly has a check box for specifying whether you buy this assembly from a vendor, as well as a field for entering a vendor name. There's no reason to use these options in an assembly, because if you're buying an assembled item, it's an ordinary single inventory item, not an assembly.*

Using Non-Inventory Items in an Assembly

By default, QuickBooks won't let you add any item that isn't an inventory part to the Bill of Materials for an assembly. That's because the items in the Bill of Materials each carry a cost, and the total cost becomes the posting to Cost of Goods when you sell the assembly.

You can edit the records of non-inventory items that you want to add to the assembly so that those items have a cost attached (or create new non-inventory items specifically for this purpose). The following item types can be used in assemblies if they're properly configured:

- Service. Useful for adding the cost of labor. Create a service item that's suitable for this if your Item List doesn't already contain one.

- Non-inventory part. Useful for adding the cost of parts that you don't track as inventory items. This could include boxes, tape, consumable goods (such as nails, screws, etc.) or other things involved in putting an assembly together.

- Other Charge. Useful for adding the cost of almost anything. Some businesses use it for overhead (calculating the approximate cost in time and utilities to build assemblies).

To configure a non-inventory item so it can be used in an assembly, select the option with a label that begins "This Service/Item Is Used In Assemblies..." (the remainder of the label text changes depending on the item type). When you select that option, the item's dialog changes to include information about cost. Fill in the cost and the expense account for that cost so QuickBooks can use it when you use this item in an assembly.

Understanding the Cost of an Assembly

The cost of an assembly is the total of the current average costs of its component parts. However, the data you see in the Bill of Materials when you create the assembly does not necessarily have any relationship to the cost of the assembly. Additionally, filling in the Cost field for the assembly is meaningless in terms of the values that are used when you build an assembly item, and when you sell it.

We spend quite a bit of time working with users, bookkeepers, and accountants who are trying to figure out why the price that's set for an assembly item doesn't produce the profits expected when the item was created. Sometimes the profits are higher than expected; sometimes the profits are lower than expected. In addition, many of these folks don't understand the numbers they see when they produce reports for sales and costs, when those reports include assemblies.

This section presents accurate information on the way QuickBooks works with the financial postings for assemblies.

Bill of Materials (BOM) Cost

QuickBooks does not display the current average cost of inventory components in the Cost column of the Bill of Materials when you create the assembly. Instead, if you filled in the Cost field of the item, QuickBooks enters that data in the Cost column.

That cost field is not necessarily the real cost of the item (in fact, as discussed earlier in this chapter, many users who have gained expertise in working with QuickBooks inventory have learned to skip that field when creating inventory items). If there is no data in the Cost field of the component's record, QuickBooks displays a zero cost in the Bill of Materials when you create the assembly item.

The real average cost is available by opening the item record and noting the average cost data at the bottom of the item record window.

When you are building the Bill of Materials, QuickBooks does not check the current average cost of the item components; instead it uses the data in the Cost field. The total cost you see for the Bill of Materials may be incorrect. Therefore, you can't trust that number to decide on the price of the assembly you're creating.

Before you create an assembly, open the record of each item component and note the current average cost. You can use that information to calculate the price of the assembly.

> **ProAdvisor NOTE**: *The numbers that appear in the Item Cost field are either the cost you enter manually, or the cost of received inventory. However, when the cost of received inventory is different from the existing cost, QuickBooks asks if you want to replace the existing cost with the incoming cost. Your decision determines what actually appears in the Cost field.*

Costing Changes When you Build an Assembly

QuickBooks changes the way it considers (and displays) costs when you build an assembly. At that point, QuickBooks ignores the value in the Cost field of each component, which means the values you might have seen in the Bill of Materials section of the assembly's item record are ignored. (The only values displayed in the BOM section that are correct are those where the value of the Cost field is exactly the same as the current calculated average cost.)

When you build assemblies, QuickBooks switches to using the current calculated average cost of the components in the assembly to post amounts to the Inventory Asset Account. It ignores the values that were displayed in the BOM section of the item record. The total of the average cost of all the components automatically becomes the average cost of the built assembly.

In fact, if you open the item record of an assembly item after you've built one or more, you can see the difference. For example, in Figure 6-11, the assembly item's average cost (located at the bottom of the window) bears no relationship to the total cost display in the BOM section.

Because QuickBooks uses the real average cost when you build an assembly, as the components are decremented and the newly built assembly is added to inventory, the amounts "wash". The result of removing components and adding the assembly doesn't change the total value of your inventory assets.

The amount displayed for Total Bill of Material Cost is meaningless, because when QuickBooks displays the cost of the inventory items that are components, it ignores the real cost (average cost).

QuickBooks only pays attention to "real" costs when you build the assembly.

Figure 6-11: The real average cost of the components is calculated and may be different from the costs in the BOM window.

Cost of a Build is Locked In

When you build an assembly, QuickBooks "locks in" the average cost of the components. If you receive component inventory items after you create the build, and the average cost of any of those items changes, the posting amounts for the build won't change when you sell the assemblies you built. That's because QuickBooks assumes you used inventory at the previous cost when you built the assembly (which is a logical assumption).

If you want to use the new average costs, you must "unbuild" the assembly and rebuild it (covered later in this chapter).

Editing Assembly BOMs

You can edit an assembly in much the same way you can edit any other item. Double-click the assembly's listing in the Item List and make the required changes.

For example, you may decide to configure other item types for inclusion in assemblies, as discussed in the previous section. In the assembly's dialog, move to the next available line in the Bill of Materials section, and add the item(s).

However, your changes only take effect the next time you build the assembly; assemblies that are already built do not change. If you want to sell the assembly with the changes right away, you must unbuild and rebuild any assemblies in stock.

Building an Assembly

After your assembly item is in your Item List, you can build it. During this process, the component inventory items are removed from inventory, and the finished assembly item is received into inventory.

Choose Vendors | Inventory Activities | Build Assemblies to open the Build Assemblies dialog. Select the assembly item (only assembly items appear in the drop-down list). If you're in the Inventory Center you can right-click the assembly item and choose Build Assemblies.

At the top of the window is the quantity information for this assembly. In the section labeled Components Needed, QuickBooks automatically fills in the components required for the assembly item, along with the QOH for each inventory component (see Figure 6-12).

ProAdvisor CAUTION: *Non-inventory components aren't tracked for QOH, so if they're not service items, you must make sure you have sufficient supplies.*

The Qty Needed column remains at zero for each component until you indicate the number of builds you're creating. The dialog displays the maximum number of builds you can create with the current QOH of inventory parts.

Figure 6-12: QuickBooks automatically provides QOH data for the assembly and for the inventory component parts.

ProAdvisor NOTE: *You can build more than the maximum number you have component parts for, but builds that are missing parts are recorded as pending builds (see the section "Managing Pending Builds").*

Enter the quantity to build, and press Tab. The component quantities are adjusted: the Qty Needed is increased to match the number of builds you indicated, as seen in Figure 6-13.

Click Build & New if you want to build another assembly, or click Build & Close if you're finished. The build is moved into inventory and you can now sell it.

Figure 6-13: After you enter the number of builds you're creating, QuickBooks fills in the Qty Needed column.

Managing Pending Builds

If you don't have enough of the components to build the number of assemblies you need, you can continue with the build process, but the build is marked Pending. Pending builds are finalized when all the components are available.

Creating a Pending Build

When you specify a number of builds that exceeds the available quantity of components, QuickBooks displays a dialog to warn you that you don't have enough components to complete this build transaction. You have two options:

- Click Cancel to return to the Build Assemblies window, and reduce the number of builds to match your QOH components.

- Click Make Pending if you want to leave the number of builds as is. The build is marked "Pending", and you can finalize the build when the missing components arrive.

The entire build is marked pending. No assemblies are brought into inventory, and no components are decremented from inventory. This is true even if sufficient quantities of some of the components exist to complete a smaller number of assemblies.

If you have enough components to build fewer assemblies than you specified in the Build Assemblies window, you should click Cancel. Then start again, reducing the number of assemblies so you can get the build into inventory and generate income.

The only time you should select the Make Pending option is when all the assemblies are for the same customer, who wants everything delivered together, so you have to wait until you can build all the assemblies.

If you create another build for the same assembly before additional components arrive, the Build Assemblies window displays the same QOH for the components as existed when you created the previous, pending, build.

For example, when you created the pending build for two assemblies, you may have had enough components to build one assembly, but not two. The next time you open the Build Assemblies window for this assembly product, you still have enough components to build one assembly. If you build the new assembly you use up components, and the pending build has more missing components than it did when you originally saved it.

ProAdvisor TIP: *To keep pending build quantities from being included in Quantity Available in the Current Availability window and the insufficient quantity dialog, enable the Quantity Reserved For Pending Builds option on the Company Preferences tab of the Items & Inventory preferences.*

Tracking Pending Builds

Check the pending builds frequently, so you can purchase components as you need them. To see a report on the current pending builds, choose Reports | Inventory | Pending Builds.

Unfortunately, QuickBooks doesn't provide a report called "components needed for pending builds". Nor is there any way to produce a stock status report that shows items that are listed on pending builds.

Lacking those useful functions, you have to double-click each listing in the Pending Builds report to see the current stock status for components. Make notes, and then buy the components you need.

ProAdvisor TIP: *An inexpensive utility named Assembly Tracker is available from www.beyondtheledgers.com. In addition to providing several useful tools for assemblies, it tracks missing components for pending builds.*

Finalizing a Pending Build

When you receive the components that are missing in a pending build, you can finalize the build and put the assembly item into your inventory. Open the pending build by opening the Pending Builds report, and double-clicking the listing for the build you're ready to finalize.

When the window opens, the current QOH of components is displayed, and the maximum number you can build is updated to match the component availability.

If you now have sufficient quantities of components to build the assemblies, click the Remove Pending Status button at the bottom of the window, and click Build & Close or Build & New to close the window. QuickBooks asks you to confirm that you want to save your changes. Click Yes. The assembly item is moved into your inventory, and the inventory item components are removed from inventory.

Disassembling an Assembly

You can disassemble a built assembly item, which automatically returns the inventory components to inventory. Perhaps the assemblies aren't selling and there are orders for the inventory components you want to fill (and don't have enough on hand because they're locked into an assembly).

Some people disassemble an assembly item because they want to rebuild it using current average costs (especially if the cost of the components has risen since the assembly was built).

While you could manually adjust inventory to move the components back into inventory, and remove an assembly from inventory, that's onerous. The quickest way to remove a built assembly item is to delete the transaction that built it.

To delete the entire build, find the build by selecting the assembly item in the Item List or in the Inventory Center and pressing Ctrl-Q to display a QuickReport on the item.

Double-click the listing for the build you want to delete to display the original build window. Choose Edit | Delete Build from the QuickBooks menu bar (or press Ctrl-D). If the build was finalized and the assembly item exists in inventory, QuickBooks readjusts your inventory appropriately. If the build is pending, no adjustments need to be made.

Deleting the build's transaction only works if the number of builds in that transaction matches the number of built assembly items you want to disassemble. For example, if the transaction was for three builds, and you only want to remove one, you can't delete the build. Instead, you can edit the original build. To do this, use the following steps:

1. Choose Reports | Inventory | Pending Builds.
2. Click Customize Report and move to the Filters tab.
3. Change the Posting Status filter to Either and click OK. This changes the report from a "Pending Builds" report to a "Builds" report.

4. Locate the build in the report and double-click it to open the Build Assembly dialog.

5. Change the Quantity To Build field to the number of builds you want to retain (two in this case) and click Build & Close.

ProAdvisor TIP: *Before you close the Pending Builds report, click the Memorize button and save the report with a new name such as Existing Builds or All Builds. It's a handy report to have available for future use.*

Managing Returned Damaged Inventory Items

If a customer returns a damaged product, you can't put it back into inventory. However, when you issue a credit to a customer, that's just what happens. QuickBooks assumes that the inventory item is good and sticks it back into inventory. This increases the Quantity On Hand for the item, even though you're probably going to return it yourself if possible, or destroy it if it's not returnable.

ProAdvisor TIP: *When the customer contacts you to report the damage, you can tell the customer to dispose of the item instead of returning it. This saves you the shipping costs you'd have to return to the customer.*

The standard method for entering a customer credit is to enter the inventory item being returned in the Create Credit Memos/Refunds transaction window, which produces the following undesirable postings:

- The Quantity On Hand of the item is increased.
- The Inventory Asset Account is increased for the average cost of the item.
- The COGS account is decreased for the average cost of the item.

The credit also reduces accounts receivable, income, and sales tax liability (if the customer and the item are taxable), which is appropriate.

There are two ways to make sure the damaged inventory isn't put back into inventory:

- Don't use the inventory item in the credit memo; instead use an item designed for the return of damaged goods.
- Use the inventory item in the credit memo and then make an inventory adjustment to remove it from inventory.

Using an Item Designed for Damaged Inventory Returns

You can create an item for this purpose, but it cannot be an inventory part. Use an item of the type Non-Inventory Part or Service.

- Name this item "Credit for Damaged Goods" or something similar.
- Link the item to the income account you use when you sell inventory.
- Do not enter a price.
- Make the item taxable, so that if the customer is also taxable the sales tax liability is automatically reduced.

Use this item in the Credit Memo. Enter an amount equal to the amount of the price you charged for the inventory item when you sold the item to the customer. In the Description field, enter the returned item name and description so you and the customer know what the credit is for.

Inventory Adjustments for Damaged Items

You can use the inventory item when you create the credit memo, and then do an Inventory Adjustment to reduce the inventory.

Create an account named Damaged Inventory (using either a COGS or Expense account, depending on your accountant's instructions). Having a discrete Damaged Inventory account provides a better audit trail for the transactions.

Use the Damaged Inventory account when you make the inventory adjustment after you receive the damaged inventory through a credit memo.

ProAdvisor TIP: *You can also use this account to adjust inventory if you find damaged items in your warehouse.*

Tracking Prepayments of Purchase Orders

Sometimes you have to provide a prepayment when you remit a purchase order for inventory items, at least until you've developed a financial history with your supplier. Some suppliers insist on a percentage of the total cost, while others may ask for the entire amount of the purchase.

Creating the Elements for Prepayments

To manage prepayments for purchase orders you need to create the following elements in your company file:

- An account to track prepayments.
- An item for prepayments.

(We're assuming you've already created the inventory item.)

Creating a Prepayment Account

To track prepayments, you must create an account of the type Other Current Asset and name it appropriately (such as Purchase Prepayments). This account receives the posting when you write the check to your supplier, and that posting is washed when you receive the items.

Creating an Item for Purchase Prepayments

In order to enter the prepayment on the purchase order, you must have an item. Create an Other Charge item named Purchase Prepayment and link it to the asset account you created. Do not enter a price.

Creating Prepayment Transactions

When a supplier requires prepayment, you have to create a purchase order and you also have to create the prepayment. It doesn't matter whether you create the prepayment before you create the purchase order, or the other way around. It's just important that you remember to do both. However, you may find it easier to keep track of what you're doing if you create the purchase order first, and then note the purchase order number in the Memo field of the check.

Creating a Prepaid Purchase Order

Create the purchase order in your usual fashion, entering the item, quantity, rate, total, and so on. On the next blank line of the purchase order, select the Purchase Prepayment item and enter the amount of the prepayment as a negative amount in the Amount column.

Click Save & Close to save the purchase order, or click Save & New if you have to create other purchase orders.

ProAdvisor NOTE*: No amounts post to your general ledger, because purchase orders are non-posting transactions.*

Creating a PO Prepayment

The prepayment can be a check, an electronic transfer of funds, or a credit card charge (assuming you gave your supplier your credit card number).

To create a check, open the Write Checks window and enter the vendor's name. If you created the purchase order first (or if any other purchase orders exist for the vendor) QuickBooks displays a message reminding you that open purchase orders exist, asking if you want to receive items from a purchase order. Click No.

Fill out the check for the appropriate amount, using the Expenses tab to post the amount to the asset account for prepaid purchases. (You could use the Items tab in the Write Checks window and select the Purchase Prepayment item, but it's a good idea to make a habit of using the Expenses tab unless you're actually receiving inventory.)

ProAdvisor TIP: *You can create the check directly in the bank account register, which is the quick way if you don't print checks.*

Sometimes suppliers ask for an electronic transfer of funds, and if this is how you want to deposit your prepayment, use the Write Checks window and follow the instructions in the previous section for creating the check.

Then, in the check number field, replace the number with the text EFT, or similar text that indicates the way this transaction is being handled. If the bank provided a transaction confirmation number, you can enter it in the Memo field.

If you arranged to use your credit card for the prepayment, the way you enter this in QuickBooks depends on the way in which you manage credit cards.

If you treat your credit card as a vendor, paying the statement in full when it arrives each month, you don't have to do anything at this point. When the credit card statement arrives, as you enter the transactions in the Write Checks or Enter Bills window, remember that the charge from your supplier must be posted to the Purchase Prepayments current asset account you created, not to an expense or to the Inventory account (the Inventory account receives the posting when you receive the items against the purchase order).

If you record your credit card transactions as they occur, using a QuickBooks Credit Card account, take the following steps:

1. Choose Banking | Enter Credit Card Charges to open the Enter Credit Card Charges transaction window.
2. Select the credit card you used for this payment.
3. If you usually enter a name in the Purchased From field (totally optional), enter the vendor's name. If you created the purchase order first (or if any other purchase orders exist for the vendor) QuickBooks displays a message

reminding you that open purchase orders exist, asking if you want to receive items from a purchase order. Click No.

4. Enter the amount and post it to the current asset account for prepayments.

5. If you don't use the Purchased From field, enter the vendor's name and the P.O. Number in the Memo column.

6. Click Save & Close to save the transaction.

Receiving Prepaid Items into Inventory

When the items arrive, receive them into inventory. If the goods arrive before the bill arrives, choose Vendors | Receive Items; then when the bill arrives, choose Vendors | Enter Bill For Received Items. Select the appropriate purchase order and receive the items into inventory.

If the goods arrive with the bill enclosed, choose Vendors | Receive Items And Enter Bill. Select the vendor and then select the appropriate purchase order to open the transaction window for receiving the goods, bill, or both.

You can add any additional expenses to the bill, such as shipping costs, or any other expense that wasn't included in the original purchase order. When you save the bill in QuickBooks, the following postings occur:

- The amount of the bill (the net due after your pre-payment) is credited to Accounts Payable. The next time you select Pay Bills from the Vendor menu, the bill appears.

- The prepayment is credited to the Purchase Prepayment asset account, which washes (zeroes out) the posting from the check, credit card entry, or electronic transfer you created to send the prepayment.

- If you used a credit card, and treat the credit card as a vendor, the credit amount remains in the Purchase Prepayment account. When the statement arrives, post the amount for that item to the Purchase Prepayment account.

- The cost of the item (not the same as the amount due after your prepayment) is debited to the Inventory account.
- The quantity of the inventory item is updated.

Taking Inventory on the Road

Sometimes your inventory travels. You may have delivery or service trucks that are stocked with certain inventory items, your sales reps may carry items as samples in their briefcases, or you may take inventory items to a trade show.

You should track inventory that's traveling outside of your warehouse, and since QuickBooks doesn't support multiple locations in the Premier editions, you have to create a tracking system manually.

This manual tracking system is a workaround that succeeds in the Premier editions because it uses sales orders, (a feature not available in QuickBooks Pro).

This workaround is not the same as maintaining multiple, permanent warehouses. If you have multiple warehouse locations you can upgrade to QuickBooks Enterprise Solutions, or purchase a third party add-on.

ProAdvisor TIP: *An inventory add-on for managing multiple warehouses is generally less expensive than upgrading to Enterprise Solutions, and often contains additional handy features for inventory management.*

This discussion is about tracking temporary movement of inventory items. Tracking inventory that's on the road is important for the following reasons:

- You need to know what inventory items are out of the warehouse so you don't create transactions that sell and ship them to customers.

- You need to know the contents of the containers that hold the inventory that's on the road to make sure you can track theft or waste.
- You need to know the value of the inventory on each container (your truck, your rep's briefcase, the delivery service that's transporting goods to a trade show site) so that if there's a problem you can document your loss.

Configuring On-the-Road Inventory

There are a couple of setup steps to take to implement this workaround. You use sales orders to move the inventory out of the warehouse and into your containers, so you need customers and jobs to link to those sales orders.

You also need to make sure your inventory is configured to tell you what items are in the warehouse and ready for sale, and what items are on sales orders. This lets you know how many items are in the warehouse so you can sell them (called *Quantity Available*, which differs from *Quantity On Hand*).

Creating On-the-Road Customers and Jobs

The most efficient way to set up the customers and jobs you need is to create a single customer and make each container a job. Because customer reports always include job details, this makes reporting faster and easier.

It's usually easier to work with the on-the-road customer by naming the customer ZZTravel. The ZZ guarantees the customer name is at the bottom of the drop-down list in the Customer/Job field, which makes it less likely that a user would inadvertently select this customer for "real" transactions.

Configure this customer as non-taxable. Then create jobs to represent the available containers. Here are some examples:

- BriefcaseAmy
- BriefcaseSam

- TradeShows
- Truck01
- Truck02

ProAdvisor TIP*: If you use numbers for components (customers, jobs, vendors, items, etc.) always use enough leading zeroes to match the number of characters in the highest number. For example, if you have more than 10 items but less than 100, start with 01 instead of a single "1". If you have more than 100 vendors but less than 1000, start with 001 instead of using a single "1". Because of the way computers sort numbers, this is the only way to make sure your lists are ordered properly. Otherwise, you'll find your lists read "1, 10, 2, 20, etc.*

Configuring the Calculation of Available Quantity

QuickBooks Premier editions offer the ability to show you what's available for sale as well as deducting what's promised on sales orders. Since you use sales orders to take items on the road, you need to know how much stock remains in the warehouse for sale to regular customers. Use the following steps to make sure you get the information you need:

1. Choose Edit | Preferences and select the Items & Inventory category in the left pane.
2. Move to the Company Preferences tab (see Figure 6-14).
3. Define "Quantity Available" by selecting the option to deduct the quantity on sales orders.
4. Tell QuickBooks to issue a warning when you try to sell an item for which there is insufficient quantity available instead of on hand (on hand is the total number of items you own).

If you use any of the following Premier editions, the dialog also includes the option to deduct items required for pending builds, which provides a "real" quantity available if you build assemblies:

- Accountant
- Manufacturing & Wholesale
- Retail

Figure 6-14: Set preferences to make sure you're warned before selling items that aren't in the warehouse.

If you build assemblies and are *not* using one of those editions, you can get the information about items assigned to pending builds by adding that information to the Item List window, Inventory Center, or by building a customized report.

Adding Quantity Information to the Item List Window

To add a column for Pending Builds, open the Item List window and use the following steps:

1. Right-click anywhere in the window and choose Customize Columns.

2. In the Customize Columns dialog select On Pending Builds in the left pane, and click Add.

3. Repeat for any other information about quantity you want to see in the Item List window (i.e. On Sales Order).

4. Click OK.

You can do the same thing in the Inventory Center by right-clicking in the left pane and choosing Customize Columns. The steps are the same.

Creating a Report on Items Needed for Pending Builds

Another option for tracking items that you can't sell because they're needed for pending builds is to create a report and print it so you can use it when you sell an item. Here are the steps to take to build this report:

1. Choose Reports | List | Item Listing.

2. Click Customize Report.

3. In the Display tab, select/deselect columns to end up with the following columns:

   - Item
   - Description (optional)
   - Quantity on Hand
   - Quantity on Sales Order
   - On Pending Builds

4. In the Filters tab, create the following filters:

   - Item: All Inventory Items
   - On Pending Builds: >= 1.00

5. In the Header/Footer tab, change the report title to Inventory Assigned to Pending Builds or something similar.

6. Click OK to return to the report.

7. Click Memorize so you don't have to do this again.

QuickBooks automatically names the memorized report "Inventory Assigned to Pending Builds" (or whatever you named the memorized report).

Creating a Sales Order for Inventory on the Road

Create a sales order using the appropriate job. Enter the inventory items you're transferring. If the inventory item you're using doesn't have a price attached, you can enter a price of zero; only the current cost matters because that's the value of the inventory you're tracking.

For users of Premier Accountant Edition, Premier Manufacturing & Wholesale Edition, or Premier Retail Edition, if there isn't enough quantity available, QuickBooks notifies you immediately, as seen in Figure 6-15.

Figure 6-15: Some Premier Editions notify you of insufficient quantity as soon as you enter the item in the sales order.

If you're using any other Premier edition, you aren't notified about insufficient quantities. Instead, QuickBooks waits until you convert the sales order to an invoice to warn you. Since you aren't going to convert this sales order to an invoice you must have your quantity report available or open the Item List window (both described earlier in this section) to make sure you can take these items out of the warehouse.

Returning Items to the Warehouse

There are two scenarios in which items in a container have to be returned to inventory:

- The items are physically removed from the container and put back into the warehouse.

- The items were sold from the container and the inventory must be returned to the warehouse so the sale can be created in QuickBooks.

Even if sales are made from the truck or briefcase, or at a tradeshow, you can't convert the sales order to a sale. Instead, the items must be sold from Quantity On Hand and the sale has to be linked to a real customer.

To tell QuickBooks that the items have been taken out of the container and returned to the warehouse, change the quantity on the original sales order to reflect the number of items returned. The quantity available changes to reflect the fact that fewer quantities are on sales orders.

If you set the quantity to zero, QuickBooks marks that line item as Closed. Don't worry, no invoice is accountant's copy created and no sales transaction is posted.

In some cases, such as items that traveled to a trade show, the quantity of every item is set to zero. QuickBooks marks the sales order as invoiced in full. You can ignore it as no transactions are posted.

Just continue to re-use the sales order, changing quantities to indicate items that are being taken on the road, and returned home.

Reports for On-the-Road Inventory

It's important to know the quantity of items that are on the road and you can track each job/container as well as each inventory item.

To know what's on the road per-job, open the customer center and select the customer. Then select QuickReport in the right pane to see a report of sales orders on a per job basis. You can drill down to open each sales order and print it. Post it so everyone has information about the inventory that's not available for sale.

To know what's on the road per item, choose Reports | Sales | Open Sales Orders By Item. This report shows all open sales orders for all customers, so you should modify it and memorize the customized settings. Click Customize Report and use the following guidelines to customize this report:

- In the Display tab, deselect all columns except Date, Num, Name, and Qty.

- In the Filters tab, select Name as the filter and then select the customer you created for this purpose.

- In the Header/Footer tab, change the name of the report to Sales Orders for <CustomerName>.

Memorize the report so you don't have to repeat the customization steps.

CHAPTER 7

Tips for Payroll and 1099 Vendors

- Payroll tips

- Managing outsourced payroll

- Subcontractors and 1099s

Payroll causes more angst, confusion, and panic calls to accountants than any other element involved in running a business. Whether a business does payroll in-house or has a payroll service, questions and problems abound.

In this chapter we'll pass along some explanations and tips for tracking payroll (either in-house or outsourced) that we've learned from clients and accountants.

Keeping Payroll Information Secure

If you do payroll in-house, your payroll records contain every employee's information. Anyone with access to employee information can see what each employee earns, whether an employee has a garnishment, and other sensitive information.

The way QuickBooks Pro/Premier editions configure user permissions makes it very difficult for business owners to prevent users from viewing payroll information for employees, bosses, owners, etc.

The permission level you must give your Accounts Payable person allows the viewing of net payroll checks. The permission level you must give a user who needs to transfer funds, create journal entries, or perform online banking chores also provides access to the Employee Center (where everything you'd want to know about employees is available). Most of the permission levels you must assign to let users do their jobs provide access to some employee payroll information.

The only way to keep in-house payroll information secure is to create a separate company for payroll. Perform all payroll tasks from this separate company, and then use journal entries to move totals (not individual transactions) into the accounts in your real company. (The same way you use journal entries to transfer totals if you outsource your payroll, which is covered later in this chapter.)

Configuring Vendors For Payroll Liabilities

Businesses that remit their own payroll liabilities often have to go through some difficult maneuvers to create the liability checks properly.

In many businesses the 941 and 940 liabilities are paid to the bank or to the IRS (electronic payments), and the state payroll taxes, UC and SDI payments are all paid to the same state agency (e.g. Department of Revenue or Department of Labor & Industry).

The business owner or bookkeeper (or even the accountant) sets up the bank or the IRS as a vendor, and sets up the appropriate state agency as a vendor. When it's time to remit liabilities, all the liabilities are selected, and QuickBooks creates one check for each vendor, representing the total of all payroll remittances.

This doesn't work, because there are always forms to fill out, or coupons to attach to each individual liability payment, and the vendor won't accept one large check for multiple types of liability payments.

What's the solution? There are two solutions; one is a pain, the other is easy.

The painful solution is to select each liability, one at a time, in the Pay Liabilities window. Create the check, print the check, attach the appropriate paperwork, and return to the Pay Liabilities window to process the next check for the same vendor. (For e-payments, substitute "record the check and fill out the appropriate form online".)

That's real work, and some of us are far too lazy to do that. Besides, we'd probably lose track and create the same payment twice.

The easy solution is to take advantage of the fact that QuickBooks presents a "Print Name On Check As" field in each vendor record, so you can have separate vendors with the same payee name.

For the federal deposits, create one vendor named 940 and another vendor named 941. Both vendors have the same name in the Print Name On Check As field (either the bank or the IRS). For the state, create separate vendors for each separate liability (payroll taxes, UC, SDI, etc.). Enter the appropriate payee name in the Print Name On Check As field (possibly the same text for all vendors).

Edit your payroll items list to reflect the vendor names (not the payee text). After you've completed this one-time-only setup chore, paying liabilities is a snap. Select all the liabilities that are due and click Create. QuickBooks creates separate checks for each liability payment.

ProAdvisor TIP: *Name all your payroll liability vendors with the form name: 940, 941, PA501 (the form for remitting payroll taxes in Pennsylvania), PA-SUTA, and so on.*

This system works well for garnishments, too. If you have employees with garnishments for child support, tax liens, etc. and the money is all sent to the same government agency, you can't send one check for all garnishments. (See the Section "Garnishments" later in this chapter.)

Posting Payroll Liabilities and Expenses

It's best to have separate payroll liability accounts for every type of payroll liability instead of posting everything to a single account named Payroll Liabilities. The same rule applies to payroll expenses. (QuickBooks automatically creates the Payroll Liabilities and Payroll Expenses accounts when you create a company file, even if you don't enable payroll.)

Separate payroll liability and expense accounts make it easier to track, and create reports on a tax-by-tax basis. In fact the best way to set up payroll accounts is as a series of subaccounts under the payroll liabilities and payroll expenses parent accounts. When you view the chart of accounts the subaccounts provide individual balance totals and you see a grand total in the parent account.

Social Security Numbers on Pay Stubs

We've had a great deal of e-mail from readers who use direct deposit and print pay stubs that are mailed to employees. The employees have asked that the social security number be omitted from the pay stubs, because they fear identity theft.

That's a valid fear, because by default the direct deposit pay stub prints not only the social security number, but also the bank account number—the kind of information someone bent on stealing identities revels in.

You can change the data that prints on pay stubs. Choose Edit | Preferences and select the Payroll & Employees category in the left pane. In the Company Preferences tab, click the button labeled Pay Stub & Voucher Printing.

The dialog that appears offers options for all the types of information that you can print, or not print (see Figure 7-1). You can disable the printing of the SSN altogether by deselecting it. You can also enable the option to print only the last four digits of the SSN and the bank account.

Figure 7-1: For safety and security, change data that prints on pay stubs.

Some states require employers to print the SSN on direct deposit pay stubs, and if you live in one of those states, check to see whether the last four digits will suffice. If your state doesn't require this information, disable the printing of the SSN altogether.

Pay Stubs Generated for Clients

If you're an accounting professional who prepares payroll for clients, the e-mail pay stub feature, which is designed to e-mail a pay stub to each employee at the employee's own e-mail address, won't work for you. Instead, you can create a single file containing all the pay stubs, and e-mail that file to your client.

The file you create is saved on your hard drive instead of being printed or e-mailed automatically from QuickBooks. It's a good idea to create a subfolder for payroll stubs in the folder you use to house the client's files. Then, if something untoward happens at the client's office, you can resend the file.

The instructions in this section cover using a PDF file or a TIFF file for the pay stubs. The file is sent to your client as an attachment, which means the sensitive information is not sent across the Internet as plain text within the e-mail message. However, it's best to take extra security measures to secure the attachment. You might be able to accomplish that with a PDF file; or, see the section "File Security" later in this section.

Using a PDF Printer

You can install a PDF printer on your computer and print all the pay stubs to a PDF file (the QuickBooks PDF printer may not work for this task). There are numerous PDF printers available that you can download from their creators. (Some are free, and none of them are expensive.) Search the Internet for the phrase "pdf converters" to find a PDF printer that suits your needs. It's best to find a PDF converter that is capable of password-protecting the file, because the contents of the file include highly sensitive information.

When you're ready to print the pay stubs, use the following steps:

1. Select the PDF printer in the Print dialog.
2. Select the folder in which to save the file.
3. Name the file with an appropriate filename, such as *<ClientName>*Payroll*<Date>*.
4. Assign a password to the document (assuming your PDF converter has that feature). Be sure to call the client and reveal the password (do *not* send the password in an e-mail message).

The resulting PDF file prints each pay stub on a separate page. E-mail the PDF file to your client, who can distribute the stubs to employees. Your client must have a PDF reader, which is available from www.adobe.com at no cost.

File Security

The file you send your client is filled with sensitive information, and it's best to make sure the contents cannot fall into the wrong hands. If you use a PDF converter with the ability to password-protect the file, and you're sure only the appropriate person at the client's site has the password, it's safe to e-mail the file. If you aren't using a password protected PDF file converter, following are some suggestions for securing the information in the pay stubs file.

Create a zipped file that is password-protected, and send that file to your client (call the client to reveal the password, don't put it into the text message). Password-protection for a Zip file is available in programs such as WinZip®.

If you have a website you probably have ftp server-based storage available. Create password-protected ftp folders for client files and upload the pay stub files so your clients can download them. Call your clients to give them the folder names, login names, and passwords (don't use message text in an e-mail to divulge this information).

Re-issuing a Lost Paycheck

You can't manage the replacement of paychecks the same way you manage the replacement of lost or destroyed vendor checks. Payroll checks and their attendant postings are more complicated than ordinary vendor checks, but if you follow these step-by-step instructions, it's easy to accomplish this task.

1. Do NOT void the original paycheck.
2. Create the employee as an Other Name. You have to use a variation of the name in the Name field, because you can't have duplicate names in your company file.

3. Use the Write Checks function to write a check for the NET amount to the Other Name entry. Post the check to any expense account (e.g. Misc expenses).

4. Print the check, write down the check number, and give it to the employee.

5. Open the bank register and find the original check (the one that was lost). Write down the check number. Edit that original check so it has the same check number as the one you just issued. When QuickBooks asks if it's OK to have duplicate check numbers, say Yes.

6. Edit the check you just wrote to the Other Name. Change its number to the old check number (the check that was lost or destroyed).

7. Now that the new check has the old number, void it.

Your records show the correct check number for the voided check, the correct check number for the check that the employee will deposit, your liabilities haven't changed, the W-2 will be correct, the Other Name listing and the expense account you used does not show a balance for this transaction.

Payroll Deductions for Employee Repayments

If you permit employees to purchase goods, get an advance on future paychecks, or borrow money from the company, a payroll deduction for repayment is the best way to ensure the employee returns the money.

ProAdvisor TIP: *You should have a standard agreement with all employees that permits you to deduct amounts owed from paychecks. Contact an attorney for the proper form.*

Setting Up Employee Repayment Elements

Before you can create transactions for employee repayments, you have to set up the list components you'll need, which are the following:

- A non-employee record for the employee. You cannot duplicate the name you use in the employee record.

You can create a Customer record, which works for all types of transactions (not just sales of products) because it's easy to create customer-based reports to track these employee transactions. To avoid duplicating the Employee name, use a nickname, or use the format "employee name-cust", such as SmithJ-Cust.

- An account to track employee debt. The account is of the type Other Current Asset. Name the account Employee Advances (or something similar).
- A Payroll Item that is a Payroll Deduction, named Employee Repayment. Link the payroll liability account for this item to the Other Current Asset account named Employee Advances/Purchases. Apply the item to Net pay (not Gross).

Creating an Employee Loan or Paycheck Advance

If you're advancing money to an employee, either as a loan or an advance against future pay, write a check to the Customer name you created for the employee. (You should never write any check except a paycheck to an Employee name.)

Post the check to the Other Current Asset account you created to track employee advances. The check posts a debit to that account. As the employee pays the debt through a payroll deduction, the amount deducted from the paycheck is a credit to that account. The goal is to get to zero.

Creating an Employee Purchase Transaction

To sell a product to an employee and collect the purchase price via a payroll deduction, you need to create an additional item. The "real" items in your Item List are linked to income accounts, and you need to post the sale to the Other Current Asset account you created for tracking employee advances. In addition, most businesses provide an employee discount for employee purchases.

Create an Item of the type Discount (because a Discount type always means a deduction, which is needed when you create a transaction of this type. Name the item Employee Purchase. The item is non-taxable, has a default amount of $0.00, and is linked to the Other Current Asset account named Employee Purchases.

Here's how to create an employee purchase transaction:

1. Create an invoice for the customer/employee.
2. Enter the services or items purchased by the employee/customer on the invoice, using the pricing structure for employees (which may or may not be the same as for other customers).
3. In the next item line, enter the discount item you created for employee purchases, and enter an amount equal to the total of the employee's purchases.

The balance of the invoice is now $0.00, so you have no A/R balance, and no money to deposit in the bank. However, the Employee Purchases Other Current Asset account has been increased by the amount for the discount item.

Deducting Payment from the Paycheck

When you create a paycheck for the employee, add the employee repayment payroll deduction item in the Other Payroll Items area of the Preview Paycheck window. You can either enter the full amount owed, or a partial amount (and deduct the rest from subsequent paychecks).

If the full amount is deducted, the Employee Purchases Other Current Asset account has no balance. If a partial payment is deducted, the remaining balance owed equals the balance in that account.

Tracking Multiple Employee Repayment Accounts

If multiple employees have advances or purchases deducted from paychecks, you don't have to set up a separate asset account for each employee. Instead, you can track each employee's current balance by creating and memorizing a report, as follows:

1. Choose Reports | Custom Reports | Transaction Detail. By default, the Modify Report dialog opens for any Custom report you create.
2. In the Dates field, select All
3. In the Display tab, select Sort By Name.
4. In the Filters tab, set the Account filter to the Employee Advances account.
5. Rearrange the report columns to suit your needs
6. Memorize the report (the name Employee Advances seems appropriate).

The report provides a breakdown of employee indebtedness on an employee-by-employee basis. Run this report on payday so you know how much should be deducted from each paycheck.

Garnishments

We receive many requests for help from small businesses who have been on the receiving end of a garnishment order. Garnishments are extremely complicated, almost impossible to automate, and can't be avoided. If a garnishment order is delivered, employers are required to collect the garnished amount and remit it to the appropriate agency.

We've never found a simple way to deal with payroll garnishments, and as a result of experimentation and troubleshooting client protocols, we've come up with some rules. These rules were established for employers who have multiple garnishment orders to deal with, but the practices established with these rules work for companies that are managing only a single garnishment order.

- You need a separate payroll liability account for garnishments.
- You need a discrete payroll item for every garnishment order, even if the agency and/or employee are the same.

- Every garnishment payroll item has to have its own agency (vendor), even if the vendor is the same for multiple garnishments. The vendor code (Name) must vary, although the payee and mailing address is the same.

- You must preview payroll checks for every employee with a garnishment deduction in order to view or change the garnishment deduction. (Some deductions vary depending on the amount of the net check, and other deductions are eliminated if the net check isn't a certain minimum amount.)

Without following these rules you won't be able to track, report on, and remit garnished wages with any level of confidence. Remember, the onus is on you—you're under orders and are obligated to do this properly. After all, in most cases, if the employee could be relied upon to make these payments there wouldn't be a garnishment order.

Garnishment Vendors

Each garnishment needs to have its own vendor, and the way you create the vendor is directly connected to its garnishment order. The reason for individual separate vendors is to create individual separate checks for each garnishment remittance.

If you send one check covering multiple garnishments to the same agency, it's almost guaranteed that the check won't be processed properly, no matter how detailed a report you attach to the check (besides, you don't want to go to the trouble of creating such a report every payday). In fact, many agencies insist on separate checks for each employee's garnishment order, and won't accept one check for multiple garnishment remittances.

Vendor Type for Garnishment Agencies

It's a good idea to set up a vendor type for garnishments; in fact, creating vendor subtypes for each type of garnishment is a better idea. Taking this step makes it easier to generate reports about garnishments—filtering a report on vendor type means you display only the specific information you need.

Garnishment Vendor Configuration

Setting up vendors properly takes a bit of time, but it's a one-time task, and that's certainly easier than going through multiple steps every payday to make sure each garnishment agency receives its remittance. Following are some guidelines for creating garnishment vendors.

In the Vendor Name field, create a code that identifies this vendor and the garnishment to which it's attached—include a reference to the employee in the code.

For example, if the employee Robert B. Whatsizname has a garnishment order for child support, and the agency is the Philadelphia County Division of Family Services, name the vendor PhilaFamServ-RBW. If the garnishment is for an unpaid student loan, and the agency is the Pennsylvania Higher Education Agency, name the vendor PHEA-RBW.

In the Company Name field, enter the name of the payee for the remittance check. QuickBooks automatically copies that name to the field labeled Print Name On Check As. No matter how many garnishments you have for child support from a single county agency, each check is processed individually, and each payment is posted against the individual deduction liability.

Move to the Payment Settings tab and enter the garnishment reference in the Account No. field. Usually this is a case number, such as S112255. The data you enter here prints on the Memo Line of the check (if you print checks), or has to be entered manually if you don't print checks (this is yet another reason to print checks in QuickBooks; manual checks are a lot of work and prone to omissions or errors).

Payroll Item for a Garnishment

You must create a payroll item for each individual garnishment order, using the following steps:

1. Choose Employees | Manage Payroll Items | New Payroll Item to open the Add New Payroll Item wizard.

2. In the first wizard window select Custom Setup.

3. In the next wizard window select Deduction.

4. In the next wizard window name the deduction, using text specific to the garnishment and the employee.

5. For instance, for a child support order for employee R.B. Whatsizname, use ChildSupp-RBW.

6. In the next wizard window enter the vendor specific to this garnishment, the account number that identifies this garnishment, and the liability account you created to track garnishments.

7. In the next wizard window which asks about Tax Tracking, select None.

8. In the next wizard window, which establishes taxes that are deducted before this payroll item is deducted, click Default to select all the appropriate taxes.

9. In the next wizard window which specifies the way the deduction is calculated, select Neither (meaning neither by quantity nor hours).

10. In the next wizard window select Net Pay.

11. If the garnishment is a percentage, it's always based on net pay; if the garnishment is a flat amount no calculation occurs when you apply it to the paycheck.

12. In the next wizard window enter the rate for this deduction.

13. If the garnishment is an amount enter it, if it's a percentage, remember to use the percent symbol (%). If there's a limit (which usually exists only for loan or other fixed-figure garnishments, not for child support) enter it. The window also has a check mark to indicate an annual limit, but it's unusual for a garnishment to establish annual limits.

14. Click Finish to save the payroll item.

Now that the payroll item exists, you can apply it to the appropriate employee.

Assigning a Garnishment Deduction to an Employee

To link the garnishment item to the employee, open the employee record in the Employee Center. Next, click the Payroll Info tab to display the available payroll options seen in Figure 7-2.

Figure 7-2: Enter the deduction for the garnishment in the employee's record.

You need to repeat all of these actions for every garnishment order you receive (with the exception of creating the liability account—you don't need a separate liability account for each garnishment order).

Viewing and Editing Garnishment Paycheck Deductions

You should always preview paychecks for employees who have garnishments, because you may have to adjust, or even remove, the deduction. Many garnishment orders include specifications about the net paycheck amount and its effect on the garnishment.

Some specifications limit the amount of the deduction depending on the amount of the employee's net pay. Other specifications remove the deduction entirely if the net pay amount is below a minimum figure.

The deduction can be edited in the Preview Paycheck window. If you have to change or remove the deduction, you need to calculate the correct amount outside of QuickBooks. (To remove the deduction, change its amount to 0.00.)

Remitting Garnishment Deductions

Your garnishment deductions appear in the Pay Liabilities window, and when you select them for payment each garnishment order has its own check, and that check is appropriately annotated with the case number. All the setup work you performed ensures this.

Returned Garnishment Checks

It's not a rare occurrence that a garnishment check is returned to you; usually because the garnishment is paid off but you weren't notified that the balance due was zero. (This tends to occur more often when the garnishment is being managed by an independent company to which the government agency has subcontracted the job of collections.)

When the garnishment check is returned, it's often accompanied by instructions that tell you to give the amount back to the employee by adding the amount to the employee's next paycheck.

Do NOT create the next paycheck with this amount added to the employee's compensation. If you do, the employee will be double taxed and the amount of total compensation on the W-2 will be wrong. A garnishment is an after-tax deduction; the employee has already paid the tax for the paycheck in which the garnishment was included.

Instead, take the following steps:

1. Void the original garnishment check you wrote. This puts the liability back into the garnishment payroll liability account.

2. Write a direct check to the employee for the amount of the garnishment check, and post it to the garnishment payroll liability account (which washes the liability and resets the account balance to zero).

Many accountants prefer to create this check to an Other Name you create for the employee. This keeps the check out of the employee's records and reports. Remember that you have to name the Other Name differently; you can't duplicate the text in the Employee Name field. One protocol for this type of transaction (and other transactions for employees, such as repayment for expenses incurred when an employee buys supplies) is to create an Other Name with the format: *<EmployeeName>-Other*. Direct repayments created in this fashion are much easier than creating payroll items and using them in a payroll run.

Tracking and Reporting Tips

If your employees receive tips from customers, those tips are taxable wages. You have to pay or report the tips on each paycheck, so that the tips are part of the income reported on the employee's W-2.

- You have to give the employees the tips if you collected the tips.

- You have to report the tips if the employee collected the tips.

In many businesses, you have to do both; that is, you have to add the employee tips you kept to the employee's paycheck, and you have to report the tips the employee kept. Usually the tips you have to provide in the paycheck are tips added to credit card charges that you didn't turn over at the time you processed the credit card. The tips that need to be reported, but not paid, on the paycheck are the cash tips the employee collected and kept at the time of customer payment.

In addition to these simple paradigms, there are lots of possible combinations and permutations in the way tips are handled. Tips may be collected in a central place (a big jar) and split evenly or split unevenly to account for job titles (servers get a larger percentage than the employees who bus the tables; colorists and stylists get a larger percentage than people who shampoo; etc. etc.).

You must have a way to track tips, because if you don't the IRS will do it for you. Employees must report the tips they collected, you must track the tips you collected and added to a paycheck, and you must track the tip jar's contents and the way those contents are distributed.

Creating an Account for Tracking Tips

You have to track the in-and-out of tip dollars, and the easiest way to do that is to create a single account for all tip activity. Commonly, the account is of the type Other Current Asset, and is named Employee Tips.

Everything you do regarding employee tips passes through that account. Tips are not a payroll liability, nor are they a payroll expense. They fall outside the payroll accounts you use to track payroll liabilities and expenses. The only connection tips have to payroll is the fact that they must be reported to the IRS, and the way to do that is to track them within paychecks (but not as liabilities or expenses).

Adding Tips to Sales Transactions

The way you manage sales transactions depends on the way your employees receive their tips:

If your employees collect their tips in cash, the tips don't affect the sales transactions. The employees must track these tips and give you the total before payday.

If you collect the tips and add them to the employees' paychecks (usually because the customer added the tip to a credit card transaction), you must post the tips to the Employee Tips account, not to the income account you use for the rest of the sales transaction. To do that, you need an item (a sales item, not a payroll item), and that's covered in the next section.

If you collect the tips and give the money to the employees from the cash register or petty cash, you must post the transaction to the Employee Tips account. The employees must track these tips as if they were directly received from the customer, and the amount must be included in the total they provide you before payday.

Creating a Sales Item for Tips

If you collect the tips, the sales transaction that includes the tips must account for those tips separately from the posting to income for the sale. That means you must have an item to use in the sales transaction. Create an item named Tips Held, using the following guidelines.

- The item type should be either an Other Charge or Service.
- The item is not taxable.
- The amount is zero (and is filled in when you create a transaction).
- The Account is the Employee Tips account you create as described earlier in this section.

Creating Payroll Items for Tips

You need to create payroll items to remit and report tips. An easy way to understand what these payroll items do is to think of them as Tips In and Tips Out.

- Tips In is an additional compensation payroll item you use to add tips to a paycheck.

- Tips Out is a deduction payroll item you use to remove the tips the employee already collected. It is a deduction from Net, not Gross.

Once both items are available for paychecks, any combination of held/collected tips can appear on a paycheck.

For example, let's say an employee received $200.00 in tips, and $100.00 of that amount was in cash and kept by the employee. The other $100.00 was added to credit card charges and you did not turn it over in cash; instead, you added it to the employee's paycheck.

- Tips In is $200.00. That's the taxable amount, and is used when creating W-2s.
- Tips Out is $100.00. That's the amount you're reducing from the Tips In total because you don't include that amount in the paycheck (the employee already has the money).

If the employee kept all $200.00 in cash at the time the customers left the tip, or if you turned over the cash after you processed the credit card transaction, then Tips In and Tips Out are both $200.00.

If you keep all the tips and remit them in paychecks, then Tips In is the amount of money you're giving the employee in the paycheck, and Tips Out is zero (and the Tips Out payroll item is omitted from the paycheck).

QuickBooks provides payroll items that work for tips, which makes configuring all of this easy. To create your tips payroll items, choose Employees | Manage Payroll Items | New Payroll Item.

In the Add New Payroll Item wizard, choose Custom Setup, and then proceed as explained in the following sections.

Creating a Payroll Item for Tips In

For the compensation item (Tips In), use the following guidelines as you step through the wizard windows:

- The payroll item type is Addition.
- The payroll item name is Tips In.
- The expense account is the Other Current Asset account you created as described earlier in this section.
- The tax tracking type is Reported Tips.
- The taxes are the default taxes (all federal, state, and local taxes).
- The calculation basis selection is Neither (because it's not compensation based on quantity or hours).
- There is no default rate nor is there a limit.

Creating a Payroll Item for Tips Out

For the deduction that covers the tips employees already received, use the following guidelines to move through the wizard:

- The payroll item type is Deduction.
- The payroll item name is Tips Out.
- There is no agency (and therefore, no identification number with an agency).
- The liability account is the Other Current Asset account you created as described earlier in this section.
- The tax tracking type is None.
- No taxes are applied (all the taxes should be deselected in the wizard window).
- The calculation basis selection is Neither (because it's not a deduction based on quantity or hours).
- The item is calculated on net pay.
- There is no default rate nor is there a limit.

Adding Tips to Paychecks

Add the tips to employee paychecks in the Preview Paycheck window in the Other Payroll Items section. When you enter the Tips In item, the totals in the Employee Summary section change (higher gross and higher taxes). When you enter the Tips Out item, the amounts are re-adjusted. You can also add them to the Payroll Info tab of the employee record.

Tips and IRA Plans

If you provide a simple IRA that involves contributions from both the employer and employee, the order in which you add the payroll items to checks is important. Tips are compensation, and the amount entered for Tips In affects the IRA contribution calculation.

QuickBooks calculates the totals "in order", which means you must enter the tips and the IRA payroll items in the following order:

- Tips In
- Tips Out
- IRA employee deduction
- IRA company contribution

If your IRA items are listed before the Tips In items the IRA calculations don't use the amount linked to tips.

Tracking Outsourced Payroll

If you don't do your payroll in-house, you have to track your payroll amounts using journal entries. If you maintain a separate bank account for payroll (recommended if you outsource payroll) you have to set up special tasks to reconcile the account. We'll cover both issues in this section.

Entering Payroll as a Journal Entry

When you receive the payroll report from the payroll service company, you should make the following journal entries:

- A Journal Entry for the payroll.
- A Journal Entry for the remittance of withholding amounts and employer payroll expenses.

If your payroll service doesn't remit withholding and pay employer expenses, don't use the second journal entry. The checks you write will take care of the postings.

Paycheck Journal Entry

To journalize the paychecks, choose Company | Make General Journal Entries to open a blank GJE transaction window. Then enter the appropriate amounts in the both the Debit and Credit columns as illustrated in Table 7-1.

Account	Debit	Credit
Salaries & Wages	Total Gross Payroll	
FWT W/H		Total Federal Withheld
FICA W/H		Total FICA Withheld
Medicare W/H		Total Medicare Withheld
State Income Tax W/H		Total State Tax Withheld
Local Income Tax W/H		Total Local Tax Withheld
State SDI W/H		Total State SDI Withheld
State SUI W/H		Total State SUI Withheld
Benefits Contrib		Total Benefits Contributions Withheld
401(k) Contrib		Total 401(k) Withheld
Other Deductions		Total Other Ded Withheld
Payroll Bank Account		Total Of Net Payroll

Table 7-1: Sample journal entry for outsourced payroll.

Payroll Liability Payments Journal Entry

If you remit your own payments, the liability payments are posted automatically when you create those checks (or ACH transfers), washing the liabilities you entered in the JE.

If your payroll service remits your payments, enter the payments in a separate JE as illustrated in Table 7-2.

Account	Debit	Credit
FWT W/H (liability)	Total Federal W/H Remitted	
FICA W/H (liability)	Total FICA W/H Remitted	
Medicare W/H (liability)	Total Medicare W/H Remitted	
State Income Tax W/H (liability)	Total State Tax W/H Remitted	
Local Income Tax W/H (liability)	Total Local Tax W/H Remitted	
State SDI W/H (liability)	Total State SDI W/HRemitted	
State SUI W/H (liability)	Total State SUI W/H Remitted	
Benefits Contrib W/H (liability)	Total Contributions Remitted	
401(k) Contrib W/H (liability)	Total 401(k) Remitted	
Employer FICA (expense)	Total Employer FICA due	
Employer Medicare (expense)	Total Employer Medicare due	
Employer Unemployment (expense)	Total Employer Unemployment due	
Federal Unemployment (expense)	Total FUTA Due	
Other Employer Payments (expense)	Total Other Deductions/ Payments Remitted	
Payroll Account		Total payments

Table 7-2: Sample journal entry for payroll liability payments.

Reconciling the Payroll Account When You Use a Payroll Service

The best way to track payroll when you use a payroll service is with a journal entry. However, the problem with journal entries for payroll is that when the bank statement comes for the payroll account, reconciling it is a bit difficult. When you open the payroll account in the Reconcile window you see the journal entry totals instead of the individual checks.

Most people find that the payroll checks are cashed quickly and clear rapidly, which always makes reconciliation easier. Payments to government agencies may not clear quite as fast.

Reconciling the Payroll Account Outside of QuickBooks

The report from the payroll service lists each check number and Payee, so you can set up a system to reconcile the account in a spreadsheet or a table in a word processing program.

Technically, you only need two columns: Check Number and Cleared. However, some users prefer to duplicate a real reconciliation window by adding columns for Date, Check Number, Payee, Amount, and Cleared.

Reconciling in QuickBooks with Fake Checks

You can't enter the paychecks in the normal fashion in your payroll account, because the JE you created already posted the amounts to that account. To create transactions that you can use when the statement arrives, you must enter the checks so they "wash", which means you post them back to the payroll account. This requires some setup, but after that one-time task you can enter each paycheck every payday.

It's easier to do this without tracking the individual payee names; instead, track the check numbers and amounts, because the statement only references that data. If a check doesn't clear, use the report from the payroll service to track the payee name against the check number. However, if you wish, you can enter the paychecks with both the check number and payee name in addition to the amount.

Create a generic employee in the Other Name list, naming it Payroll or Employee. If you want to track payee names, you have to create each employee as an Other Name list entry, using a slightly different version of the real employee name (because you can't have duplicate names in your company file). For example, you can insert a fake middle initial, such as X, in each name to create the listing in the Other Name List.

Enter the paychecks by opening the account register for the payroll account, and taking the following actions:

1. On the next available transaction line, enter the payroll check date.
2. Tab to the Number field and enter the first check number on the payroll service report.
3. Enter the generic payee you created (unless you've entered all your employee names as Other Name types, in which case enter the appropriate name).
4. Enter the amount of the net paycheck.
5. In the Account field, choose the Payroll account. QuickBooks displays a message warning you that you're posting the payment to the source account. Click OK. (In fact, click the check box that tells QuickBooks to omit this warning in the future.)
6. Click the Record button to save this check, and then enter the next check.
7. Continue the process until all the checks are entered.

You can also enter the checks the payroll service wrote to transmit your withholdings and employer payments. As long as the postings were entered into the journal entry you can post everything back to the payroll account. You're "washing" every transaction, not changing the balance of the account. Then, when you want to reconcile the payroll account, the individual checks are there. The fact is, this procedure is quite easy and fast and you only have to do it on payday (or once a month if you want to wait until the bank statement arrives).

Net To Gross Paycheck Calculation

Available only in the QuickBooks Enhanced Payroll services, the net to gross feature is handy for special paychecks in which you want to make sure the employee receives a certain amount in the net check.

This scenario occurs when you want to give an employee taxable pay above and beyond the regular salary or wages—the most common reason is a bonus check. If you're tracking bonuses separately from regular paychecks, be sure to create a payroll item for bonuses. (You can also treat a bonus as a regular Salary payroll item.)

ProAdvisor TIP: *If you don't subscribe to one of the QuickBooks Enhanced Payroll Service offerings, you can find net-to-gross calculators on the Internet. Enter the words "net to gross payroll" in your favorite search engine.*

Use the following steps to create a net to gross paycheck:

1. In the Enter Payroll Information window, make sure there's a check mark next to the employee's name, and then click the name to open the Preview Paycheck window.

2. In the Earnings section of the window, select a Bonus or Salary payroll item from the drop-down list in the Item Name column. Don't enter anything in the Rate column.

3. Click the option labeled Enter Net/Calculate Gross at the bottom of the window.

4. The Check Amount field displays the current amount of the net check (which is either 0.00, or a negative figure if the employee has an automatic deduction).

5. Replace the current amount of the check with the net amount you want this employee to receive.

6. Press the Tab key to automatically calculate the gross amount, the taxes, and any automatic deductions that result in the net amount you specified.

7. Click Save & Close and then continue to follow the procedures for creating paychecks.

Subcontractors and 1099s

At the end of the calendar year you must send Form 1099 to independent contractors for services/goods rendered. Most of the time, sending accurate 1099s is easy to accomplish. As long as you've configured the appropriate vendors for 1099s, and you've linked the appropriate account(s) for 1099s, any 1099 vendors linked to 1099 accounts are automatically tracked properly in QuickBooks.

However, tracking 1099s gets complicated when:

- You have to withhold federal taxes from 1099 vendor payments.
- You want to reimburse independent contractors for expenses incurred, and you don't want the reimbursed amounts included on the 1099s.
- You must withhold garnishments from 1099 vendor payments.

In the following sections we'll go over the methods you can use to manage these scenarios.

Form W-9

You must have a signed copy of IRS Form W-9 from every subcontractor. The form provides information about the subcontractor's business as well as a Tax Identification Number (TIN). The TIN is either a social security number or an EIN number. You shouldn't issue any payments until you receive the signed form. You can download, print, and send the form to the subcontractor, or you can have the subcontractor download, print, sign, and send the form to you.

ProAdvisor TIP: *When you read the instructions for Form W-9, you (the business hiring the subcontractor) are the "requester".*

1099 Backup Withholding

You must withhold federal taxes from 1099 vendor payments under any of the following circumstances:

- You don't have a TIN for the subcontractor, but you want to issue a payment.
- You have been notified by the IRS that the TIN you were given is not valid.
- You have been notified by the IRS that you must withhold taxes because the subcontractor owes taxes.
- The subcontractor notifies you that he/she has been told by the IRS that taxes must be withheld from 1099 payments.

This withholding is called *backup withholding*, to distinguish it from federal withholding connected to payroll.

Configuring QuickBooks for Backup Withholding

The 1099 paradigm has changed significantly from earlier QuickBooks versions (2011 and before). The old dialog box mapping accounts to boxes on the 1099 is gone. You now have to access the QuickBooks 1099 Wizard.

Begin by creating an Other Current Liability account named Backup Withholding. Next, choose Edit | Preferences to open the Preferences dialog. Then select the Tax: 1099 icon in the left pane and the Company Preferences tab in the right. Click the Click Here link in the If You Want To Map Your Accounts To Boxes On Form 1099-MISC option to open the wizard. If you've posted at least one vendor payment to this account, it automatically appears in the list. If you don't see it, change the Show 1099 Accounts field to Show All Accounts, and scroll down to find the new account. Highlight the account and select Box 4: Federal Tax Withheld, from the Apply Payments To This 1099 Box drop down list.

ProAdvisor TIP: *If you have more than one subcontractor for whom you must withhold taxes, create a parent account named Backup Withholding and a separate subaccount for each contractor. Always post transactions to the subaccount, never to the parent account.*

You also have to configure the vendor to remind yourself that backup withholding must be deducted from payments. Custom fields don't work because you can't customize the Write Checks or Enter Bills windows to add the field. Relying on your memory, or applying sticky notes to your monitor rarely works.

The best way to create a reminder is to change the Name field in the vendor record. Because you can configure a separate Payee Name for checks, the text in the Name field isn't used in transactions. Edit the vendor so that when you use the vendor in a transaction, the information about backup withholding is in front of your face. As you can see in Figure 7-3, this vendor's name includes the information that backup withholding is in effect, along with the rate.

Figure 7-3: The vendor's name includes backup withholding info.

Creating a Vendor Payment with Backup Withholding

When you enter a bill or write a direct check, you have to post the full amount due, and then deduct the backup withholding. Use the following steps to make sure all the amounts post properly:

1. Enter the total amount due the vendor, and post it to the expense account you use for this type of payment (such as Outside Contractors). That expense account must eventually be linked to your 1099 configuration.

2. Enter the backup withholding as a negative amount and post it to the Other Current Liability account you created for this purpose.

3. If you didn't enter the net amount in the header section of the transaction, click Recalculate to create a check for the net amount.

Remit the backup withholding with Form 945, posting the check to the same Other Current Liability account you used to post the withholding amount. Creating the check "washes" the amount you deducted from the vendor's payment.

When you print 1099s at the end of the year, the amount posted to backup withholding appears in Box 4 of the form.

Remitting Backup Withholding to the IRS

You have to track the backup withholding and remit it to the IRS periodically. Each year you must file Form 945 and indicate the amount you deposited. Additional backup withholding due is remitted along with Form 945.

Deposit backup withholding to the IRS using the online filing system at the IRS website, or an IRS-issued coupon (delivered to the bank that has the account from which you pay vendors and keep withholding amounts). Your deposit schedule depends on the amount of backup withholding you expect to have for the calendar year:

- Monthly deposits if your total annual backup withholding is less than $50,000.00.

- Semiweekly deposits if your total annual backup withholding exceeds $50,000.00.

Reimbursing 1099 Vendor Expenses

Technically, it's not appropriate to reimburse subcontractors for expenses; that's a transaction reserved for employees. The subcontractor tracks the total amount of your payments as income, and indicates the expenses in his or her tax return. Separating expenses from earned fees should be part of the subcontractor's bookkeeping process.

However, many users have written to say they prefer to reimburse 1099 vendors for expenses without including that amount in the 1099 (frequently because the contract between the user and the subcontractor provides that directive).

The bookkeeping process for this scenario means that the expense is your expense rather than the vendor's expense. Therefore, when you enter a bill from the subcontractor or write a direct check to the subcontractor, enter the reimbursed expense on its own line item in the transaction window, and post the expense to an account that is not included in the 1099 linked accounts configuration.

For example, perhaps you owe the vendor $2000.00 for a fee, and $100.00 for out-of-pocket reimbursable expenses. When you create the vendor bill or direct check, post $2000.00 to the expense account that is linked to 1099s (such as Outside Contractors or Subcontractors), and post $100.00 to the appropriate expense account.

If you're using items to pay the vendor's fee, after you enter the data for the vendor's fee in the Items tab, then move to the Expenses tab and enter the reimbursed expense(s).

ProAdvisor TIP: *Many users don't realize you can use both the Items tab and the Expenses tab when entering a bill or a direct check. The amount of the bill/check must equal the total for both tabs.*

Subcontractor Garnishments

If you receive a garnishment notice for a subcontractor you must withhold and remit the garnishment amount. The process is similar to collecting and remitting garnishments for payroll described earlier in this chapter.

Create an Other Current Liability account named Garnishments. Use that account to reduce the payment to the vendor when you enter a bill or a direct check. Use the same account when you post the remittance to the agency requesting the garnishment.

ProAdvisor TIP: *If you have more than one subcontractor for whom you must collect garnishments, create a parent account named Garnishments and a separate subaccount for each contractor. Always post transactions to the subaccount, never to the parent account.*

CHAPTER 8

Sales and Use Tax

- Sales tax
- Use tax
- Resolving common sales tax problems

Sales tax is becoming a complicated issue and has created an enormous administrative burden for small businesses. In recent years, many states have created multiple sales tax authorities within the state (by county, city, town, or even zip code), and each location has its own tax rate. As a result, there are many thousands of tax rates within the United States.

Businesses in some of those states must remit the sales tax they collect to both the state and the local sales tax authorities (or multiple local sales tax authorities). In other states, businesses remit all the sales tax to the state, but the remittance form includes taxable/nontaxable sales on a location-by-location basis.

As a result, tracking sales tax properly (which means in a manner that makes it possible to fill out all the forms for all the authorities) has become a very complicated process. To avoid audits, fines, and annoying communications from a variety of tax authorities you need to pay careful attention to the way you set up, configure, collect, and track sales tax.

In addition, most states are beginning to press businesses about Use Tax, sending reminders, forms, and even warnings about tracking and remitting any use tax due to the state.

Sales Tax

The QuickBooks Help files provide details for setting up and implementing sales tax. Setting up sales tax requires multiple steps, briefly described here.

Enable Sales Tax

Enable sales tax by choosing Edit | Preferences and selecting the Sales Tax icon in the left pane of the Preferences dialog. Move to the Company Preferences tab to enable sales tax and configure the sales tax feature.

Configure Sales Tax Codes

A sales tax code indicates tax liability (whether tax should be applied). The entity to which the code is linked (a customer or an item) is deemed taxable or nontaxable, depending on this code. Tax codes contain no information about the tax rate or the taxing authority; they just offer a Yes or No answer to the question "Is this taxable?"

Linking a sales tax code to customers and items lets you (and Quick-Books) know whether sales tax should be calculated for that item for this customer. A customer's sales tax liability is like a light switch; it's either on or off. However, if a customer is liable for sales tax, it doesn't mean that every item you sell the customer is taxable, because some items aren't taxable—like a customer, an item has a tax liability switch that operates as an on/off switch. For sales tax to kick in, both the item and the customer must have their tax liability statuses set to "taxable".

QuickBooks prepopulates the Sales Tax Preferences dialog with the following two sales tax codes:

- Tax, which means liable for sales tax
- Non, which means not liable for sales tax

For many businesses that's enough; no additional tax codes for customers or items are needed. However, for some companies, those two tax codes aren't enough. Some taxing authorities care about the "why"—most often they want to know why a customer *isn't* liable for sales tax. Is a customer nontaxable because it's out of state and the rules say you don't have to collect taxes for out-of-state sales? Is the customer nontaxable because it's a nonprofit organization, or a government agency? Is the customer nontaxable because it's a wholesale business and collects sales tax from its own customers? If your state requires this information, you must create tax codes to match the reporting needs required by your state. For example, you could create tax codes similar to the following for nontaxable categories:

- NPO for nonprofit organizations
- GOV for government agencies
- WSL for wholesale businesses (resellers) for which you have the sales tax license numbers
- OOS for out-of-state customers (if you aren't required to collect taxes from out-of-state customers)

For nontaxable customers who are resellers, don't forget to record the tax exemption number (QuickBooks provides a Resale Number field for this information on the Sales Tax Settings tab of the customer record.)

ProAdvisor CAUTION: *In some states, tax-exempt reseller certificates that make a customer nontaxable are only for the state tax. If there are local sales taxes in addition to the state tax, some local tax authorities do not recognize reseller tax exceptions.*

Configure Sales Tax Items

A sales tax item is a collection of data about a sales tax, specifically the rate and the agency to which the sales tax is remitted. The agency has to be set up as a vendor.

Sales tax is an item because, like your service and product items, it's used on sales transaction forms. QuickBooks uses sales tax items to calculate the amount in the Tax field at the bottom of sales forms, and to prepare reports for tax authorities.

Creating Sales Tax Items

When you enable sales tax in the Preferences dialog, you must specify the most common sales tax, which means you must create a sales tax item. Click the button labeled Add Sales Tax Item to open the New Item window with Sales Tax Item preselected in the Type drop-down list. Press Tab to display the New Item window seen in Figure 8-1:

It's entirely possible that your most common sales tax item is not an individual tax; instead it may be a sales tax group (two sales tax items, one for the state and one for the county or city). However, you can't create a sales tax group until you've created the sales tax items that make up the group (see "Sales Tax Groups", later in this section).

To configure the dialog for a single sales tax (you can come back and change it if you create a group later on), take the following steps:

1. Enter a name for the sales tax, and make it descriptive. For instance, use your state abbreviation if your state has a single sales tax structure, or you do business in one of the state's counties or cities that isn't required to collect local taxes along with the state tax.

2. Optionally enter a description of this sales tax.

3. Enter the sales tax rate (QuickBooks automatically adds the % sign).

4. Select the Tax Agency from the drop-down list if you've already created a vendor record for the tax agency. If the vendor doesn't exist, select <Add New> and add the tax agency to your vendor list.

Figure 8-1: A sales tax item must have a name, a rate, and a tax agency.

Notice that Figure 8-1 displays an agency name that's a vendor code, not the real name of the sales tax authority. If you remit sales tax to your state's Department of Revenue, it's highly likely you remit other payments to the same department. Using vendor names that are codes ensures that the right vendor gets the right check for the right type of payment. Because QuickBooks has a field for the payee in the vendor record, the checks are made out to the right payee. This field is called Print Name On Check As, and is found on the Payment Settings tab. For example, if you were in Pennsylvania you might have the following vendors in your system, all of which have the "PA Department of Revenue" in the Print Name On Check As field.

- PA501 (vendor for remitting employee withholding for state income tax—501 is the form number).
- PACorp (vendor for paying state corporate taxes).
- PACorpEst (vendor for remitting estimated corporate taxes).
- PASalesTax (vendor for remitting sales tax).
- PAUC (vendor for remitting unemployment tax).

This paradigm makes it easy to create checks and track history.

When you finish configuring this sales tax item, click OK to return to the Sales Tax Preferences dialog. QuickBooks inserts this tax as the most common sales tax item. If this is the most common sales tax item (or the only sales tax item you need), you're finished.

When you click OK, QuickBooks asks whether it should configure all your existing customers, non-inventory, and inventory items as Taxable. If most of your customers and items are taxable, let QuickBooks configure them automatically.

QuickBooks does not insert the most common sales tax you configured into the records of existing customers; however, as you create new customers the most common sales tax is automatically linked to the customer (see the section Assigning Sales Tax Items to Customers, later in this chapter).

Create Sales Tax Groups

In some states, the tax imposed is really two taxes, and the taxing authority collects a single check from you but insists on a breakdown in the reports you send. For example, in Pennsylvania, the state sales tax is 6%, but businesses in Philadelphia incur another 2% and businesses in Allegheny County (largely Pittsburgh) incur another 1%.

One check is remitted to the state's revenue department, but the report that accompanies the check must break down the remittance into the individual taxes—the total taxable and nontaxable sales for the 6% tax, and the amount of tax due, and the same data for the surtax.

In other states, the basic state sales tax is remitted to the state, and the locally added sales tax is remitted to the local taxing authority.

Your challenge is to display and calculate a single sales tax for the customer and report multiple taxes to one or more taxing authorities. Tax groups meet this challenge.

A sales tax group is a single entity that appears on a sales transaction, but it is really multiple entities that have been totaled. QuickBooks inserts the sales tax amount in the sales transaction window by calculating taxable sales at the "combo" rate—the total of the two (or more) rates in the group.

Create a sales tax item for each sales tax you need to add to a group. If you're liable for sales tax collection for five counties (or other local subdivisions) in your state, you'll need five groups. Each group contains the state's basic sales tax as well as one of the county sales taxes. When you create the additional sales tax items you need, be sure to name them appropriately so you have an easy time creating your groups.

After all your individual sales tax items are in the system, use the following steps to create a sales tax group item.

1. Open the Item List by choosing Lists | Item List.
2. Press Ctrl-N to open the New Item dialog.
3. Select Sales Tax Group as the type.
4. Enter a name for the group.
5. Optionally enter a description.
6. In the Tax Item column, choose the individual sales tax items you need to create this group. As you move to the next item, QuickBooks fills in the rate, tax agency, and description (if one exists) of each sales tax item you select. The calculated total (the group rate) appears at the bottom of the dialog (see Figure 8-2).
7. Click OK.

Figure 8-2: Create a Sales Tax Group to apply two (or more) taxes
at once to sales transactions.

Select this item for the appropriate customers when you're creating
sales transactions.

Assign Sales Tax Items to Customers

Each customer's taxable status (the sales tax code) and linked sales tax
item are on the Sales Tax Settings tab of the customer's record, and you
can edit each customer's record to make changes to either field.

Adding the sales tax item to every customer record can be a pain. If
you already created a great many customers, opening each record to make
changes is onerous, and there are three ways to remedy this:

- Wait until you use each customer in a sales
  transaction. Then, in the transaction window,
  change the customer's tax item. When you save
  the transaction, QuickBooks cooperates with this
  approach by asking you if you want to change the
  customer's tax information permanently. Click Yes.

- Use the Add/Edit Multiple List Entries feature to add
  the correct sales tax item to each customer.

- Export your customer list to an IIF file, change or create the tax code and tax item for each customer, and then import the file back into QuickBooks (see Appendix B for details about using IIF files).

Sales Tax Rates that Differ by Item

Suppose you offer several products or services in a state that imposes one tax rate for some products and another tax rate for other products? The taxes are remitted to the same tax authority; this isn't a matter of "one rate for residents of X and another rate for residents of Y".

For example, in the hospitality industry, some states impose one tax rate for alcoholic beverages, another tax rate for restaurant food, and yet another tax rate for hotel rooms. Your state may have different rate structures for another set of products and services.

If you sell items or services that have different sales tax rates, it's not an easy task to prepare a single sales transaction for a customer who is purchasing items that have differing tax rates.

For tax rates based on an item, creating a Tax Group doesn't work, because a Tax Group represents the total tax of differing rates applied to all the taxable items you sold, and that's not what's needed in this case. The workaround for this complicated situation has two parts:

- Creating the sales tax items you need.
- Learning how to enter those items on a sales transaction.

Create Items for Item-Based Tax Rates

You have to create multiple sales tax items to be able to apply different tax rates in the same sales transaction. Obviously, you have to create an item for each tax rate, but you also have to create two other items:

- A subtotal item (which you may already have) that lets you create a subtotal for all items with the same tax rate.

- A fake tax item to satisfy the QuickBooks need for a tax rate for the entire invoice (the field that appears at the bottom of the invoice).

Create the Special Tax Items

You need to create a tax item for each tax rate. Open the Item List by choosing Lists | Item List, and press Ctrl-N to create a new item using the following guidelines:

- The Type is Sales Tax Item
- The Sales Tax Name is the specific tax, e.g. Food Tax. The Description should be specific, such as Restaurant Food Tax. Don't leave the Description field blank. You want the customer to see what the line item tax is.
- In the Tax Rate field, enter the appropriate rate (QuickBooks adds the % character automatically).
- In the Tax Agency field, enter the name of the tax authority (a vendor) to which you remit this tax.

Create a Placeholder Tax Item

When you want to enter taxes as line items, QuickBooks throws up two impediments:

- It continues to tax the total taxable sale at the rate of the default tax item for the customer, which is displayed at the bottom of the transaction form.
- It won't let you enter a line item tax if that tax is already assigned to the customer or item, and is automatically listed at the end of the sales transaction (e.g. Food Tax).

The solution is to have a tax item that has a zero percent rate, and has a description that the customer will understand. Here are some guidelines for creating this item:

- The Item Type is Sales Tax
- The Item Name is Placeholder
- The Tax Rate is zero percent
- The Description is Other Sales Tax
- The Tax Agency is a vendor you must create named "No Tax", and the vendor has no address or other information, just the name.

ProAdvisor NOTE: *The vendor named No Tax will appear on all sales tax reports, but since no money is involved, it won't affect your numbers, nor will QuickBooks create a payment when you remit your sales tax.*

Create a Subtotal Item

In order to apply taxes as line items properly, you need a subtotal for each set of taxable line items. You have two ways to do this:

- You can create one item of the type Subtotal, named Subtotal (which may already exist in your Item List). Then, when you prepare a sales transaction, you can type in the description, such as "Total Taxable Food" before applying the applicable tax (in this case, the food tax).
- You can create one item for each subtotal you need, such as Subtotal-Food, and enter an appropriate description, such as "Total Taxable Food", which saves you the effort of entering the description when you prepare the sales transaction.

The second choice works best, because it's always more efficient to do a little extra setup work to save the extra efforts needed on a daily basis.

Creating Multi-Rate Sales Transactions

In the Invoice or Sales Receipt transaction window, enter the Customer Name, and change the Tax field at the bottom of the line item section to the Placeholder tax item you created. Then, take the following steps:

1. Enter all the items that are subject to one of the taxes, followed by the subtotal item for that tax. (You must enter a subtotal item even if there's only one item for the tax category).

2. Enter the appropriate sales tax item. QuickBooks calculates the tax based on the subtotal.

3. Enter the items that are subject to the next tax, followed by the subtotal item for that tax.

4. Enter the appropriate tax item for this subtotal.

5. Continue to enter items, subtotals, and tax items (see Figure 8-3).

Figure 8-3: This transaction tracks all taxes properly.

You can make the printed version easier to read by inserting blank lines after each tax line (to separate the sections). To insert a blank line, place your cursor on the line below the place where you want the blank line, and press Ctrl-Ins (or Ctrl-Insert, depending on your keyboard's text).

Special Tax Rates

Some states have a long list of circumstances under which a sale that is normally taxable may be nontaxable (or the other way around). In this section we'll discuss some of the common complications and their solutions.

On Premises Vs. Off Premises Tax Rates

Some states and/or local tax authorities differentiate between goods that are used/consumed on your premises and goods that are purchased for use/consumption at home. The most common example (and perhaps the only example) is food. Sales tax on food works as follows in many states (usually, states that don't tax grocery items):

- You must apply tax to the diner's bill for food that is consumed on the premises.
- Take-out customers don't pay tax.

The solution for this is to create separate items, such as Food (taxable) and TakeOut (not taxable). QuickBooks calculates the total tax due for the taxable item at the bottom of the sales form.

Incremental Sales Tax

An incremental sales tax has a per-item limit for applying the tax. If the item limit is $5000.00, the sales tax is only applied to that amount, and then it disappears. For example, if the sales tax is 5%, then a $6000.00 item carries a tax burden of $250.00 (5% of the first $5000.00).

Some states have devised incremental sales taxes that kick in with the opposite formula—tax exemptions at the beginning and tax applications at a particular point (essentially, a tax exemption with a maximum). For example, a state may say that the first $100.00 of a particular item type (e.g. clothing) is tax free (per item) and then the sales tax kicks in. For other types of purchases no such scalable tax rate applies.

To make it worse, in some states the exemption to a certain amount for certain types of items is ignored by the local sales tax authority.

QuickBooks cannot manage incremental taxes, because, unlike most of its competition, it does not have a tax table that lets you create tax items with formulas (similar to the way payroll items are configured). Hopefully this will change in the future.

We've looked at some QuickBooks users' workarounds for this, but none of them works properly. For instance, users have entered an item for the first $5000.00 (or other threshold), applied the combo tax as a line item, and then entered the same item with the balance of the real price, selecting Non as the tax code for that item.

If the item is an inventory item, you've removed two pieces of inventory in QuickBooks (and one item from the physical inventory) and registered some really strange price structures and COGS calculations. In addition, the customers don't understand the printed sales receipt, and trying to explain it to each customer as a line of waiting customers grows impatient, is not good business.

You can build a set of formulas in Excel, calculate the taxes in Excel, and then enter the tax amount manually, but that's a lot of work and wastes a lot of time. Instead, think about using an external sales tax calculator.

Some states have online calculators (e.g. Kansas and Iowa, and perhaps others). You fill out the form (including the purchaser's address or local tax code), and the calculator provides the sales tax amount(s). Use a line item to apply the sales tax to the sales transaction form, and select a tax rate of zero to avoid additional tax being imposed automatically by QuickBooks (see the discussion on the zero-percent Placeholder tax, earlier in this chapter).

The Streamlined Sales Tax Project, the national organization that's working to streamline sales taxes, has certified some tax calculator software solutions. Among QuickBooks users, we've found that Avalara (www.avalara.com) is popular and deemed reliable (and it has a specific product for QuickBooks).

Remitting Sales Tax

Periodically (at the interval stated on your sales tax license), you have to remit the sales tax you've collected, to the appropriate government agencies. This discussion assumes you've created the sales tax items you need, and each item is linked to the right vendor (tax authority). You also have to remit Use Tax, which is covered later in this chapter.

QuickBooks provides a feature called Manage Sales Tax (see Figure 8-4) that acts as a "home page" for information and help, and contains links to the reports and payment forms covered in this section. You can open the Manage Sales Tax window by choosing Vendors | Sales Tax | Manage Sales Tax.

Figure 8-4: The Manage Sales Tax window has links to sales tax functions.

You can use the links in this dialog to display your sales tax reports and use the Pay Sales Tax function to remit sales tax to the appropriate tax authorities.

Adjusting Sales Tax Amounts

If you need to adjust the amount of sales tax due (some states offer a discount for timely payment), click the Pay Sales Tax button, select the appropriate sales tax item in the Pay Sales Tax window, and click the Adjust button to open the Sales Tax Adjustment dialog seen in Figure 8-5.

Figure 8-5: Adjust the sales tax amount before remitting the payment.

Specify the amount by which to reduce (or increase, if you're late and paying a penalty) the tax amount. Specify an Adjustment Account (you can create a specific account for this adjustment), and click OK to return to the Pay Sales Tax window, where the amount has been changed to reflect your adjustment.

If you remit sales tax to multiple tax agencies, create an adjustment for each tax vendor that requires an adjustment.

Use Tax

Use tax is an amount due to your state sales tax authority to make up for lost sales tax revenue when you purchase or use something that's taxable without paying sales tax. Each state that imposes sales taxes defines the conditions under which use tax is due.

For example, you may purchase goods or services from a vendor in another state where the purchase isn't taxable, but it would be taxable in your state. Or you may take a product out of your inventory to use in your business instead of selling it to a customer.

Unlike sales tax, which is money you collect from customers and turn over to the state (making it neither income nor expense), use tax is a business expense.

QuickBooks has no built-in mechanism for tracking and remitting use tax, so you must develop your own system. Generally, there are three scenarios in which you may owe your state use tax:

- You purchased goods or services that are taxable in your state from an out-of-state vendor, and paid no tax.

- You purchased taxable items for resale (inventory) without paying sales tax because you have a sales tax license, but you used an item in your business instead of selling it.

- You purchased taxable items for resale (inventory) without paying sales tax because you have a sales tax license, but you gave an item away (as a charitable donation, as a sample, or as a premium for a customer).

In this section, we'll provide procedures for these scenarios. There is no "one and only way" to track use tax, but these processes have worked for the businesses we've configured.

The way you track use tax depends on your state's reporting requirements. Some states include use tax remittances on the same form that you use to remit sales tax, and you'll need the same detailed information you need for sales tax reports. Other states just ask you to declare the value of the untaxed items and remit the appropriate amount of tax.

ProAdvisor TIP: *Some states are "audit happy", so even if you only have to report and remit total use tax due (without filling out details of each purchase), you need to make sure you have detailed records for each occurrence of use tax liability.*

Tracking Use Tax for Purchases

The safest way to track use tax is to record it as part of the purchase transaction that created the use tax liability. This makes it easy to remit the use tax you owe, and creates the details you need to pass an audit. To track use tax for purchases, you need two accounts:

- A use tax liability account (Other Current Liability).
- A use tax expense account.

When you record the expense, whether it's a check, a vendor bill, a credit card transaction in the credit card liability account, or a check written to the credit card vendor, you also record the use tax due (a liability) and the use tax expense (an expense). Use the following steps to record a purchase and its attendant use tax.

1. Enter the expense account and the amount for the purchase you made.
2. On the next line, enter the use tax amount due to your state and post it to the Use Tax expense account.
3. Enter the same amount you entered in Step 2 as a negative amount and post it to the Use Tax Due liability account.

Because the last two items cancel each other out, you haven't changed the amount of the transaction. However, you have the postings you need to track and remit use tax:

- The use tax expense is recorded and appears in your Profit & Loss report.
- The use tax liability is sitting in the liability account, reminding you that you owe use tax.

When you remit Use Tax to the state, post the payment to the Use Tax liability account to wash the amounts you've posted. The accumulated amount you posted to Use Tax Expense is a deductible expense.

Use Tax for Inventory Items Used in Your Business

If you remove inventory that's available for resale from your warehouse to use in your business, you owe use tax on those items. The state knows that if you'd sold the inventory to a customer, you would have collected and remitted sales tax.

You need to record every pencil, notebook, computer part, light bulb, etc. you remove from your warehouse for in-house use. Tracking this is a two step process: First, adjust the inventory; second, create a journal entry to track the use tax.

Adjusting Inventory for In-House Use of Items

You need to remove the inventory item(s) you're appropriating and post the adjustment to the right expense. For example, if you're removing office supplies, post the adjustment to the Office Supplies expense. Here are the steps:

1. Choose Vendors | Inventory Activities | Adjust Quantity/ Value On Hand.
2. Select Quantity as the Adjustment Type.
3. Select the appropriate expense account for the type of material you're removing from the warehouse (Figure 8-6

shows the posting for removing a computer monitor to be used in the office).

4. Reduce the quantity on hand by the number of items you're removing.

Figure 8-6: Adjust inventory to remove the item you're using in your business.

Posting Use Tax for In-House Use of Items

To track the use tax, create a journal entry as follows:

- Debit Use Tax expense.
- Credit the Use Tax liability account.

When you remit the use tax, post the payment to the Use Tax owed liability account. The expense stays on your books as a deductible expense.

ProAdvisor NOTE: *Most states impose use tax for withdrawn inventory items based on the current cost of the item, not your retail price. Be sure to check the law in your state to make sure you can create the transaction based on cost.*

Use Tax for Inventory Giveaways

If you send a sample or premium to a customer or make a donation of an inventory item to a nonprofit organization, your state may want to collect use tax for the transaction.

Use the instructions in the previous section to track the use tax. When you adjust the inventory quantity, post the transaction to Advertising and Marketing (for a sample or premium sent to a customer) or to Charitable Contributions if you're making a donation to a nonprofit organization. The journal entry to track the use tax is the same explained in the previous section: debit Use Tax expense and credit Use Tax liability.

Common Sales Tax Problems

Based on the reader questions we receive at CPA911 Publishing LLC and at our website www.cpa911.com, there are some problems users run into as they try to manage sales tax. We'll cover the most frequently encountered problems in this section.

Payments to State Didn't Reduce Sales Tax Liability

Most states require that sales tax reports and remittances be submitted online. After filling out the report and approving the ACH transfer from the bank account, many users enter the check in the bank register (sometimes after downloading transactions from the bank). The sales tax liability account isn't reduced.

You *must* use the Pay Sales Tax feature to remit payment to the state. If you don't, your bank register displays a payment of the type CHK or BILLPMT (even if you post the payment to the Sales Tax liability account). You need to replace the incorrectly posted check with a real liability payment, as follows:

1. Make a note of the date and amount of the check. If you didn't pay online with an ACH transfer, also note the check number.
2. Void the transaction.

3. Use the Pay Sales Tax feature to create the transaction properly. Use the date, amount, and check number of the payment you voided. The bank register shows a transaction type TAXPMT.

4. If the original payment cleared the bank and was reconciled, mark the replacement payment as reconciled.

Sales Tax Charged to Exempt Customer

The following scenario is not uncommon: You send an invoice to a customer with tax included. When the payment arrives, the sales tax has been deducted and a copy of the customer's tax certificate is included in the envelope.

You have to mark the invoice closed (paid in full) and reduce your sales tax liability. To accomplish this task, create a credit memo with following guidelines:

- Leave the customer status as taxable.

- Enter the same item(s) that were on the invoice, marking them taxable.

- Then enter the same item(s) with a minus sign, marking them nontaxable (this is a reverse credit, or a debit memo).

The net amount of the credit memo is the amount of the sales tax. Your total taxable income and total nontaxable income figures have been adjusted properly, so you can file an accurate report with the tax authorities.

Now you can go to Receive Payments and post the payment, using the credit to pay off the difference between the amount of the invoice and the amount of the payment. (Don't forget you also have to change the customer's record to include the certificate number and configure the customer as non-taxable.)

CHAPTER 9

Accountant Edition

- Using Accountant Edition in your practice
- Client support tools
- Client troubleshooting tips

The Premier Accountant Edition differs from all the other Premier editions. It contains features, tools, and add-on programs that aren't included in the other Premier editions. The Premier Accountant Edition is designed to serve two purposes:

- Provide a robust accounting application for running an accounting practice.
- Provide tools and features that make it easy to support QuickBooks clients.

In this chapter we'll go over some of the most useful features in the Premier Accountant Edition.

Premier Accountant Plus

Before we delve into the workings of Premier Accountant, a quick word about Accountant Plus. This is a subscription based service which provides the Premier Accountant desktop software plus two cloud based services:

- Client Collaborator
- Accountant's Copy File Transfer Service

The Client Collaborator feature enables you to maintain an online conversation thread with your client about specific QuickBooks transactions. You open a transaction, ask a question, which is added to the online conversation, and send the client a notification. The client opens the thread from within QuickBooks, responds, and sends a notification back to you. Once you subscribe, the Client Collaborator icon on the menu bar (next to the Alerts icon) becomes functional.

The Accountant's Copy File Transfer Service allows you to exchange the Accountant's Copy file and the changes file with your client from within QuickBooks. Once you've subscribed to the service your client can send the file to you by selecting File | Accountant's Copy | Send To Accountant. When you've made your changes you send them back to the client using the service.

Using Accountant Edition in Your Practice

The best part of purchasing QuickBooks Premier Accountant Edition is that you've really bought all the QuickBooks editions. In addition to the Premier Accountant Edition, you can also run QuickBooks Pro, QuickBooks Premier (non-industry specific), and all of the QuickBooks Premier industry specific editions (Contractor, Manufacturing & Wholesale, Nonprofit, Professional Services, and Retail). To switch among QuickBooks editions:

1. Choose File | Toggle To Another Edition to open the Select QuickBooks Industry-Specific Edition dialog.

2. Select the edition you want to use, and click Next. QuickBooks displays a window confirming the edition you've selected.

3. Click Toggle to close the currently loaded edition and open the selected edition.

ProAdvisor NOTE: *If a company file is open at the time you toggle, that file is loaded when QuickBooks opens again in the new edition.*

In this section, we'll go over some of the features in Premier Accountant Edition that you'll find helpful for running your own practice. Most of the information will also help you work with client files.

Company Data File

QuickBooks provides a wide range of options for tracking clients, projects, and income. The flexibility built into QuickBooks lets you set up your company data file in the way that best meets your needs.

Proving the old legend of the shoemaker's children, we've found many accounting firms that spent years operating without full-featured accounting software. They have a time and billing program for receivables and payments, and they use write-up software to record revenue totals and disbursements.

Fixed assets and liabilities are tracked in spreadsheets, and a variety of other software documents keep track of other financial details. They have an outside payroll service, but they don't track the weekly payroll (at the end of a quarter or year, they enter the totals provided by the payroll service). Preparing the firm's tax return must be a real joy!

Many of these firms, especially those who support clients using QuickBooks, have begun installing QuickBooks for their own use—and the Premier Accountant Edition is in use at many accounting practices. Unfortunately, it's not uncommon to find the company file lacks configuration options that make QuickBooks truly useful.

As a result, a lot of after-the-fact work (especially the calculation of subtotals and the process of analyzing revenue) continues to be performed in spreadsheet applications. Very little of the work done outside of QuickBooks would be required if the configuration options were more carefully considered. Old habits are hard to break.

Configuring the Chart of Accounts

QuickBooks creates a partial chart of accounts for accounting firms, but it's missing many accounts. In addition, the accounts are not numbered by default (and we've met very few accountants who didn't prefer numbered accounts).

To number your accounts, choose Edit | Preferences and select the Accounting category in the left pane of the Preferences dialog. On the Company Preferences tab, select the option Use Account Numbers, and also select the option Show Lowest Subaccount Only (to avoid having to scroll through parent and subaccount names when you're selecting an account in a drop-down list).

If you added any accounts to the chart of accounts that was installed automatically by QuickBooks, they will not be automatically numbered, and selecting the "Show Lowest Subaccount Only" option produces an error message (when you try to close the Preferences dialog) that tells you that you must create numbers for all accounts before you can enable this option.

After you enter account numbers for the accounts you added manually, return to the Accounting category of the Preferences dialog to enable the Show Lowest Subaccount Only option.

Incidentally, the reason selecting "Use Account Numbers" works without a hitch is that QuickBooks actually provides account numbers for the chart of accounts it establishes automatically during company setup. Even though numbers are attached to every account, QuickBooks sets the default configuration for the chart of accounts so it doesn't display those numbers. The numbers are there, most accountants prefer account numbers, why not display them?

When you've enabled account numbers, check the number scheme to make sure it matches your own preferences. QuickBooks uses the standard numbering paradigm for an Accountant/CPA chart of accounts:

- 10000 starts the asset accounts
- 20000 starts the liability accounts
- 30000 starts the equity accounts
- 40000 starts the income accounts
- 50000 starts the cost of goods sold accounts
- 60000 starts the expense accounts
- 70000 starts the "other" income accounts
- 80000 starts the "other" expense accounts

Configuring Customers and Jobs

Many accountants track only customer names, omitting jobs from the configuration of their company data files. Specific types of work for clients are tracked by items, or by posting revenue to specific income accounts.

Using Jobs

If you use service items or revenue accounts to track types of services, analyzing any individual client's history requires quite a bit of work. You have to customize a report so it filters items and/or revenue accounts.

All of the information is available, without customization, on a job report. If you want to view individual client histories to analyze your work and income stream, you should consider tracking clients by jobs.

Incidentally, jobs are not restricted to projects with start and end dates ; a job can be defined as a specific type of work. For example, you might decide to create the following jobs for clients:

- Business tax preparation
- Personal tax preparation
- Bookkeeping services
- Audits (performing or attending)
- Planning (preparing proformas, business plans, and so on)

Using Customer Types

If you choose Accounting as the industry type during company file setup, QuickBooks prepopulates the Customer Type List for specific business types. You can view and manipulate those customer types by choosing Lists | Customer & Vendor Profile Lists | Customer Type List. Figure 9-1 shows the customer types that QuickBooks automatically adds to your data file.

Figure 9-1: The prepopulated customer types may not suit your practice.

Most accountants find that these customer types don't work, because this isn't the type of information that's useful for creating the reports they need. Many accounting firms use the month of the fiscal year end for business clients, as customer types. Create twelve customer types, from January to December. Then assign the appropriate type to each customer record. Every month, run a report for the customer type two months hence, and begin the steps for year-end work, which could encompass any of the following:

- Use the Write Letters feature in QuickBooks to send a note reminding clients of the things they must do to close their books and produce reports. Include a request to call the office to make an appointment.

- If you use pretax preparation worksheets (a copy of last years figures and a line for clients to enter the current totals), use the Print Labels feature to send the packages to the appropriate customer type.

- Print a Customer listing of only the appropriate type, and have a staff member set up the appointments.

Add your own end of year protocols to this list of chores, and you'll find that it's easy to identify the right clients because almost all Quick-Books reports let you filter for a customer type.

Managing Items

Items are the services and products a company sells. As an accountant, you sell services, and your item list can be as simple or as complex as your client services and invoicing standards require.

Most accounting firms need service items such as tax preparation (both personal and business), audits, tax planning, business planning, write-up or other bookkeeping services, and special services such as preparing business plans or projections. Create an item for each service you provide.

Using Price Levels

Price levels provide a way to fine-tune your pricing in situations where you want to pass along a discount (or a higher rate) on an item. QuickBooks Premier editions offer two types of price levels:

- Fixed percentage price levels
- Per item price levels

To use price levels, you must first set up your items. If your items have no assigned rates, you can use price levels to set all rates for the item. If your items have been assigned a rate, you can create price levels based on that rate. (Chapter 2 contains the information you need to create and apply price levels.)

Using Billing Rate Levels

The Billing Rate Level List lets you assign a billing rate to a person performing a specific service. This list is only available in the following Premier Editions:

- Accountant Edition
- Contractor Edition
- Professional Services Edition

After you create billing rate levels, and associate them with service providers, invoicing for services becomes almost automated. Every time you create an invoice with billable time, QuickBooks automatically fills in the correct rate for the service, based on the person who performed the work.

For instance, you can have one rate for audit activities that are performed by a senior partner, and another rate for audit activities performed by a junior partner. The senior partner rate for creating business plans may differ from the audit rate (and the junior partner rate for creating business plans may also be unique). The permutations and combinations are almost endless, which makes this a very powerful feature. Learn how to create and apply billing rate levels in Chapter 2.

Entering Transactions in a Batch

One useful feature found only in the Premier Accountant Edition is the ability to enter checks, deposits, credit card transactions, bills, bill credits, invoices, and credit memos in batches. This can come in handy if you're entering a large number of these transactions manually, or transferring them from a spreadsheet. It is similar to the Add/Edit Multiple List Entries feature found in all versions of QuickBooks. Choose Accountant | Batch Enter Transactions to open the Batch Enter Transactions window shown in Figure 9-2.

Figure 9-2: Transferring large numbers of transactions is a lot
easier with the Batch Enter Transactions feature.

You can enter the transactions manually and take advantage of the Copy Down and Duplicate Row commands found on the right-click shortcut menu to speed up the process. You can even copy and paste from an existing table or spreadsheet. Just make sure you line up the columns correctly.

If you find that not all the fields you need are visible, click the Customize Columns button to display the Customize Columns dialog. From there you can select the columns to view or hide.

Client Support Tools

The Premier Accountant Edition is built from the ground up to help you support QuickBooks clients. In this section, we'll go over some of the features designed for client support.

Working Trial Balance

The Working Trial Balance is a spreadsheet-like display of general ledger activity over a specified period (see Figure 9-3). You can use it with a client's company file that you've opened in Premier Accountant Edition, or with the Accountant's Copy of a client's file. To access this tool, choose Accountant | Working Trial Balance.

For each account, the report displays the opening balance, the closing balance, and the total transactions (using QuickBooks transaction windows and adjustments made with journal entries) that created the closing balance. In addition, this tool has the following powerful options:

- You can hide the display of accounts that have no activity.
- Double-clicking an account listing opens the account's record so you can edit it (e.g. change the name, description, or account number).
- Double-clicking the amount in a column opens a detailed report on the transactions that created the amount displayed.
- You can create a journal entry for any account by selecting the account and clicking the Make Adjustments button.
- You can use the Workpaper Reference column for notes if you make any changes.

Figure 9-3: Use the Working Trial Balance to view and manipulate account activity.

Accountant's Copy

An Accountant's Copy is a copy of a company file that's sent from the client to the accountant or bookkeeper. The Accountant's Copy feature is designed to let the client continue to work in the company file at the same time the accountant is working in the Accountant's Copy, although there are limitations on the work that both the client and the accountant can perform.

When the accountant is finished working in the Accountant's Copy, a change file is returned to the client so that the accountant's changes can be merged into the client's company file.

Following is the process in chronological order:

1. The client creates an Accountant's Copy of the company file and sets the dividing date (see the next section, Accountant's Copy Dividing Date). This file is the Accountant's Copy transfer file, which has a file extension .QBX.

2. The client sends the file to the accountant, either on removable media or by uploading the file to a secure server that QuickBooks provides.

3. The accountant opens the transfer file (.QBX) which is automatically saved as an Accountant's Copy working file, with a file extension of .QBA.

4. When the accountant finishes working on the file, the changes are exported into the Accountant's Copy changes file, which has a file extension .QBY, and the file is sent to the client.

5. The client opens the file and reviews the changes, then imports the data into the company file.

Accountant's Copy Dividing Date

The dividing date, selected by the client when creating the Accountant's Copy, determines who can do what. Following is an oversimplified overview:

- The accountant can work on existing transactions that are dated on or before the dividing date, and can create transactions on both sides of the dividing date.

- The client can work on transactions (editing existing transactions or creating new transactions) that are dated the day after the dividing date, or later.

Even though the client selects the dividing date, that date should be determined with input from the accountant. The dividing date should match the period for which you need to examine your client's records and make needed changes. The period could be a previous year, quarter, or month. Some clients need an income statement and/or balance sheet covering a specific period for a bank because of an existing or potential line of credit. Other clients may need an "accountant approved" report for the company's partners or a nonprofit association's board.

To give yourself a period in which to insert changes such as adjusting journal entries or reversing journal entries, have your client set the dividing date about two weeks after the end date you need.

Working in an Accountant's Copy

An Accountant's Copy can only be opened in the Premier Accountant Edition. The file has to be opened (as a transfer file) and then saved (as a working file). The working file is loaded in the QuickBooks window so you can begin using it. Use the following steps to accomplish these tasks:

1. Choose File | Accountant's Copy | Open & Convert Transfer File. QuickBooks displays a window that provides an overview of the way the Accountant's copy works.

2. Click Next to see an explanation of the permitted transactions. The message includes the statement that if you want to do more than the Accountant's Copy permits, you can convert the Transfer File to a full company file and do anything you wish (see Creating a Company File from a Transfer File, later in this section).

3. Click Next and navigate to the folder that contains the file you received from the client.

4. Double-click the file's listing. QuickBooks displays a message explaining that the file is about to be converted to an Accountant's Copy working file. Click OK.

5. The Save As Accountant's Copy dialog opens, displaying the same folder you selected to retrieve the file. By default QuickBooks retains the filename, changing the extension to .QBA. Unless you have some reason to change the folder, click Save.

6. QuickBooks converts the file, which takes a few minutes, and then opens the file.

7. If the file contains users and passwords, the Login dialog appears with the Admin user entered in the User Name field. You must enter the Admin password to continue.

8. QuickBooks displays another message reminding you that this is an Accountant's Copy. Click OK to begin working.

The title bar of the QuickBooks window displays the company file-name along with the parenthetical text (Acct Copy, Div Date MM/DD/YYYY). Once the file is converted to an Accountant's Copy working file, you can close and open it the same way you open any company file in QuickBooks. To open the file choose File | Open Or Restore Company, and click Next. Navigate to the folder that contains the file and open it.

Creating the Accountant's Copy Change File

While you're working in the Accountant's Copy, you can review the work you've done by choosing File | Accountant's Copy | View/Export Changes For Client.

When you've completed your work, and you're ready to send the file back to your client, open this window and click Create Change File to save a file to your local hard disk.

ProAdvisor NOTE: *If you have a subscription to the web based file exchange service you can click Send Changes To Client to upload the file to the Intuit servers. The client can then download the file free of charge.*

The Save Accountant Change File To dialog opens, and defaults to the folder that stored the working file (you can change the location). The file is renamed with the format <*CompanyFileName*> (Acct Changes). QBY. QuickBooks issues a success message when you save the file. Send the file to your client via e-mail (it's a small file), or on a CD.

Creating a Company File from a Transfer File

QuickBooks provides a command that lets you convert the transfer file you received from a client into a full-blown company file. The explanation for providing this function is "If the restrictions on using Accountant's Copy won't accommodate your situation, you can convert an Accountant's Copy to a regular company file".

This is *not* a good reason to convert the file. Your client sends you an Accountant's Copy because it's a way for you to work on the file while he or she continues to run the business with QuickBooks. If you convert the file, your file overwrites the client's file when you return it, and all the work the client did is lost.

If you want to do full-scope data entry on a client's file, either go on site, or ask the client for the full file and explain that the client must stop working until you complete your work and return the file.

A valid reason to convert an Accountant's Copy to a company file is to replace the client's file if the client doesn't back up regularly and suffers a computer crash while the Accountant's Copy exists. Give the converted file to the client, along with a lecture about daily backups.

Portable Files

A portable company file is a copy of a QuickBooks company file that has been condensed to save disk space. Portable files not only take up less room on a disk, they also save upload and download time if you send the file over the Internet. Generally, the process of creating and using portable company files proceeds as follows:

1. A company file is saved as a portable file (with the extension .QBM).
2. The portable file is sent to a recipient (e.g. client sends to accountant).
3. The portable file is opened in QuickBooks at the recipient's computer, and the process of opening the file expands it to its original size and adds the .QBW extension (making it a regular company file).
4. After the file has been changed, updated, fixed, etc., the process is repeated in the other direction.

The significant (and potentially dangerous) part of the process is the fact that the file is saved as a .QBW file, and therefore overwrites the existing <*CompanyFileName*>.QBW file in the same folder.

When an accountant receives the file from a client, that's usually not a problem, because even if the same company file exists in the accountant's folder, it's an older version of the file dating back to the last time the client sent the file.

On the client side, however, if an accountant returns the portable file, it overwrites the existing company file. If the client was working in the company file, when the returned portable file is opened, all the work that was done since the portable file was created is gone.

This differs from the use of an Accountant's Copy, which has two properties that the portable company file lacks:

- The changes made in an Accountant's Copy can be merged back into the company file from which it came.
- The Accountant's Copy has limited functions available.

Because the changes an accountant makes to an Accountant's Copy can be merged into the client's company file, the client continues to work in the company file while the accountant is working in the Accountant's Copy.

You must explain to your clients who send you a portable file that they cannot work in their company files until they've replaced the existing file with the portable file you return. You must also realize that data entry tasks are piling up at the client's office, so you must work on the file in a timely fashion and return the file to the client quickly.

Creating a Portable Company File

Take the following steps to create a portable company file:

1. Choose File | Create Copy.
2. In the dialog that opens, select Portable Company File and click Next.
3. Click Save to create the file. QuickBooks displays a message telling you it has to close the company file in order to save the portable company file. Click OK.

By default, QuickBooks names the file in the format <*CompanyFile-Name*> (Portable).QBM and saves it to the Desktop of the computer on which the user is working.

If you're taking the file to the recipient location (office, client site, or home), select a USB flash drive if you have one (if you don't, you should). If you're going to copy the file to a CD or upload it to the client via an FTP service, save it in a convenient folder.

It takes a while to create the file (the amount of time depends on the size of the file, but even a new, small file takes several minutes to convert to a portable company file). When the file is saved, QuickBooks issues a success message. Your company file is reopened, and you can go back to work.

Installing a Portable Company File

On the recipient side, installing a portable company file may mean overwriting the current company file with the portable file. If the company file is already open and you import the portable company file, it will automatically overwrite the existing file. However, if the company file is closed, QuickBooks will not allow you to overwrite the existing file with the portable file. It insists you rename the portable file before opening it.

To install a portable company file on your computer, follow these steps (provide these instructions to your client when you return the file):

1. Choose File | Open Or Restore Company.
2. In the dialog that appears, select Restore A Portable File and click Next.
3. In the Open Portable Company File dialog, navigate to the folder or drive that holds the portable file.
4. Double-click the file's listing to open the wizard-like window that explains your next step is to decide on the location for saving the file.
5. Click Next to open the Save Company File As dialog.
   - Accountants should save the file in a folder designed to hold files from clients.
   - Clients should select the folder in which their company file resides.

For clients, since the company file already exists, and since portable files are restored with a .QBW extension, QuickBooks automatically overwrites the company file if the company file is open during this process. If, however, you started with a different company file, or no company file open, QuickBooks will not allow you to overwrite the existing file. In that case you must rename the file (e.g. <*company file name*>NEW.QBW). If you try to restore it with the same name as the original file QuickBooks issues a warning that you are about to overwrite an existing file. When you click Yes to confirm the replacement QuickBooks issues another warning, telling you that the file is "read-only" and that you must rename it before restoring.

After the portable company file is uncompressed and saved, it's loaded in the software window, ready to be used.

Client Data Review

Client Data Review (CDR) is a one-stop location for troubleshooting problems and potential problems in a company file. Within the Client Data Review feature you'll find tools and reports that help you examine probable trouble spots in QuickBooks data files.

The Client Data Review command is only available under the following circumstances:

- You are using Premier Accountant Edition. (The Client Data Review command is on the Accountant menu).

- You are using any other Premier edition of QuickBooks, or QuickBooks Pro, and you are logged in as an External Accountant. (The Client Data Review command is on the Company menu.)

ProAdvisor NOTE: *Some CDR tools that are available in Premier Accountant Edition are not available in other editions, or when you're working with an Accountant's Copy. Those exceptions are noted in the discussions that follow.*

External Accountant

An External Accountant is a specific type of QuickBooks user who has the same rights as the QuickBooks Admin with the following exceptions:

- External Accountant cannot create, edit, or delete users.
- External Accountant cannot view customer credit card numbers if the QuickBooks Customer Credit Card Protection feature is enabled.

When you log in to the company file as a user designated as an External Accountant, the Client Data Review feature becomes available on the Company menu. If you, or a bookkeeper on your staff, go to client sites to perform work, you should have your clients create an External Accountant user (or log in as the Admin and create this user yourself).

ProAdvisor TIP: *Even if you're working on a client's file in Premier Accountant Edition where the CDR is available for the user named Admin, it's a good idea to log in as an External Accountant. The Audit Trail report distinguishes changes made by the External Accountant from those made by the Admin.*

Creating an External Accountant

To create a user who is an External Accountant, you must be logged into QuickBooks as the Admin (only the QuickBooks Admin can create users). Then take the following steps:

1. Choose Company | Set Up Users And Passwords | Set Up Users.
2. In the User List dialog, select Add User.
3. Enter the User Name and Password and click Next.
4. Select External Accountant and click Next.
5. QuickBooks asks you to confirm this action – click Yes.
6. Click Finish to create the External Accountant user.

Close the company file and re-open it, logging in with the User Name and Password that belongs to the external accountant.

Converting an Existing User to an External Accountant

Many companies have already set up a user name for the accountant. Even if the accountant's login provides full permissions, the Client Data

Review tool isn't available on the Company menu unless an External Accountant user is logged in (except in Premier Accountant Edition). You can edit the accountant's user account to convert it to an External Accountant.

Select the accountant's user account and click Edit User. Don't change the user name and password data. Click Next, and in the following window, select External Accountant and follow the prompts to save this user name as an External Accountant.

Client Data Review Tools

In the Client Data Review (CDR) center (see Figure 9-4), listings that display the CDR tool icon are tools that perform functions available only in the CDR utility. Listings that don't display the CDR icon provide convenient access to existing QuickBooks functions and reports (eliminating the need to access those functions from the menu bar). As mentioned earlier, some tools are only available in the Premier Accountant Edition.

Figure 9-4: The CDR center provides good troubleshooting tools.

Account Balances Tools

The Account Balances section of the CDR has two tools: Troubleshoot Prior Account Balances, and Reclassify Transactions.

ProAdvisor NOTE: *The Account Balances section also has a link that opens the Working Trial Balance window (discussed earlier in this chapter), where you can view beginning balances, changes by transactions, changes by adjustments, and ending balances for all accounts. If you open the Working Trial Balance window from the CDR window, the date range matches the review dates you selected in the CDR.*

Troubleshoot Prior Account Balances

Use this tool to find changes in transactions that caused differences between an account balance at the end of the prior period and the original balance for that period. When a problem is displayed, you can make adjustments to resolve the problem.

The first time you use the Troubleshoot Prior Account Balances tool, the file has no ending balances from a prior period stored in the CDR file. Therefore you have no opening balances in the left pane (labeled Balances In Accountant's Records). The balances in the right pane (labeled Balances In Client's File) are retrieved from records in the company file.

ProAdvisor NOTE: *If you used this tool previously, but the From date of the current review period is not the day after the To date of the last review you performed, the left pane doesn't load the last balances you saved.*

You have two ways to get the Balances In Accountant's Records data into the window:

- Fill in the previous period data manually, using data you have from other sources, such as a report you prepared and saved (e.g. Balance Sheet, Profit & Loss

Statement, etc.) or other records you saved from the last tax return.

- Click Copy Balances to copy the contents of the right pane into the left pane, and then change only those balances that don't match your own records. (Usually, most or all of the balances remain the same. Differences indicate that the client made changes to the existing balances you recorded by creating, changing, or removing transactions within the "closed" date range.)

The next time you use this tool for this client file, the balances you save are loaded automatically in the left pane. If there aren't any differences between your records and the data taken from the client's file, your work is done. When you close the window your data is saved for the next time you work in the client's file.

Resolving Differences

If there's a difference between the balances, the amount of the difference is displayed in the Difference columns. You have several ways to explore the cause, and then take the appropriate action to resolve the problem.

Audit the Transaction(s) That Caused the Difference

Double-click the amount in the Difference column (it's displayed in blue) to see if there's an Audit Trail report for the transaction in question. (Clicking the button at the top of the window that's labeled View Changed Transactions opens the same report.)

If the report displays data, you may find that a transaction was entered on a date after the original "closed" balance was established, but the transaction itself carried an earlier date—a date within the period in question. Either open the transaction and change the date, or create a journal entry to remove the amount from the "closed" period and then enter a reversing JE for the first day of the "new" period.

The audit trail may show you a transaction from the "closed" period that was changed, voided, or deleted. More often than not, this is a client mistake, and after you question the client about the reason, it's usually easy to determine that the transaction should be changed back to its original state.

You can also select the cell displaying the difference and click the button labeled "View Suggested Adjustments". QuickBooks opens a JE window that contains an adjustment to fix the problem. If this is the way you want to adjust the difference, save the journal entry.

Find List Changes that Caused the Difference

Sometimes the client makes configuration changes to list items that affect prior records. For instance, the client may change the income account link, or the expense account link (for two-sided items) for an item. QuickBooks asks if historical transactions should be changed, and if the client responded Yes, that affects postings in the "closed" period (although you should see an equal and opposite change in the original account).

You can confirm whether this was the cause of the differences by selecting the account in the window, and then clicking the button labeled View List Changes. If the difference isn't due to a list change, a message displays to tell you that; otherwise a window opens to display the changes made to the list that affected the account totals.

If the changes are due to a list change, you can also select the cell displaying the difference and click the button labeled "View Suggested Adjustments". QuickBooks opens a JE window that contains an adjustment to fix the problem. If this is the way you want to adjust the difference, save the journal entry.

Reclassify Transactions

Does this sound familiar? You learned from a client (or from your bookkeeper who visited the client on-site) that a slew of bills or direct checks to a vendor were posted to the wrong account. Sometimes, some checks were posted correctly but others were not.

The question you heard is, "Is there a way to change all the wrong postings without opening all 55 transactions, one at a time, and changing the account?"

Your answer was, "No sorry, there's no way to do this except one transaction at a time." Now you can say, "Of course, we can do this for you."

The same problem exists if some of the transactions were posted to the wrong class, and you can also fix that in one fell swoop.

Reclassify to Fix Vendor Transactions

Reclassify Transactions is only available if you're working in the Premier Accountant Edition. If you're working as an External Accountant in another edition of QuickBooks, selecting this tool results in an error message.

Open the Reclassify Transactions window and select the Vendor from the Name field to view the transactions and postings (see Figure 9-5).

Figure 9-5: This vendor is an outside contractor and all postings should have been to the Subcontractors account to make sure Form 1099 is accurate.

Select the transactions that need to be changed, select the Account To check box, and then select the right account. Click Reclassify to change all the transactions at once.

> **ProAdvisor CAUTION**: *You cannot use the Reclassify function in batch mode for any transaction that uses an item, nor for any transaction that posts to A/P or A/R. Instead, you have to make the changes one transaction at a time.*

If all the transactions you're changing also need to have the class reclassified to the same class, select the check box labeled Class To and then select the right class. Otherwise, reclassify the classes in a separate step.

In the transaction shown in Figure 9-5, the Show Transactions field shows the selection Non-Item-Based (Reclassify TO Account). The drop-down list for this field also includes the selections Item-Based (Reclassify Class Only), and All (Reclassify TO Account Only). If you select either of these, the select check box is grayed out for transactions that can't be reclassified automatically. However, you can double-click any listing to open the original transaction window and change the item or the class (of course this is not batch mode, it's the old one-at-a-time function).

In addition, you can select the option labeled Include Journal Entries if your clients (or you) ever adjust A/P or A/R via JEs instead of using a transaction window (which is not a good idea).

Reclassify Transactions is not limited to vendors; you can perform the same batch changes for payments made to names in the Other Names list.

The drop-down list in the Name field at the top of the window also includes customers and jobs, but you should never see transactions that can be reclassified if you select a customer or a job, because customer transactions always include an item. If you do see a transaction that can be reclassified, there's a problem; see the next section on using this tool to fix the error.

Reclassify to Fix Customer Transactions

One of the most frustrating exercises is trying to figure out the sales linked to specific customers when some sales don't appear in the Customer Center. When that happens, you'll also find that the totals in sales reports don't equal the totals for income accounts for the same period. You may also find that item reports (especially inventory items) and sales tax reports are erroneous.

These problems occur when users enter customer sales in the Make Deposits window or directly into the bank register instead of using a Sales Receipt transaction. When you use either of those shortcut methods, the normal links required for tracking sales properly are missing. Items aren't entered, inventory items aren't decremented, COGS isn't posted, item reports are wrong, sales tax isn't tracked, and the transaction never appears in the customer's record in the Customer Center.

Luckily, the Reclassify Transactions tool displays customer sales transactions that were entered improperly. Figure 9-6 shows the Reclassify Transaction window with the Show Transactions option set to "Non-Item-Based (Can Be Reclassified)". Because you can't reclassify transactions with items, and all customer transactions should have items, any customer transactions that appear were entered improperly (without items) or they wouldn't be displayed.

Figure 9-6: No customer transactions should appear in this window.

Notice that the transaction type is DEP, which says that the transaction was entered in the Make Deposits window or directly into the bank account register. You can't edit or fix these transactions; instead you must remove them and replace them with the proper transaction, using the following steps:

1. Note the customer, date, amount, and other transaction information.
2. Determine the appropriate item (often, your client can provide this information).
3. Open the bank register to see if the transaction is reconciled.
4. Double-click the entry to open it.
5. Choose Edit | Delete from the QuickBooks menu bar.
6. Open a Sales Receipt transaction window and enter the transaction.
7. If you use Undeposited Funds, move the funds into the bank account.
8. If the deleted transaction had been reconciled, open the bank register and mark the transaction as reconciled.

Review List Changes

This section of the CDR has tools to display list elements that were added, modified, deleted, or merged by your client since the last CDR review. You can see both the previous and current data for any list elements that were changed. The following lists are included in the tool:

- Chart of Accounts
- Items
- Fixed Asset Items
- Payroll Items.

The Review List Changes section also has links you can use to open the list window for any of these lists, as well as links to the Customer Center, the Vendor Center, and the Change Name Types dialog. You can use these links to view configuration and transaction details.

Accounts Receivable Tools

This section of the CDR offers three tools: Fix Unapplied Customer Payments And Credits, Clear Up Undeposited Funds Account, and Write

332 Running QuickBooks 2014 Premier Editions

Off Invoices. The Accounts Receivable section of the CDR also provides a link to the A/R Aging Summary Report.

Fix Unapplied Customer Payments And Credits

This tool displays credits that were recorded but not applied to open invoices.

Select each customer in the left pane to display credits and invoices. Select a credit and choose an invoice (or multiple invoices) to use for that credit. Click Apply to apply a credit to an invoice. (If you change your mind, there's an Unapply button.) Click Save & Close when you're done.

Applying credits to invoices doesn't change the A/R balances in your client's company file. Applying credits merely makes detailed reports on A/R activity smaller. We have received complaints from clients telling us that a customer balance is zero, but the customer appears on the A/R aging reports, and a detail report on the customer's aging is filled with transactions – these conditions result when credits aren't applied to invoices.

Be careful about performing this process; it's not a good idea to do this without discussing these credits with your client. Remember that when your client created the credit, QuickBooks asked what to do with the credit, offering the following choices:

- Retain As An Available Credit (which is the choice the user made or these credits wouldn't appear in this window).
- Give A Refund
- Apply To An Invoice

If your client didn't understand the choices, and clicked OK with the Retain As An Available Credit option selected (it's the default option), you should explain the meanings of those choices and ask if it's OK to apply the credits to existing invoices.

Many times, the client leaves the credit open (a floating credit) because of some arrangement with the customer. Perhaps the customer sends payments that reflect credits taken, with specific instructions about the invoice to which the credit is applied. In that case, if you apply credits without any knowledge of the arrangements between your clients and their customers, you're creating customer invoice balances that don't match the records your client's customer is keeping.

ProAdvisor TIP: *Sometimes floating credits exist because of a barter arrangement – the customer is also a vendor, and at various intervals credits are applied to complete the barter trade-offs.*

Usually, most unapplied credits result from one of the following actions:

- A floating credit was never applied to an invoice with an open balance. (This often results in queries from your client asking, "Why is the customer balance zero when there are transactions for this customer in the A/R Aging reports?")

- A Journal Entry exists that credits Accounts Receivable and has a customer name attached. This type of credit is almost always "safe" to apply to any invoice, because it's almost always the case that a Credit transaction should have been entered instead of using a JE.

Click the Vendors tab in the left pane to view vendor payments and vendor bills. The process is the same for vendors as for customers. If you have multiple A/P accounts (or A/R accounts for customers) be sure to select the correct one from the drop-down list.

Clear Up Undeposited Funds Account

This tool lets you see cash receipts currently waiting in the Undeposited Funds account (the list on the right) that were also deposited directly into a bank account (the list on the left).

Match the undeposited amount against the deposited amount and click Apply, then click Save. QuickBooks reverses the entry that was deposited directly into the bank, and moves the Undeposited Funds entry into the bank.

Write Off Invoices

This tool lets you write off selected A/R balances in batch mode. It is only available if you're working in the Premier Accountant Edition.

The functions available in this tool make it much faster and easier than creating an individual credit and applying it to the appropriate invoice one write-off at a time. (The tool displays any existing unapplied credits, and you should apply those credits to existing open invoices before writing off balances.)

Select the invoices to write off, select the date for the write-off, and then select the write-off item. (If you don't have a write-off item, choose <Add New> at the top of the drop-down list and create the item you need.)

Click Preview & Write Off to display a preview report of the affected invoices. If anything seems amiss click Cancel and return to the Write-off tool. When the preview is correct, click Write Off to create the transactions.

The write-off transaction is a credit memo which appears in the customer's record in the Customer Center. When you open the invoice you'll see it's marked Paid, and the Memo section has the text "Written off by <user name> (Admin/External Accountant) on MM/DD/YYYY".

Accounts Payable Tools

The only tool in the Accounts Payable section of the CDR is Fix Unapplied Vendor Payments And Credits. This is the flip side of the Fix Unapplied Customer Payments And Credits tool. Just select the appropriate tab.

The Accounts Payable section also provides links to the 1099 account mapping configuration options in the Preferences dialog, and the Unpaid Bills report.

The Fix Unapplied Vendor Payments And Credits tool lets you match unapplied vendor credits to open vendor bills. As stated earlier in this section, when discussing using the CDR tool to apply customer credits to invoices, tread carefully – don't just dive in and apply the credits. Your client may have some arrangement with vendors that caused these credits to be held for some future transactions.

Sales Tax Tool

This section of the CDR offers a single tool: Fix Incorrectly Recorded Sales Tax. The tool locates payments to sales tax vendors that were created as direct disbursements or bill payments instead of payments created through the Pay Sales Tax Liability function.

Select the payments that were created improperly and click Void & Replace. QuickBooks replaces the voided transactions with TAXPMT transactions with the same date, check number, and amount. The reconciliation status of the improperly prepared payment is also retained.

If you're logged into a non-Premier Accountant edition as an External Accountant user, the tool name changes to Find Incorrectly Paid Sales Tax. Clicking this link displays the problem transactions in a report so you can change them manually.

Inventory Tools

Inventory tracking is probably the most vulnerable part of QuickBooks, because many users don't understand the way financial data is posted for inventory. User errors abound.

The CDR supports two useful tools (covered in the next sections) to help you find and correct common problems with inventory tracking, but these tools are only available if you're working in the Premier Accountant Edition. (The links to reports in the Inventory section of the CDR are available in all editions, when the logged in user is an External Accountant user.)

Compare Balance Sheet and Inventory Valuation

Use this tool to see whether the balance of the inventory asset account matches the balance of the Inventory Valuation Summary report for the same date (it should). The tool checks those balances as of the last day of the review, and displays the results.

If the balances don't match, a yellow warning triangle appears and the difference between the accounts is displayed. Some of the most common reasons for discrepancies between these balances include incorrect setup of items, transactions for inventory items being posted to non-inventory accounts, and journal entries that affect the inventory asset account. The tool also provides links to reports that can help you find the cause of the difference.

As an example, a discrepancy in a client file and was resolved by selecting the link to the report that shows non-inventory transactions using an inventory asset account. The report showed a JE that posted a debit to the Inventory Asset account and a credit to the Work In Process asset account. This is not the proper method for moving WIP totals into inventory; and it's a frequent user mistake. Instead, the client should use the Adjust Quantity/Value On Hand transaction, using the WIP asset as the offset account. Voiding the JE and adjusting inventory properly resolved the issue.

Troubleshoot Inventory

Selecting this tool opens a window that displays a great deal of information about the inventory items (including assemblies) in the company file. If any item has a problem (usually the result of it being sold into negative quantity at some point), a yellow warning triangle appears in the Status column.

Usually, when an item is sold into negative quantity, the item was physically available, but no adjustment was made before selling the item. This wreaks havoc with the average cost used for postings when the item is sold. You can resolve the problem by creating an adjustment that predates the sale that brought the item into negative quantity (or by changing the date of an adjustment that was entered after the sale so the date is prior to the date of the sale).

You can change the criteria for displaying the items in the top of the window, which enables you to perform a more comprehensive analysis of the client's inventory—you're not limited to finding problems.

For example, if the client uses automatic markups, you can see the markup percentage for every item; perhaps you want to advise the client to raise or lower some markups (depending on the current state of business). You can use the links in the window, or double-click an item, to change whatever needs to be changed.

Payroll Tool

In the Payroll section of the CDR, the only tool is Find Incorrectly Paid Payroll Liabilities. Similar to the sales tax liability payments problems cited in the earlier section, this tool locates payments to vendors that were created as direct disbursements instead of through the Pay Scheduled Liabilities function. This means that payroll liabilities (and the attendant reports such as Form 941) have incorrect amounts.

QuickBooks doesn't fix these transactions; it finds them so you can fix them. Use the Pay Liabilities transaction window to create the check (which has a transaction type LIAB CHK) and delete the incorrect payment check (which has a transaction type CHK). If the original (wrong) check cleared, mark the new check as cleared.

The Payroll section also provides links to helpful QuickBooks tools: Review Payroll Liabilities, Review Employee Default Settings, and Enter After-The-Fact Payroll.

ProAdvisor NOTE: *The Bank Reconciliation, and Miscellaneous sections of the CDR Center do not have CDR tools. They have links to the QuickBooks functions and reports needed to resolve questions and troubleshoot problems.*

Working in the CDR Center

In addition to the tools and functions available with a click of the mouse, the CDR center has features that help you work efficiently.

Tracking CDR Progress

Each task (CDR tool or link to QuickBooks functions/reports) has a status field that the accountant can use to track the progress of a review. A drop-down list offers several selections: Not Started (the default selection), In Progress, Completed, and Not Applicable. If you track your progress, it's easier to return to pick up where you left off the next time you open the CDR.

Creating CDR Task Notes

As you perform tasks, the ability to create notes on each task provides "memory joggers" for the session. To create a task note, click the Task Notes icon (a clipboard) to the right of the task listing. In the Task Notes entry screen, enter the note and click Save.

A Task Notes icon is displayed next to each CDR tool/function. If you've entered notes, the icon has lines in the clipboard (imitating text), instead of a blank clipboard. Hovering the mouse pointer over the icon displays the contents, or you can click the icon to open the text window.

Creating Review Notes

Review notes are designed to be more generic than task notes, and they're always visible in the upper right side of the CDR center. To create or edit review notes, click the Edit (pencil nub) icon above the Review Notes box at the top of the CDR.

Review Notes can be saved for future reviews, so the next time you review the file the Review Notes from the last review are available.

Closing the CDR Center

You can close the CDR center at any time, and all the work is saved automatically (including the current status of each task, and the task notes). No "Save" button exists on the CDR center; the choices are Close and Mark Review Complete (see "Completing the Review" in the next section).

Printing the Review

You can print the review, or create a PDF file of the printout at any time. The printed report displays the state of the review; actually, it's a printout of the CDR center with the status selections. In addition, the printout includes task notes and review notes. To create a PDF copy, click the Save As PDF button and choose a filename and location.

Customizing the CDR Center

Not all clients have the same system setup, so you can customize the CDR center to eliminate unneeded tasks by clicking the gear icon to the right of the Cleanup Tasks tool. Deselect tasks you don't need, so that working in the CDR center is more efficient.

> **ProAdvisor NOTE**: *CDR detects basic system configurations automatically. For example, if Sales Tax is not enabled, tasks related to Sales Tax won't appear in the CDR center.*

Completing the Review

When all the work you want to accomplish is complete, clicking the button labeled Mark Review Complete begins the process of wrapping up the review. QuickBooks asks for confirmation that the review be marked complete, and offers the option of setting a closing date and password for the company file in addition to completing the review.

> **ProAdvisor NOTE**: *The next time you use the Client Data Review command in this company file, QuickBooks offers the option to re-open the completed review, or start a new review.*

Fixed Asset Manager

All versions of QuickBooks have a Fixed Asset Item List, which you can use to store information about fixed assets. This list is meant to track data about the assets you depreciate. Unless it's opened in QuickBooks Premier Accountant Edition, this is merely a list, which neither provides any method for calculating depreciation, nor the ability to link to any depreciation software. It's designed only to keep a list of assets.

QuickBooks Premier Accountant has a nifty tool, Fixed Asset Manager, that can synchronize data with the Fixed Asset Item List from any edition.

Fixed Asset Manager doesn't require the presence of the Fixed Asset Item List, so if your client hasn't used the list, you can still manage fixed asset depreciation.

Fixed Asset Manager calculates depreciation for fixed assets, so you can create journal entries using the calculated amounts. It works with the currently open QuickBooks company data file (usually a client's company file).

ProAdvisor TIP: Fixed Asset Manager integrates with Intuit's ProSeries Tax products, so you can automatically pass asset data from QuickBooks to ProSeries Tax.

In the following sections, we'll provide an overview of the Premier Accountant Edition Fixed Asset Manager. The program is complex and powerful, and it's beyond the scope of this book to go over all its functions. You can use the Help files in the Fixed Asset Manager to learn the step-by-step procedures for all the functions.

ProAdvisor NOTE: You can also use Fixed Asset Manager with an Accountant's Copy provided by your QuickBooks client, but you might lose some of the functionality of Fixed Asset Manager. Details are available in the Help files.

Creating a Fixed Asset Manager Client File

Fixed Asset Manager must know the type of tax form a business files. Before you open Fixed Asset Manager, make sure the right tax form is configured for the company file that's open. In fact, make sure the tax form information isn't blank, which is often the case. To see the tax form information, in the company file choose Company | My Company. To change the tax form click the Edit icon (pencil nub) and then the Report Information link on the left.

With the QuickBooks company file (the client file) open, choose Accountant | Manage Fixed Assets. When the Fixed Asset Manager software opens for the first time, it looks for an existing Fixed Asset Manager client data file for the currently open company. If no previous client data file exists you must create one.

In the opening software window, select the option Create A New Fixed Asset Manager Client, and click OK. The Fixed Asset Manager New

Client wizard launches. As with all wizards, you must click Next to go through all the windows.

Configuring Company Information

The wizard takes information from the QuickBooks file that's open, displays the company information, and then queries you about the following data:

- Current fiscal year
- Prior short years
- For corporations, qualification for the "small corporation" exemption from AMT
- Depreciation bases
- Default depreciation method for each selected basis

The wizard also asks how you want to synchronize fixed asset data between the company file and the Fixed Asset Manager client file it's creating. The first question asks how you want to bring data from Quick-Books into Fixed Asset Manager. The following window asks how you want to move data from Fixed Asset Manager into QuickBooks. What all of this is doing is setting up synchronization options between the company file and Fixed Asset Manager. In the future, the files will synchronize so you stay on top of the client's fixed asset purchases and depreciation.

The last wizard window is a summary of the QuickBooks company information. If any information is incorrect, use the Back button to return to the appropriate wizard window and make changes. When all the information is correct, click Finish.

Importing the Fixed Assets

Fixed Asset Manager finds the Fixed Asset Item List, and displays a log report. Fixed Asset Manager identifies the assets using the text in the Purchase Description field of the QuickBooks Fixed Asset Item List—not the name assigned to the asset.

Click OK to close the log report and open the Fixed Asset Manager software window. A robust set of functions is available on the menu system, and in the various tabs.

> **ProAdvisor NOTE**: *If an asset isn't transferred to Fixed Asset Manager, the log report indicates that fact. Usually, the reason is a date of purchase that is later than the end date of the fiscal year you indicated in the wizard. For example, if you're creating a file in 2015 for 2014 depreciation, assets purchased in 2015 are not transferred.*

Entering Fixed Assets Manually

If the client's company file has no entries in the Fixed Asset Item List, but has maintained information about the purchase of fixed assets, you can enter the data manually. Click the Add icon on the toolbar, and enter the appropriate data by scrolling through both sections of the window.

Importing Data from Other Software

If asset and depreciation records are tracked in another software application, you can import the data to Fixed Asset Manager. In the Fixed Asset Manager window, choose File | Import. The only import file format on the submenu is Comma Separated Value (CSV) file.

If the other program can't export data to a CSV file, but can save data in a file format that is readable by Microsoft Excel, open the file in Excel, and then save the file in CSV format.

> **ProAdvisor NOTE**: *You must map the fields in the import file to the fields in Fixed Asset Manager. Fixed Asset Manager provides help for this task during the import.*

If you've been managing fixed assets for the client in ProSeries tax software, you can import data directly from that software into Fixed Asset Manager. If ProSeries is available (installed on the computer), choose File | Import | ProSeries Tax from the QuickBooks Fixed Asset Manager menu bar.

Viewing and Editing Assets

As mentioned earlier in this section, we're not going over all the features and functions of Fixed Asset Manager (because it would fill a separate book), but we'll present a few guidelines that should help you get started.

Schedule Tab

In the Schedule tab, Fixed Asset Manager identifies the assets using the text in the Purchase Description field of the QuickBooks Fixed Asset Item List—not the text in the Name field. In fact, Fixed Asset Manager doesn't even import the name field from the QuickBooks Fixed Asset Item List.

Fixed Asset Manager assigns a number to each asset, and that number becomes the asset's name (think of it as a code) in the Fixed Asset Manager client file. If the assets were obtained automatically from a QuickBooks Fixed Asset Item List, the numbers represent the order of assets in that list.

The asset that's currently selected in the Schedule tab is the asset used when you visit any of the other tabs at the top of the software window.

Asset Tab

Use the Asset tab to enter information about tax forms, posting accounts, and other data about the selected asset.

The upper section of the tab is the place to enter general information for the selected asset, including any classification fields. The bottom section of the Asset tab is the Basis Detail section. Enter the cost, date acquired, tax system, depreciation basis, recovery period, and other information needed to calculate the asset's depreciation. You can also configure Section 179 deductions here, if appropriate for this asset.

Disposal Tab

Use the Disposal tab to dispose of assets. Fixed Asset Manager displays the cost basis, and any Section 179 deductions. Enter the sales price, the expense of sale, and any other relevant information about the disposal.

For ProSeries client file exports, select a property type from the drop-down list to determine where the disposal information will appear on Form 4797, Sales of Business Property.

Projection Tab

Use the Projection tab to determine the best depreciation method for the selected asset by reviewing its projected depreciation. Use the Bases tabs at the bottom of the window to see the projections.

ProAdvisor TIP: *You can change information in the Asset tab to alter the projections available in the Projection tab.*

The other tabs on the Fixed Asset Manager window are informational. The Notes tab is a blank window where you can write notes and reminders. The Calendar tab displays information about an asset on the selected date (select date acquired, date of disposal, or both).

Configuring Depreciation

Use the Tools menu to set up depreciation, using the following tools:

- Prepare For Next Year. This process removes disposed assets from the asset list, adds the current year depreciation to each asset's record, updates unrecovered basis fields for each asset, and calculates depreciation for next year. Be sure to print reports on the current status of each asset before using this tool.

- Recalculate All Assets. This process recalculates the current depreciation for each asset. Prior depreciation is calculated and posted according to the rules you configure in the dialog.

- 179/40% Test. This process applies the Section 179/40% test to the appropriate assets. You can select the convention you want to use for the test.

Using the Section 179/40% test

To determine whether the Section 179 deductions claimed for the current year are within allowed limits, or to calculate the percentage of assets acquired in the last three months of the year, use the Section 179/40% test.

Perform these diagnostics after you enter client asset information and before you print reports or link the file to the client's tax return. To perform these tests, choose Tools | 179/40% Test from the Fixed Asset Manager menu bar. Review the Section 179 test, then click the 40% test tab to review mid-quarter totals.

Reviewing Section 179 limitations

The Section 179 test determines the total cost of all eligible Section 179 property, the total Section 179 expense deduction made, and how much of the deduction exceeds federal limits for the active year

Reviewing the Mid-Quarter 40% test

Fixed Asset Manager totals the cost of all assets purchased in the active year and all assets purchased in the last quarter of the active year. If the percentage of assets purchased in the last quarter is greater than 40%, you can convert these assets to the mid-quarter convention.

Using the Client Totals Summary

Use the Client Totals Summary to review the accumulated cost and depreciation before and after current-year calculations for each basis supported in a client file. To see the Client Totals Summary, choose View | Client Totals.

Calculating Depreciation

When the selected asset is properly configured, go to the Asset tab and choose Asset | Calculate Asset. If the command is grayed out, Fixed Asset Manager does not have all the information it needs to perform the calculation. Check all the fields to make sure you've entered the required information about this asset.

ProAdvisor TIP: *You can configure Fixed Asset Manager to automatically calculate assets after making modifications. To select this setting, choose Tools | Program Options. Select the Automatically Calculate Assets When Modified option, and click OK to save the change.*

Posting a Journal Entry to QuickBooks

Fixed Asset Manager automates the process of creating a journal entry for depreciation expense and/or accumulated depreciation. Choose QuickBooks | Post Journal Entry To QuickBooks, and then enter the appropriate information.

Creating Reports

Fixed Asset Manager provides a variety of report options, including pre-configured report templates. Choose Reports | Display Report to view the available reports.

To organize a report list, choose Reports | Report List Organizer. Select the reports you want to associate with this client file (you're creating a custom report list). You can also opt to print reports in batches.

Select a report list from the drop-down list (or create a new report list by clicking New). Then select and deselect the reports you want to include.

Exporting Depreciation Data

Fixed Asset Manager has built in tools for exporting depreciation data, and then importing the data to another software application. The following file formats are supported:

- ProSeries
- Microsoft Excel
- Microsoft Word

- ASCII (text) file
- CSV file
- Tax Worksheets

Creating Tax Worksheets

Fixed Asset Manager automatically creates tax worksheets, using the information in the client file. Choose Reports | Display Tax Worksheet to open the Print Preview dialog. Select the worksheets you want, and click OK to preview them, and then print them. The following tax worksheets are available:

- Form 4562 Part I — Section 179 Summary Copy
- Form 4562 Part II & III— Lines 15, 16 and 17
- Form 4562 Part III — Lines 19 and 20
- Form 4562 Part IV — Summary
- Form 4562 Part V — Listed Property
- Form 4562 Part VI — Amortization
- Form 4626— Depreciation Adjustments and Tax Preferences
- Form 4626— ACE Worksheet
- Form 4626— Gain/Loss Adjustments
- Form 4797 Part I — Property Held More Than One Year
- Form 4797 Part II — Ordinary Gains and Losses
- Form 4797 Part III — Gains from Disposition of Depreciable Property

Fixed Asset Manager Synchronization

When you open and close Fixed Asset Manager, data is synchronized between the software and the QuickBooks company file (and a log is displayed). You can also manually update the asset information between QuickBooks and Fixed Asset Manager. The commands and the default settings for automatic synchronization are on the menu named QuickBooks.

Before you synchronize, be sure to print reports about the asset list from both software applications, so you have a way to track changes.

Remember, if you dispose of an asset in Fixed Asset Manager, the synchronization process removes the asset from the QuickBooks Fixed Asset Item List.

File Manager

The QuickBooks File Manager is a separate program that lets you organize and access your clients' company files. You can launch it within QuickBooks by choosing Accountant | QuickBooks File Manager, but QuickBooks doesn't have to be open to use this program. You can also open it directly from the Programs menu within the QuickBooks program folder, or use the desktop icon that was installed when you installed the Premier Accountant Edition.

This is a powerful program that is capable of performing many tasks that will help you keep track of client files. In this section we'll provide an overview of both the functions and features included in File Manager.

When you first open File Manager you see an informational window. Click Launch QuickBooks File Manager to begin using the program. (You can select the option labeled Do Not Show This Message Again to stop the informational window from appearing in the future.)

Organize Client Files

The File Manager offers three options for organizing and grouping client files to match your needs (see Figure 9-7).

You can use the Add/Update Clients Wizard, drag and drop files and folders from Windows Explorer, or enter them one at a time using the Add Client Dialog.

- Add/Update Clients Wizard. This wizard offers two choices when selected. You can have the wizard

search for files using QuickBooks company file names.
The second choice uses folder names to add clients.
Either way you have to click the Browse button in the
next wizard window and tell the File Manager where
you want to search.

• Drag & Drop From Windows Explorer. If you click this
option, Windows Explorer launches and you are left
on your own to navigate to the folders containing the
files you want to add. When you find them, just drag
them from Windows Explorer into the QuickBooks
File Manager.

• Add Client dialog. Click this option to open the Add
Client dialog, which offers a text field in which to
enter the client's name, and a browse button to search
for client files.

Figure 9-7: Tell File Manager how to search for QuickBooks data
files.

ProAdvisor NOTE: *You can access these options any time by
selecting Clients | Add Clients Via from the icon bar.*

Using the file names as client names, File Manager builds a Clients list (see Figure 9-8). Select a client name in the left pane to display information about the data files for that client.

Figure 9-8: Details about the files for each client are displayed.

ProAdvisor TIP: *You can use the Merge feature in File Manager to merge multiple clients into a single client listing. Select the client listings in the left pane, right-click, and then choose Merge Selected Clients from the shortcut menu that appears.*

Create Client Groups

It's usually efficient to group your clients by a scheme designed to make it easier to work on their files. File Manager pre-populates the program with groups for each version (year) of QuickBooks you support and moves the appropriate data files into each group. However, if that's not the way you want to work, you can create your own groups. To accomplish this, click the Groups icon on the File Manager icon bar and choose Add/Edit Groups.

In the Add & Edit Custom Client Groups dialog, name the group and move the appropriate data files into the group by selecting the client name and clicking the right-pointing arrow. For example, Figure 9-9 represents the creation of a group named with the initials of one accountant in the firm. That accountant's clients will populate this group.

Figure 9-9: This accounting firm creates a group for each accountant.

Store Passwords

Client files are usually password-protected (if they're not, they should be). Every time you open a client file you have to know the password for the Admin user (or for another user with administrative rights). Keeping track of passwords on a per-file basis is a major problem; imagine having that many sticky notes affixed to your monitor (unfortunately, that's one of the most popular ways to store client login information).

File Manager offers a password vault where you can store the password for each client file. As you open each data file, the password is automatically passed to the file so you don't have to enter any login text.

To begin, click the Password Vault icon and select Open Password Vault. Then create a login name and password for the vault, as seen in Figure 9-10. The password must be a "strong password", which means it has to contain complex characters (explained on the dialog). Next, select two challenge questions and supply their answers. This ensures that in the event you forget the master password to the Password Vault, you'll be able to retrieve it by providing the correct answers to the challenge questions.

Figure 9-10: Set up your password vault user name and login.

Now you can enter the login name and password for each client file, as seen in Figure 9-11. If you have multiple files for a single client and the password is different for each file, click the Client Login Options button and select the option to provide unique user names and passwords for each data file and then enter the login and password for each file.

Figure 9-11: Store login names and passwords in a vault instead of entering them every time you open a client file.

Open Client Files in the Correct Version

Accountants have to maintain several versions of QuickBooks because some clients don't upgrade their software version every year (and some clients wait several years to upgrade).

File Manager automates the process of opening a client file by launching the correct version of QuickBooks when you select the file's listing from within File Manager.

Upgrade Client Files in Batches

If you do the bookkeeping for your clients (and they don't run QuickBooks), it's easy to upgrade all your client files to the latest version. Without File Manager you'd have to open each file from within QuickBooks and go through the steps required for upgrades; that means waiting to make a backup and then selecting a name and location for the upgraded file. File Manager automates this process and does every step invisibly in the background.

To use the batch upgrade feature, close QuickBooks and click the Batch Upgrade icon on the File Manager icon bar. Then select files to upgrade, as seen in Figure 9-12.

Figure 9-12: Upgrading data files in File Manager is a snap.

The upgrade can take quite a bit of time, even if the data file isn't very large. During a batch upgrade you cannot use QuickBooks (it's actually running, but not visible or accessible), so only do a few files at a time and start the process when nobody in your firm needs to run QuickBooks. It's best to come in to the office very early so the upgrades finish before the rest of the staff arrives, or start the upgrade before you leave at the end of the day.

The upgrade process requires no user intervention – no user input. Here are the guidelines for using the batch upgrade feature successfully:

- If the file is password-protected, the user name and password must be in the password vault.

- The user name in the password vault must have Admin or External Accountant permission levels (no other type of user can upgrade a file).

- You can click Stop if you need to use QuickBooks, but the upgrade for the file being upgraded currently will finish before the batch upgrade process stops.

If the upgrade is successful, the Status column displays the text "Success". If the upgrade doesn't work properly the reason for failure appears in the Status column. You can click Last Unsuccessful Upgrades to see a detailed report on failures along with suggestions for remedies.

Open Two Company Files in QuickBooks

You can open two company files at the same time, which is especially useful for working with clients who maintain two businesses in separate files. Instead of entering all the intra-company transactions into one file and writing yourself notes to make sure you remember the transactions you have to enter in the other company later, you can switch between companies easily.

ProAdvisor NOTE: *You're actually running two instances of QuickBooks; you're not loading two files in a single instance of the software.*

After opening QuickBooks and loading a company file, select File | Open Second Company from the menu bar.

ProAdvisor CAUTION: *Do not use either of the other Open commands to open a second file within the first instance of QuickBooks; they merely replace the current open file with a different file.*

When the second file opens the title bar text changes as follows:

- The word "Primary" is inserted after the filename in the first file you opened.

- The word "Secondary" is inserted after the filename in the second file you opened.

Switch between the files by clicking the appropriate icon on your Windows Taskbar.

Restrictions When Working with Two Files at Once

When you're working in two files, there are some restrictions on the actions you can perform; there are more restrictions on the secondary file than on the primary file. If you need to perform work that's restricted, close one of the files. The Help files have a comprehensive list of restricted activities.

The restrictions on both files are mostly concerned with activities that take place outside of the QuickBooks transactions, such as Fixed Asset Manager, features that are based on Intuit's websites (data sync, licenses, registration, product updates, etc.), and third party applications.

The restrictions on the secondary file are more comprehensive, including some setup functions, planning and budgeting features, and customization of templates.

ProAdvisor NOTE: *You can only open the Help system in the Primary company file.*

Send General Journal Entries

One task that many clients find challenging is creating journal entries. Not only do the clients find the process challenging, but most accountants find cleaning up the resulting confusion somewhat challenging as well. To eliminate all that potential confusion, Premier Accountant now lets you open the client's file, create journal entries, and send them back to the client for import into the client's company file. It's easy to do:

1. Choose Accountant | Make General Journal Entries to open the Make General Journal Entries window.
2. Create the Journal Entry.
3. Click the Send GJEs icon on the ribbon bar of the Main tab to open the Send General Journal Entries window.

4. Select the entries to send.

5. If you're sending more than one JE and you want the client to be able to choose which JEs to import, check the Allow Recipient To Select Which GJEs To Post To File option.

6. Click the Email As Attachment button to e-mail the journal entries to the client. If you want to deliver them using a different method, click the Save As File button.

The safest method for importing the JE into the client's company file is as follows:

1. Open the e-mail and save the attachment to the hard drive.

2. Open the company file into which the JEs are to be imported.

3. Select File | Utilities | Import | General Journal Entries.

4. Locate the saved .QBJ file and double-click it.

5. Review the JEs in the Add General Journal Entries To Your File window.

6. Select the JEs to import (only available if the Allow Recipient To Select Which GJEs To Post To File option was checked by the sender).

7. Click the Add GJEs button.

ProAdvisor TIP: *Be sure to advise the client that it is possible to import the JEs into any (i.e. the wrong) company file, and that QuickBooks will allow the client to import the JEs multiple times into the same company file. In both cases QuickBooks issues a warning, but the client can choose to ignore it and proceed with the import.*

Client Troubleshooting Tips

Accountants who support QuickBooks users (or users of any accounting software application) spend a lot of time troubleshooting problems. Most of the problems are user-induced rather than software bugs. Some of the predicaments users find themselves in are the result of plunging ahead on a task without calling an accountant first.

In this section, we present tips, tricks, workarounds, and trouble-shooting techniques that we've used, or learned about from accountants. It's impossible to cover every possible dilemma, and it's even impossible to cover every possible facet of a particular predicament (users are *so* inventive), so you'll have to view this section as a much-shortened course in QuickBooks problem solving techniques.

The topics presented are those about which we receive the largest number of queries or comments. They're presented in random order, because it's difficult to create logical groups out of the subject matter offered here.

Managing Uncashed Checks

An accountant asked us to solve a problem that involved a check sent to a vendor that wasn't cashed, and never would be cashed. The check was written to pay a bill that had been previously entered in QuickBooks.

The accountant voided the check in the bank account, which, of course, put the vendor bill back into the "Bills to Pay" window, and also put the bill into A/P aging reports. When the A/P manager brought this to the accountant's attention, he did what accountants often do — he created a journal entry (accountants seem to gravitate to JEs automatically, even though a JE is almost never the right tool).

The journal entry debited A/P and credited the original expense account, and the accountant entered the Vendor name in the JE. Now the A/P aging reports showed correct totals, but the A/P manager reported that the bill continued to appear in the Pay Bills transaction window, and on QuickReports for this vendor. The accountant told her to ignore the bill's listing because the company's books were in balance (the A/P totals were correct).

However, the A/P manager insisted that the bill be removed from the Pay Bills window, and the accountant didn't know how to proceed.

To remove a bill from the Pay Bills window, you have to pay the bill, either with a check or a credit. When the accountant created the JE with the vendor name, a credit was created for the amount posted to A/P.

The credit is floating, so all the bills from this vendor in the Pay Bills window are eligible for the credit. Obviously, the credit should be applied to the bill that was paid with the voided check, and that bill is the same amount as the floating credit (making it easy to select it in the Pay Bills window).

Select the bill, click Set Credits, apply the credit, and click Pay & Close. When the Pay Bill window closes, QuickBooks issues a message telling you that one or more bills were paid by credits and no check was issued. That's what you wanted to happen, so click OK.

The best approach to this is not a JE, which only creates the extra step of the JE. Instead, open the Enter Bills window and select the Credit option at the top of the window. Fill out the transaction form so that QuickBooks posts it correctly, and creates accurate reports.

Vendor Bills Paid with Direct Disbursements

Sometimes users write direct checks to pay vendors for whom they've entered bills, instead of using the Pay Bills feature. Most of them use the bank account register to record checks they wrote manually.

When you enter a vendor name in the Write Checks window, Quick-Books warns you to use the Pay Bills feature if there are outstanding bills for this vendor, which many users ignore <sigh!>, but you see no warnings if you record checks directly in the register.

After a while, these users notice they have a very large Accounts Payable balance, and running an A/P report displays open balances for vendors who have been paid.

In addition, expenses are higher than they should be, because the expense was posted when the bill was entered, and then posted again with the direct disbursement.

ProAdvisor TIP: *Most people who do this use the vendor's physical bill to create the check. Insist that clients mark the physical bill to indicate the fact that the bill was entered into QuickBooks in the Pay Bills transaction window, so they can avoid this problem. Put a 'Q' or a 'QB" on the part of the bill that's retained (not the portion returned to the vendor).*

The easiest way to fix the problem is to replace the direct disbursement check with a "pay bills" check. In order to do this, you need to create a list of checks so you know where the problems are.

Choose Reports | Banking | Check Detail, and modify the report as follows to make it easier to find the direct disbursements.

1. Change the date range to go back to the date of the first incorrect direct disbursement.

2. Click Customize Report, and then click the Filters tab.

3. In the Filter list, select TransactionType, and select Check from the TransactionType drop-down list. (This eliminates the checks that were correctly written as the type Bill Payment).

4. If there are only a few vendors that are affected, select Name from the Filter list, and then select Multiple Names in the Name drop-down list. When the Select Name dialog appears, select the affected vendors. If many vendors are involved, skip this step.

5. Click OK to return to the report window, and print the report.

Now that you have a list of the checks and their check numbers, you can open the Pay Bills window and begin paying the bills that were already paid by a direct disbursement.

1. Use the Filter By drop down list to select the first vendor.

2. Check the vendor's bill (or multiple bills if the check covered more than one bill). If credits were applied when

the check was written, click the Set Credits button to apply those credits.

3. Change the Payment Date to match the date of the check that was written and sent.

4. When the bills are selected, and the amount of the check matches the direct disbursement check, select the option Assign Check Number at the bottom of the Pay Bills window.

5. Click Pay Selected Bills to open the Assign Check Numbers dialog.

6. In the Assign Check Numbers dialog, enter the check number that was used for the direct disbursement (the Check Detail report has the check number).

7. When QuickBooks warns you that the check number has already been used, select Keep Number.

8. In the Payment Summary dialog, click Pay More Bills if you have more checks to clean up, otherwise click Done.

When you're finished paying the bills that were already paid, using the check numbers you've already used, open the check register. Here's what you'll find:

- The bank balance is much smaller than it should be.

- Each check number you just used appears twice, once for the direct disbursement (check type CHK), and once for the bill payment you just made (check type BILLPMT).

Void or delete every duplicate check that is of the type CHK. The bank balance returns to its proper amount, and the expense account is adjusted to reflect only the expenses posted when the vendor bills were originally recorded.

Vendor Pays Off a Credit with Checks

A user has an open credit with a vendor for a large amount. She no longer uses this vendor, so the vendor has agreed to refund the credit amount in installments. She has to enter each check, deposit it into the bank, and reduce the credit at the same time. She wants to be able to track the history of this credit and the installment payments against it (which is a good idea, because it means that any disputes with the vendor can be easily resolved).

This is actually quite easy to accomplish, assuming that when you created the credit, you used the Enter Bills transaction window, selected the Credit option, and posted the credit amount to the expense account that was originally used for the purchase.

Now, checks from the vendor begin to arrive. To pay down the credit, when each check arrives, open a General Journal Entry window and proceed as follows:

1. In the Account column, choose the bank in which you're depositing the funds, and debit it for the amount of the check. This deposits the money into your bank account.

2. You can also debit the Undeposited Funds account, instead of the bank account, and when you open the Make Deposits window, this amount is on the list of payments to deposit.

3. In the Name column of the Make General Journal Entries window, enter the name of the vendor.

4. On the next line, choose Accounts Payable. QuickBooks will automatically insert a credit equal to the debit you entered. Enter the vendor in the Name column.

5. Save the JE.

Do this each time you receive a check. When you check the A/P balance of this vendor, you'll notice the credit balance has declined by the amount of the check.

Open the Pay Bills window, where the entry you made shows up as a payable (an open bill). When you select that bill, QuickBooks displays a message saying there's a credit available. Select the Set Credits window, and apply the appropriate amount (the amount of the bill you selected). Eventually, the last check will pay off the vendor credit balance. If the checks don't continue to arrive, you'll have an accurate record of the balance the vendor still owes, and an audit of the transactions to date.

Applying Additional Credits to a Paid Bill

After entering a credit and applying it to a vendor's bill, you create the check in the Pay Bills transaction window. Then you realize you need to add more credits to the bill. After voiding the check, the credit already applied to the bill disappears, and it seems as if you can't apply it. What's going on?

When you create a credit for a vendor, and then use the Pay Bills window to apply the credit, the resulting check is for the net amount. For example, if the original bill is $1000.00, and you apply a credit of $100.00, the check amount is $900.00 after you use the Set Credits feature to apply the credit you created.

To add more credits after you void the check, open the Enter Bills window, select the Credit option at the top of the window, and enter another credit for this vendor (for this example, $100.00). You've now applied a total of $200.00 credits to this vendor, and the vendor had originally submitted a bill of $1000.00, so you should only have to pay the vendor $800.00.

When you open the Pay Bills window, the bill listing that appears for this vendor is for $900.00, not the original $1000.00. That first $100.00 credit has been "absorbed" into the current balance due. If you select the bill's listing and click Set Credits, you'll see the second $100.00 credit you created. The window also displays the bill's "history" - the original amount, the first credit, and the current balance due. The current balance due should equal the original amount less the original credit that was applied. Just apply the second credit to change the new balance due.

The net amount of the check will be mathematically correct – you just don't see the individual listing for the credit you originally applied, because it's been taken into account for this bill.

If you really want to start over and enter all the available credits just before paying the original bill, you could void the original credit transaction after voiding the check. But that's extra work, and unnecessary, because QuickBooks is tracking the net amounts.

If you select the Vendor's listing in the Vendors list and press Ctrl-Q, you see a list of all the transactions, including the bill, the original credit, and the additional credit(s).

Reimbursable Cost of Goods

It's unusual to encounter a situation in which a customer is invoiced for reimbursement of cost of goods, but after receiving several inquiries from business owners and accountants on this subject we figured out a way to do this.

In each case, the object was to charge the COGS account, not to move an inventory item in or out of inventory. We're assuming these inquiries involve businesses that aren't tracking inventory items, and are posting COG amounts directly when they have an expense directly connected to sales items or services.

Each inquiry we received included the information that when the COGS account was selected in the Enter Bills or Write Checks transaction window, QuickBooks did not permit the transaction line to be marked as "billable" after the user entered a customer name. Therefore, the amount never showed up in the Time/Costs list when the customer's invoice was created.

QuickBooks doesn't recognize a COGS account as a customer-reimbursable expense if you enter the account in the Expenses tab in the Enter Bills or Write Checks transaction window. The workaround is to use the Items tab in the transaction window. For reimbursement for non-inventory purchases, it's best to create an Item specifically for this purpose.

Creating an Item to Use for Reimbursable COGS

Create an Other Charge type of item and name it appropriately, such as Goods Supplied, or Services Supplied. This is a generic name, and a generic type of item, because it's used in a variety of scenarios. If you wish, you can set up multiple specific items, but it's usually not necessary.

- Select the option labeled This Item Is Used In Assemblies Or Is A Reimbursable Charge, which changes the dialog so that you can enter an account for the cost, as well as an account for the revenue (when you bill customers).
- In the Expense Account field, enter the COGS account you want to post to when using this item. (If you send 1099s to vendors for transactions using this account, be sure to include this account in your 1099 setup.)
- In the Income Account field, enter the Income account you want to use when billing customers for this expense.

Using the Item in Vendor Transactions

When you enter a vendor bill, or write a check, use the Items tab instead of the Expenses tab to enter the transaction.

If the cost is being passed on to a customer, or if you're using job costing without invoicing the customer, enter a customer or job. The "Billable" option is automatically selected. If you're going to invoice the customer for the expense, you don't have to do anything else. If you're merely tracking job costs, deselect the check mark in the Billable column

Including the Amount in Form 1099

QuickBooks only tracks vendor payments for Form 1099, which means that if you use the Enter Bills transaction form, the amount is not transferred to the vendor's 1099 record until you pay the bill. Form 1099 payments are calculated on a Cash basis, not an Accrual basis.

Invoicing the Customer for the Expense

When you invoice the customer, after entering current charges (if there are any), click the Add Time/Costs button on the Create Invoices window and move to the Items tab. Select the item(s) you marked billable to include them on the invoice.

You can also include the billable item(s) if you're using a Sales Receipt transaction for this sale instead of an invoice.

Managing Outside Sales Reps

The reason we're asked so often about managing commissions for outside sales reps is probably the lack of an automatic commission calculator in QuickBooks. Some accounting applications let you enter the commission rate in the rep's record, and then automatically calculate the commission (and some software automatically creates the checks). QuickBooks doesn't, which makes the issue of sales reps and commissions seem more complicated than it is.

Configuring QuickBooks to Track Reps

In order to track sales for which outside reps receive commission, you must create sales reps, and enter the rep on every affected sales transaction. (Chapter 2 covers setting up sales reps).

To enter the reps when you're creating transactions, you have to add the Sales Rep field to all the sales transaction templates you use (Sales Orders, Invoices, Sales Receipts, etc.). Some of the industry specific Premier editions provide a sales order template with the rep field included, but if such a template isn't available, create customized templates that contain a Rep field.

When a sales rep is linked to a customer, the rep's initials are automatically placed in the Rep field when that customer is selected in a sales transaction template. However, even if the rep is linked to that customer, if you use a transaction template without a Rep field, the transaction is *not* linked back to the rep.

ProAdvisor TIP: *You cannot split a sales transaction among multiple reps. If you need to pay commissions to more than one rep, create a rep that is an alias for two reps, and then split the commission appropriately for that duo-rep.*

Sales Transactions and Sales Rep Commissions

Most of the time, all the items (services and products) in a sales transaction can be posted to the sales rep's record, so the rep gets a commission on the total sale. QuickBooks does not include sales tax amounts in the sales total posted for commission tracking.

Sales Reports for Reps

To create a report on sales by rep, choose Reports | Sales and then select one of the following reports:

- Sales By Rep Summary, which displays the total amount of sales credited to each rep for the period selected in the report.
- Sales By Rep Detail, which displays every sales transaction for each rep, totaled for each rep.

You can use a calculator to add the amounts and multiply by the commission rate. If you have a lot of sales reps and a lot of sales, export the report to Excel and perform your calculations there.

ProAdvisor TIP: *If you only pay sales reps on paid sales, and want to omit open invoices, change the report to Cash Basis.*

Write the commission check, posting the amount to the account you set up for that purpose. For sales reps that receive 1099 forms, use an expense account that you've configured as a 1099 account.

Remittance Documents for Reps

You can attach a detailed report with the rep commission payment by modifying the Sales By Rep Detail report for each rep as follows:

1. Choose Reports | Sales | Sales By Rep Detail.
2. Click Customize Report and move to the Filters tab.
3. In the Filter column, select Rep.

4. In the Rep field, select a rep.

5. Click OK to return to the report window, where only this rep's sales are displayed.

6. Click Memorize and memorize the report, using the rep's name.

7. Repeat for every rep.

Each time you issue rep commissions, select the appropriate report from the Memorized Reports list, print it, and attach it to the check.

ProAdvisor TIP: *Create a Memorized Report Group for rep commission reports, and put all these memorized reports in that group. This makes it easier to find the report you need when you pay the commissions.*

Paying Reps Who Collect Payments

Some reps bring invoices to customers when they deliver goods, and collect cash payments from some customers. The reps want to deduct their commissions from the total collection, and remit the balance to the business owner.

That's a common situation, and it's not difficult to manage it in QuickBooks, as long as you understand the basic rules:

- The customer's invoice must be totally paid off in QuickBooks.

- The reps must have their commissions tracked (especially if they're 1099 recipients).

- You must deposit the money to Undeposited Funds, not directly to a bank account; otherwise you cannot deduct the commission the rep already took.

When you receive the money from the rep, open the Receive Payments window, enter the customer's name, select the appropriate invoice, and indicate the full amount the customer turned over to the rep as the amount received.

Choose Banking | Make Deposits to open the Payments To Deposit window. Select this payment for deposit, and click OK.

In the next Make Deposits window, make the following entries in the row below the deposit listing:

- Select the Rep's name in the Received From column.
- Select the account you use for posting commissions in the From Account column (this account is linked to 1099 payments if the Rep gets a 1099).
- Optionally, enter a comment in the Memo column (e.g. Commission on Inv#1234).
- Skip the Check Number column.
- Optionally, choose Cash in the Payment Method column (it's not essential, but you may want to track this as cash).
- Assign a class in the Class column (if you're tracking classes).
- In the Amount column, enter the amount the Rep kept, *using a minus sign.*

The net amount is transferred to the bank account as a deposit. Your customer's record are accurate, your rep's records are accurate, and your 1099s will be accurate.

Bartering

It's amazing how much e-mail we receive asking how to manage relationships with customers who are also vendors. Bartering isn't complicated if you configure QuickBooks properly to manage it.

Bartering kicks in when you send an invoice to a customer, and your customer contacts you to buy something from his company. You buy the product or service and then either you or your customer suggests that a credit against the invoice is the easiest way to pay (either partially or in full, depending on the amounts) for the purchases. It works the other way around, too — you may have a vendor who wants to buy your products or services and use a credit for payment or partial payment.

Configuring Elements for Bartering

To manage bartering, you need the following elements in your QuickBooks company file:

- A duplicate customer account for each vendor with whom you barter (and the other way around, a duplicate vendor account for each barter customer). Use the same text in the Name field for both, adding "V" and "C" to the names to make the names unique.

- An Other Current Asset account to track barter transactions. Name the account Barter or Exchanges.

- An item to use in transactions, of the type Other Charge. Name the item To/From Exchange (or Barter, or whatever text works for you). Link the item to the Other Current Asset account you created.

Entering Barter Transactions

Once you've agreed to barter transactions with your Customer/Vendor, entering transactions is the same as it was before. When there's a barter balance, you credit the appropriate transaction using the barter item. You have to follow two rules to make this work:

- Always use an invoice when the vendor/customer purchases goods or services—never use a sales receipt. You can only apply credits against invoices.

- Always use a bill when you purchase from the vendor—never use a direct disbursement. You can only apply credits against bills.

Let's go through the processes so this is clear:

- You sell a customer (who is also a vendor) products or services, and the total invoice is $540.00.

- You order a product or service from the vendor (same as the customer above) for $400.00, and agree to a barter arrangement.

- The Vendor sends a bill for $400.00, which you enter in the Enter Bills transaction window.

QuickBooks now shows that you have an A/R entry in the amount of $540.00 and an A/P entry for $400.00, which in "barter-speak" means you have an A/R for $140.00. (This works identically the other way around—when the A/P is a larger amount than the A/R.)

Now you have to take $400.00 off the original invoice, and clear the vendor bill because you're not going to write a check to pay the bill.

1. Choose Customers | Create Credit Memos/Refunds.

2. Select the barter customer.

3. Select the barter item you created and enter the amount (in this case $400.00).

4. Save the transaction.

5. QuickBooks displays a message asking how you want to apply the credit. Choose Apply To An Invoice and click OK.

6. In the Apply Credit To Invoices dialog, select the original invoice (in this case, for $540.00) and click Done.

QuickBooks debits $400.00 to the Barter account. Now you have to enter a vendor credit and apply it to the vendor's bill. QuickBooks will credit the Barter account, which ends up with a zero balance.

1. Choose Vendors | Enter Bills to open the Enter Bills transaction window.

2. Select the Credit option at the top of the transaction window.

3. Select the vendor.

4. Move to the Items tab and enter the Barter item.

5. Enter the amount of the credit (in this case, $400.00).

6. Save the transaction.

Now you have to clear the bill.

1. Choose Vendors | Pay Bills

2. Select the vendor bill that is part of the barter agreement.

3. Because the existing credit is the same amount as the bill, QuickBooks immediately applies the credit and displays a message telling you that no check will be created.

4. Click OK.

5. Click Pay Selected Bills. QuickBooks displays a summary of the Pay Bills activities, including this bill (which has no real payment).

Once you're rolling along with barters, it's not this "neat and clean", of course, because you won't always have near-simultaneous barter transactions. The invoices and bills you create, and the credits you enter against them for barter activities, produce balances on one side or another of the Barter account. Sometimes you'll enter a customer credit with no existing invoice, saving the credit for future use. At other times, you'll enter a vendor credit with no existing bill. This is normal for ongoing bartering.

When needed, you can enter the Barter item as part of a normal invoice to your customer, in addition to the services or products that appear on that invoice. You can also enter the barter item as an A/P credit and use it against any invoice from the vendor (if you've received multiple invoices). When the vendor credit is less than the amount owed, apply the credit and QuickBooks creates a check for the balance due.

Tracking Barter Balances

To see the current state of the barter balances, create a QuickReport on the Barter Item (select the item in the Item List and press Ctrl-Q). Choose All as the date range to see a report on the item's transactions.

> **ProAdvisor TIP**: *Change the Sort By field to Name so you have all the customer side and vendor side transactions listed contiguously.*

The balance of the QuickReport should always match the current balance of the Barter account.

Inter-company Transactions

Some businesses create multiple QuickBooks company files to manage separate companies or separate divisions. Many of these businesses find that it's common to have inter-company transactions. Sometimes it's not easy to figure out the best way to manage these transactions, so we'll present the solutions that seem to work best for the following common inter-company transactions:

- One company invoices the other company
- A customer pays invoices from two separate companies with one check
- One company sells items on behalf of the other company

One Company Invoices Another Company

During a seminar for users, an accountant explained that inter-company receivables shouldn't be mingled with standard customer A/R figures. The accountant recommended setting up an Other Current Asset account to track the inter-company receivables and instructed attendees to create a journal entry after creating an invoice for the other company. The JE moves the invoice total from the A/R account to the Other Current Asset account (credit A/R and debit the Other Current Asset account).

When payment is received, treat it like a regular customer payment, and then make a journal entry to move the reduction in A/R to the Other Current Asset account (debit A/R and credit the Other Current Asset account). This washes the Other Current Asset account for the transactions.

After the seminar, attendees who wanted to keep inter-company invoices separate from regular customer invoices asked whether there's an easier way to manage these transactions. There is, and it involves a few easy tasks:

- Create a second A/R account (named Intercompany Receivables or something similar). When you have multiple A/R accounts, QuickBooks adds a field to the Create Invoices and Receive Payments transaction windows for selecting the A/R account from a drop-down list of all the A/R accounts.

- Select the appropriate A/R account when you create the invoice.

- Don't forget to select the same A/R account when you receive the payment (or the invoice won't show up in the Receive Payments window when you select the customer).

ProAdvisor TIP: *QuickBooks lets you use a separate invoice numbering scheme for each A/R account, which is very handy.*

Multiple A/R accounts can be quite useful in a number of scenarios, because you can track receivables and customers (or customer types) quickly, without the need to customize standard reports by selecting complicated filters.

For example, nonprofit organizations usually track different types of receivables (grants, contracts, pledges, dues, etc.) in their own A/R accounts. Some businesses track wholesale and retail customers separately, and there are probably many other scenarios in which you'd find it advantageous to use the power of multiple A/R accounts.

To make it all work properly you just need to remember to select the appropriate A/R account every time you create an invoice or receive a payment. (Most businesses that move to this paradigm find that after a few false starts that cause some confusion, remembering to select an A/R account becomes a habit.)

Using the Net Balance Between Companies

Some users who have transactions between two companies prefer to track what's owed and what's paid on a net balance basis. For example, if Company #1 owes Company #2 $1000.00, and Company #2 owes Company #1 $400.00, they have Company #1 pay $600.00 to Company #2 instead of exchanging remittances for the full amount of each debt.

This system is really *bartering* and can be managed using the instructions for bartering earlier in this chapter.

Customer Pays Separate Company Invoices with One Check

Many readers who maintain multiple QuickBooks company files have written to ask how to handle customer payments that cover two invoices, when each invoice is from a different company. Usually these readers tell us that they opened one company file and filled out the Receive Payments window with the full amount of the check, and selected the invoice being paid. Of course, the amount of the check is larger than the selected invoice, and the extra funds can be held as a customer credit.

For example, a customer sent $185.60 to pay an invoice from one company in the amount of $85.60, and pay an invoice from the other company in the amount of $100.00.

Many users enter the entire amount of the check ($185.60) in the Amount field of the Receive Payments window for one company; causing QuickBooks to reserve the overpayment as a customer credit. These users write to ask how to use the credit to pay the open invoice in the other company.

The steps required to change the credit into a payment that's received into the other company are often more complicated than changing the way you enter the original "double-payment" check. We'll go over both methods in the following sections.

Another Problem with Overpayments

If the customer in question has multiple open invoices, when you enter the full amount of the customer's check, QuickBooks automatically pays off the selected invoice and then applies the remaining funds against another open invoice. Many users don't notice that another invoice has had a check mark inserted until they save the transaction and see a dialog that asks if they want to maintain the underpayment or forgive it. Underpayment? These users expected an overpayment, not an underpayment.

If this occurs, you must re-open the transaction window and remove the check mark from the second invoice. When you close the transaction, QuickBooks displays the dialog that lets you select the option to reserve the credit.

Creating an Account for Inter-Company Transactions

For both solutions described in the following sections you need to create an account of the type Other Current Liability and name it Due To OtherCompany, or something similar. (Do this in both companies so you can manage transactions like this in either direction.)

Converting a Customer Credit into a Payment to Another Company

First, in case you've already received the payment and created a credit, we'll go over the way to remove the credit you created, and turn it into a payment that you'll remit to the other company on behalf of the customer.

However, the earlier section, "Customer Pays Separate Company Invoices with One Check", presents a better method — so read that if you haven't already entered the transaction into QuickBooks and created a credit.

To convert a customer credit into a payment for another company, open the company file for the company where you received the payment (and generated the credit) and take the following steps:

1. Create an item of the type Other Charge or Service. Name the item Collections For OtherCompany and link it to Other Current Liability account you created.

2. Create an invoice for the customer for the amount you need to send to the other company, using the new item that links to the Other Current Liability account.

3. Apply the existing credit for the overpayment to this invoice, creating a paid invoice.

4. Save the invoice.

5. Write a check to the other company, posting it to the Other Current Liability account that is tracking money owed to the other company.

The following postings take place:

- When you create the "fake" invoice to wipe the credit, QuickBooks debits A/R (to remove the money previously credited to the customer) and credits the Other Current Liability account that is tracking money owed to the other company.

- When you write the check to the other company QuickBooks debits the Other Current Liability account (washing the previous transaction) and credits your bank account.

Now open the company file for the other company and perform the following tasks to pay off the customer's invoice:

1. Open the Receive Payments window and select the customer in question.

2. Enter the amount of the check you wrote in the other company, and select the appropriate invoice to pay with this payment.

3. In the Check # field, enter the check number of the customer's original check (which provides a clear audit trail of the transactions in case you have to discuss these payments with the customer).

4. In the Memo field, enter a note describing your action, such as "Xfer from OtherCompany Chk#XXX" (where XXX

is the check number of the check you wrote to transfer the money).

ProAdvisor NOTE: *If you transferred the money between the two companies electronically, use EFT or other similar text for your check number.*

Posting Checks Between Companies

It's much easier to manage customer payments that have to be split between companies if you don't receive all the money in the Receive Payments window of the company named as the Payee on the customer's check.

Instead, create the Other Current Liability account to track and remit monies owed to the other company, as described earlier in this section. Then open the company to which the customer made out the check, and use the following steps to allocate the payment properly:

1. In the Receive Payments window, select the invoice being paid, and enter the amount of that invoice in the Amount field at the top of the transaction window. (This figure is lower than the actual amount of the check).

2. Post the payment to the Undeposited Funds account, not directly to the bank account (to make it easier to reconcile the bank statement).

3. Save the transaction.

Now you must deposit the customer's entire check. To do so, perform the following tasks:

1. Select Banking | Make Deposits, to open the Payments To Deposit window.

2. Choose this payment.

3. Click OK to open the Make Deposits window.

4. In the Make Deposits window, click the From Account column in the *next* line and enter the Other Current Liability account you created to track monies owed to the other company.

5. In the Memo column, enter a note to indicate the fact that this is a transfer and a check is being sent to the other company.

6. In the Chk No. column, enter the customer's check number (the same check number used for the deposit of the payment).

7. In the Amount column, enter the amount that was intended to pay the invoice from the other company.

8. Save the transaction.

The amount being deposited now equals the full amount of the customer's check.

Write a check to the other company, posting it to the Other Current Liability account that is tracking money owed to the other company.

Now use the check you wrote to apply the customer's payment to the invoice in the other company. To accomplish this, open the other company file, and perform the following tasks:

1. Open the Receive Payments window and select the customer in question.

2. Enter the amount of the payment, and select the appropriate invoice to pay with this payment.

3. In the Check # field, enter the check number of the customer's check.

4. In the Memo field, enter a note describing your action, such as "Xfer from OtherCompany Chk#XXX" (where XXX is the check number of the check you wrote to transfer the money).

When you've finished, the postings, the customer's payment records, the bank deposits, and the transaction histories are correct in both companies.

Selling Items on Behalf of Another Company

A number of our readers who maintain two companies use one of those companies to sell products for both companies. This is common for companies that have credit card sales because they don't want to maintain two merchant card accounts (and pay two monthly fees).

To do this easily and properly, you have to go through some configuration steps, and follow some guidelines for creating transactions. The following sections cover those issues.

Configuring the Company that Accepts the Sales

To configure the company that is accepting orders so that it's easy to manage this scenario, perform the following tasks:

- Create an account of the type Other Current Liability to collect the money for the other company. Name it Owed To OtherCompany, or something similar.

- Set up items that are sold by the other company, and link them to the Other Current Liability account instead of to an income account.

- Be sure the items are named in a way that makes it easy to tell which items are sold by the other company and which are sold by the company that is making the sale. For example, if the company recording the sales is Ajax Sales and the other company is Foombah Supplies, name the items you're selling for Foombah F-xxx, where xxx is the item name/code.

- If the other company is tracking inventory, do not use inventory items in the company that is recording the sales and collecting the money. Inventory is decremented in the second company when the first company remits payment to the other company.

In addition, following are some guidelines for managing these sales (tested by trial and error in companies that deal with this scenario).

For Internet or telephone sales, use a generic customer (named CreditCard or something similar). Don't create a new customer in QuickBooks for each person who makes a purchase (you'd be surprised how fast you can hit the customer limit of 10,000 and completely shut down your company file). When you fill out the billing and shipping address blocks in the Sales Receipt transaction window, QuickBooks keeps the information and you can search for a particular customer later if you need to. If you want to keep customer information about the sale, use Excel or a database program.

ProAdvisor TIP: *Create the generic customer name in both companies; in fact, you can use the same generic customer name (e.g. CreditCard).*

Do not store credit card numbers on your computer (except the last four digits), unless your computer is protected by the security features that exist on secure computers that collect sensitive information on the Internet. If you must, be sure to enable Customer Credit Card Protection.

If the company collecting the money (Company#1) is not required to collect sales tax, but the company that owns the products is reporting sales tax (Company#2), do not configure Company#1 for sales tax. Instead create an item of the type Other Charge, name it SalesTax, and link it to the Other Current Liability account. Add this item (and the appropriate amount) as a line item in the transaction. If Company #2 has complicated sales tax issues (sales tax groups that combine jurisdictions, or different sales tax rates for different types of products), duplicate those sales tax items as Other Charge items.

ProAdvisor CAUTION: *Don't forget to add the Other Charge items you're using for sales tax on customer credits when you accept a return.*

Creating Sales Transactions

You create sales transactions for the other company the same way you create those transactions for a single company. (Most credit card sales are processed using the Sales Receipt transaction window, not an Invoice.)

If the customer is buying multiple products and the list includes products from both companies, it's perfectly fine to include all the products in a single sales transaction. The items are automatically linked to the appropriate accounts.

Creating Reports on Sales for the Other Company

At regular intervals, you must create a report to determine the amount of money owed to the other company, and, of course, you must also write a check to remit that amount. The report you create is also used to enter quantities and prices in the other company.

The easiest way to create this report is to customize the built-in report named Sales By Item Detail (in the Sales submenu of the Reports menu). By default, this report shows all sales information for every item in the current month to-date, so you must customize it as follows:

- Set the date range to match your needs. For example, if you remit the money you've collected on a monthly basis, it's probably a good idea to set the date range for Last Month (unless you always create the report on the last day of the current month, even if it falls on a weekend).

- In the Filters tab, select Account, and then select the Other Current Liability account you created to track these sales.

- In the Display tab, you can remove two of the columns that are included on the report: Name (assuming you're using a generic name for the customer) and Memo (unless you use the Memo field in the transaction window for some important special purpose).

- In the Header/Footer tab, change the report title to make its contents clear (e.g. Monthly Sales for Company #2).

Memorize this report after you've customized it so you don't have to go through the customization steps in the future. Then print it so you can use it to enter the sales in the other company.

Entering Sales Information in the Other Company

Armed with the printout of the sales transactions, open the other company and enter the total for each item as a line item on a single Sales Receipt transaction. You can use the same generic customer name you used in the first company for the transaction.

CHAPTER 10

Contractor Edition

- Contractor company files
- Managing the sale of materials
- Handling customer deposits
- Job costing
- Estimates
- Handling change orders
- Managing retainage
- Managing checks with two payees

Q uickBooks Premier Contractor Edition includes features and functions designed for businesses in the construction industry. Our experience with contractor clients includes generals, subs, and independent trade businesses (plumbers, electricians, and so on), and the QuickBooks Contractor edition has features for all of those contractor business types. In this chapter, we'll cover the issues that arise most frequently.

ProAdvisor NOTE: *QuickBooks Premier Contractor Edition has a great many preconfigured reports of use to contractors. You can view the list by choosing Reports | Contractor Reports. The list of reports is quite comprehensive (and the report names are self-explanatory).*

Contractor Company Files

If you're just starting with QuickBooks, you have to create a company file. QuickBooks has a predefined company file for contractors that works extremely well. The predefined company file for contractors isn't marked as such when you create a new company file. It's merely listed as an industry type, with no indication that it contains a suitable chart of accounts, and some prepopulated entries in lists. (This is what we call an "undocumented feature".)

You can create a company file using the predefined file either with the Express Start feature or by clicking Advanced Setup and using the EasyStep Interview. In the wizard window for selecting your industry, choose the appropriate construction trades listing.

Because this is a preconfigured company file, many of your preferences are already set up, and quite a few of the lists are populated with entries. Open the lists so you can delete the entries that aren't specific to your business, and rename the entries you need if the supplied names aren't appropriate. In this section we'll discuss some of the prepopulated lists and make suggestions about changing those list entries to make them more useful.

If you're upgrading a previous version of QuickBooks to the Premier Contractor edition, you already have a company file, lists, and settings.

Classes for Contractors

The predefined company file for contractors contains classes that are deemed desirable for contractors. As you can see in Figure 10-1, these classes track job related revenue and costs.

Figure 10-1: The predefined classes probably won't suit your needs.

These classes are neither useful nor appropriate. These predefined classes are for tracking costs, and there are two things wrong with that approach:

- The best use of classes is to provide separate Profit & Loss Statements for each class. We've never met a business owner or an accountant who wanted to see a Profit & Loss Statement based on equipment rental costs. It's more common to want to see a Profit & Loss Statement based on jobs or types of jobs.

- You already track costs by posting transactions to expense accounts in the chart of accounts. If your chart of accounts is well designed, you can learn everything you need about your expenses from standard QuickBooks reports.

In the following paragraphs, we'll discuss some of the scenarios we've encountered with contractor clients, and the way we set up classes to meet their reporting needs.

Creating Virtual Branch Offices with Classes

If you perform work in more than one city, town, county, or state, you probably have expenses that are specific to each location (such as taxes, permits, and licensing expenses). For example, you may have to pay taxes based on gross receipts or net profits earned in some localities, as well as payroll taxes for employees (including yourself) who perform work in that locality.

If the local income taxes are based on gross receipts or net profits, you need to track the income you generated in each location, and also track the costs you incurred for work in that location. Those are the numbers you need in order to create a Profit & Loss statement. In addition, many local authorities impose yearly or per-job fees for permits, licenses, and other specific costs of doing business in those localities. Some have license rules and you must pay for courses and tests to obtain a license to work in the locality.

Some accountants take the total gross or profit for the company, and then report these local earnings by applying a percentage. For example, if you have a net income of $100,000, and you tell your accountant you do 15% of your work in East Overcoat Township, your accountant files a tax return with the East Overcoat tax authority that assumes a tax liability based on $15,000.

We've had calls for help from contractors who couldn't defend the numbers produced by that approach when they were called in for an audit by a local taxing authority. Besides, suppose the work you do in East Overcoat isn't as profitable as the work you do in Hollow Spoon Township, but the East Overcoat tax rate is much higher? You might want to raise your prices for work in East Overcoat, or charge customers an additional flat fee to cover the increased tax rate.

If you treat each local authority as a branch office (by using a class), you can produce Profit & Loss reports for each class. Furthermore, you can assign a percentage of your overhead expenses to each class, using a formula that's based on the real numbers produced by your P & L By Class reports.

Here are some guidelines for using classes for this purpose:

- Create a class for every location/taxing authority, and also create a class named Administration (for general overhead expenses that aren't specific to any class or job).

- Post every income transaction to the appropriate class.

- Post every expense that is specific to the local authority to the appropriate class (such as permits, licenses, and taxes).

- Assign classes to expenses that are job related. For example, if you write a check to a supplier for something you purchased for a specific job, link the expense to the appropriate class for that job.

- Split expense postings when you write a check that covers costs for multiple jobs. Each line of the vendor bill or check should be assigned to a class, and the line items must total the payment to the vendor.

- Create payroll items to match your classes, and track the hours your employees spend in each locality. If you use a payroll service, ask them to help you set up a way to track employee time by locality. Remember to post your employer payroll costs to classes, too.

Tracking the Source of Work with Classes

If Profit & Loss reports by locality aren't an issue, you might want to know the profit margins of work that you obtain in different ways. You can use classes to track the source of your work. Then your P & L By Class reports provide a way for you to analyze where the best profits are.

For example, perhaps you get customers who call you directly (usually referred by one of your happy customers or because they saw your sign on the lawn of a customer), and customers who are referred by hardware stores or do-it-yourself chain stores with whom you've registered your services (or you put a sign on a corkboard). And then, of course, there's advertising such as the local yellow pages, or ads in the community newspaper.

If you track your net profits by source for a while, you may discover a pattern, and you can adjust the way you look for work to match the pattern. If you learn that referrals from the local hardware stores turn out to provide more profit than referrals from any other place, visit more hardware stores to arrange for referrals.

If you learn that the least profitable jobs come from paid advertising (don't forget to post the advertising costs to this class), you can save some money by cutting back your advertising budget.

Using classes for this purpose only lets you track profits (and assign overhead intelligently) by broad general categories. If you want to track the profit by each referring entity (specific hardware stores, or specific advertising contracts), you need to track customers and jobs by type (covered later in this chapter).

Tracking the Type of Work with Classes

Depending on your specific type of business, you might want to track the profitability of different types of jobs. For example, you may have some jobs that fit into rather easy-to-define categories, such as:

- New construction (includes additions in existing homes)
- Restoration of historical properties
- Rehab of rundown properties
- Equipment installation in existing homes
- General repair work

To track profits and losses for each type of work, create the appropriate classes. The particular categories we mention here are used by local contractors we've worked with. Restoration is a big issue in some areas, and generally contractors charge more because they need to do research about the original plans for the house, and historical societies keep an eye on the finished work they produce. Often, rehabs are government subsidized and require additional expenses, such as filling out complicated RFPs (Request For Proposal), and obtaining professional certification. Your own professional categories may vary, but this list gives you some ideas for determining how different types of work can be classified.

The class-based reports you create can provide more than just the P & L figures you need for tax forms. These reports give you insight on the financial advantage (or disadvantage) of each division of your business. If you learn that your bottom line for rehab work is much better than your bottom line for new construction, perhaps it's time to turn your company into a rehab specialty business.

Tracking General vs. Subcontractor Profits with Classes

If you act as a general contractor for some jobs, and as a subcontractor for other jobs, you're almost running two different businesses. To report net profits from your general contractor work separately from your subcontractor work, create a class for each type of work.

Customer Types for Contractors

You should create entries representing the customer types you want to track, and then apply the appropriate type to each customer. The predefined customer types in the QuickBooks contractor company file are:

- From Advertisement
- Referral
- Retail
- Wholesale

This list doesn't work properly because it isn't consistent. Customer types should separate a specific piece of information into categories, and should be designed to avoid confusion or overlapping. In this case, the first two listings have nothing to do with the next two listings; in fact, most of your customers could be typed as "one of the first two listings and also one of the last two listings". This is not going to work!

The first two customer types provide an excellent method of tracking the way you obtain jobs. You can easily use the information you gain to increase business. Of course, these customer type entries don't work unless you specifically ask each customer how he or she learned about your business.

The Retail and Wholesale types are more suited to businesses that sell products to both retailers and wholesalers. You can delete those types and add other types that reflect other methods that bring you business.

If tracking referrals shows you get more business in one particular way, or the least amount of business in one way, test the referrals paradigm. Do something to increase referrals (besides the obvious ploy of doing a good job and making your customers happy), and then track the results.

For instance, when you send your final invoice, enclose a flyer that offers something for every referral that turns into a job. Buy merchandising gifts that fit your business, and send a gift to each customer that refers a new customer. Depending on the type of contractor business you have, a suitable gift may be a tape measure, a stud-finder, polish for plumbing fixtures, a flashlight, or any other inexpensive and useful gift. Print small labels with your name, logo, and telephone number, and affix one to the gift.

If referral business increases, continue to reward referring customers. If referral business doesn't grow, and advertisements continue to be more effective, increase your advertising budget. Test one new medium at a time, and track the results.

You can also use these predefined customer types as the basis of more complex, and more meaningful, customer types. For example, you could have the following customer types:

- Ad-yellow pages
- Ad-local paper
- Ad-cable TV
- Ad-broadcast TV
- Refer-Joe's hardware
- Refer-Bob's hardware
- Refer-customer

ProAdvisor NOTE: *You can use up to 31 characters for a Customer Type entry.*

Sometimes, the source of business isn't important to you. Perhaps you don't feel you need to spend money on advertising, or you don't need to track the source of business because all your business comes from a store or a general contractor. In that case, use customer types that provide another quantifying description for customers, and track those descriptions in reports.

For example, you may find it useful to sort customers by the type of work. Depending on your type of contractor business, you could use New and Rehab as customer types. Alternatively, examine the list of suggestions for using classes earlier in this section, and use one that isn't suitable for your own Class List, but may work nicely as your Customer Type List.

Job Types for Contractors

Use the Job Type List to sort jobs in some manner that's useful for analyzing the work you do, creating profit reports for job types, or creating job-costing reports for each type of work. The QuickBooks predefined company file for contractors contains several job type entries, seen in Figure 10-2.

If any of the predefined job types don't work for you, delete the useless ones and create your own descriptive types, based on the types of jobs you take on.

Figure 10-2: The pre-loaded job types are useful for some types of construction businesses.

Vendor Types for Contractors

You can track vendors by type, to analyze the categories in which you spend your money, and to contact vendors appropriately. The QuickBooks predefined company file contains some built-in vendor types, but they may not be applicable to your business. For some of these, expense accounts in the chart of accounts provide the same information.

We prefer to use vendor types to categorize vendors in a way that makes it easier to contact them for specific reasons. For example, vendors who are your subcontractors need to be contacted when you need bids for a potential job. In that case, we suggest vendor types that sort appropriately when you need to get a bid. The following examples illustrate the possible vendor types for a plumber:

- Demolition
- Digging/back hoes
- Gas line install
- Wiring
- Duct cleaning

Items for Contractors

The entries you put into the Item List should be well thought out, because you use them constantly. You need an item for every category of sale you make, but not for every single individual product or service—the word "category" is the important keyword to consider.

The predefined company file for contractors has an Item List you should examine. This list almost certainly doesn't match your exact needs (it's a wide-ranging list covering all types of contractor businesses), but you can get a sense of the way an Item List can be put together. Delete the items you don't need, and add any items you need that are missing.

> **ProAdvisor TIP**: *You can edit the items you keep from the predefined list to get rid of the numbers at the beginning of the item name. Many contractors find it easier to use the items in alphabetical order when they're selecting an item in a drop-down list of a transaction window.*

Managing the Sale of Materials and Parts

Most contractors don't need to track inventory formally, because they don't buy parts for resale the way a retail store does. Instead, they keep parts in stock for use in jobs (which is a form of resale, but not the same as running a retail parts store).

Many independent contractors have a long list of parts, both inventory and non-inventory, in their Item Lists. Frequently, the lists contain multiple entries of the same item.

For example, we've seen item lists in electrician's files that included Plate Covers-2hole, Plate-Covers-4hole, and so on. Plumbers have listings such as PVC-4', PVC-8', and so on. Plumbers who do this probably add a new inventory item every time they buy a different length of PVC. This is almost always totally needless, and makes the time you spend on record keeping longer than necessary.

It's much better to keep a short list of items. For example, create an item named PVC Pipe. If your customer cares about the number of feet of pipe you used, enter that information in the Description column of the invoice (I'll bet most customers don't care). Even better, use an item named Materials in your invoices, and then use the Description column to inform your customer that it was pipe.

When appropriate, use a per-unit cost and price. For example, you can have an item named Wood and enter the per-running-foot price. Then, when you use 25 feet of that wood on a job, enter the item, enter a quantity of 25, and let QuickBooks do the math.

Applying Units of Measure to Materials

The best way to manage the sale of materials without creating a mile-long list of different sizes, lengths, and amounts is with the Units of Measure feature. See Chapter 6 for details on using this handy feature.

The Premier Contractor Edition supports multiple units of measure (U/M), which means you can create a base U/M and then devise multiple conversions of that base U/M to permit sales of different quantities of the same item. Multiple U/Ms support the following types of measurements:

- Count (e.g. single, dozen, package, case, etc.)
- Length
- Weight
- Volume
- Area
- Time
- Self-configured (invent your own)

This list contains every possible useful measurement calculation for contractors. (Learn how to create Multiple U/Ms in Chapter 6.)

Handling Customer Deposits

When you receive a deposit from a customer, you cannot record the money as income. You haven't yet earned the money; it still belongs to the customer. You can turn it into income by completing the work (or a portion of the work, as agreed to with the customer). Until that time, that money is a liability to your company.

Elements for Tracking Customer Deposits

To track the money you receive as deposits separately from money you earn as income, you need to set up an account to track the deposits. When you earn the revenue, it's moved to an income account. In order to create the transaction, you need to create an item that you can use in the transaction. We'll cover both these elements in the following sections.

Creating a Liability Account for Customer Deposits

You need a liability account to track customer deposits, and you use this account when you receive a deposit from a customer. If you used the predefined company file for contractors (trades, not general contractors), the account already exists as Customer Deposits Received.

If you have to create this account, open the chart of accounts and press Ctrl-N to create a new account. Select the account type Other Account Types and then select Other Current Liability from the drop-down list. Click Continue, and name the account Customer Deposits Held, or something similar.

Creating an Item for Customer Deposits

You need an item for customer deposits, which you use when you create transactions involving those deposits. To create the item, open the Item List, and press Ctrl-N to open the New Item dialog. Then create the item using the following guidelines:

- The type of item is Service
- The name is descriptive, such as CustomerDeposit.
- The rate is zero, because it's customer-specific, and the amount is entered at the time you create the transaction.
- The item is not taxed (if you've enabled Sales Tax).
- The account to which it's linked is the liability account you created to track customer deposits.

Recording a Customer Deposit

When you and your customer agree on the amount of the deposit, you can either create an invoice or a direct sale (called a Sales Receipt in QuickBooks).

- If the customer needs a reminder to send the deposit, create an invoice.
- If the customer gives you the deposit at the time you're discussing the job and signing the contract, create a sales receipt.

In either case, use the CustomerDeposit item you created, and enter the appropriate amount.

Here's what happens in your general ledger when you record the deposit:

- The liability account you created to track deposits (linked to the CustomerDeposit item) is credited for the amount of the deposit.

- If you created an invoice, Accounts Receivable is debited for the amount of the deposit.

- If you created a sales receipt, the bank account (or undeposited funds, which gets moved to the bank account when you actually deposit the funds) is debited for the amount of the deposit.

- The customer's record is updated to record the transaction.

ProAdvisor NOTE: *Just a reminder that Asset and Expense accounts are debit side accounts and Liability, Income, and Equity accounts are credit side accounts. That means that in this case, the Customer Deposits Received (Liability) account is increased by the credit and the Accounts Receivable (Asset) account is increased by the debit. For a sales receipt, the bank (Asset) account is increased by the debit.*

Applying the Customer Deposit to an Invoice

When you're ready to send an invoice to a customer who gave you a deposit, you have to apply the deposit against the invoice total. You can do this at the end of the job, with a total invoice, or if you send invoices periodically, you can apply the deposit to the first invoice (if the invoice amount is larger than the deposit), or apply a portion of the deposit on each invoice.

To create the invoice, press Ctrl-I to open the Create Invoices transaction window. Fill out the invoice with all the services and materials you've sold the customer. For the last item, use the customer deposit item you created, and enter the amount of the deposit with a minus sign.

QuickBooks posts the invoice in the following manner:

- The income account(s) attached to the item(s) on the invoice are credited.
- The Deposit account (the liability account) attached to the customer deposit item is debited (this "washes" the credit you posted when you recorded the deposit).
- The A/R account is debited for the balance due.

When the customer pays the bill, the A/R account is credited, and your bank account is debited.

Reporting on Customer Deposits

You need to keep track of the customer deposits you've collected, so you know which customers have given you deposits, the amount of each deposit, and which deposits have already been applied to invoices.

You need this information when you prepare invoices for each customer, so you can enter the correct amount in the invoice item in which you're applying the deposit.

QuickBooks does not have a report that gives you this information, so you have to build it. The process takes a few minutes, so after you've created this report you must memorize it to avoid doing the work again. Use the following steps to build a report that tracks the current state of customer deposits:

1. Choose Reports | Custom Reports | Transaction Detail, which automatically opens with the Modify Report dialog displayed.
2. In the Date field, select All from the drop-down list.
3. In the Columns field, select and deselect column names to end up with the following columns:

    - Type
    - Date

- Source Name
- Amount
- Balance

4. In the Total By field, select Customer from the drop-down list.

5. Move to the Filters tab.

6. In the Filter list, select Item.

7. In the Item field, select the item you created for customer deposits.

8. Move to the Header/Footer tab.

9. In the Report Title field, replace the title with a title that matches this report, such as Customer Deposit Status.

10. Click OK to return to the report, which should now list all the information about customer deposits (see Figure 10-3).

11. Click Memorize and name the report, using the name you entered as the report title.

Figure 10-3: Keep track of customer deposits.

Notice the following about this report:

- The report is sorted and subtotaled by customer. Each job attached to the customer is listed, along with its own total.

- Positive amounts are amounts received as a deposit.

- Amounts that are negative are amounts credited on an invoice, and only the amount linked to the liability account is displayed (the actual invoice total is usually higher).

- The total balance matches the amount currently in the liabilities account you created to track deposits.

To generate this report whenever you need it, choose Reports | Memorized Reports, and select the name you gave it when you memorized it.

Deposits that Are Just Payments in Advance

Sometimes, a customer deposit is nothing more than an advance payment. This generally means that the job is completed in a short time—usually a couple of hours or a single day.

In this circumstance, you don't have to treat the advance payment as a liability. Instead, you create an invoice upfront (before beginning the job), apply the advance payment, and then leave the balance unpaid until you finish the job and ask for the balance.

It's best to do everything in advance, during your initial conversation with the customer. Give the customer the price for the job, and tell the customer how much you need as an advance. Then, back at the office, create the invoice, apply the deposit, and print the invoice. Take the printed invoice to the job, and get the advance check/cash. When you've completed the work, hand the invoice to the customer and get a check for the balance (or a promise to mail the check).

Creating an Advance Payment Item

To use an advance payment, you must create an item for it. In the New Item dialog, select Payment as the Item type, and name the item Advance

Payment or Payment in Advance. As you can see in Figure 10-4, items of the type Payment don't have a lot of fields to fill out.

Figure 10-4: Set up an item to handle advance payments on an invoice.

The description field is optional, but you should enter the text you want to appear in the invoice, to make it clear to the customer that the advance has been applied to the invoice. Don't enter a payment type because you don't know how the customer will make the payment.

Select the Undeposited Funds account as the account that receives the deposit. If you don't use the Undeposited Funds account, select Deposit To and choose your bank account from the drop-down list (and then consider using the Undeposited Funds account, which is much more efficient).

Applying an Advance Payment to an Invoice

In QuickBooks, you receive this type of advance payment and create an invoice at the same time. The advance is not treated separately as a sales receipt or a payment against an existing invoice. You can create the scenario for the advance payment in any of several ways:

- Create the invoice, including the advance payment, and take it to the customer. Get the advance check at the same time. (This assumes you've made these arrangements with the customer.)

- Ask the customer to send you the advance, and when it arrives don't use a Sales Receipt transaction to record it. Instead, create the invoice with the advance payment included.

To create the invoice, enter the item(s) you're selling the customer, and then enter the Advance Payment item. Do **not** enter a minus sign; QuickBooks knows that a Payment type item is a deduction and automatically enters the minus sign. The invoice total is the amount of the sale less the advance payment.

Virtual Bank Accounts for Customer Deposits

You don't need to open a separate bank account to hold customer deposits (only businesses that keep escrow funds, such as lawyers, are required to do that). However, if most of your jobs are long-term, and you're holding on to customer deposits for an extended period of time, you might want to think about opening a money market account (or another type of business bank account that pays interest).

If you deposit customer deposits into your regular business bank account, you must make sure you don't spend down into the deposit money. You can keep a post-it note that tracks the total of customer deposits you're holding, and maintain that balance in the bank. Or, you can configure your bank account so that it tracks two sets of totals; the total funds for customer deposits, and the total funds for the money you can spend.

If your customer deposits and regular funds are commingled in a single account, you can use virtual bank accounts to separate deposit funds from operating funds. When you use the operating account to pay your business expenses, the balance won't include the deposit amounts you're holding. This makes it easier to avoid spending the money you're holding as customer deposits.

In addition, having a bank account for customer deposits (whether real or virtual) provides a quick way to check the status of those funds. The amount in the bank account should always equal the amount in the customer deposit liability account.

Virtual bank accounts are subaccounts of your business bank account. The bank account you've already created in your chart of accounts is the *parent account*.

Create two subaccounts: one for your operating (regular) funds, and one for the customer funds you're holding. To do this, open the chart of accounts window and create subaccounts as follows:

1. Press Ctrl-N to open the Add New Account dialog.
2. Select Bank as the account type and click Continue.
3. Enter a number for the virtual operating account (if you're using account numbers). Use a number ten digits higher than your bank account. For example, if your bank account number is 10100, make the new account 10110.
4. Enter a name for the new account, such as Operating Funds.
5. Select the option Subaccount Of, and select your bank account from the drop-down list in the text box.
6. Optionally, enter a description of this account.
7. Click Save & New to open a blank Add New Account dialog, which has Bank selected as the account type.
8. Enter the next number as the account number (if you're using numbered accounts).
9. Enter a name, such as Customer Deposit Funds.
10. Select the option Subaccount Of, and select your bank account from the drop-down list in the text box.
11. Optionally, enter a description.
12. Click Save & Close.

In the chart of accounts window, your new subaccounts are listed (and indented) under your bank account.

Transferring Funds to Subaccounts

After your bank subaccounts are created, you need to transfer the appropriate amounts into each subaccount.

- The total amount of customer deposits is the current balance of the liability account you use to post the customer deposits.

- The remaining amount represents your operating funds.

When you finish, the parent bank account displays the total of the balances of the subaccounts when you view the chart of accounts.

Create a journal entry to transfer the funds by choosing Company | Make General Journal Entries. Enter the entire current balance of the bank account in the Credit column to remove the funds (you're emptying the account virtually, not for real).

In the next rows, debit the appropriate amounts for each sub-account (see Figure 10-5). The debit for the virtual customer funds account is the total of customer deposits you're holding. The debit for the virtual operating funds account is everything that's left in the bank account.

Figure 10-5: Empty the parent bank account, and fill the subaccounts.

ProAdvisor TIP: *If you enter the debit for the Customer Deposit subaccount after you credit the entire balance of the real bank account, QuickBooks does the math and automatically enters the correct amount for the debit to the Operating Funds subaccount.*

When you open the Chart Of Accounts window, the balance displayed for the main bank account is the total of the balances in the subaccounts.

When you create reports that include the bank account (such as a Balance Sheet), QuickBooks displays the totals for each bank subaccount, and the grand total for the bank account.

ProAdvisor CAUTION: *Never use the parent bank account for transactions; it automatically tracks the amounts in the subaccounts and the displayed balance should equal the totals of the subaccounts. The only time you use the parent account is when you reconcile the bank account.*

Depositing Funds to Subaccounts

Your QuickBooks company file configuration probably enabled the Undeposited Funds account. This means when you create transactions for received funds (customer payments of invoices, or cash receipts), the money is deposited into the Undeposited Funds account. (If you haven't configured your company file to use Undeposited Funds, you should, because it makes reconciling your bank account much easier.)

When you deposit the funds in the bank, you use the Make Deposits feature to transfer the funds into a bank account. This is the best way to manage bank deposits because it matches the way your bank statement reports deposits. However, if you're using virtual bank accounts via subaccounts, it means you have to be careful about the way you deposit money into your new virtual bank accounts.

When you move revenue from the Undeposited Funds account into the appropriate bank account, you have to separate regular income from customer deposit income. Select all the regular income, and deposit that in the operating funds subaccount. Select all the customer deposit receipts, and deposit them in the customer deposit subaccount.

Often, this isn't an easy task, because you can't tell which income is for regular earned income, and which is for customer deposit payments.

The way to resolve this dilemma is to come up with a solution that announces itself in the Payments To Deposit window. Using the Memo field in a customer payment transaction window doesn't work, because memo text isn't displayed in this window.

For our clients, we solved the problem with a new payment method, named CustomerDeposit, with a payment type of Other. To create a new payment method, use the following steps:

1. Choose Lists | Customer & Vendor Profile Lists | Payment Method List.
2. Press Ctrl-N to open the New Payment Method dialog.
3. Name the new method CustomerDeposit.
4. Select the Payment Type "Other" and click OK.

When customer deposits arrive, either as a customer deposit or as a payment, the sales transaction window has a field for the Customer Deposit Payment type. The transaction window also provides a field to accept the customer's check number (always important to record in case of any disputes with the customer).

- In the Receive Payments transaction window, when you select CustomerDeposit (or any other payment method classified as Other), the Check # field changes its name to Reference #.

- In the Enter Sales Receipts transaction window, when you select CustomerDeposit (or any other payment method classified as Other), the Check No. field doesn't change its label.

When you use the new CustomerDeposit payment method in transactions, the Payments To Deposit window is much easier to work with. As you can see in Figure 10-6, customer deposits are clearly discernible in the Payment Method column.

Figure 10-6: Select the CustomerDeposit payment type for your deposit into the right bank subaccount.

It's easy to deposit different payment types into different bank accounts, and QuickBooks provides two methods: one works if you only have a few listings in the Make Deposits window; the other works best if you have a lot of listings in the window.

If you only have a few deposits listed in the Payments To Deposit window, use the following steps to separate your deposits by bank account:

1. In the Sort Payments By field at the top of the window, select "Payment Method".

2. Put a check mark next to each deposit of the type CustomerDeposit.

3. Click OK to open the Make Deposits window.

4. Select the Customer Deposit Funds subaccount from the drop-down list in the Deposit To field at the top of the window.

5. Click Save & New to return to the Payments To Deposit window.

6. Click Select All to select all the remaining deposits.

7. Click OK, and in the Make Deposits window select the Operating Funds subaccount.

8. Click Save & Close.

If you have a great many deposits listed in the Payments To Deposit window (perhaps you've been storing checks in your desk and haven't been to the bank for a long time), or if you use other Payment Methods such as credit cards, cash, electronic transfers, etc. use the following steps:

1. Click the arrow next to the View Payment Method Type field at the top of the Payments To Deposit window, and choose Selected Types from the drop-down list.

2. In the Select Payment Types dialog, choose Other.

3. Click OK to return to the Payments To Deposit window, where only your customer deposit payments are displayed.

4. Click Select All to select all your customer deposit funds, and then click OK to open the Make Deposits window.

5. Select the Customer Deposit Funds subaccount, and then click Save & New to return to the Payments To Deposit window.

6. Make sure All Types is selected in the field at the top of the window, and click Select All to select the remaining payments.

7. Click OK to open the Make Deposits window, and select the Operating Funds subaccount.

8. Click Save & Close.

Reconciling Bank Accounts with Subaccounts

When you reconcile the bank account, use the parent account. Because your subaccounts are virtual bank accounts, instead of real separate bank accounts, the parent account actually maintains all the activity in the bank register.

After you fill out the Begin Reconciliation window and click Continue, the Reconcile dialog displays all the transactions for both accounts. Quick-Books doesn't pay any attention at all to the fact that there are subaccounts; this is just a regular bank reconciliation and no transaction shows any indication of being initiated from a subaccount.

The first time you reconcile after moving the money into the subaccounts, you'll see a check/payment for the total amount of the checking account that was moved into the subaccounts. On the deposits side, you'll see the two journal entry transactions that put the money into the two subaccounts. They wash when you check them off.

Transferring Deposits Held to Operating Funds

When you earn the money, it's not a customer deposit any more, it's not a liability any more; it's income, and it's yours to spend.

When you create the invoice and give the customer the credit for the deposit, as described earlier in this chapter in the section, " Applying the Customer Deposit to an Invoice", that action turns the deposit into income.

Now that it's income and you can spend it, you have to move the funds into the Operating Funds subaccount. You can tell how much to transfer by opening the Chart Of Accounts window and looking at the balances for the Customer Deposit Funds subaccount and the Customer Deposits Received liability account. The liability account has been reduced as customer deposits were applied to invoices; now it's time to move those deposits to the operating account.

The current difference between the liability account and the customer deposit bank account is the amount you've now earned and can declare as income. The easiest way to do that is to transfer funds between accounts, as follows:

1. Choose Banking | Transfer Funds to open the Transfer Funds Between Accounts transaction window.

2. In the Transfer Funds From field, select the Customer Deposit Funds subaccount.

3. In the Transfer Funds To field, select the Operating Funds subaccount.

4. In the Transfer Amount field, enter the total of the customer deposits that can be moved to operating funds.

The balance remaining in the Customer Deposit Funds subaccount matches the balance in the Customer Deposits Received liability account (those totals must always match).

Job Costing

Job costing means tracking the cost of each job so you can keep an eye on your costs and your profits.

Going over all the processes involved in setting up and implementing job costing involves far more information than we could present here. Each type of construction business has different needs, and you'll find as you use QuickBooks, and create reports, you'll think of other job-costing details you want to track. As a result, you'll be continuously tweaking your company file and creating new rules for entering transactions.

ProAdvisor TIP: *For job costing to work properly, every job should be a QuickBooks job. If you have a customer that you believe is a one-time-only customer, create a job anyway.*

Linking Expenses to Jobs

The least complicated method for job costing is to make sure that every expense related directly to a job is linked to that job. To accomplish this, when you enter vendor bills, or write direct checks, you must select the appropriate job in the Customer:Job column of each line item in the transaction window.

By default, when you fill in the Customer:Job column, the Billable column adds a check mark to indicate that you plan to send an invoice to the customer to reimburse you for the cost. However, for job costing you deselect the Billable check mark.

If the bill you're entering or the check you're writing is for expenses that involve multiple jobs, or is for expenses that include some job related cost and some general costs, you must split the line items on the transaction windows so that you enter the specific amounts for each job.

For example, if you're tracking long distance charges and your telephone bill is $200.00, and $20.00 is related to Job A and $10.00 is related to Job B, you need to split the amount of the telephone bill.

In the heading section, enter the total amount of the bill. In the first line in the Expenses tab enter details as follows:

1. In the Account column select the expense account for Telephone.
2. In the Amount column enter the amount linked to Job A.
3. In the Customer:Job column select Job A.
4. In the Billable column deselect the check mark.
5. Repeat for Job B (and any other jobs to which the jobs are linked).
6. In the last line omit any jobs (this is your general administrative charge for this expense).

If you select the Billable option, when you invoice the customer, the charges will be waiting in the Choose Billable Time And Costs dialog (click Add Time/Costs in the invoice window), and you can add them to the invoice.

Using Items for Job Costing

You can also use items to track job costs, but you need to make sure you have all the items you need in your Item List. That means items that describe the materials and services you provide, as well as the materials and services you purchase. Use the following guidelines when you set up items:

- Create an item for each type of work you perform, and for materials you sell as part of that work.

- Create an item for each phase of work, when the work you perform has multiple phases. (This is especially useful if one phase is subcontracted.)

- Use subitems to refine both your invoicing and job costing activities. For example, if you have an item for Permits & Licenses, create subitems for the specific types of permits and licenses you need to perform your work.

- Items for materials should be generic; use lumber as an item instead of creating multiple items for different types or sizes of lumber.

- Don't enter cost and sales prices when you create an item unless it's an item or a subcontracted service that you always buy and resell at a specific cost and price.

When you create your items, select the check box labeled This Item Is Used In Assemblies Or Is Purchased For A Specific Customer:Job even if the item doesn't seem to fit that definition. In QuickBooks we call this a "two-sided" item. (You can edit an existing item to make it "two-sided" instead of creating a new item.)

Selecting this option changes the New Item (or Edit Item) dialog by adding fields for tracking both costs and sales (see Figure 10-7).

Figure 10-7: Set up your item to track both costs and sales.

In the Expense Account field, select the account to which you post job-related costs. Your accountant may want this account to be of the type Expense or Cost of Goods—it might be an account named Materials, or an account named Subcontracted Work (if this item is something you usually job out). In the Income Account field, select the income account to which you post job revenue.

Then, when you pay a vendor for materials or subcontracting work that's related to a job, link the expense to both an item and a job. You do this whether you're entering the vendor's bill in the Enter Bills transaction window, or you're using the Write Checks window to pay a vendor for whom you didn't enter a bill.

To do this, you use the Items tab instead of entering expense accounts in the Expenses tab. Enter the item connected to the expense, the amount of the expense, and the job for which you incurred this expense.

If the vendor bill covers more than one job, enter the information over multiple lines, to make sure that postings for each item and job are applied to each job properly. For example, if a vendor bill of $2905 is split between two jobs where material for one job is $1260.00 and $1645.00 for the other, enter the bill as seen in Figure 10-8.

Figure 10-8: Track job costs by splitting vendor bills to reflect individual jobs.

If you select the Billable option, when you invoice the customer, the charges will be waiting in the Time and Costs dialog (click Add Time/ Costs button on the Main tab in the invoice window), and you can add them to the invoice.

If you don't want to invoice the customer; instead you just want to keep track of your costs, deselect the Billable check mark.

Tracking Material That Isn't Job-Specific

As described in the previous section, when you purchase materials or services for a specific job, you link the purchase to the job by entering the job in the Customer:Job column of the vendor bill or the Write Checks window. Sometimes you invoice the customer for reimbursement for the purchase; sometimes the purchase is included in the job price and you use the information to track job costs.

However, when you use warehoused materials on a job (the stuff you buy just to keep because you frequently use it on jobs), you should track that usage in QuickBooks, so you can keep track of your job costs.

Most contractors keep all sorts of materials and supplies in a warehouse (or the garage, basement, truck, etc.). They have these items in their Item Lists. Sometimes they list the items on the customer's invoice, but they either use an estimated price or leave the price at zero (just to let the customer know the item was used on the job).

Many contractors have asked how to use these item types in job costing. Each contractor has mentioned several types of items (the types differ depending on the type of contractor). For example, plumbers want to track soldering materials, small pipe fittings, washers, etc. Carpenters have nails, screws, cement, etc. You get the idea. None of these are purchased for any specific job; instead, these are materials that are used all the time and have to be kept on hand.

To track these generic parts and materials as part of job costing, you can use a system we call "paying yourself back for the consumed parts". To pay yourself (which doesn't involve any real payments), you link a previously purchased product to a job.

Let's say you purchased $1000.00 worth of materials, posting the purchases to an item named Materials. As you use the materials, you want to track them against a job (and perhaps invoice the customer).

To accomplish this, create a new account in your chart of accounts named Adjustment Register. The account type is Bank. If you're using numbered accounts, use a number that falls at the end of the number range for your other (real) bank accounts.

You'll use this account to record a zero amount check by creating two entries—one positive entry and one negative entry, which washes the total. During the entry process, you allocate the cost to a customer or job, and to a class (if you're tracking classes). Here are the steps:

1. Press Ctrl-W to open the Write Checks window.
2. In the Bank Account field, select the Adjustment account.

3. In the Date field, enter the date you used the material.

4. Don't enter anything in the payee field.

5. In the Items tab at the bottom of the window, select the item.

6. In the Description column, optionally enter a description of the material you used.

7. Skip the Qty and Cost columns and enter the cost (not an estimated retail price) in the Amount column.

8. Select the Customer:Job (and select a Class if you're using classes). If you want to include the item in an invoice, make sure the Billable column has a check mark. If you're merely tracking job costs, deselect the check mark.

9. On the next line, fill in the exact same information for all columns except the Customer:Job and Class columns, using a negative amount equal to the amount in the first line. (If you filled out the Customer:Job and Class columns, you'd be setting the charge to the customer and class to zero, which you don't want to do.)

10. Click Recalculate. The amount of the check changes to zero.

11. Click Save & Close.

If you marked the item Billable, when you invoice the customer the charges will be waiting in the Choose Billable Time And Costs dialog and you can add them to the invoice. If you deselected the Billable check mark, the cost you entered is for the purpose of tracking job costs.

Reporting Job Costs

You can see the income, job costs, and net profits for each job by choosing Reports | Job Costing | Profit & Loss By Job. The report displays a column for each job along with a total for each customer.

For a detailed report on an individual job, select the job in the Customer Center and click the link labeled Job Profitability in the right pane. The report displays the costs by type (costs associated with items and expenses linked to the job), along with the income and the amount of the difference between the costs and income for each type of cost (the amount of profit or loss). Choose Customize Report to add a column for the percentage difference.

Estimates

Estimates are a necessity for contractors, and creating an estimate in QuickBooks is a straightforward process. Choose Contractor | Create Estimates & Change Orders to open the Create Estimates transaction window.

Enter the customer, item(s), and financial information, including a markup if you're using markups. QuickBooks calculates the total. When you print the estimate for your customer, only the total amounts appear; any cost and markup rates you entered are not printed.

If the job has phases (for instance a demolition phase, then a building phase, then a finishing carpentry phase, and finally a cleanup phase), you should think about creating separate estimates for each phase. This makes progress billing less complicated, and also provides a way to track estimated-to-final costs on a phase-by-phase basis (which is valuable information to have when you create an estimate for another similar job). In addition, if you subcontract any of the phases, it's easier to track the subcontractor on a specific phase and estimate.

Change Orders

Change orders are a common fact of life for both general and sub contractors. QuickBooks Premier Contractors Edition supports this feature, which makes your business life easier. (QuickBooks editions that don't have the change order feature merely change the original estimate when you make changes.) With the change order feature, you see all your change order items on the estimate form

Unfortunately, many independent contractors don't bother to create or track change orders, and sometimes this leads to misunderstandings (and occasionally, serious disputes) with customers.

It only takes a few seconds to create a change order, and you should get into the habit of using this feature for any changes to the original estimate. In fact, if you're not bothering to create estimates for every job, you should change that habit, too.

Creating a Change Order

To create a change order, you must have saved an estimate. Change orders don't exist by themselves; they're linked to estimates. To create a change order, follow these steps:

1. Open the original estimate.
2. Make changes to the quantity, price, or other line item components.
3. Click Save & Close.
4. QuickBooks displays a message asking if you want to record your changes. Click Yes.
5. QuickBooks displays the Add Change Order dialog (see Figure 10-9) asking if you want to add this change order to the estimate. Click Add.

Figure 10-9: Track your changes by adding them to the estimate.

You can add a note to the text displayed in the Add Change order dialog to explain the change.

Making Additional Changes to an Estimate

It's not uncommon to require multiple changes to an estimate, especially if the estimate has many entries. Frequently, you may have to add services or items, due to some unexpected event as you complete the job.

You can continue to add or remove items in the original estimate, creating an audit trail of the job's changes. However, you have to be careful about the way you add further items.

When you view the original estimate, the change order(s) appear below the line items. A blank line sits between the line items and the change order(s), as seen in Figure 10-10.

Figure 10-10: A blank line appears between the estimate and the change order.

You should use the blank line above the change order to add items (or to remove items by entering them with a minus sign), so your change orders remain below the list of line items. If you select an item in the Item column of the same line that contains the change order to use that row, the change order info is replaced with the item description. If you accidentally erase the change order data, click the Revert button to restore it.

If you need more than one new line, right-click the Item column of the existing new line, or the line in which the change order appears, and choose Insert Line. A new blank line appears above the line your cursor is on.

To be sure you don't forget the estimate now has a change order you might want to select Custom Change Order from the Template drop-down list. It changes the form title (both onscreen and in the printed version) to Estimate With Change Order. It also removes the Ship To field and adds the Class field (if you're using classes) to the body of the estimate.

Managing Retainage

Construction contracts frequently contain a *retainage* clause (sometimes called a *retention* clause). This clause specifies that a certain percentage of the total price of the job will not be invoiced to the customer until all parties agree that the job is completed satisfactorily.

The retainage percentage is usually ten percent, and it means that you can only invoice ninety percent of the job until the terms governing retainage are met. If you use progress invoicing (invoicing a percentage of the contract price as the appropriate percentage of the work is completed), you must deduct the retainage percentage from the total of each invoice.

ProAdvisor NOTE: *Some contractors negotiate retainage so that progress invoices don't deduct retainage, and the entire ten percent of the total is deducted from the last invoice. This provides a better cash flow for covering costs of the work. This method only works if the progress invoicing structure results in the last invoice being large enough to cover the entire retainage amount.*

If your business encounters a retainage clause, you have to configure QuickBooks to track and report the retainage figures. This means creating accounts and items, and then entering the appropriate transactions.

Configuring QuickBooks for Retainage

To track retainage you need an account, and items. The money involved in retainage is part of the contract you signed, and is technically yours because you're expected to earn it. Therefore, it's an asset.

Creating a Retainage Account

You need to create an account to track retainage. The common account type is Other Current Asset, and you can name the account Retainage, Retentions, or anything similar.

Creating Retainage Items

You need several items to include on your sales forms to implement retainage:

- An item to deduct the percentage
- An item to subtotal the sales form before deducting the percentage
- An item to use when it's time to collect the retainage due to you.

Retainage Deduction Item

To create the retainage deduction item, follow these steps:

1. Choose Lists | Item List to open the Item List window.
2. Press Ctrl-N to open the New Item dialog.
3. Select Other Charge from the Type drop-down list.
4. Name the item Retainage Deduction (or Retention Deduction).

5. Enter Deduction for Retainage (or something similar) in the Description field.

6. Enter -10% in the Amount Or % field – note the minus sign and the percent sign. (If you have multiple retainage rates, create an item for each, such as Retainage10, Retainage15).

7. Enter a non-taxable tax code in the Tax Code field (which only exists if you've enabled Sales Tax).

8. In the Account field, select your retainage asset account.

9. Click OK.

Retainage Subtotal Item

The retainage item is a percentage, and QuickBooks calculates percentages against the line immediately above the percentage item on the sales form. Therefore, you must subtotal all the items on your sales form before you enter an item that calculates a percentage. This requires a discrete subtotal item in your Item List.

Create a new item, using the following configuration settings:

• The item type is Subtotal.

• Name the item Subtotal (or something similar).

• Optionally, enter a description that will appear on your sales forms ("Subtotal" works fine).

Retainage Collection Item

After the job is approved, you bill the customer for the retained amount, so you need an item to include on your invoice form. Use the general instructions described earlier to create the retainage deduction item. However, use the following configuration settings:

• The item type is either Service or Other Charge. Other Charge is probably better since it keeps the listing near the retainage deduction charge.

- Name the item Retainage Collection (or something similar).
- Optionally, enter a description to appear on sales forms.
- Do not enter a rate or amount—you'll fill that in when you create the sales form.
- In the Account field, select the retainage asset account.

Using the Retainage Item in Sales Forms

You must use your retainage items whenever you create a sales form for a customer that has a retainage clause in the contract.

During the course of the job, create invoices as usual. After all the applicable line items are entered for each invoice, insert the subtotal item in the next line. Then, insert the retainage deduction item in the line after the subtotal item. QuickBooks will use the percentage figure and calculate the invoice correctly.

When the job is done, and the terms for collecting the retainage amount are met, the retainage can be released to you. Create an invoice, and use the retainage collection item to bill the customer for the withheld funds. Enter the amount due in the Amount column of the invoice.

Of course, to enter the amount due, you have to discover the correct amount. No built-in QuickBooks report exists to provide this amount, so you must create a report for this purpose. Use the following steps to determine the retainage amount you've deducted for a specific customer or job:

1. Choose Reports | Customers & Receivables | Customer Balance Summary.
2. Click Customize Report.
3. Go to the Filters tab.
4. Select Account in the Filter list.
5. In the Account list, scroll down the list to find and select your retainage asset account.
6. Click OK.

7. In the report window, locate the customer or job, and note the amount (which is the total amount you deducted over the course of all invoicing for this customer or job).

Memorize this report to avoid the need to set the filters next time you need this information for a customer. Click the Memorize button and name the report Retainage Totals (or something similar).

Holding Retainage for Subcontractors

Sometimes retainage works the other way around; you hold back a percentage of an agreed total from a subcontractor, and remit the retainage when the job is completed satisfactorily. For lack of a better term, we'll call this "Retainage Payable".

Configuring QuickBooks for Retainage Payable

The money you hold back for retainage is not yours; it belongs to the subcontractor and must be paid when the terms of the contract are met. Therefore, it's a liability.

Creating a Retainage Payable Account

You need to create an account to track retainage payable. Use an Other Current Liability account named Retainage Payable.

Entering Retainage Payable on a Bill

When you receive a bill from the subcontractor, enter the amount of the bill on the first line of the details section in the Enter Bills transaction window. If you're tracking job costs, enter the job.

On the next line, enter the Retainage Payable liability account you created, and enter the appropriate amount (usually 10%) with a minus sign. Do not enter a customer/job on this line, because it has nothing to do with the costs applied to the job. The bill amount displays the net amount (the amount billed less the retainage amount).

When you pay the bills, the net amount appears in the Pay Bills window, and you remit that net amount.

Do this for every bill that arrives from this subcontractor until you receive the final bill.

Paying the Retainage Payable

When the job is complete, and the final bill arrives, you add back the retainage you've held. In the Enter Bills window, after you enter the amount of the bill, enter the Retainage Payable liability account, and enter the total amount of retainage due (without the minus sign, of course).

The bill amount changes to the total of the latest bill plus all the retainage due to the subcontractor. When you pay the bill, you've completed your payments to this subcontractor.

Tracking Retainage Payable

You need to create periodic reports on retainage payable so you know how much money that's in your bank account doesn't really belong to you (and therefore cannot be spent for any purpose except to send retainage to subcontractors).

To create a report on the retainage payable you're holding, select the Retainage Payable account in the Chart Of Accounts window, and press Ctrl-Q. Change the date range to All. If you're managing retainage payable for multiple subcontractors, sort the report by Name.

QuickBooks does not display subtotals for each name, so you can either print the report and enter the subtotals manually, or export the report to Excel and enter formulas to subtotal each subcontractor's postings.

To produce a report for an individual subcontractor (useful to enclose when you send the final check), click Customize Report. In the Filters tab, choose Name as the filter and select the subcontractor.

ProAdvisor TIP: *If you're a general contractor who frequently holds retainage amounts for subcontractors, you might consider opening a separate bank account, or at least creating a virtual bank account to keep the money separate. See "Virtual Bank Accounts for Customer Deposits" earlier in this chapter for details.*

Depositing Checks with Two Payees

If you're in the construction business, and you're a subcontractor, the checks from the general contractor frequently arrive with two payees.) This scenario often occurs when you're working in a "time and materials" environment. You sell a customer (usually a general contractor) a product or a service that you sub out to a vendor. The vendor charges you $1000.00. You enter the vendor's bill and send the sub or the product to the job.

You send the customer (the general) an invoice for $1000.00. The check arrives from the customer, and there are two payees: you and the vendor.

You can't deposit the check into your bank account, and then write a check to the vendor, because your bank won't take a check that isn't endorsed by both payees. Here's the solution

1. Create a fake bank account named "Passthrough Payments" (or something similar).
2. Open a Receive Payments window and pay off the customer's invoice with the check. Be sure to note the check number for later reference.
3. Deposit the check to the fake bank account.
4. Select Pay Bills, and choose the fake bank account in the Payment Account field. Select the appropriate vendor bill and use the same check number to pay the bill.

5. Endorse the check and send it to the vendor with a copy of the vendor's bill.

The transactions you entered "wash" the fake bank account, so it has a zero balance. If that account shows a balance, you've forgotten to take one of the steps:

- If the account has a positive (debit) balance, you received payment for the customer invoice, but you didn't pay the vendor's bill.

- If the account has a negative balance, you paid the vendor's bill, but you didn't enter the receipt of the payment for the customer's invoice.

When you open the register for the fake bank account, you can see a history of every check you treated in this manner.

CHAPTER 11

Manufacturing and Wholesale Edition

- Stock status for sales orders
- Customizing purchase orders
- Customer RMAs
- Returning products to a vendor
- Tracking damaged and missing inventory
- Customized reports

Manufacturing and distribution businesses were among the first business types to install computerized accounting systems. Many of the larger companies purchased software systems designed specifically for their types of businesses. Those systems are called "vertical applications" and are written specifically for certain types of manufacturing or distribution businesses.

For smaller businesses, it's certainly possible to track some of the same accounting processes with QuickBooks, and the Premier Manufacturing and Wholesale Edition includes features to help you do just that.

If you think about it, the paradigm is always the same:

- You buy stuff at a certain price, and you sell it at a higher price (wholesale distribution).
- You buy stuff to build stuff you sell (manufacturing).

Many businesses do both. This is all very straightforward, and small manufacturing and wholesale businesses can easily manage their finances with QuickBooks.

Stock Status Information for Sales Orders

The QuickBooks Premier Manufacturing & Wholesale Edition offers advanced functions for tracking sales orders. Two important and useful advanced features are built into this edition of QuickBooks Premier:

- Stock shortage warnings when creating a sales order.
- One-click access to stock status reports in the Create Sales Orders transaction window.

These features are only available in the Premier Manufacturing & Wholesale, Retail, and Accountant editions. The other Premier editions don't warn you about stock shortages until you convert a sales order to an invoice.

Stock Status Configuration Options

By default, QuickBooks warns you about inventory stock shortages when the Quantity on Hand (QOH) is less than the quantity you enter on a sales order. However, when you're creating a sales order, the QOH isn't necessarily the only thing you need to be warned about.

If the QOH of a product is 10, and you want to sell 5, the math isn't as simple as it seems. If existing sales orders (that have not yet shipped and been converted to invoices) include that product, and those sales orders add up to 6 units, you don't really have 10 units available when you're creating a new sales order, you only have 4 units available.

Similarly, if the QOH is 10, and the people in the warehouse have begun assembling products that use that inventory part, a substantial number of the QOH may be in the process of going into an inventory assembly (called a *build*, and covered in Chapter 6).

You need to configure QuickBooks to track the quantity available, not the quantity on hand in the warehouse.

To access this option, choose Edit | Preferences, and select the Items & Inventory icon in the left pane. Move to the Company Preferences tab, and make the appropriate adjustments to the options (see Figure 11-1).

Figure 11-1: Configure the stock status options that help you manage sales of inventory efficiently.

Control the way QuickBooks calculates available stock by selecting either or both of the options in the dialog:

- *Quantity Reserved For Pending Builds* means QuickBooks checks the list of pending builds for assemblies to see if the item you're entering in a sales form is included; if so, it deducts the total number of units of the item involved in the pending builds from the quantity available for sale.
- *Quantity On Sales Orders* means QuickBooks checks all existing sales orders and deducts the total units of the item included on sales orders from the quantity available for sale.

Specify the conditions under which a warning about insufficient inventory is displayed. You can choose QOH or Quantity Available, although it makes more sense to select Quantity Available.

Out of Stock Warnings

If an item is out of stock (QOH is zero), QuickBooks issues a warning as soon as you select the item in the sales order, even before you enter the quantity (see Figure 11-2). You can continue with the sales order, and wait until stock is available before converting the sales order to an invoice.

Not Enough Quantity	
You don't have sufficient quantity available to sell 1 ea of the item 5030-03-02	
Quantity on hand	0
Quantity on other Sales Orders	14
Quantity Reserved for Assemblies	0
Quantity available	-14

OK

Figure 11-2: When there's no stock on hand, QuickBooks tells you as soon as you enter the item in the sales order.

Insufficient Stock Warnings

If you've configured QuickBooks to issue warnings when stock is on hand, but is not available because it's committed on existing sales orders or for pending builds, you see a message similar to Figure 11-3.

Figure 11-3: This item isn't out of stock, but all the stock is promised.

You can continue with the sales order and wait until stock is available before converting the sales order to an invoice, or negotiate an exchange of stock with the person who created the other sales orders. This is one of those times when you need to consider whether one customer should take priority over another customer.

It's possible to free up stock that's available (but promised) to make sure your best customers receive their orders quickly. See "Modifying Sales Orders to Obtain Promised Stock", later in this chapter.

Checking Stock Status Details

One of the nifty enhanced functions in the Premier Manufacturing & Wholesale Edition is the ability to check stock status, in detail, right from the sales order transaction window. After you enter the item in the sales order, whether you receive a stock status warning or not, click the icon that appears on the right side of the Ordered column.

QuickBooks calls this icon and resulting report Current Availability. This is a report on the current status of this item. As you can see in Figure 11-4, this report has more information than the stock status warnings QuickBooks displays.

Figure 11-4: There's a limit to the quantity you can enter on this sales order, but a purchase order exists so more should arrive soon.

You can learn even more about the stock status of this item by clicking the Show Details button. Then choose the type of information you want to see by selecting one of the following topics from the drop-down list:

- **Sales Orders**. This choice displays all the current sales orders that contain this item. See "Modifying Sales Orders to Obtain Promised Stock" to remove items from one of those sales orders so you can invoice and ship the current sales order.

- **Pending Builds Using <*item name*>**. This choice displays all the pending bills that include this item.

- **Purchase Orders**. This choice displays all the current purchase orders for this item, including the expected date of arrival (see Figure 11-5).

The Purchase Order due date is probably not accurate. The default PO in QuickBooks uses the date the PO is created as the delivery date.

See the section "Customizing Purchase Orders" to learn how to make POs more efficient.

Figure 11-5: If more stock is due to arrive soon don't convert the sales order to an invoice until after it's been received into inventory.

Modifying Sales Orders to Obtain Promised Stock

When you click the Show Details button, and select Sales Orders, QuickBooks displays a listing of the sales orders containing the item you want to include in the sales order you're creating.

If the sales order you're creating is for a customer you think should be shipped product faster than the customers on the existing sales orders, you can modify any of the displayed sales orders to reduce the item's quantity.

Double-click the listing for the sales order you want to change. However, since you have a sales order in process in the Create Sales Orders window, and QuickBooks can neither open a second sales order in the window, nor open another instance of the Create Sales Orders window, you have to decide how to remove the current sales order from the window. QuickBooks displays a message that offers three choices for handling the current sales order:

- **Save Changes**. Save the current sales order with its current items and quantities, and open the selected existing sales order in the Create Sales Orders window. You can return to the sales order you saved to adjust the quantity, after you finish modifying the older sales order.

- **Discard Changes**. Close the current sales order without saving it, and open the selected existing sales order. You can create the new sales order after you've adjusted the quantities in the existing sales order.

- **Continue Editing**. Forget about opening an existing sales order, and return to the sales order you're currently working on.

Unless the sales order you're trying to create is for an important customer who doesn't accept back orders, and no additional stock is expected in the near future, it's best to continue working on the current sales order.

When stock arrives, you can ship to this customer first by converting this sales order to an invoice before the earlier sales orders are converted. See the next section, "Sales Order Fulfillment Worksheet", to learn how to allocate stock to sales orders.

Sales Order Fulfillment Worksheet

The QuickBooks Premier Manufacturing & Wholesale Edition has a Sales Order Fulfillment Worksheet that you can use to decide how to fill sales orders if there is insufficient stock to fill all sales orders.

To open the worksheet, choose Customers | Sales Order Fulfillment Worksheet. When the worksheet opens (see Figure 11-6), its appearance is determined by the availability of the stock entered in sales orders, and the way you sort the data. You can sort the display of sales orders by selecting a sort order from the drop-down list.

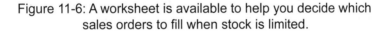

Figure 11-6: A worksheet is available to help you decide which sales orders to fill when stock is limited.

In the sales order listing at the top of the window, QuickBooks uses symbols to indicate the fulfillment status of each sales order:

- An empty square with a red X means there is no stock available to fill the order.

- A solid green circle means there is sufficient stock to fill the order.

- A half filled amber circle means there is sufficient stock to ship a partial order. This could mean that less stock than ordered is available for the items in the sales order, or one (or more) items on the sales order is out of stock (even though there is sufficient stock to fill the order for another item).

Select any order to display stock status details for that order in the bottom of the window. QuickBooks uses the same symbols to indicate the fulfillment capabilities of each item in the sales order.

The fact that more than one sales order has a green circle doesn't mean you can fulfill all the "green circle" sales orders. Depending on stock availability, it could mean that you can fulfill one order, and when you do, an item is used and the other sales orders won't be able to ship (and their symbols will change).

Click the button labeled Choose For Me to display a variety of choices you can select to have QuickBooks automatically determine the sales order to fill (see Figure 11-7).

To choose sales orders manually, select a listing and click the check box in the first column. The bottom of the window inserts the number of items required to fill the order (or partially fill the order if the sales order does not have a green circle) in the To Fulfill Qty column. If this action uses up the available stock, the symbols for other sales orders that include this stock, change to an empty square with a red X.

Selecting a sales order does not turn it in to an invoice, nor does it lock the available stock so that it belongs to this sales order. This is a worksheet, an informational window. However, you can begin the process of converting a sales order to an invoice from the worksheet window.

Figure 11-7: Decide how you want to handle filling sales orders.

The first step is to make sure that the reported availability numbers match what's actually on the shelves. Select the sales order you want to fill, and select the Pick Lists option at the bottom of the window. Click the Print button to print the pick list, and then send the printed pick list to the warehouse to make sure the sales order can be filled to match the quantity in the To Fulfill Qty column.

ProAdvisor TIP: *If you're on a network, install a printer near the stock shelves, and select that printer when you print pick lists.*

If enough stock is available to fill the order, double-click the sales order listing at the top of the window to open the original sales order. Then click the Create Invoice button on the Main tab ribbon bar and follow the prompts to turn the sales order into an invoice.

When you return to the worksheet, the symbols on the worksheet change to indicate the new status of order fulfillment, because at this point you've actually removed product from inventory.

You could also close the worksheet window, convert the appropriate sales orders to invoices, and then check the worksheet stats again when new product arrives. This worksheet is an ad-hoc document, which means that any information you entered in the window wasn't saved, and each time you open the worksheet the data in the window displays real time information as of the moment you open it.

Customizing Purchase Orders

The default Purchase Order template (named Custom Purchase Order) is selected by default when you create POs. It lacks some fields that are important. However, it's quite easy to customize the template to make sure all the information you need appears on the PO. QuickBooks provides two ways to customize this template:

- Customize the Custom Purchase Order template.
- Create a new customized template, with a different name, based on this Custom Purchase Order template.

The latter approach is preferable since the former changes a basic template. It's better to keep the basic template available for other, different, customizations.

This is a two-step process: First, duplicate the default PO template and give it a new name, then customize the new template.

Duplicating a Template

Use the following steps to duplicate the default PO template:

1. Choose Lists | Templates to open the Templates window.
2. Select (highlight) the Custom Purchase Order listing.
3. Click the Templates button at the bottom of the window and choose Duplicate.
4. In the Select Template Type dialog, select Purchase Order and click OK.
5. The Templates window displays a listing named Copy Of: Custom Purchase Order.
6. Double-click it to open the Basic Customization dialog.
7. Click Manage Templates and in the right pane of the Manage Templates dialog, change the name of the template. Use a name that describes your customization— in this case we used the name PO With Due Date.
8. Click OK to return to the Basic Customization dialog.

In this dialog you can make minor changes to the template, such as changing fonts, colors, the company information that prints on the transaction document, and so on.

However, in this case you want to make major changes to the template; you're adding fields or columns to the document.

Customizing the Purchase Order Template

With your new template displayed in the Basic Customization dialog, click the Additional Customization button at the bottom of the dialog to open the Additional Customization dialog (see Figure 11-8).

Figure 11-8: Customize the PO template to make sure all the information you require is included.

On the Header tab you can include or exclude fields for the on-screen version, the printed version, or both. For example, if you've created custom fields for vendors and you want to include the data in the custom field for the vendor receiving the PO, that might be data only needed on the screen as you prepare the PO.

ProAdvisor NOTE: *Many businesses don't mail purchase orders; instead, they phone the information in and only create the PO to have a record of its existence.*

The most important change for POs is to include a field for the expected delivery date on the PO. The default template created the first time you open the Create Purchase Orders window does not include this field. To add it, click both the Screen and Print check boxes next to the field named Due Date. You can change the Title text to suit your needs.

Examine the other fields in the Header tab to see if you want to make any other changes (such as including the Ship Via field in the template).

ProAdvisor NOTE: *As you make changes, QuickBooks may display a message about using the Layout Designer to make sure all the elements you're changing fit properly in the template. Most of the changes described here don't require a complete overhaul of the layout, so you can select the option to stop displaying the message. Keep an eye on the preview panel in the right pane, or click Print Preview to see if changes you're making cause fields or columns to overlap. If so, you can use the Layout Designer to move fields and columns (it's easy to use because it's visually logical).*

Move to the Columns tab (see Figure 11-9) to see if there are any columns you want to select or deselect.

Figure 11-9: Customize columns for your purchase orders.

If you don't usually order items specifically for a customer (or, if you do, you link the purchase to the customer when you receive the bill), you can remove the Customer & Job column.

If you're tracking the Manufacturer's Part Number in your inventory item records, add that column to your PO template.

Click OK when you finish customizing fields and columns, and then click OK in the Basic Customization dialog to save the new template and add it to the Template drop-down list when you create POs. Use this template for your purchase orders.

Adding Purchase Order Info to the Item List

One of the quickest ways to ascertain the current availability level of an item is to open the Item List, which displays information about availability. However, by default the list does not include information about the number of items currently on order via POs.

To add PO information to the Item List, right-click anywhere in the window and choose Customize Columns. Select Quantity On Purchase Order in the left pane of the Customize Columns dialog, and then click Add to include this column in the list window.

To make the list even easier to work with, select the Quantity On Purchase Order listing in the Chosen Columns list and click Move Up to put the new column next to the On Sales Order column.

Units of Measure

A unit of measure (U/M) is a way to establish specific information about the basis on which you sell quantities of goods and products. For example, if you sell an inventory item named Chocolate Syrup, you can specify the U/M as a bottle, a 6-pack, or a 24-unit case.

U/Ms are attached to items—each item has its own U/M. QuickBooks provides two ways to track and assign U/Ms:

- Single U/M per item, in which you can assign one U/M to an item.
- Multiple U/M per item, in which you can create a base U/M and then devise multiple conversions of that base U/M to permit sales of different quantities.

The Premier Manufacturing and Wholesale Edition supports both types of U/Ms, and you can learn how to set up and configure them in Chapter 6.

Customer Return Merchandise Authorizations

RMAs (sometimes called RAs) are a fact of life in your business. You have to deal with customer returns, but you can, and should impose rules and protocols; otherwise, tracking the financial consequences becomes extremely difficult.

One rule you should impose is that no merchandise can be returned unless an RMA number that you provide is on the packing slip and/or the shipping label.

Creating RMAs

When a customer wants to return an item, QuickBooks has a way for you to assign an RMA number, and track it with a Microsoft Word document. Of course, you must have Word installed on your computer to take advantage of this feature.

Choose Mfg & Whsle | Inventory Activities | Customer Return Materials Authorization Form. (QuickBooks uses the word "materials" but most wholesale/manufacturing businesses use the word "merchandise".) Word opens with the form loaded in the software window (see Figure 11-10).

The document doesn't really exist as a discrete file (you can see that the title bar lacks a file name), so the first thing to do is save this document so you can access it from Word.

Choose File | Save As, and name the document. By default, Word saves the document in your My Documents folder. You should create a folder for your QuickBooks documents and forms so they're easy to find.

Save the document before you fill anything out, so you have a boilerplate you can open directly in Word. You can use this form whenever you need a customer RMA. The form is configured as a Word table, so you can enter data into all the appropriate cells. Every time you fill out the form, use the Save As (not Save) command to save the document with a new filename that includes the customer's name.

Print a copy of the filled-in form for your bookkeeper, who can issue a credit in QuickBooks when the material comes back from the customer.

You should also print a copy for your warehouse personnel, so they know the material is due.

Figure 11-10: QuickBooks provides a form for tracking RMAs.

ProAdvisor TIP: *If you name each RMA document with the format XXXX-<CustomerName> (where XXXX is the RMA number), when you open the folder in which you're storing RMAs, you can automatically determine the next RMA number.*

This form is inert, which means it has no automatic functions connected to QuickBooks or your QuickBooks company file. You have to track RMA numbers manually, outside of QuickBooks.

Additionally, the form provides fields that make it easy for you to create a credit memo for the customer when the products are returned. However, the data in your QuickBooks file, such as Item Name and Invoice #, don't automatically appear—no drop-down lists exist because you're not working in, or linked to, QuickBooks.

Processing Customer Returns of Inventory

When a customer returns inventory, you have to track the inventory return and the customer's financial status in a way that fits the scenario. For example, the customer may have already paid for the inventory and is returning it because it's damaged. Or the customer may not have paid for the inventory, and is returning it "just because".

The condition of the inventory (whether it is damaged, or is fine and can be resold), and the state of the customer's indebtedness to you are the factors that determine the type of transaction you create.

Creating a Credit for a Paid Invoice

If the customer paid the invoice that covers the damaged returns, you must enter a credit memo, or issue a refund check. The credit memo/refund should cover only the returned items, not the entire invoice (unless the only item on that invoice was the product being returned).

When you create the credit memo, enter the returned item(s) in the line item section of the transaction window. You should also credit any shipping charges (proportionately, if the credit memo is for an invoice that included more items than those being returned).

When you save the credit memo, QuickBooks asks if you want to save the credit for future use by the customer, create a refund check, or apply the credit to an existing invoice.

If you opt to save the credit or apply it to an existing invoice, Quick-Books makes the following postings:

- Debits the Inventory Asset account (puts the product back into inventory).
- Credits the COGS account (removes the cost expense).
- Debits the sales account connected to the item (lowers your income).
- Credits the A/R account (lowers the total receivables).

In addition, appropriate changes are made to your sales tax liability account and to any shipping charges you include in the credit. Of course, for any sales tax adjustments to be made, both the customer and the item must both be taxable.

If you create a refund check, QuickBooks makes the following additional postings:

- Debits Accounts Receivable (reversing the action taken when you saved the credit memo)
- Credits the bank account (removes the money from the bank).

After the customer's record is updated, you must adjust your inventory to remove the damaged goods that QuickBooks put back into inventory. See the section "Adjusting Inventory for Damaged Goods".

Voiding an Unpaid Invoice

If the customer has not yet paid the invoice, and the invoice only contains the product being returned, void the invoice. QuickBooks makes the following postings:

- Debits the Inventory Asset account (puts the product back into inventory).
- Credits the COGS account (removes the cost expense).
- Debits the sales account connected to the item (lowers your income).
- Credits the A/R account (lowers the total receivables).

If the invoice contains additional items, do not void it. Instead, issue a credit for the returned item, and when you save the credit choose the option to apply the credit to a specific invoice, and then choose the invoice that contains the inventory item being returned.

Providing Credits for Damaged Inventory

If the inventory being returned by your customer is damaged you can't put it back into your warehouse. However, you need to credit the customer's account, which automatically puts the inventory back into stock. You have two methods available to accomplish this:

- Use an item on the credit that's designed for this situation. The real item isn't returned to inventory.
- Use the original item on the credit, and then create an inventory adjustment as explained in the following sections.

Use a Damaged Inventory Item for Damaged Inventory Credits

If you create an item for damaged inventory, you can use that item in a credit to avoid putting the inventory item that's being returned back into inventory. Create the item and link it to the inventory adjustment account you use to adjust inventory.

It's best to create a separate damaged inventory account, in addition to the inventory adjustment account. For example, most accountants recommend the following Cost of Goods Sold accounts:

- Cost of Goods Sold
- Inventory Adjustments
- Damaged Inventory

The advantage of using an item specifically for returned damaged goods is that it's a one-step adjustment. However, it doesn't provide the full history of the interaction with the customer, so you may want to use the method of receiving the damaged item back into inventory and then creating an adjustment to remove the damaged item (explained next).

Adjusting Inventory for Returned Damaged Goods

You must remove the damaged inventory that QuickBooks put back into your system when you created the customer's credit memo using the original inventory item. To do this, choose Vendors | Inventory Activities | Adjust Quantity/Value On Hand to open the Inventory Adjustment transaction form seen in Figure 11-11.

In the Adjustment Account field, select the Inventory Adjustment account or the Damaged Inventory account.

Figure 11-11: Adjust your inventory to remove damaged products.

In the item's listing adjust the number of units by the number of returned damaged units. You can either enter data in the New Quantity column (mentally subtracting the returned number from the displayed Qty On Hand number), or enter the number of returned items in the Qty Difference column (don't forget the minus sign). It's a good idea to use the memo field for details, so when you see this transaction in reports (or your accountant sees it) you can explain it.

In addition, if you purchased this inventory, you must return it to your vendor (usually the manufacturer), and you can also track the details by using the Damaged Goods Log. These functions are discussed in the next section.

Returning Products to a Vendor

When you return products to a vendor you have to enter the appropriate transaction in QuickBooks. The actions you take differ, depending on the scenario:

- You have a PO in the system, but haven't entered the receipt of goods or bill (because you noticed damage when the product arrived).

- You have a receipt of goods in the system, but have not yet entered the bill (because it didn't arrive with the package).

- You have entered both a receipt of goods and a bill into the system.

Voiding or Modifying a Purchase Order

If you haven't yet created the receipt of goods/bill transaction for the PO that covers the damaged products, you can void the purchase order. This only works if the PO contains only the damaged products, and all of the products were damaged (which would be an unusual occurrence).

If the PO contains a quantity larger than 1 of the item, and some of the items aren't damaged, you can void the PO and create a new one with the correct data. Be sure to notify the vendor about this action, telling them to ignore the original PO and look for a new PO number.

You can also modify the PO by reducing the quantity to reflect the number of items you're returning. Notify the vendor that you've changed the PO and ask them to adjust their records.

Voiding or Modifying a Receipt of Items

If you received the items into inventory (without the bill), you can void or modify the receipt of goods transaction. The quickest way to locate the original Item Receipt is to open the Vendor Center, select the vendor, and select Item Receipts from the Show field drop-down list in the right pane.

> **ProAdvisor TIP**: *You can also open the Inventory Center (Vendors | Inventory Activities | Inventory Center), locate the item in the left pane, and select Item Receipts from the Show drop-down list in the Transactions tab on the right.*

If the receipt covers only this item, and if the entire quantity of items is damaged, void the receipt. If the receipt covers multiple items, and/or only some of the quantity received of a single item is damaged, adjust the data in the Qty column, and click Recalculate to adjust the total.

Voiding or Modifying a Receipt of Items and Bill

If you received the items into inventory and also entered the vendor's bill, adjust your transactions according to the contents of the receipt and bill. If everything covered in the receipt of items/bill is damaged, void the transaction.

If you only need to adjust the quantity of an item to reflect the damaged goods you're returning, adjust the data in the Qty column, and click Recalculate to adjust the total.

Entering a Vendor Credit for a Paid Bill

If you paid the vendor before returning damaged goods, you need to create a credit with this vendor. Use the following steps to accomplish this:

1. Choose Vendors | Enter Bills
2. Select the Credit option at the top of the Enter Bills window.
3. Select the vendor.
4. Use the Items tab in the line item section of the window to enter the item and the amount of the credit (don't use a minus sign, QuickBooks knows what a credit is).
5. If appropriate (i.e. you and the vendor agree), enter a credit on the Expenses tab for shipping costs you incurred for the delivery, or will incur for the return of goods.

You can use the credit against existing or future bills from this vendor.

Entering a Vendor Refund

If the vendor agreed to send you a refund check, enter a credit as described in the previous section. The credit applies the appropriate postings to your inventory and A/P accounts. When the check arrives, use the following steps to enter it into your QuickBooks system:

1. Choose Banking | Make Deposits to open the Payments To Deposit window.

2. If there are deposits listed that you are ready to take to the bank, select them.

3. Click OK (even if you haven't selected any deposits) to open the Make Deposits window.

4. If you have multiple bank accounts select the correct one.

5. In the first blank line make the following entry:

   • Enter the Vendor in the Received From column.

   • Enter Accounts Payable in the From Account column (this washes the A/P posting you entered when you created the vendor credit memo).

   • Optionally, enter a note in the Memo column, enter a check number, and select the payment method in the appropriate columns.

   • Enter the amount of the check in the Amount column.

6. Save the deposit.

Saving the credit memo and depositing the check into the bank created all the right postings to your general ledger. However, the postings did not specifically match the vendor credit to the vendor's check. You have to accomplish that step manually:

1. Choose Vendors | Pay Bills to open the Pay Bills window.

2. Select the vendor from the Filter By field drop-down list.

3. Find the bill you created when you entered the refund check. It's easy to spot since, unlike the other listings in the Pay Bills window, this bill has no due date.

4. Select the bill for payment by clicking in the left most column to insert a check mark in the check box.

5. Click Pay Selected Bills to complete the transaction.

If you didn't configure QuickBooks to use credits and discounts automatically, click the Set Credits button after you select the bill. This action opens the Discounts And Credits window seen in Figure 11-12. Select the credit and click Done.

Figure 11-12: Select the credit you created in order to apply it to the bill that represents the vendor refund.

Click Pay Selected Bills in the Pay Bills window. QuickBooks displays the Payment Summary window, showing a zero amount paid. Click Done if this is the only bill payment you're creating.

ProAdvisor NOTE: *You can configure QuickBooks to use discounts and credits automatically by choosing Edit | Preferences, and selecting the Bills icon in the left pane. The option is on the Company Preferences tab.*

Creating a Non-Conforming Material Report

After you have an RMA number from your vendor, you can track the details about the return of damaged goods with the Non-Conforming Material Report, which is a Word document QuickBooks installs for this purpose.

Choose Mfg & Whsle | Inventory Activities | Non-Conforming Material Report to open the document in Word. Fill out the appropriate cells, and use Word's Save As command to save the document with an appropriate name for this return. Print a copy to use as a packing slip (see Figure 11-13).

Non-conforming Material Report

Use this form to record information about material that does not conform to the vendor's specifications. Include a copy of the form when returning the material to the vendor.

Inspector _____   Vendor _____

Inspected on _____   Vendor RMA # _____

Non-conforming Material

Part	Part #	Vendor Part #	Qty	Description of non-conformance	PO #	Date

Recommended Actions

Production Manager _____

Manufacturing Engineer _____

Quality Engineer _____

Customer Support _____

Figure 11-13: Track details for merchandise you return to the vendor.

You can copy this template to the My Documents folder of the person in charge of handling vendor returns, and access it directly from Word instead of working through QuickBooks. Save the document as a Word document, instead of a Word template, as described in the preceding section on the Customer Return Materials Authorization Form.

Tracking Damaged and Missing Products

If you want to keep a log of inventory products that are damaged internally (or go missing) you can use the Damaged Goods Log that QuickBooks installs. This is a Word template that you open in Word, as explained in the previous sections on other Word documents.

To open the log from within QuickBooks, choose Mfg & Whsle | Inventory Activities | Damaged Goods Log. When the Word document opens (see Figure 11-14), you can fill it in.

Use the instructions presented earlier to copy this Word template to the My Documents folder of the person who tracks damaged and missing inventory.

Damaged Goods Log

Part Name	Part #	Qty	Description of Damage	Date Adjusted in QuickBooks

Figure 11-14: Track details about damaged or missing inventory items.

ProAdvisor TIP: *You should create a second document, changing the name to Missing Goods Log, so you can track damaged and missing goods separately.*

Damaged inventory that isn't returned to vendors should be physically removed from inventory so it's not accidentally counted the next time you do a physical count.

When inventory is damaged, or disappears, you must adjust your inventory, using the following steps:

1. Choose Vendors | Inventory Activities | Adjust Quantity/Value On Hand.
2. In the Adjust Quantity/Value On Hand dialog, select the Adjustment Account from the drop-down list.

3. Select the listing for the missing or damaged item.

4. In the Qty Difference column, enter the number of missing or damaged units of this item with a minus sign. QuickBooks automatically calculates the New Quantity column.

If inventory is missing, it could be the result of a miscount or an item being placed on the wrong shelf, or in the wrong room. However, if this happens more than a couple of times, you need to look for another reason. There are two common scenarios to explain missing inventory items:

- Sales personnel take inventory and hide it in their own offices to make sure they can service their customers. This is common for inventory items that have high turnover and are frequently out of stock before the next order arrives from the vendor.

- Employees are helping themselves to inventory items (yes, that means stealing). Employee theft of inventory items is a common occurrence, and the jargon for this is *shrinkage*.

No software can solve either problem, although, usually when accounting software is installed, and inventory tracking is part of the software, shrinkage slows down. To accomplish the change in attitude (the existing attitude of "nobody will notice if you steal"), you need to make an announcement that when there's a difference between the software's inventory numbers and the physical count, you're going to believe the software's numbers.

Manufacturing and Wholesale Reports

QuickBooks includes many customized and memorized reports that are designed to be useful to your type of business. To view the list of reports choose Reports | Manufacturing And Wholesale Reports. The report titles are self-explanatory. You can customize any of these reports further to suit your own needs, and then memorize them with the same name or a different name, for future use.

CHAPTER 12

Nonprofit Edition

- Unified chart of accounts for nonprofits

- Using Classes

- Equity accounts

- Customized templates for transactions

- Data entry shortcuts to avoid

- Memorized reports for nonprofits

The Premier Nonprofit Edition isn't really designed for optimum nonprofit use. However, the Premier Nonprofit Edition includes the Unified Chart of Accounts for nonprofits, customized templates you can use to record specific types of income, and some useful customized reports.

You have to adapt your use of QuickBooks to use it successfully for nonprofits. In this chapter, we provide an overview of some of the basic issues involved in using QuickBooks for nonprofit transactions.

ProAdvisor NOTE: *Adapting QuickBooks for nonprofit accounting is a rather complicated endeavor; more than can be covered in a chapter. Because of the demand for this information, we've published a book on the topic. Look for "Running QuickBooks in Nonprofits" from CPA911 Publishing at your favorite bookstore or buy it online from the publisher's website, www.cpa911.com.*

Unified Chart of Accounts (UCOA)

Most nonprofits have to file a great many detailed reports about their financial activities. Federal and state governments have filing requirements, and grant-givers frequently require financial information. Except for the Form 990 model on the federal level, there's no particular across-the-board standard you can take for granted (although most states will accept the Federal Form 990).

The Unified Chart of Accounts (UCOA) is an attempt to standardize the way nonprofits keep financial records, and report them. The UCOA is based on Form 990, but it's useful and efficient even for nonprofit organizations that don't file Form 990.

Developed by the California Association of Nonprofits and the National Center for Charitable Statistics (NCCS), UCOA provides a way to unite all of your reporting needs into one set of accounting records. By using UCOA as a model for your own chart of accounts, you'll find it easier to produce reports for all who demand them.

When you create a new company file and select Non-Profit as your type of business, QuickBooks offers to install a chart of accounts suitable for nonprofit organizations. The file that's installed is the UCOA.

Renaming Accounts

Some of the accounts have generic names, and you should go through the account list to rename the accounts to fit your circumstances. Select each account you want to rename, and press Ctrl-E. The account record opens in Edit Mode, and you can change the name.

Importing the UCOA

If you updated an existing QuickBooks company file (that did not have the UCOA) to QuickBooks 2014 Premier Nonprofit Edition, you can import the UCOA. Then you can edit and merge accounts to make sure your current balances are properly transferred to the UCOA accounts you want to use.

When you installed QuickBooks Premier Nonprofit Edition, the UCOA file was installed on your computer. To import it, simply choose Nonprofit | Import Nonprofit Chart Of Accounts (UCOA).

When the file is imported, QuickBooks issues a success message. Open the chart of accounts and see if you have duplicate, or nearly duplicate, accounts (your original chart of accounts may have the same, or similar, accounts as the UCOA). If so, delete unneeded duplicate accounts, or merge your original accounts with the new accounts that were installed with the UCOA.

Many nonprofit organizations need only a small percentage of the accounts that are included in the UCOA. The best time to remove accounts you won't need is before you start working in QuickBooks. (If you inadvertently use an account in a transaction, you won't be able to remove it.)

The UCOA is so large that it's easier to remove unneeded accounts in Excel. Go to the folder into which QuickBooks was installed, make a copy of UCOA.iif and rename it UCOA_original.iif. Then open UCOA.iff in Excel. Delete the rows you don't need and save the file. Return to Quick-

Books and select Nonprofit | Import Nonprofit Chart of Accounts (UCOA) from the QuickBooks menu bar. (For additional information on working with IIF files, see Appendix B.)

Accounts Receivable

For nonprofits, tracking income source and income type is far more complex than it is in the for-profit business world. Tracking accounts receivable means creating transactions and reports about money owed or expected. That money has to be categorized by the type of income.

Using Multiple A/R Accounts

If you're using the UCOA, you have multiple A/R accounts, so you can track receivables by type. This makes it easy to report receivables by category to the appropriate committees (many nonprofits have committees for these categories).

Depending on the type of income you generate, you may need to add more A/R accounts to your chart of accounts (and remove those you don't need).

If you're not using the UCOA, you can manually add the A/R accounts you need. Following are some of the A/R accounts we've entered in client files. These may not mirror your needs, but they should stimulate your thinking as you plan the A/R section of your chart of accounts.

- Accounts Receivable: Used for invoices for services or goods you sell. (QuickBooks creates this account automatically as soon as you open an Invoice (Pledge).
- Grants Receivable: Used for invoices entered to track expected grants.
- Contracts Receivable: Used for invoices entered to track expected service contracts (commonly from government agencies).
- Tuition Fees Receivable: Used for invoices for tuition (if you are a school, or if you offer classes).

- Pledges Receivable: Used for invoices for pledges from individual donors.
- Dues Receivable: Used for invoices for membership dues.

Using A/R Accounts in Invoice Transactions

If you have multiple A/R accounts, all invoice transaction windows have a field named Account above the transaction header. You have to remember to enter the appropriate A/R account for the invoice you're creating.

> **ProAdvisor NOTE**: *As a nonprofit organization, many of your invoices are really internal records of pledges from donors, or of expected grants or contracts. They're not mailed; instead, you post them so you can track revenue you're expecting from pledges and grants.*

Entering the A/R account does more than post the transaction to the right account—it affects the invoice numbering system. Invoice numbers are automatically incremented, using the last invoice number in the A/R account being used for the invoice transaction. This means each set of invoice types has its own, discrete, numbering system, which is quite handy.

Reporting on Receivables

Maintaining multiple A/R accounts means you can create a report on the money you're expecting (called an *aging report*), and display the information by category. This lets you keep an eye on the amounts due, by source.

You can see how much money is due from grants, contracts, membership fees, pledged donations from individuals, and so on by choosing Reports | Customers & Receivables | A/R Aging Summary. The aging report displays the monies you're expecting, including the age of each receivable.

You can also customize an aging report for a particular category by filtering the report for a specific A/R account, using these steps:

1. Choose Reports | Customers & Receivables | A/R Aging Summary.
2. Click the Customize Report button at the top of the report.
3. Move to the Filters tab, where the Account field displays All Accounts Receivable.
4. Click the arrow in the Account field, and select the specific A/R account you need for this report.
5. Click OK.

The customized report displays the aging for the selected A/R account.

Using Classes

Nonprofit organizations can't use QuickBooks without using classes to track transactions. Without classes, getting the reports you need for funding agencies, government agencies, and your board of directors is extremely difficult. You either have to spend many hours (or days) analyzing each transaction and creating tallies outside of QuickBooks, or spend a lot of money to have your accountant perform tasks that wouldn't be necessary if you'd used classes.

You can think of a class as a division, or department. In the for-profit world, a business that has a main office in Philadelphia, and a branch office in Camden, would create classes named Phila and Camden to track the respective profits (or losses). Every transaction is assigned to a class, so the business owner can determine the income and expenses for each location. Because that business owner tracks income and expenses by class, he or she can create a Profit & Loss Statement for each class.

In the nonprofit world, you do the same thing by using classes to break down income and expenses by the categories you need to track. You can produce a Statement of Activities (the nonprofit term for an income statement) for each class.

At the very least, when you create reports or tax returns, you must provide the total amount for expenses in each of the following three categories:

- Program services
- Management (administration)
- Fundraising

In addition to preparing reports and tax returns with these categories, these are the expense breakdowns that funding agencies want to see when they consider your organization for grants. And, your board of directors probably wants to see expenses broken down by these categories.

Therefore, these are the classes to start with. You can create any additional classes and subclasses you need. For example, many nonprofit organizations create a class for capital improvement projects (and a subclass for each specific project).

Also, you have to create classes to track the status of funds that are linked to programs or have some time of restriction on the way those funds can be spent.

Create the following classes to ensure that you can track income properly:

- Restricted (also called Permanently Restricted). Restricted funds are funds that are earmarked for a particular program or goal. A building fund for a new building, roof, addition, etc. is a good example of a restricted fund. The funds are spent only for the linked programs.
- Temporarily Restricted. Temporarily restricted funds are earmarked for a particular program, and are restricted until restraints on the use of the funds are lifted. For example, funds received for next year's sports programs are temporarily restricted, and the restriction is lifted when the new year begins.
- Unrestricted. Unrestricted funds are monies that can be spent for any programs.

Program Classes

"Program services" is a generic category that applies to the programs you run (the services you provide). You should have a specific class for each program, or for each program type (such as Education), and a subclass for each specific program of that type (such as Youth, Seniors, etc.).

Having a class for each program lets you create a Statement of Activities for each class, and present the appropriate report to the funding agencies for programs. Figure 12-1 is a sample Class List for a community organization.

Figure 12-1: This community organization can track income and expenses for each funded program.

Customers and Jobs

QuickBooks didn't bother to change any component names or field names for the Premier Nonprofit Edition, so you have to live with the terms "customers" and "jobs".

- A customer is a donor, which is any entity (individual or organization) from which you receive a donation.

- A job is a grant or a contract from a particular donor. Each grant/contract from a donor that requires reporting must be entered as a discrete job under the customer you create for the donor.

Customers that don't require reports don't need jobs. This definition fits any entity that provides unrestricted funds, such as individual donors, tuition-payers, or members who send you membership fees for activities not connected with a specific program.

Equity Accounts

QuickBooks provides one equity account automatically: Opening Balance Equity. This equity account doesn't work properly for nonprofits. It used to offer a Retained Earnings account which you would have had to rename to Unrestricted Net Assets, but fortunately, it's now automatically named properly.

A nonprofit organization requires multiple equity accounts (called *net asset* accounts in the world of nonprofits), to wit:

- Permanently Restricted Net Assets
- Temporarily Restricted Net Assets
- Unrestricted Net Assets

If you're using the Unified Chart of Accounts, these equity accounts are available. If you're creating your own chart of accounts, or updating an existing chart of accounts, you must add the equity accounts required for nonprofits.

ProAdvisor CAUTION: *When you're using an account that has subaccounts, never post to the parent account, only post to the subaccounts.*

Balance Sheet By Class Report

You can create a Balance Sheet report that provides class totals for balance sheet accounts (assets, liabilities, and equity accounts). To see the report, select Reports | Company & Financial | Balance Sheet By Class.

If you see totals under the column labeled Unclassified, drill down into those transactions to assign a class.

ProAdvisor TIP: *To ensure optimum results with the Balance Sheet By Class Report do not assign more than one class to those transactions that accept multiple classes.*

Customized Templates for Transactions

QuickBooks Premier Nonprofit Edition includes some templates you can use for tracking income. These templates are for donations from individuals, not for grants.

Pledges (Invoices)

Many donations start out as pledges, and nonprofit organizations have a number of creative methods for obtaining pledges from friends of the organization. You may have a pledge form that you hand out, a sign-up sheet that's passed around at an event, or even a website that contains a form to make a pledge.

Whatever you do to get pledges, when a pledge is promised you should record it in QuickBooks to make sure your financial reports are complete (a pledge, like an invoice in the for-profit world, is part of your accounts receivable asset).

QuickBooks Premier Nonprofit edition provides a template for a pledge, which is really a standard QuickBooks invoice that's been customized. To open a blank pledge transaction window, use one of the following actions:

- Choose Nonprofit | Enter Pledges (Invoices) from the menu bar.
- Press Ctrl-I to open a blank invoice form and choose Intuit Standard Pledge from the drop-down list in the Template field (in the upper right corner of the window).

When the Pledge form opens, it looks like Figure 12-2. If you're using the UCOA, select the Pledges Receivable account in the Account field at the top of the form. If you're not using the UCOA, you should add a Pledges Receivable account to your system. Notice that the title bar of the Pledge window contains the name of the A/R account you've assigned to the transaction.

You can print each pledge as you create it, or you can check the Print Later option and print all the pledges you create in a batch. To print a batch of pledges choose File | Print Forms | Invoices. When you print pledges, the unprinted forms are separated by A/R account – select all the A/R accounts you used to print all the pledges you created.

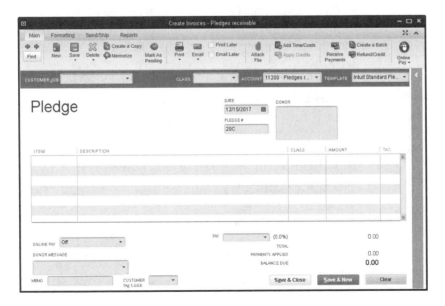

Figure 12-2: A Pledge is an accounts receivable transaction.

Donations (Sales Receipts)

Donations differ from pledges because a donation is money received "spontaneously" instead of in response to an invoice (there's no invoice recorded in your QuickBooks file).

ProAdvisor NOTE: *For most small nonprofits, donations are the normal method of receiving donations. Invoices are generally not necessary.*

When you want to record a donation, QuickBooks Premier Nonprofit Edition has a template named Intuit Standard Donation, which is better suited to this situation than the regular sales receipt template (which is named Custom Sales Receipt). To open this template, take one of the following actions:

- Choose Nonprofit | Enter Donations (Sales Receipts).

- Choose Customers | Enter Sales Receipts, and select the transaction form named Intuit Standard Donation from the Template field at the top of the window.

The Intuit Standard Donation template looks like the Custom Sales Receipt template, but it differs in several ways (see Figure 12-3):

- The word Donation appears in the header, at the top of the form, instead of Sales Receipt.

- The address block is labeled Donor instead of Sold To.

- The Sale No. field is changed to Donation No.

- The Customer Message field becomes the Donor Message field.

Figure 12-3: The Standard Donation template works perfectly for receiving donations.

Avoid Data Entry Shortcuts

Tracking and reporting income and expenses is more complicated for nonprofits than it is for regular for-profit businesses. A nonprofit isn't a closed corporation; instead, its records must be available to donors and government agencies. You're not working with earned money (profits), you're working with other peoples' money and you made promises about the way that money is used.

In order to report your financial transactions properly, every transaction must have a class assigned. Income should be tracked by item in addition to class, because item reports provide information to you (and to your donors) about the type of income you're receiving.

Do NOT use the Make Deposits transaction form to enter donations. That form does not track items (which means you can't get accurate reports on items connected to programs), nor does it post information to sales reports (which means your total income and your total sales won't match – a problem for your accountant and auditor).

Reports for Nonprofits

The Premier Nonprofit Edition provides useful reports that have been customized for this QuickBooks Premier edition. Choose Reports | Nonprofit Reports, and select one of the following memorized reports:

- Biggest Donors/Grants
- Budget vs. Actual By Donors/Grants
- Donors/Grants Report
- Donor Contribution Summary
- Budget vs. Actual By Programs/Projects
- Program/Projects Report
- Statement Of Financial Income And Expense
- Statement Of Financial Position
- Statement Of Functional Expenses (990)

You can customize any of these reports to meet your own needs, and then memorize them.

CHAPTER 13

Professional Services Edition

- Configuring your company file
- Managing retainers
- Managing customer deposits
- Managing escrow
- Customized templates
- Customized reports

QuickBooks is extremely well suited for service businesses, and the Premier Professional Services Edition extends that innate strength. In this edition you have built in transaction templates, customized reports, and other features that are designed with professional service providers in mind.

Company File

If you're just starting with QuickBooks, you have to create a company file. QuickBooks Premier Professional Services Edition has a predefined company file that works extremely well.

The predefined company file for professional services isn't marked as such when you create a new company file. It's merely listed as an industry type, with no indication that it contains a suitable chart of accounts, and some prepopulated entries in lists. (This is what we call an "undocumented feature".)

You can create a company file using the predefined file either with the Express Start feature or by clicking Advanced Setup and using the EasyStep Interview. In the wizard window for selecting your industry, choose the Professional Consulting listing.

Because this is a pre-configured company file, many of your preferences are already set up appropriately, and quite a few of the lists are populated with entries. Open the lists so you can delete the entries that aren't specific to your business, and rename the entries you need if the names aren't appropriate.

Lists

Most of the industry choices for Professional Services result in a company file that has been pre-populated with elements in some lists (such as the Customer & Vendor Profile Lists). In this section we'll discuss some of the concepts you should consider for developing lists.

Customers and Jobs List

Most professional service businesses should track jobs for customers. Even if the work you do for a customer doesn't seem to fit the description of a "job", it's best to set up a job, so you can track additional work for the customer with specific jobs.

Even if some customers don't want reports and invoices on a job basis, tracking jobs gives you internal information about your business finances. You can track job costs and profitability, and analyze the types of jobs or projects that generate the most income.

ProAdvisor TIP: *Lawyers who have personal injury practices often provide advance money for doctors and other expenses before a case is settled. A job cost report works well as a settlement sheet when the insurance check arrives.*

Items

Most of the items you create for a professional service company are of the item type Service. You should plan your items to make sure you can track each type of service for job costing, and for profitability reports.

If you have services that are provided by non-employees, be sure to set up service items for that scenario. Create a service item and select the option This Service Is Used In Assemblies Or Is Performed By A Subcontractor Or Partner. Selecting that option changes the New Item dialog to include fields for tracking both costs and revenue. This means you can track profitability for the service, and for the customers to whom you sell the service.

If you're going to track time, remember to set up service items for unbillable time so you can track those totals. Create a parent item named Unbillable Time, and then create subitems to cover meetings, proposal writing, sales calls, general administrative tasks, and so on. Using those services with the QuickBooks Timesheet feature lets you track your expenses accurately, including overhead.

> **ProAdvisor NOTE**: *In QuickBooks 2014 you can create multiple weekly timesheets for employes who are all performing the same, or similar tasks. After you open the weekly timesheet, Choose Multiple Names (Payroll) or Multiple Names (Non-Payroll) from the Name drop-down list and then select names to include. Keep in mind that only employees whose records have the Use Time Data To Create Paychecks option enabled appear when you choose Multiple Names (Payroll).*

Customer and Vendor Types

Create customer types and vendor types to match the way you want to separate customers and vendors when you produce reports. In addition, bear in mind the types you need for analyzing your business—where your business comes from, and where you spend money. For example, you may want to track customers by referral type, which lets you analyze the effectiveness of your advertising and marketing expenditures.

On the other hand, you may prefer to use business types as your customer types, separating lawyers, doctors, engineers, and so on. Then, you can contact customer types if you expand your service offerings to match a need of a specific business type. You can create reports on profitability and receivables by type, and if you discover that some types of customers don't pay well, or aren't profitable, you can adjust the way you plan sales calls.

If you selected a predefined company file during setup, your file may already have entries in the Customer Type and Vendor Type Lists. Some of these pre-loaded entries may not suit your purposes, so you can remove them and create your own.

Billing Rate Levels

The Premier Professional Services Edition includes the Billing Rate Level List, which lets you assign billing rates and automatically enter the appropriate rate in a sales transaction.

For example, you can have a partner's rate for a specific type of work, and a lower rate for the same type of work if that work is performed by a supervisor. You can apply these rates to employees and subcontractors.

If a manager sometimes acts as a senior associate, or performs some task that involves more responsibility, you can assign a higher billing rate to that different job, for that same person.

This feature provides a great deal of flexibility, to ensure that you're billing time at a rate higher than the cost of that rate. All the instructions you need to create, assign, and apply billing rate levels are in Chapter 2.

After you create billing rate levels, and associate them with service providers, invoicing for services becomes almost automatic. Every time you create an invoice with billable time, you can select the correct rate for the service, linked to the person who performed the work.

Classes

Classes let you track your business in a divisional manner, and then produce divisional Profit & Loss reports. The way you use classes depends on the organization of your business. Here are a few of the common class tracking scenarios for service businesses (to stimulate your thinking):

- Tracking multiple offices.
- Tracking partners.
- Tracking service divisions. A law firm may have a domestic relations division and a personal injury division. An advertising agency may have a creative division, and a media buying division.

Income is linked to the appropriate class when creating sales transactions. Expenses that are specific to a class are linked to that class during vendor transactions (bills, checks, or credit card purchases).

Allocating Overhead to Classes

Create a class for general administration, so you can allocate overhead among the divisions you're tracking with classes. Allocations are performed with a journal entry at a regular interval. You can allocate expenses monthly, quarterly, or at the end of your fiscal year.

General office expenses are posted through normal transaction entries (vendor bills, direct checks, or credit card purchases). All of these transactions are posted to the Administration class. These expenses can include rent, payroll (including employer payroll expenses), utilities, insurance, web hosting, online services, and so on. At some regular interval, some of these overhead expenses are allocated to each class.

To allocate overhead expenses, create a journal entry that moves the funds from the Administration class to the divisions you're tracking by class. Chapter 4 has detailed instructions for creating allocation journal entries to classes (and also covers allocating overhead to jobs, if you want to track overhead when you track job costs).

Retainers

Many professional service providers work with some (or all) customers on a retainer basis. The customer sends a certain amount of money that is applied to future invoices. When the retainer is spent down, more retainer funds are collected; the customer is always being invoiced against retainer funds.

When you receive a payment for a retainer, it isn't income. It becomes income when you earn it, at which point you create an invoice to turn it into revenue.

To manage retainers, you need to set up the following components in your company file:

- A liability account to track retainer funds.
- A retainer item.

Ideally, you should also create a QuickBooks bank account to hold retainer funds. That doesn't mean a real, separate, bank account; instead, you can use a virtual bank account to make sure you keep retainers (unearned funds) separate from regular operating funds. (See the section entitled "Virtual Bank Accounts for Retainers" later in this chapter.)

A virtual bank account for retainers not only ensures you don't spend down into retainer funds before they're earned, it provides a way to track a balance against the balance in the liability account you use to post retainer funds—the two numbers must be identical.

Lawyers are required to maintain separate bank accounts for client funds (escrow accounts), but in most states, that rule doesn't cover retainers. Many professions besides lawyers work with retainer agreements for some or all clients, such as advertising agencies, technical support companies, and others.

ProAdvisor NOTE: *Escrow funds for clients have to be deposited into a separate escrow bank account. Service businesses, such as real estate professionals, agents, and other professions that temporarily hold money for clients, also maintain escrow accounts. See the section "Managing Escrow", later in this chapter for more information.*

Liability Account for Retainers

To track retainers you need an Other Current Liability account named Retainers or Retainers Held. You may also need a liability account to track other client funds that you're holding, such as upfront deposits that are connected to a specific job and are applied against the future invoice for that job. Upfront deposits are not constantly renewed with additional funds the way retainers are. See the section "Managing Upfront Deposits" later in this chapter for details.

Some businesses prefer to separate retainers from other types of upfront deposits by creating multiple liability accounts. Or, you can create an Other Current Liability account named Client Funds Held, and then create subaccounts for deposits and retainers. Only use the subaccounts in transactions. When you view the chart of accounts, or create reports that include your liability accounts, the parent account reports the total of the amounts in the subaccounts.

Retainer Items

You need an item for retainers, which you use when you create transactions involving retainers. Retainers are usually Service items. If you manage both retainers and upfront deposits, you should have two items, so you can track them (and create reports about them) separately.

To create an item for retainers, use the following guidelines:

- The type of item is Service.
- The rate is zero, because it's customer-specific, and is therefore entered at the time you create the transaction.
- It is non-taxable (taxes are applied when you create an invoice).
- The account to which it's linked is the liability account you use to track retainers.

Virtual Bank Accounts for Retainers

Most companies put retainer funds into the regular business bank account. If your retainer and regular funds are commingled in a single account, you should consider using virtual bank accounts to separate retainer funds from operating funds. When you use the operating account to pay your business expenses, the balance won't include the retainer amounts you're holding. This makes it easier to avoid spending retainer money.

In addition, having a bank account (whether real or virtual) for retainer funds provides a quick way to check the status of retainer funds. The amount in the bank account should always equal the amount in the retainer liability account.

Creating Virtual Bank Accounts

Virtual bank accounts are subaccounts of your business bank account. The existing bank account in your chart of accounts becomes the parent account.

You must create two subaccounts under the parent account: an operating account and a retainer account. The operating account assumes the same role as a single bank account—it holds your operating funds. The retainer subaccount is where you deposit retainer fees, and then move the appropriate amounts to the operating subaccount as the retainers are earned and turned into income. Use the following steps to create the subaccounts:

1. Open the Chart Of Accounts window.
2. Press Ctrl-N to open the Add New Account dialog.
3. Select Bank as the account type, and click Continue.
4. Enter a number for the virtual operating account (if you're using account numbers). Use a number ten digits higher than the number of your bank account. For example, if your bank account number is 10000, make the new account 10010.
5. Enter a name for the new subaccount, such as Operating Funds.
6. Check the Subaccount Of option, and select your bank account from the drop-down list in the text box.
7. Optionally, enter a description of this account.
8. Click Save & New to open a blank Add New Account dialog, which has Bank selected as the account type.
9. Enter the account number if you're using account numbers.
10. Enter a name, such as Retainer Funds.
11. Check the Subaccount Of option, and select your bank account from the drop-down list in the text box.
12. Optionally, enter a description.
13. Click Save & Close.

In the Chart Of Accounts window, your subaccounts are listed (and indented) under your bank account.

Transferring Existing Funds to Subaccounts

After your bank subaccounts are created, you need to transfer the appropriate amounts from your original bank account into each subaccount. When you complete this task, the parent bank account should have a zero balance, although it displays the total of the balances of the subaccounts when you view the chart of accounts.

You must know the amount you're holding as retainer funds, as of the date you adjust the real bank account. Often these records are kept outside of QuickBooks, in spreadsheets or on paper. When you have the total, you're ready to begin transferring money to your subaccounts.

Create a journal entry to transfer the funds by choosing Company | Make General Journal Entries. In the Make General Journal Entries transaction window, credit (remove) the entire current balance of the parent bank account, and debit (add) the appropriate amounts for each subaccount (see Figure 13-1). Remember that this is a virtual exercise; the money is in your real bank account.

Figure 13-1: Empty the parent bank account, and fill the subaccounts.

Hereafter when you open the chart of accounts window, the balance displayed for the main bank account is the total of the balances in the subaccounts. Balance sheet reports and trial balance reports display the balances of the subaccounts and the total for the parent account.

Making Deposits into Subaccounts

Your QuickBooks company file configuration should specify the Undeposited Funds account as the default depository of monies. This means when you create transactions for received funds (customer payments of invoices, or cash receipts), the money is deposited into the Undeposited Funds account.

To deposit the funds in the bank use the Make Deposits feature. This is the best way to manage bank deposits; because it matches the way your bank statement reports deposits.

However, if you're using subaccounts you have to separate regular income from retainer income so the monies are deposited into the appropriate virtual account. First, select all the regular income and deposit that in the operating funds subaccount. Then select all the retainer receipts, and deposit them in the retainer funds subaccount.

Often, this isn't an easy task, because you can't tell which income is for regular earned income, and which is for retainer payments. The Payments To Deposit transaction window doesn't provide any clues about which receipts are for retainers, and which are for regular income.

The way to resolve this dilemma is to come up with a solution that announces itself in the Payments To Deposit window. Using the Memo field in a customer payment transaction window doesn't work, because memo text isn't displayed in this window.

Solve this problem with a new payment method, named Retainer, which you create using the following steps:

1. Choose Lists | Customer & Vendor Profile Lists | Payment Method List.
2. Press Ctrl-N to open the New Payment Method dialog.
3. Name the new payment method Retainer.
4. Select Other as the Payment Type.

5. Click OK to save the new payment method.

When retainers arrive, either as a payment against an invoice you sent for retainer funds, or as a sales receipt for retainer funds that arrived without an invoice, be sure the transaction window is marked with the Retainer payment type. The transaction window also has a field for entering the customer's check number (always important to record in case of any disputes with the customer).

- In the Receive Payments transaction window, when you select Retainer from the More Payments Type dialog (or any other payment method classified as Other), the Check # field changes its name to Reference #.

- In the Enter Sales Receipts transaction window, when you select Retainer from the More Payments type dialog (or any other payment method classified as Other), the Check No. field doesn't change its label.

When you use the new Retainer payment method in transactions, the Payments To Deposit window is much easier to work with. As you can see in Figure 13-2, retainers are clearly discernible.

Depositing the receipts in the proper accounts requires the following steps:

1. Select the Retainer payments and click OK.
2. In the Make Deposits window select the Retainer Funds bank subaccount.
3. Select the date on which you took the receipts to the bank.
4. Click Save & New to return to the Payments To Deposit window.
5. Click Select All to select the remaining (non retainer) receipts.
6. Click OK.
7. In the Make Deposits window select the Operating Funds bank subaccount.
8. Click Save & Close.

Figure 13-2: You can separate payments by type when depositing
funds into a bank account.

You can automate the way you select payment types in the Payments To Deposit window, which is important in either of the following scenarios:

- You have a very large list of receipts in the window and you don't want to click off the retainer methods one at a time.

- You have other types of payment methods that have to be deposited separately (such as credit card payments which your bank handles separately on your statement).

To deposit different payment types in groups, use the following steps:

1. Click the arrow next to the View Payment Method Type field at the top of the Payments To Deposit window, and choose Selected Types from the drop-down list.

2. In the Select Payment Types dialog, choose Other.

3. Click OK to return to the Payments To Deposit window, where only your retainer payments are displayed.

4. Click Select All to select all your retainer deposits, and then click OK to open the Make Deposits window.

5. Select the Retainer bank account, and click Save & New to return to the Payments To Deposit window.

6. If you have credit card receipts to deposit, repeat Steps 1 and 2, selecting the appropriate credit card type in Step 2. Then repeat Steps 3 through 5 (unless a credit card receipt was for a retainer, in which case it has to be handled separately and deposited in the Retainer Funds account).

7. Click OK to open the Make Deposits window, and select the Operating bank account.

8. Click Save & New to return to the Payments To Deposit window.

9. In the Selected Types dialog, choose All Types, because all the remaining receipts should be standard income receipts.

10. Click Select All, and click OK.

11. Choose the Operating Funds bank account.

12. Click Save & Close.

Reconciling Bank Accounts with Subaccounts

When you reconcile the bank account, use the parent account. Because your subaccounts are virtual bank accounts, instead of real separate bank accounts, the parent account actually maintains all the activity in the bank register.

Select the parent account for reconciliation, not a subaccount. After you fill out the Begin Reconciliation dialog and click Continue, the Bank Reconciliation window displays all the transactions for both accounts. In fact, the parent account doesn't pay any attention at all to the fact that there are subaccounts; this is just a regular bank reconciliation and no transaction shows any indication of being located in a subaccount.

Moving Existing Income to Retainers

If you haven't been tracking retainers in a liability account, you've been bringing those funds into your bookkeeping as income. Hopefully, you're tracking the amount of income that's really retainer funds separately (in a spreadsheet or on paper).

Now it's time to move those funds out of an income account and into the liability account you created to track retainers. The current total of the funds you're holding as retainers has to be moved from the income account into the liability account.

Choose Company | Make General Journal Entries to open the Make General Journal Entries transaction window. If you have one income account in your chart of accounts, this is an easy task:

- Debit the income account for the total amount of retainer funds you're currently holding.

- Credit the Retainers (current liability) account for the same amount.

If you've been tracking income by category and have multiple income accounts, you have to figure out how much of each income account is really retainer income that you're still holding as retainers. Then debit each income account for the appropriate amount and credit the Retainers liability account with the total.

Applying Retainers to Invoices

The retainers you hold aren't your funds; they belong to your customers. They become your funds when you earn them, at which point they become revenue. When you invoice your customer for services performed, you transfer retainer funds to income.

To invoice a retainer customer and apply retainer funds, create an invoice as usual, using the following guidelines:

- Enter the appropriate items in the line item section of the invoice.

- The last line item in the invoice is the retainer item; enter the amount with a minus sign.

- If the retainer balance is larger than the invoice amount, apply a retainer amount equal to the invoice amount.

- If the retainer balance is smaller than the invoice amount, apply the entire retainer balance.

- In the Memo field, enter text to indicate retainer funds were applied to the invoice.

- Save the invoice.

You can print and send the invoice to the client, but many businesses don't bother sending individual invoices to retainer customers (especially because the invoices almost always have a zero total). Instead, they periodically send a report on the retainer balance.

Unfortunately, there's a big problem with the above scenario. The invoice window doesn't display the client's current retainer balance. You must ascertain that information before you create invoices. To do that, you have to create a report on retainer balances (covered next).

Tracking Retainer Balances

You need to keep an eye on customer retainer balances, so that when you create invoices you know whether there are sufficient funds to apply against an invoice. To do this, you must create a Retainer Report, using the following steps:

1. Choose Reports | Customers & Receivables | Customer Balance Detail.

2. In the report window, click Customize Report.

3. In the Display tab, deselect the Class and Balance columns in the Columns list (this makes the report easier to read).

4. In the Filters tab, select Account in the Filter list.

5. In the Account field, select the Customer Retainers liability account.

6. In the Header/Footer tab, change the name of the report to Retainer Balances or something similar.

7. Click OK to return to the report window.

8. Click Memorize and name the report using the new report name you just created.

To open the memorized report in the future, choose Reports | Memorized Reports, and select this report. The totals displayed are updated to display current balances whenever you open a memorized report.

Postings for Applying Retainer Funds

When you create an invoice and apply retainer funds to the invoice, QuickBooks posts the amounts as follows:

- The income account(s) attached to the items in the invoice are credited, and Accounts Receivable is debited.

- The Customer Retainers liability account is debited, and Accounts Receivable is credited (because the line item is a negative amount).

This means your general ledger tracks the full amount of the income in the invoice, and reduces the customer's receivable by the application of the retainer amount. Your Profit & Loss report, and reports on the customer's activity, all show the full amount of the income you invoiced.

ProAdvisor NOTE: *If the amount of the retainer applied equals the invoice total, the invoice is a zero amount invoice. If you view the invoice, you'll see the PAID stamp in the transaction window.*

Moving Retainers to the Operating Bank Account

After you invoice retainer customers, the retainer amounts you applied to the invoices are no longer the customers' funds; instead, they're your funds. You've earned them and you can spend them. In addition, your retainer liability account balance no longer matches the retainer bank subaccount balance.

Both of these circumstances are resolved by transferring the funds in the retainer funds bank subaccount to the operating funds subaccount.

The easy way to accomplish this is to use the Transfer Funds transaction window (on the Banking menu), as seen in Figure 13-3.

ProAdvisor NOTE: *If you're keeping retainer funds in a separate bank account instead of using subaccounts, write a check or use an online transfer to move the funds to your operating account.*

Figure 13-3: Move funds from the retainer subaccount into your operating subaccount.

Managing Upfront Deposits

Under certain circumstances, you may ask a customer for an upfront deposit against a job. This is particularly important if the job requires you to lay out substantial funds, perhaps to hire a subcontractor, or purchase a product. This is not the same as a retainer; it's an advance payment for a particular project or job (retainers are constantly refreshed and refilled so the customer is always working against the retainer amount).

When you receive a deposit, you cannot record the receipt as income. You haven't yet earned the money; it still belongs to the customer. Therefore, it's a liability to your company.

Creating Accounts for Upfront Deposits

You need a liability account to track customer deposits, of the type Other Current Liability. Name it Customer Deposits, or something similar.

If you also collect retainers from customers, you could use a single account for both types of funds. However, to avoid confusion, it's preferable to have separate liability accounts.

If you have both retainers and upfront deposits to track, you can also set up another virtual bank subaccount for upfront deposits. See the discussion on creating virtual bank accounts with subaccounts in the previous section on tracking retainers. However, most upfront deposits are already earmarked for spending, and the outlay of the upfront funds usually occurs rather rapidly, so it's usually fine to deposit the money into your operating funds bank account.

> **ProAdvisor TIP**: *Another way to handle a mixture of retainers and upfront deposits is to create a liability account named Customer Funds, and then create separate subaccounts for retainers and upfront deposits.*

Creating Items for Upfront Deposits

You need to create an item for upfront deposits, so you can record the deposit activities in sales forms. Usually the item type is Service, and it is not taxable. Link the item to the liability account you created for customer upfront deposits.

Receiving Upfront Deposits

Often, the receipt of an upfront deposit is the result of a conversation or a written proposal. You may not have created an invoice for the deposit, so when the customer's check arrives it's a sales receipt.

Whether you use an invoice or a sales receipt, the way you fill out the transaction window remains the same. Select the upfront deposit item, and enter the amount.

If you use an invoice, QuickBooks posts the transaction as follows:

- Debits Accounts Receivable
- Credits the Upfront Deposit liability account.

If you use a sales receipt, QuickBooks creates the following postings:

- Debits the Undeposited Funds account.
- Credits the Upfront Deposit liability account.

(If you don't use the Undeposited Funds account, and instead you deposit the funds to a bank account, that bank account receives the debit posting.)

If you use the Undeposited Funds account, and you want to deposit the funds into the Customer Deposits subaccount of your bank account, use the instructions earlier in this chapter for separating the funds in the Payments To Deposit window. Create a new Payment Method named Upfront Deposit and make it a type Other, and use the drop-down list in the Payments To Deposit window to display only the type Other.

Applying an Upfront Deposit to an Invoice

To create the invoice against which you need to apply the upfront deposit, open the Create Invoices transaction window. Fill out the invoice with the items for the services you've delivered to the customer.

For the last item, use the upfront deposit item you created, and enter the amount of the deposit that you're applying to the invoice, with a minus sign.

QuickBooks posts the invoice in the following manner:

- The income account(s) attached to the item(s) on the invoice are credited.

- The liability account attached to the deposit item is debited.
- The A/R account is debited for the net balance due.

If you're maintaining subaccounts of your bank account to separate upfront deposits from operating funds, transfer the amount of the deposit you applied, to the operating funds. (See the instructions earlier in this chapter for transferring funds between bank subaccounts.)

Upfront Deposits that are Just Payments in Advance

Sometimes, a customer deposit is nothing more than an advance payment. This usually means that the job or product is delivered to the customer in a short time. (You shouldn't hold deposits for long jobs unless you treat the deposits as liabilities.)

In this circumstance, you can create an invoice, apply the advance payment, and then hold the invoice until you deliver the services or products. You don't have to treat the advance payment as a liability.

Creating an Advance Payment Item

To use an advance payment, you must create an item for it, as follows:

1. Choose Lists | Item List.
2. Press Ctrl-N to open the New Item dialog.
3. Select Payment as the item Type.
4. Name the item Advance Payment or Payment in Advance.
5. If you take credit cards or receive cash in addition to receiving checks, don't enter anything in the Payment Method field.
6. Click OK.

The description field is optional, but you should enter the text you want to appear in the invoice to make it clear to the customer that the advance has been applied to the customer's account.

Applying an Advance Payment to an Invoice

Usually you receive an advance payment and create an invoice at the same time. The advance is not treated as a separate transaction, or as a payment against an existing invoice.

Enter the item(s) you're selling the customer, and then enter the Advance Payment item. Do *not* enter a minus sign; Payment type items are always deducted from the total because QuickBooks automatically enters the minus sign. The invoice total is the net of the sale less the advance payment.

Depositing Advance Payments

When you apply an advance payment to an invoice, QuickBooks automatically deposits the money. If you linked the advance payment item to the Undeposited Funds account, the next time you use the Payments To Deposit window, the advance payment is there. The payment is differentiated by the code INV in the Type column.

Managing Escrow

Managing escrow funds (also called *trust funds*) differs from managing retainers and customer deposits in two respects:

- The funds belong to your client, but are not collected from that client. Instead, they're collected from a third party on behalf of your client.

- The rules for managing escrow funds are mandated by state law and the rules of your professional association.

All states require attorneys to maintain a separate bank account for escrow funds, and to impose bookkeeping procedures for tracking escrow funds as liabilities. Professional associations impose similar rules on other professions, such as realtors, agents, and others who collect funds on behalf of clients.

Configuring Escrow Components

To manage escrow you must open a separate bank account for escrow funds, and you must have an item for escrow funds.

Escrow Accounts

You must create the following accounts in your chart of accounts:

- A bank account for your escrow account.
- A current liability account to track escrowed funds (usually named Funds Held In Trust).

If you open more than one escrow bank account, you must create a bank account in your chart of accounts for each account. If you have multiple escrow bank accounts, you can still use one liability account for escrowed funds. Because all transactions are linked to a customer, your customer reports make it easy to ascertain which funds in the liability account belong to which customer. On the other hand, you may be more comfortable using subaccounts to separate the liability account by category (the categories you create match the reasons for opening additional escrow accounts).

All financial activity that involves an escrow account, whether it's money in or money out, must follow certain rules, and there are ***never*** any exceptions to the rules:

- The transaction must be posted to the Funds Held In Trust liability account.
- A customer or job must be linked to the transaction.

Escrow Item

You need an item for escrow funds that are received. You can name it Proceeds Received, or any other name that matches the way you describe money coming in to the escrow account. Use a Service item, make it non-taxable, and link it to the liability account you created to track escrow transactions.

You may prefer to create multiple items for escrow funds. For example, a law firm may have separate items to track proceeds of court cases separately from proceeds of out-of-court settlements. Some law firms create an item named Proceeds with subitems for each type of proceeds received. No matter how many items you create, each item must be linked to the Funds Held In Trust liability account.

Receiving Funds into an Escrow Account

Usually, escrow funds are deposited using a Sales Receipt transaction form because it's not the norm to issue an invoice. The typical transaction is similar to Figure 13-4. The item used in the account is linked to the Funds Held In Trust liability account.

Figure 13-4: This case is settled and the check has arrived.

Deposit the check into the escrow bank account. The balance in the bank account matches the balance in the liability account because the item is linked to the liability account.

Disbursing Funds from an Escrow Account

Depending on your profession, a variety of payments are due after funds have been deposited in an escrow account. Attorneys usually have the most complicated set of payments, so we'll use a legal example. Typically, disbursements include repayments of costs paid in advance by the law firm, internal costs incurred by the law firm, the legal fee due the law firm, and the client's proceeds.

ProAdvisor NOTE: *Be sure to separate real costs (hard costs) advanced from internal costs incurred (soft costs) by posting them to different accounts. The IRS tends to be unhappy when hard and soft costs are mixed. To learn how to track internal costs, see Chapter 3.*

Repayment of Costs and Fees Advanced by the Firm

Attorneys often pay costs related to the case out of their operating account. This is quite common for attorneys who handle personal injury cases. Those costs are usually posted to a Current Asset Account or an Other Expense Account, and the customer or job is linked to each transaction. The costs are recovered from the proceeds.

ProAdvisor NOTE: *Some attorneys ask clients to reimburse them for costs as they're incurred, or to provide a retainer to cover those costs. In those circumstances, costs are not distributed from the proceeds received into the escrow account.*

Tracking Advanced Costs

When you pay costs for a client in advance, and don't ask the client for reimbursement or a retainer, you have two methods available for tracking those costs as you write checks for those costs: Marking them Billable, or removing the Billable check mark.

In either case, you should print a report for the client to make sure the reimbursement check you write is understood by the client.

Using Billable Costs

If you selected Billable when you wrote checks for costs, create a report of unbilled costs (Reports | Jobs, Time & Mileage | Unbilled Costs By Job). It displays all the transactions marked Billable, but not yet billed. Customize the report using the Filters tab and select Name as the filter. Then select the client.

Create an invoice for the client. QuickBooks finds the billable costs when you enter the client's name in the Create Invoices transaction window and offers to add the costs to the invoice. Accept the offer, but don't mail the invoice; the client isn't going to send a payment. Instead, the invoice is used to show the client advanced costs that are owed to your firm.

When you create the check from the escrow account to repay the firm for the advanced costs, link the payment to the customer or job. This creates a credit. Then use the Receive Payments window to apply this credit to the invoice you created.

Using Non-billable Costs

If you remove the Billable check mark, you're using the Customer field for job costing. This eliminates the need to create an invoice, create a credit, and then apply the credit.

To track the job costing, create a memorized report as described here, and then use that memorized report for each case. Take the following steps to create the basic memorized report:

1. Choose Reports | Jobs, Time & Mileage | Unbilled Costs By Job. (If no costs were marked Billable, the report should be empty.)
2. Click Customize Report.

3. In the Filters tab, choose Billing Status in the Filter list, and select Any.

4. You could select Not Billable, but users sometimes forget to deselect the Billable check mark, and those transactions won't appear on the report unless you select Any as the filter. Open the listing of any cost marked Billable and remove the Billable check mark.

5. In the Display tab, select and deselect columns to match the columns seen in Figure 13-5.

6. In the Header/Footer tab, change the text in the Report Title field to Costs Advanced and deselect the Subtitle field.

7. Click OK.

8. Click Memorize to memorize the report. QuickBooks automatically names the memorized report to match the text you entered in the Report Title field.

Figure 13-5: This report provides details about the check you'll write for recovering advanced costs.

To use the memorized report, open it and click Customize Report. In the Filters tab, choose Name and select the appropriate job. Print the report for the client.

Disbursing the Costs and Fee

Most attorneys create separate checks for the firm's advanced cost repayment and the firm's fee. Following are the guidelines for these checks:

- Use the trust account (escrow) bank.
- Make the checks payable to the firm.
- Post the checks to the trust liability account.
- Enter a description in the Memo field (e.g. Costs Repaid or Fee).
- Link the expense to the job in the Customer:Job column.

Disbursing the Proceeds to the Client

When you write the check to the client to turn over the proceeds due, follow all the guidelines in the previous section for writing the fees/cost repayment checks (except, of course, make the check payable to the client).

Printing a Settlement Sheet

Because you linked the client to the checks you wrote, those transactions are available in the memorized report described earlier. Open the report, and change the text in the Report Title field in the Header/Footer tab to something more appropriate, such as Settlement Sheet (see Figure 13-6). Print the report and give it to the client along with the check for proceeds.

Figure 13-6: The total in this report equals the total amount of the proceeds received.

Customized Templates

The Premier Professional Services Edition offers several customized templates you can use to create transactions. You can use these templates as-is, or as the basis of further customizations.

Customized Invoice Templates

The customized invoice templates are designed to tweak standard Intuit invoice templates so they use the right jargon (which is a slick professional touch). For example, the Time & Expense invoice template has a column named Hours/Qty instead of the standard Qty heading which is more appropriate for product sales. The Fixed Fee invoice template has a simplified design that omits any columns for quantity, and adds a Due Date column.

Customized Proposal Template

Proposals are estimates with a different name. If you create proposals, QuickBooks has a Proposal template available when you choose the Create Estimates command from the Customers menu or the Create Proposals & Estimates command from the Professional menu.

To use proposals you must enable the feature by choosing Edit | Preferences and selecting the Jobs & Estimates category in the left pane. In the Company Preferences tab, select the Yes option in the section labeled Do You Create Estimates?

The Proposal template has a column titled Est. Hours/Qty. If you wish, you can customize this template to eliminate the text Qty from the column heading (making the column title Est.Hours).

ProAdvisor TIP: *Use the Create Invoice icon on the Proposal template to turn the proposal into an invoice automatically when it's time to invoice your customer.*

Customized Reports

The Premier Professional Services Edition includes a well thought out list of reports that have been customized for service providers. Choose Reports | Professional Services Reports to display the list. The reports are useful and relevant (and the titles are self-explanatory).

CHAPTER 14

Retail Edition

- Company file elements

- Recording sales

- Upfront deposits

- Layaways

- Gift certificates

- Selling on consignment

- Traveler's checks

- Point of Sale add-ons

The Premier Retail Edition is designed to help you track retail sales efficiently. While you wouldn't want to use QuickBooks to run a supermarket or a hardware store that has to track thousands of inventory items, the Premier Retail Edition works well for small retailers, including restaurants.

In this chapter, we'll discuss ways to understand and use some of the features and functions available in your copy of QuickBooks Premier Retail Edition software.

Company File Elements

Your company file needs to be set up with elements required to run your retail business. If you're just starting in QuickBooks, when you create your company file, either with the Express Start or with the EasyStep Interview (click the Advanced Setup button), choose Retail Shop Or Online Commerce as the industry type. This action automatically creates the basic elements you need to start running your business in QuickBooks.

In this section we'll provide a brief overview of a few of the important elements in your company file.

Chart of Accounts

You need to make sure your chart of accounts contains the accounts you need to run your business. When you create your company file in QuickBooks, many accounts are automatically loaded in the chart of accounts, but you have to create a number of accounts yourself.

- You need to create an account of the type Bank for each bank account (operating account, payroll account, money market, business savings, etc.).

- You need an additional bank account for the cash you keep in the register. You can name the account Cash in Register, Cash in Till, or something similar.

- For Assets, you need an account for inventory (if you're tracking inventory in QuickBooks). QuickBooks creates it for you the first time you set up an inventory item.

- For Liabilities, you need Sales Tax Payable (if you're liable for collecting sales tax), which QuickBooks installs in your chart of accounts as soon as you set up sales tax items.

- For income, you need an account of the type Income (name it Sales or Revenue or another similar name). Usually, retailers have no need to track a variety of income types with additional income accounts. However, it's a good idea to have an account of the type Income named Sales Discounts. If you offer a discount for quantity, or for any other reason, you should track that amount so you can analyze the effect of discounts on your gross and net income.

- You need an account for Cost Of Goods Sold, which tracks sales of inventory items (if you're tracking inventory in QuickBooks). QuickBooks creates the account for you the first time you set up an inventory item.

- You need an account for tracking merchant card fees, and you should ask your accountant whether those fees should be posted to an account of the type Cost Of Goods Sold, or Expense. If you create a retail company, QuickBooks automatically includes an account of the Cost of Goods Sold type in your chart of accounts.

- You need accounts of the type Expense for all your business expenses.

In addition, you may have to add accounts to track special circumstances, such as layaways, gift certificates, and so on. Those topics, and the accounts you need to create for them, are discussed later in this chapter.

Inventory

Inventory is a topic you must discuss with your accountant (Chapter 6 covers advanced inventory issues; for basic inventory setup and transactions, see the QuickBooks help files.)

For many retailers, including restaurants, tracking inventory in QuickBooks is more trouble than it's worth. You can probably work out a data entry system, with the help of your accountant, that lets you post purchases to Cost Of Goods Sold (COGS). Then, periodically (perhaps yearly, at tax time) adjust your inventory and COGS accounts as follows: debit Inventory and credit COGS for the amount (cost amount) of unsold Inventory. Your accountant may want to handle this slightly differently, so it's best to have a conversation about the topic.

If you have a super-duper fancy cash register, and/or bar code readers, you can let that equipment track and report inventory data. Then, turn that data over to your accountant, along with product purchasing totals, and have your accountant tell you how to enter the adjusting journal entry in QuickBooks.

Items

You can't sell anything in QuickBooks without creating items, because all sales transactions require an item. If you selected Retail as your industry type when you created your company file, QuickBooks automatically created two items:

- Total Sales-Taxable
- Total Sales-Non-taxable

Depending on the way you operate your business, you may need one or more of the following items in addition to the built-in items:

- Customer Deposits
- Discount
- Subtotal

- Sales Tax
- Over and Short

Over and Short items are discussed in the section " Handling Over and Short ", later in this chapter. Sales tax is covered in Chapter 8.

In addition, you may have to add items to track special sales, such as layaways, gift certificates, and so on. Those topics, and the items you need to create for them, are discussed in this chapter.

Customers

Most small retailers don't track customers; instead, they create one generic customer in QuickBooks, named Customer, or Sale, or RetailSale. If you collect sales tax, make the customer's tax code Taxable.

If some of the products you sell aren't taxable, a customer who is taxable isn't charged sales tax for the purchase of those non-taxable products. Sales tax kicks in when both the customer and the item are taxable.

If you have customers who are not required to pay sales tax (such as nonprofit associations), create another generic customer named CustomerNoTax (or something similar). Configure that customer as nontaxable.

If you want to track some individual customers (required if you extend credit to certain customers), create those customers in addition to the generic customers.

Payment Methods

It's important to create all the payment methods you need, because your bank deposits vary by payment method. For instance, cash and checks are deposited separately from credit card payments. Visa and Mastercard payments (deposits from the merchant account into your bank account) may be handled differently from American Express payments. Some retailers take checks to the bank with a deposit slip and deposit cash in a bag provided by the bank.

To create a payment method, choose Lists | Customer & Vendor Profile Lists | Payment Method List. Press Ctrl-N to open a blank Payment Method List dialog. Name the new payment method and select the appropriate payment type.

If you chose Retail as the industry when you created your company file, the list is already populated with payment methods commonly required for retailers (see Figure 14-1).

METHOD	TYPE
American Express	American Express
Cash	Cash
Check	Check
Debit Card	Debit Card
Discover	Discover
E-Check	E-Check
Gift Card	Gift Card
MasterCard	MasterCard
Visa	Visa

Figure 14-1: The payment methods displayed here cover the needs of most retailers.

The Payment Method named E-Check is for electronic deposits of checks instead of taking the check to the bank. It's a service you can buy through the QuickBooks merchant service. The merchant service also supports scanned checks, a service that lets you scan both sides of a check and upload the image for deposit (saving you a trip to the bank).

Handling Over and Short

Most retailers find that when they count the money in the till at the end of the day, the recorded income doesn't match the cash in the till. This is a common problem with cash.

You have to know how to handle this in your bookkeeping system. QuickBooks is a double-entry bookkeeping system, which means the left side of the ledger has to be equal to the right side of the ledger. If you post $100.00 in cash sales but only have $99.50 to take to the bank, how do you handle the missing 50 cents? You can't just post $100.00 to your bank account (well, you could, but your bank reconciliation won't work and, just as important, you're not practicing good bookkeeping).

The solution to the Over/Short dilemma is to acknowledge it in your bookkeeping procedures. Track it. You'll be amazed by the way it balances — short one day, over another. (Of course, if you're short every day, and the shortages are growing, you have an entirely different problem and the first place to look is the person who stands in front of the cash register.)

Create Over and Short Accounts

To track Over/Short, you need to have some place to post the discrepancies, which means you have to create some accounts in your chart of accounts, as follows:

- Create an account named Over, using the account type Income.
- Create an account named Short, using the account type Income.

If you're using numbered accounts, use sequential numbers on the next level from your regular Income accounts. For example, use 41000 if your regular Income accounts are 40000, 40100, 40200, and so on.

If you want to see a net number for Over/Short (a good idea), create three accounts. Create the parent account first and name it Over-Short (or Over&Short), and then make the Over and Short accounts subaccounts of the parent account. If you use account numbers, make the three numbers sequential; for instance:

- 41000 Over/Short (parent account)
- 41010 Over (subaccount)
- 41020 Short (subaccount)

Create Over and Short Items

When you track cash sales in a Sales Receipt transaction, you need items for your overages and shortages (in QuickBooks, you need items for everything that's connected with entering sales data in a transaction window). Create items for overages and shortages using the following guidelines:

- Create two Other Charge items, one named Overage, the other named Shortage.
- Don't assign a price.
- Make the items nontaxable.
- Link each item to the appropriate account (or subaccount) that you just created for Over/Short.

Now that you have the necessary accounts and items, use the Over and Short items right in the Enter Sales Receipts window to adjust the difference between the amount of money you've accumulated in the cash-sale transactions and the amount of money you're actually depositing to the bank. Remember to use a minus sign before the figure when you use the Short item.

Recording Sales

The big difference between retailers and other types of businesses is the overwhelming presence of direct sales. A direct sale is a sale for which you don't have to create an invoice, because the exchange of product and payment occurs simultaneously. This also means that there's no period of time during which you have money "on the street". You can have a direct sale for either a service or a product, although it's far more common for retailers to deal exclusively in products.

There are two ways to handle direct sales in QuickBooks:

- Record each sale in its own transaction record. This method is useful when you sell to a customer for whom you want to keep a history of transactions.

- Record sales in batches (usually one batch for each business day). This method tracks income and inventory when you have no need to maintain historical information about each customer.

Recording Individual Sales

If you don't have a cash register capable of producing detailed information that you can enter as a batch transaction, or you want to track the history of certain customers for some reason, you can enter each sale in its own transaction form.

If you're not tracking a specific customer by name, create a generic customer and enter that customer on the sales form. Then, choose Customers | Enter Sales Receipts from the menu bar, which opens the Enter Sales Receipts transaction window (see Figure 14-2).

Figure 14-2: Use the Custom Sales Receipt template to track a single sales transaction.

Recording Sales in Batches

If your cash register gives you a breakdown of sales in terms of taxable and nontaxable, and also provides payment information (cash, check, and each credit card you accept), you have everything you need to enter your totals in QuickBooks.

The best way to make use of a cash register report is to include sales and deposits information (bank deposit information) in one QuickBooks transaction form. The bottom line is zero (sales in, deposits out). To do this you have to set up a couple of accounts and items so that everything posts properly.

If your cash register can track the items you sell, you don't need to track those items in your QuickBooks sales transaction (you can periodically adjust item quantities separately, using journal entries or inventory adjustment transactions). You use the daily summary transaction to get the numbers into your general ledger.

Create Items to Match the Sales and Payments You Enter

You need to create items to use on your batch sales receipt transaction. We'll go over the simple method for this, and once you understand how it works you can add any additional items you want to track.

Sales Items

For sales, you need the following:

- An item for taxable sales
- An item for nontaxable sales

If these items weren't automatically created when you set up your company file, create them using a Non-Inventory Part Type.

Sales Tax Items

For sales taxes, you need the following:

- A sales tax item or group. You probably already have this item configured in your company file.
- If needed, a separate sales tax item to apply a line item for items subject to special taxes by your state or local tax authority (such as specific taxes for alcoholic beverages, or other items your government agencies tax at a different rate)
- A "placeholder" sales tax item, with a zero rate, to apply to the batch transaction if tax items are applied as line items to specific types of items.

Read Chapter 8 to learn how to set up sales tax items and groups, including special tax items for goods and services with separate tax rates.

Payment Items

Payment items track payments (money out of the till, including bank deposits), and to do so, they deduct amounts from sales transactions. This means you don't use a minus sign when you enter a Payment type item; QuickBooks automatically adds the minus sign. To track payments you need the following Payment items:

- Cash
- Check
- Visa
- MasterCard
- Other credit cards you accept
- Debit cards

To set up Payment items, take the following steps:

1. Open the Item List

2. Press Ctrl-N to open the New Item dialog.

3. Select Payment as the Item Type.

4. Enter the Item Name, such as Visa.

5. Select the appropriate payment method from the drop-down list.

6. Select the option labeled Group With Other Undeposited Funds.

Repeat this for every payment type you accept.

To set up these Payment items, you must have created the appropriate payment methods (so they appear in the drop-down list of the Payment Item dialog). To accomplish this, choose Lists | Customer & Vendor Profile Lists | Payment Method List. Press Ctrl-N to create a new payment method if the payment method you need isn't available.

Creating the Summary Sales Transaction

Armed with the report from the cash register, choose Retail | Enter Daily Sales. The Daily Sales Summary template should appear automatically. If it doesn't, select it from the drop-down list in the Template field.

In the Daily Sales Summary template, select the generic customer and fill out the form as follows:

1. Enter the total of nontaxable sales.

2. Enter the total of taxable sales (QuickBooks automatically calculates the tax and inserts the amount at the bottom of the transaction window).

3. Enter the total payments for each of the payment types.

When you're finished entering sales and payments, the total for the transaction should be zero (see Figure 14-3). If the total isn't zero, use the

Over or Short item discussed earlier in this chapter to balance the transaction. Then save the transaction.

Figure 14-3: It's easy to summarize the day's activities when the sales and payments are equal.

Depositing the Day's Funds

When you choose Banking | Make Deposits, the Payments To Deposit window displays each payment method, so you can select each method separately, to match the way deposits are listed on your bank statement.

If you deposit cash and checks together, select both items and click OK to add them to the Make Deposits window. Then click Save & New to return to the Payments To Deposit window.

If your credit card merchant accounts are fairly consistent about depositing proceeds, select each credit card and enter the total deposit in the Make Deposits window, but adjust the date to reflect the usual delay.

For a merchant card company that deducts the fee before depositing the proceeds, deduct the fee in the Make Deposits window before transferring the funds to the bank account:

1. In the line below the deposit, select your merchant card fee expense account in the Account column.

2. In the Amount column, enter the fee with a minus sign.

3. The deposit totals the net payments, which matches what will show up in your bank statement.

ProAdvisor TIP: *If your merchant card company takes its fee from each transaction, call and ask them to deposit the full amount and then take their fees at the end of the month. This makes it easier to deposit your daily payments. At the end of the month enter the total fee in your bank register, posting it to the Merchant Card Fee expense.*

Upfront Deposits

Deposits are funds a customer gives you before taking delivery of a product. It's common to ask for a deposit when you're selling a customized product that you have to special-order. There are two ways to treat upfront deposits: as liabilities, or as upfront payments that are applied to an invoice.

Managing Upfront Deposits as Liabilities

Theoretically, upfront money is money you've collected that continues to belong to the customer. Because the money isn't yours until you earn it by delivering the product, it's a liability. If you're going to hold the customer's money for more than a few days, you need to treat the upfront deposit as a liability.

To track upfront deposits as liabilities you need to create two components in your company file:

- A Current Liability account named Customer Deposits.
- An Item (use either an Other Charge or Service type) named Customer Deposit, which you link to the liability account.

The transaction for a deposit has two steps: Record the deposit, and then apply the deposit to the invoice or sales receipt transaction you create when you deliver the product.

Use a Sales Receipt transaction to post the deposit. QuickBooks creates the following postings:

- Debits the Undeposited Funds account (or the bank account, if you don't use the Undeposited Funds account).
- Credits the Customer Deposits liability account.

Applying an Upfront Deposit to an Invoice

To create the invoice against which you need to apply the upfront deposit, open the Create Invoices transaction window. Fill out the invoice with the items you've sold the customer. For the last item, use the upfront deposit item you created, and enter the amount of the deposit that you're applying to the invoice, with a minus sign.

QuickBooks posts the invoice in the following manner:

- The income account(s) attached to the item(s) on the invoice are credited.
- The liability account attached to the deposit item is debited (washing the original credit).
- The A/R account is debited for the net balance due.

Applying an Upfront Deposit to a Sales Receipt

If the customer is paying for the product at the time of delivery, you can create a sales receipt instead of an invoice.

In the Enter Sales Receipts transaction window (using the Custom Sales Receipt template), enter the item(s) you've sold the customer. For the last item, use the upfront deposit item you created, and enter the amount of the deposit that you're applying to the sale, with a minus sign.

QuickBooks posts the sale in the following manner:

- The income account(s) attached to the item(s) on the sales receipt are credited.
- The liability account attached to the deposit item is debited (washing the original credit).
- The Undeposited Funds (or bank) account is debited for the net balance collected.

Managing Upfront Deposits as Regular Payments

Sometimes, a customer deposit is nothing more than a down payment. This usually means that the job or product is delivered to the customer in a short time (you shouldn't hold deposits for a long time unless you treat the deposits as liabilities).

The easiest way to manage a sale that has a down payment is to create a standard invoice, and then immediately accept the customer's deposit against it. Asking for a deposit is an acceptable and common way of doing business, particularly when a customer wants a special item.

In this circumstance, you can create an invoice, apply the advance payment, and then hold the invoice until you deliver the services or products. You don't have to treat the advance payment as a liability.

Creating a Down Payment Item

To use an advance payment, you must create an item for it. Use Payment as the Item type, and name the item Down Payment or Advance Payment. Link the item to the Undeposited Funds account or your bank account, depending on how you manage bank deposits.

The description field is optional, but you should enter the text you want to appear in the invoice, to make it clear to the customer that the advance has been applied to the invoice.

Applying a Down Payment to an Invoice

You should receive a down payment and create an invoice at the same time. The advance is not treated as a separate transaction, or as a payment against an existing invoice.

Enter the item(s) you're selling the customer, and then enter the Advance Payment item. Do *not* enter a minus sign; Payment type items are always automatically deducted, so QuickBooks automatically enters the minus sign. The invoice total is the net of the sale less the advance payment. Use the Receive Payments transaction window to record the invoice payment.

Layaways

Layaways require you to take an item out of stock for the period of time that the customer makes payments. You should have a policy on layaways that clearly spells out the payment schedule, and what happens if the customer stops making payments. That policy should be printed and given to the customer along with the invoice or sales order.

Using Sales Orders for Layaways

Technically, since a layaway isn't a completed sale until all the payments are made, you can consider a layaway a sales order. A sales order is a pending order, and doesn't post any amounts to accounts. The item isn't removed from inventory, but inventory reports display the item as linked to a sales order.

What's complicated about using sales orders for layaways is that you cannot accept payments against a sales order—the sales order is not a financial transaction.

If you want to use sales orders for layaways, the payments you receive are managed as credits, and when the final payment is made you can create the invoice, apply all the credits (creating a zero balance invoice) and give the customer the product.

After you create the sales order (using the Layaway Sales Order template), you have two methods for tracking layaway payments:

- Use a Receive Payments transaction (receiving payments against a non-existent invoice actually creates a customer credit) and let the payments pile up until you create the invoice, at which point you can apply the payments to the invoice.

- Use a Create Memos/Refunds transaction for each payment, and then apply all the credits against the invoice you create when the product is paid for.

Using Invoices for Layaways

You could use an Invoice for layaways, but your accountant probably won't like it. You're creating income that you don't really receive for quite some time in the future. Technically, the item isn't really sold, because a real sale decrements the inventory quantity, applies the amount of the invoice to income, and applies the cost of goods as an expense. For a big-ticket item, such as furniture or major appliances, this is a significant amount of money.

If the terms of the layaway state that the item will be paid for in a short period of time (a few days or a couple of weeks), then an invoice may be appropriate. Create an invoice for the sale (use the Memo field to indicate the sale is a layaway). As each payment arrives, use the Receive Payments transaction window to apply it.

Service Charges for Undelivered Layaways

It's common, and perfectly acceptable, to assess a service charge if the customer doesn't finish paying for the layaway. When the customer shows up to tell you "I've changed my mind", you return the customer's money, less the service charge. (Some businesses call this a restocking charge, or a handling charge.)

If you want to assess a service charge, you must create an item for it. Make the item a Service or Other Charge item, and link it to an income account for service charges. Don't specify a price for the item; instead, when you invoice the customer for the charge, you can enter an amount that matches your layaway policy.

Gift Certificates

To sell and redeem gift certificates, you need to set up accounts and items to manage those sales. A gift certificate isn't a real product, so when you sell a gift certificate, you haven't received money that qualifies as income. Instead, you've put cash on the street that can be redeemed for a product in the future.

You need to set up a liability account to track your gift certificates, and you also need items for selling and redeeming the gift certificates.

Creating an Account for Gift Certificates

The funds you receive for the sale of the gift certificate aren't yours; they belong to the certificate holder. Because you're holding funds that belong to someone else, you've incurred a liability.

You must create a liability account to track the sale and redemption of gift certificates. The account type is Other Current Liability, which you should name Gift Certificates or something similar.

Creating Items for Gift Certificates

To sell a gift certificate, you need two items: One item for the certificate itself, and another item for the income you receive when you sell a certificate.

Create the item for gift certificates with the following configuration options:

- The item type is Other Charge
- The item name is GiftCert, Gift Certificate, or something similar.
- Do not enter text in the Description field or the Amount field (you use those fields when you sell the gift certificate).
- The item is not taxable.
- In the Account field, select the liability account you created for gift certificates. (Because you don't record income for a gift certificate, the item isn't linked to an income account.)

Now you need a way to post the money you received to your bank account without creating a sale. QuickBooks offers an item type of Payment for this purpose.

Create another item, of the type Payment. Name it Paymt-GiftCert (or something similar). Configure the item for deposit to the Undeposited Funds account,or to a bank account, depending on the way you usually handle bank deposits.

Selling Gift Certificates

Usually you sell gift certificates over the counter, so a Sales Receipt is the appropriate transaction type. Most of the time, it's not necessary to track customer activity for this type of sale, so you can create a generic customer named GiftCertificate. Use the following steps to sell a gift certificate:

1. Choose Customers | Enter Sales Receipts.
2. Enter the customer name (the generic customer for gift certificates).
3. Enter the gift certificate item in the Item column.
4. Enter the gift certificate number in the Description column.

5. Enter the amount of the gift certificate in the Amount column.

6. On the next line, enter the payment item you created for gift certificates.

7. In the Amount column, enter the amount of the payment (which must equal the amount of the gift certificate). Don't enter a minus sign, because QuickBooks automatically assigns a minus sign to payment items.

8. Save the transaction.

When you save the transaction, QuickBooks makes the following postings:

- The gift certificate liability account is credited.

- The bank (or Undeposited Funds) account is debited.

Redeeming Gift Certificates

When a customer redeems a gift certificate, use a sales receipt as the transaction type. Take the following steps to redeem the gift certificate:

1. Fill out the transaction window with the item(s) the customer purchased and the prices.

2. In the last line of the transaction, enter the gift certificate item (you can include the gift certificate number in the Description field or in the Memo field).

3. Enter a negative amount for the gift certificate. Do not exceed the amount of the sale if the gift certificate is larger than the total sale.

- If the total sale is more than the amount of the gift certificate, the customer must pay the balance.

- If the total sale is less than the amount of the gift certificate, you should issue a new physical certificate for the balance (do not enter that certificate in QuickBooks).

When you save the transaction, QuickBooks makes the following postings:

- The gift certificate liability account is debited.
- The income accounts connected to the items you sold are credited.

If the gift certificate was larger than the sales total, and you entered an amount equal to the sales total, but smaller than the certificate, you didn't "wash" the entire amount of the certificate in the liability account.

Issue a new physical certificate for the balance due on the original certificate. When that certificate is redeemed (assuming it's not larger than the next sale), entering its amount will wash the rest of the original posting to the liability account.

Consignment Sales

A consignment sale is a sale you make on behalf of another seller. Instead of purchasing goods from the seller, you offer the products to your customers, acting as an agent for the seller. When (or if) the goods are sold, the seller is paid, and you get your commission.

You have several choices about the way you want to track consignment sales in QuickBooks. You should ask your accountant to help you decide which paradigm to follow. In the following sections, we'll go over some of the options available to you.

Configuring QuickBooks for Consignment Sales

To track consignment sales accurately, you need to create components in your company file that let you separate consignment transactions from the transactions involving your purchased products. You need the following components:

- A vendor record for each consignor.

- Items for consigned products (see the following sections regarding inventory and non-inventory consignment items).
- A custom field for items, to track the consignor.
- An income account to track consigned item sales.

ProAdvisor TIP: *In addition to setting up QuickBooks for consignment sales, you need to establish an identification system for consigned products. Each product must have a sticker or tag that identifies it as a consigned item, and identifies the consignor by name or by a code you've created.*

Custom Fields for Consigned Items

To facilitate transactions and reports, you should add a custom field to your Item List, and use it to track the consignor for consigned items. When you create a custom field in any item, it's available for all items and all item types except sales tax items and groups, and subtotal items. Use the following steps to accomplish this:

1. Double-click any item in the Item List to open its record.
2. Click Custom Fields. If this is the first custom field you're creating, QuickBooks displays a message telling you there are currently no custom fields. Click OK.
3. In the Custom Fields dialog, click Define Fields.
4. In the Set Up Custom Fields For Items dialog enter the text for the field's label (Consignor), and select the Use check box.
5. Continue to click OK until you close all dialogs and return to the Item List.

As you create consignment items, you can use the custom field to enter the name of the consignor. You must also add the custom field to the transaction templates you use to sell those items. See the section "Customizing Templates for Consignment Sales".

Consigned Products as Inventory Parts

It's not a good idea to track consigned products as inventory if you have a large variety or volume of consignment sales. You'll find the amount of work involved is onerous if you sell more than a few consigned items a month. In addition, inventory Cost Of Goods Sold postings require a purchase price, and often you don't purchase the goods you sell on consignment; instead you receive a commission on the sales price.

However, if you or your accountant insists on tracking consigned products as inventory parts, we'll go over the tasks you need to perform to accomplish this.

First, you must separate the consigned inventory from your regular inventory (the inventory you purchased and own). Create the following accounts:

- A separate inventory asset account named Consigned Inventory. (Inventory accounts are Other Current Assets.)
- A separate Cost Of Goods Sold account named COGS-Consigned Inventory.

You assign those accounts to the inventory parts you create for consigned items.

Creating Inventory Items for Consigned Products

If you want to track inventory for consigned products, each product must have its own discrete item listing. Use the following guidelines when you create the inventory part:

- Use a special convention for the Item Name/Number to make it easy to identify consignment items in the drop-down list in transaction forms. For example, start each item name with **X-**.
- In the Cost field, enter the amount you have to pay the consignor.

- In the COGS Account field, enter the COGS account you created for consigned inventory.
- In the Preferred Vendor field, enter the name of the consignor.
- In the Sales Price field, enter the price of the item.
- In the Tax Code field, enter the appropriate tax code.
- In the Income Account field, enter the income account for consignment sales.
- In the Asset Account field, enter the inventory account for consignments.
- Click Custom Fields, and in the Custom Field labeled Consignor, enter the consignor's name, and click OK. (The data appears on your customized transaction templates.)

Click Next to create another consigned inventory part, or click OK if you're finished.

Receiving Consigned Products into Inventory

If you're tracking consigned products as inventory, you must receive the products into inventory. This action increments the value of your consignment inventory asset, and updates the quantity available for the items. Use the following steps to receive the items:

1. Choose Vendors | Receive Items to open the Create Item Receipts transaction window.
2. Select the vendor (consignor).
3. Move to the Items tab and select the item from the dropdown list in the Item column.
4. Enter the number of items in the Qty column. The cost should appear automatically from the item's record. If you didn't enter a cost when you created the item, enter the cost per item in the Cost column. (QuickBooks automatically calculates the quantity and cost to enter

data in the Total field at the top of the transaction window.)

5. If necessary, continue to receive items for this shipment.

6. Click Save & New to receive another shipment. Click Save & Close if you're finished.

When you sell the items, QuickBooks automatically posts the cost of goods, and decrements the inventory asset.

Consigned Products as Non-Inventory Parts

To manage your consigned items outside of inventory, use a Non-Inventory Part type for the items.

You can create a special naming convention, such as a prefix of **X**, to separate your consignment items from your purchased items. Or, you can create a parent item, named Consigned, and make all your consigned items subitems. The subitem paradigm is easier to manage, and it also makes it easier to see totals in reports.

If you're using subitems, when you create the parent item don't enter any information except the expense and income account. Then, for the subitems, enter information about cost, price, description, and vendor, as follows:

1. Create a New Item of the type Non-Inventory Part.

2. Name the item.

3. Select Subitem Of, and enter the parent consignment item.

4. Select the option This Item Is Used In Assemblies Or Is Purchased For A Specific Customer:Job. Even though the option doesn't fit the way you sell consigned items, selecting the option changes the dialog by adding the cost fields you need.

5. Enter the Cost (the consignor's share) and the account to which the cost is posted (usually Cost Of Goods Sold).

6. Enter the Preferred Vendor (the Consignor)

7. Enter the Sales Price, and the account to which you post the income.

8. Specify whether the item is taxable in your state.

9. Click Custom Fields and enter the consignor name.

Customizing Templates for Consignment Sales

You need a customized template for sales transactions, so you can track consignor information. Most retailers use a sales receipt template, so we'll go over the customizations for that form. However, if you use invoices, you can make the same changes to an invoice template.

To create a customized template, use the following steps:

1. Choose Lists | Templates to open the Templates window.

2. Select the template named Custom Sales Receipt, click the Templates button, and choose Duplicate from the menu.

3. In the Select Template Type dialog, choose Sales Receipt and click OK.

4. Double-click the new listing, named Copy Of: Custom Sales Receipt to open the Basic Customization dialog.

5. Click Manage Templates.

6. In the right pane, enter Consignment Sale in the Template Name field, and click OK to return to the Basic Customization dialog.

7. Click Additional Customization (at the bottom of the dialog), and then make the following changes:

    • In the Header tab, change the text in the Default Title field to Consignment Sale.

    • In the Header tab, deselect the check mark for the Project/Job field (the check mark is for the printed version of the sales receipt).

    • In the Columns tab, go to the Consignor entry (the custom field you created for items), and click the Screen option. This puts the column on the on-screen version of the template so you can enter the consignor's name in order to track sales for this consignor. Enter Consignor in the Title field.

Selling Consigned Items

When a customer purchases a consigned item, choose Customers | Enter Sales Receipt and select the template you created for consignment sales. Enter the item, and the rest of the row should be filled in automatically, using the information in the item's record.

Tracking Consigned Item Sales

You need a consignment sales report in order to pay your consignors. Several reports can be modified to produce information about your consignment sales. Here are the instructions for creating the customized report we recommend:

1. Choose Reports | Custom Reports | Transaction Detail (this report automatically opens in Modify Report mode).

2. In the Display tab, go to the Columns list and select Consignor. Then deselect all the selected columns except for the following:
   - Date
   - Item
   - Amount

3. In the Filters tab, make the following changes:
   - Select Account in the Filter box. Then select the income account to which you post your consignment sales.
   - Select Item in the Filter box. If your consignment items are subitems, select the parent item. If you use items with special letters for the first character choose Multiple Items and select all the items.

4. Click OK to return to the report window.

5. In the Total By field, select Total Only.

6. In the Sort By field, select Consignor.

7. Click Memorize and give the report a recognizable name. You don't want to have to go through all this work the next time you need this report.

Unfortunately, there isn't any way to list costs (the amount you owe the consignor). However, when you pay the consignor, the cost information is available (see the next section on paying consignors).

Paying Consignors

The way you pay consignors depends on whether you set up your consigned items as inventory parts, or non-inventory parts. Regardless of your method, use the customized report on consignment sales you created as your basis of information.

Paying for Inventory Consignments

If you use inventory parts, you received the items with the inventory item receipt transaction. To remit payment, choose Vendors | Enter Bill For Received Items. In the Select Item Receipt dialog, choose the Vendor, and the list of item receipt transactions appears in the dialog.

Choose the appropriate receipt of goods transaction and click OK to open the Enter Bills window. All of the data is filled in automatically.

The Qty column displays the Qty received. If you received more items than you sold, change the number to reflect only the number of sold items, and click Recalculate. Then follow the usual procedures to pay the bill.

Paying for Non-inventory Consignments

If you track consigned goods as non-inventory parts, it's easiest to write a check to pay the consignor. Choose Banking | Write Checks. Enter the vendor, and move to the Items tab. Enter the items and quantities of the products you sold.

Traveler's Checks

If you receive a traveler's check, the odds of a customer spending exactly the amount of the check fall somewhere between "hardly likely" and "are you kidding?".

Traveler's check transactions are complicated when the check doesn't match the amount of the sale.

- When a customer purchases something that costs more than the amount of the check, you can ask for cash or a credit card to make up the difference. However, a sales receipt transaction can't have two payment methods selected in the Payment Method field.

- When a customer purchases something that costs less than the amount of the check, you have to give change. However, your transaction must include the full amount of the traveler's check, because that check is what you deposit in the bank.

You can solve both of these problems by configuring QuickBooks properly for traveler's checks. Once you have the right components, traveler's check transactions are entered as zero-based sales receipts (similar to a daily summary transaction discussed earlier in this chapter).

Traveler's Checks Configuration

To create transactions involving traveler's checks, you need the following components in your QuickBooks company file:

- A Payment Method named TravelerChk, of the payment type Other (for traveler's check transactions that exactly match the amount of the sale and for transactions where you must give change).

- Items of the type Payment for cash, Mastercard, Visa, and other payment types you accept. (If you configured

QuickBooks for a daily summary sales transaction, these payment items already exist.)

- An item of the type Payment named TravelerChkPayment (for traveler's check transactions in which the check is less than the amount of the sale).

- A bank account representing the till/petty cash, which you may already have in your chart of accounts (for traveler's check transactions where you have to give change).

- An item for the change you give after accepting a traveler's check. This is usually an Other Charge item named TravCheckChange that is linked to the till bank account (for traveler's check transactions where you have to give change).

Traveler's Checks that Are Less Than the Sale Amount

If the amount of the traveler's check is less than the amount of the sale, you have to create a sales receipt that covers two types of payments: The traveler's check, and the cash/check/credit card for the difference between the check amount and the total sale.

Because a sales receipt transaction doesn't permit multiple payment methods, you have to enter the payments as line items. This, of course, results in a zero based transaction (similar to the daily summary transaction discussed earlier in this chapter). Here's how to create the sales receipt:

1. Enter the items/services sold.

2. Select the payment item named TravelerChkPayment and enter the amount of the traveler's check. Don't enter a minus sign because Payment items are automatically changed to a negative number by QuickBooks.

3. Select the payment item for the type of payment the customer used to make up the difference (usually cash or credit card), and enter the amount. Don't enter a minus

sign because Payment items are automatically changed to a negative number by QuickBooks.

The resulting sales receipt transaction should look similar to Figure 14-4.

When you use the Make Deposits function, you'll see both of the payments you recorded as line items and you can deposit them into your bank account.

Figure 14-4: This zero-based transaction records two payment types.

Traveler's Checks that are More than the Sale Amount

Traveler's checks are more complicated when you have to give change, because you have to deposit a check that is more than the total of the sale. The solution is to create a zero-based transaction that posts both the traveler's check and the change as line items. That way, the check can be deposited even though it's larger than the sale amount, because the change you give the customer creates the correct sale amount.

Create the transaction in the Sales Receipt transaction window as follows:

1. Enter the item(s) the customer purchased.
2. Select the TravelerChkPayment item and enter the amount of the traveler's check (do not enter a minus sign, QuickBooks automatically enters the minus sign for a payment item).

The Sales Receipt now displays a total with a negative value, which is the change you owe the customer.

On the next line, select the item you created for giving change to a customer who presents a traveler's check, and enter the amount that offsets the negative total (and give this amount to the customer). Now you have a zero-based transaction, which is appropriate for this scenario.

Everything posts properly; you have the correct amount for the bank deposit, your till/petty cash account is reduced by the amount of change you gave the customer, and the amount of the sale posts to your Income account.

Point of Sale Add-ons

For many retailers, it's difficult to track everything you want to track without a robust POS add-on. In fact, it's probably not possible to run anything beyond a small boutique retail business without help from a POS. There are two common POS approaches:

- A powerful cash register that provides detailed reports about sales. You manually enter the totals into your QuickBooks company file.

- A software add-on that runs the "front end" of your sales. The software should be able to integrate with QuickBooks, so you can transfer data into the general ledger of your company file.

A POS software program is more convenient, of course, and many applications are available for QuickBooks.

QuickBooks POS

Start by investigating QuickBooks POS, which is built from the ground up to integrate with your company file. QuickBooks POS runs the "front" – sales, inventory, and payments, while QuickBooks Premier Retail Edition tracks your postings and other accounting data.

QuickBooks POS transfers sales totals to your general ledger. In addition, as you add vendors, customers, and items into the POS software, that data is transferred to your company file.

You can learn more about this software by visiting www.quickbooks.com, and following the links to the products.

Third Party POS Applications

A number of third-party developers have created POS applications that integrate with QuickBooks. You can investigate their offerings by traveling to www.marketplace.intuit.com.

APPENDIX A

Importing Lists from Excel

- Configuring the import files

- Mapping data categories

- Importing data

- Add/Edit Multiple List Entries

- Third party add-ons

Importing the contents of your lists is an efficient way to get the data you need into your QuickBooks company file, without going through all the work of entering each entry by filling out a dialog one entry at a time.

You can import data into QuickBooks directly from Excel or a CSV file. (QuickBooks supports both .XLS and .XLSX Excel files.) In this appendix, we'll go over the steps for importing Excel/CSV files. In addition, we'll discuss the Add/Edit Multiple List Entries feature that's built into QuickBooks.

Importing Excel or CSV Files

While the ability to import data directly into QuickBooks from Excel is attractive, it's a limited feature. You can only perform a direct import for the following lists:

- Chart of accounts
- Customer list
- Vendor list
- Item list

Additional limitations include the inability to import complex listings, such as nonposting accounts, or detailed information about entries (for example, custom fields). After you import your list, you have to fill in those details.

Configuring an Excel or CSV File as an Import File

The data format of your Excel/CSV file must follow a set of conventions and rules in order to be recognized as an import file by QuickBooks. In addition, some of the data in the import file must contain text that matches QuickBooks keywords (see the section "Data Keywords" later in this appendix).

ProAdvisor NOTE: *Each worksheet (or spreadsheet, if only one worksheet exists) must contain data for a single list. Other lists you want to import must be in their own discrete worksheets or spreadsheets.*

Header Row

The top row must contain headers that categorize the data in each column. You can enter the header text that QuickBooks requires (header keywords), or leave the header text from the export file you created, and *map* that text to the QuickBooks keywords when you perform the import. Mapping is covered later in this section.

If your worksheet doesn't have a header row, insert a blank row at the top of the worksheet, and enter the QuickBooks column heading keywords. For Excel and CSV files, QuickBooks uses plain English phrases for keywords. All of the keywords are documented in this appendix.

ProAdvisor NOTE: *For IIF files, QuickBooks requires specific (less user-friendly) keywords for each category, but IIF files can import more types of data. IIF files are covered in Appendix B.*

It's possible to import an Excel/CSV file without having a header row, because QuickBooks will use the Column Names that Excel displays (Column A, Column B, and so on) when it maps the categories. However, this means you either have to memorize the type of data in each column, or print at least one row of the spreadsheet to use as a reference.

Understanding Mapping

Mapping is the process of linking the category title text you used in your file to the specific text QuickBooks requires. Specifically, it means matching the titles of the columns (column headings) in your spreadsheet document to the "official" field names in the QuickBooks list.

For example, QuickBooks uses the text "Name" for an entry's name in the list. Your exported file may use different text for that category, such as CustName for your customer's names. QuickBooks needs to know which column holds the data for the category Name. If your file has the column heading CustName, you map "CustName" to "Name". QuickBooks uses the data in the column named CustName as if the column were called Name.

Data Keywords

Mapping, the ability to match your text to the text QuickBooks needs, is only available for column headings (categories). Certain data in your file must match the text QuickBooks is expecting, called *keywords*.

The data categories that require keywords vary, depending on the list you're importing. For example, QuickBooks requires specific text for account types in the chart of accounts, and requires a Y or N (for Yes and No) in some fields of other lists (such as whether a vendor is configured for Form 1099). See the sections on Keywords for Excel/CSV Import Files later in this appendix for details.

It's possible (in fact, it's probable) that your Excel/CSV file contains data that requires keywords, in which case you can add that data later, either by using an .IIF file (covered in Appendix B) or the Add/Edit Multiple List Entries tool (covered later in this appendix).

When your file is ready (with the data arranged in columns by category, and the data that requires keywords appropriately entered), save the file with the extension .xls, xlsx, or .csv, depending on the spreadsheet program you use.

To import the data, open QuickBooks, and open the company file for the company into which you want to import the list. Before you begin the import, back up the company file (just in case something goes wrong during the import process).

Selecting the Import File

Select the file you want to import by choosing File | Utilities | Import | Excel Files. If QuickBooks displays a message asking if you want to use the Add/Edit Multiple List Entries feature, click No.

The Add Your Excel Data To QuickBooks dialog opens. This dialog is aimed at people who want to copy and paste listings from an existing spreadsheet, which we're not discussing in this appendix because copying and pasting an entire list is inefficient and time consuming.

The dialog has a button labeled Advanced Import. Click that button to open the Import A File dialog seen in Figure A-1. (Even though the feature seems to be exclusively for importing Excel files, it also works for CSV files.)

Figure A-1: The utility can handle XLS, XLSX, and CSV files.

Click the Browse button and locate the file you want to use to import your list(s). When you select the file, QuickBooks enters the filename in the File: field of the dialog.

QuickBooks also opens Excel to examine the file. If the file is an .XLS or .XLSX file that has multiple worksheets, QuickBooks notes the worksheet names (and then closes Excel).

If QuickBooks finds multiple worksheets, it populates the drop-down list of the field labeled Choose A Sheet In This Excel Workbook with the worksheet names. Choose a worksheet from the drop-down list. (If the file is a CSV file, it only has one worksheet, so you can skip this step.)

> **ProAdvisor NOTE**: *Many Excel workbooks have multiple worksheets, so even if you only used one worksheet the other worksheets still exist (unless you deleted them). The drop-down list displays the names of all the worksheets in the selected file.*

If you renamed the worksheet you used for your list, you'll see it on the drop-down list. If you didn't rename the worksheet you see Worksheet1, Worksheet2, and so on. Select the Worksheet that contains the data for the list you're importing.

ProAdvisor TIP: *If you have multiple worksheets that contain data, open your spreadsheet in Excel before importing the list. Either rename each worksheet to specify the contents (e.g. Chart of Accounts, Customers, and so on), or make yourself a note about the contents of Worksheet1, Worksheet2, etc.*

If the file doesn't have a header row, deselect the option labeled This Data File Has Header Rows. During the mapping process, QuickBooks will map the column labels (e.g. Column A, Column B, etc.) to the appropriate keyword text. Of course, you must have made notes about the type of data in each column; otherwise you won't be able to map the columns to QuickBooks titles.

Mapping the Data Categories

A QuickBooks *mapping* is a set of data linking the text in the header row of an import file to category names that match the fields of the list being imported. For example, if you're importing an Excel or CSV file that has a column named VendorName (because that's how you or your previous application described vendor names), you must map that text to the QuickBooks text "Name" (the field name QuickBooks uses for the vendor name).

QuickBooks mappings are created for specific lists, so you must create a mapping for each type of list you're importing. You can save your mappings and use them again for re-importing the same type of list.

To create mappings for the list you're currently importing, click the arrow to the right of the Choose a Mapping field, and select <Add New> to open the Mappings dialog seen in Figure A-2.

Figure A-2 Name the mapping scheme you're creating, and select the type of list you're importing.

Give the mapping scheme a name (make sure the name is a hint about the list it's intended for), and select the list type you're importing from the drop-down list in the Import Type field.

> **ProAdvisor TIP**: *Once you create a mapping scheme and name it, you can select it in the future for importing the same QuickBooks list. If a list you want to import in the future has different column headings in your file, you can edit this mapping scheme to change the text that maps to the appropriate QuickBooks fields. This is easier than building the mapping scheme from scratch.*

In the left pane, QuickBooks displays the text it uses for field names for the type of list you're importing (see Figure A-3).

Figure A-3: You need to link each field name to the text in your worksheet.

Click inside the Import Data column (the right pane), to the right of the first QuickBooks field name for this type of import file. QuickBooks reads the column headings of your worksheet (or the column labels if you don't have a heading row) and displays them. Select the column heading that matches the QuickBooks field (see Figure A-4).

Continue to map your worksheet column headings to the QuickBooks text for the fields in this list.

Usually, QuickBooks offers more fields than your worksheet contains, because you weren't tracking all the information available in QuickBooks. If you decide to enter data for the fields you haven't been using, you can edit each record after you import the file (manually, via an IIF file, or with the Add/Edit Multiple List Entries feature).

Click Save when you've finished mapping your column headings to the QuickBooks field names. Your mappings are saved, using the name you provided, and you're returned to the Import A File dialog.

Figure A-4: Map the text in your column headings to the text
QuickBooks requires for the list you're importing.

Setting Preferences for Importing Data

Move to the Preferences tab of the Import A File dialog to specify the way
QuickBooks manages duplicate records and errors (see Figure A-5).

Figure A-5: Specify the way to manage problems.

Duplicate records occur if your list already has entries that are also in your import file. For cxample, if you're importing the chart of accounts, QuickBooks created a basic chart of accounts when you set up a company file so there may be duplicates.

Errors occur if any data is incorrectly configured. For example, you may have the wrong text for a field that requires a QuickBooks keyword, or your data may use more characters than QuickBooks permits in a given field.

Managing Duplicate Records

Here are the guidelines for selecting your options for duplicate records:

- **Prompt me and let me decide**. Don't select this option because the message you see (the prompting message upon which you're expected to make a decision) doesn't name the record in question. Blind guesses don't work well as a problem solving technique.

- **Keep existing data and discard import data**. This tells QuickBooks to skip the imported data and keep the existing record.

- **Replace existing data with import data, ignoring blank fields**. Existing data is replaced, and a blank field in the import file won't overwrite any existing data in that field.

- **Replace existing data with import data, including blank fields**. Existing data is totally replaced with imported data. If an existing field in the record has data, but the import file field is blank, the blank field overwrites the existing data.

Managing Duplicate Records When You're Importing a List

If you're importing a list for which you've already made entries, the option Keep Existing Data And Discard Import Data is the best choice. It means that the import won't disturb any records you've already created.

If you don't have any records, and you're using the Import function to create a list from scratch, it doesn't matter which option you choose for managing duplicate records.

Managing Duplicate Records When You're Modifying a List

If you're importing a list for the purpose of modifying the data in an existing list, select either of the options that start with Replace Existing Data. You can decide which of those options to select depending on the current state of your QuickBooks list, and the data in your import file.

For example, you may be changing the numbering scheme for a chart of accounts, or you may be adding or changing the Type field in a customer or vendor list.

If you're changing the data in a list, it's often easier to export your original list, make changes in Excel, and then import the list back into QuickBooks. Excel has handy features for sweeping changes such as "Search and Replace". Importing the modified data back into QuickBooks is quicker and easier than opening every record in the list in QuickBooks and making changes.

Managing Error Handling

Use the following guidelines for selecting the way to manage errors:

- **Import rows with errors and leave error fields blank**. This option works best. It means that, except for any fields that have data errors, your records are imported. You can edit the imported records later to enter the data that wasn't imported.

- **Do not import rows with errors**. If you select this option, the entire record is skipped if any field has an error. You'll have to enter the entire record manually.

Previewing the Import

It's always better to preview the import to see if your data has any problems. Click Preview to have QuickBooks test the data and display the results in the Preview dialog, which also tells you how many rows (records) were processed, and how many errors were found.

> **ProAdvisor NOTE**: *Unfortunately, the Preview feature doesn't catch all errors, just some data entry errors. You could still have errors when you import the file.*

Managing Preview Errors

QuickBooks displays the results of the test import in the Preview dialog, along with the row number, and an explanation of the problem. By default, the Preview dialog shows all the import data, not just the errors, and you have to scroll through the list to find the errors.

> **ProAdvisor NOTE**: *Usually, the Customer and Vendor lists have no errors, because they don't rely on keywords the way the Item List and Chart of Accounts do.*

To make it easier to locate errors, select Only Errors from the drop-down list in the field labeled In Data Preview Show, at the top of the dialog.

You can correct errors in the Preview dialog, instead of canceling the import, opening your worksheet, changing the data, and starting the import again. To correct an error, select the record in the top part of the dialog, and then change the text in the Data column in the bottom part of the dialog. When you've made all the corrections, click Preview to see if any errors still appear (and fix them). If the errors are gone, click Import.

Importing the File

When there are no errors in your file, click Import. QuickBooks displays a message asking if you want to continue with the import, rather than cancel it in order to back up your company file. If you've just backed up the file, as I suggested earlier, click Yes to continue. Your list is imported into your QuickBooks company file.

Viewing the Import Error Log

After QuickBooks imports your data, it saves an error log that contains details about errors, or warnings about problems (if any were encountered). A message appears to ask if you want to save the error log.

Click Save, because you should always save and inspect the log. In the Save Import Error Log As dialog, select a location for the error file, and give the file a name (e.g., customer-import-errors). The file is saved as a CSV file, which you can open in your spreadsheet program.

Open the error log to examine the problems. In many cases, an error prevents the record from being imported. Here are some of the common errors:

- A field had the data that is linked to another list, and that other list doesn't yet exist (most common for importing customer and vendor terms – you must first create the terms in the QuickBooks Terms List)
- A required field had no data
- The record name (or number, if the file is a chart of accounts with account numbers) is already in use
- The format of the data did not match QuickBooks requirements, which is frequently a problem with the way you enter dates
- The number of characters your data uses exceeds the number of characters allowed in the field
- A job or subaccount was not imported because the parent account did not exist. This means the parent account may have had a data problem and was not imported, or it was listed below the subaccount in your worksheet—it must be listed first.

You can correct the problems in your worksheet, and re-import, but if you only have a few errors it's easier to open the list in QuickBooks and manually edit or enter data.

Re-using Mappings

Once you save a mapping, you can use it again for another import of the same list. As long as the worksheet you're importing uses the same columns and has the same heading text as the existing map, QuickBooks will import the data to any company file.

If you plan to import lists to multiple companies (a common task for accountants), use a generic name when you save the mapping. For example, you can name the mapping for a chart of accounts "COA". Essentially, you're creating a mapping template.

Editing a Mapping

If a new worksheet is slightly different from the saved mapping, you don't have to create a whole new mapping. Instead, you can edit an existing mapping. For example, if you receive the data for a list from your client you may face one or more of the following scenarios:

- The worksheet uses different text for one or more of the column headings.
- The worksheet omits a column that exists in your mapping.
- The worksheet contains a column that doesn't exist in your mapping.

To edit a mapping so it matches the worksheet you want to import, follow the steps enumerated earlier in this appendix to import an Excel/CSV file. When all the fields on the Import A File dialog are populated with data, follow these steps:

1. Choose Edit from the drop-down list in the field labeled Choose A Mapping to open the Mappings dialog.
2. Select the mapping you want to edit.
3. Change whatever needs to be changed.
4. Click Save to return to the Import A File dialog. If you plan to use the original mapping as well as the edited version, use the Save As command to retain both versions.
5. Preview, and then import, the list.

Deleting a Mapping

To delete a mapping, click the Mappings button on the Import A File dialog to open the Mappings dialog. Select the appropriate mapping name and click Delete. QuickBooks asks you to confirm the fact that you want to delete the mapping. Close the Mappings dialog to return to the Import A File dialog, where you can create a new mapping, edit an existing mapping, or close the dialog if you're not ready to import a file.

Data Keywords

Two types of keywords are required for a direct import of an Excel or CSV file:

- Heading keywords, which are category names that match the names of the fields in the list. In your worksheet, these appear as column headings. You don't have to use the keywords in your spreadsheet document, because you can map your text to the keyword text QuickBooks needs.

- Data keywords (only for certain fields), which are the text entries that must match text that QuickBooks expects (keywords).

The heading keywords are the name of the field for each component of the data record. When you import a list using an Excel/CSV file, Quick-Books uses plain English that matches the text you see if you're creating list entries directly in QuickBooks. If the heading row of your import file doesn't match the text QuickBooks requires, you can map your text to the QuickBooks text (as described earlier in this appendix).

For the data keywords (which are actually the choices you see in drop-down lists in the dialog when you're creating an entry directly in QuickBooks), you must be sure to use the keyword text in your worksheet data. In the following sections we'll provide the data keywords you need for each list you can import via an Excel or CSV file.

Chart of Accounts Excel/CSV Headings

When importing the chart of accounts, you must enter data in all required fields, and can optionally enter data in the other fields. Table A-1 describes the headings and data requirements for the chart of accounts.

Heading	Data
Account Type (Required)	The type of account. You must use the text QuickBooks expects for the account type (covered in the next section).
Account Number	The number you want to assign to the account.
Account Name (Required)	The account name.
Description	A description of the account.
Bank Acct. No/Card No./Note	The number for a bank account, credit card, or loan.
Opening Balance	Don't use this field; see the discussions in this book about the reasons to avoid opening balances.
As Of (Date)	The date for the opening balance you're *not* going to enter.
Remind Me To Order Checks	The check number you'll be entering at the point you want to be reminded to order checks.
Track Reimbursed Expenses	Enter Yes or No to specify whether you want to track reimbursed expenses for this account. See the section "Understanding Reimbursed Expenses Accounts".
Income Account For Reimb. Expenses	The name of the income account to use to track reimbursed expenses.
Account Is Inactive	Enter Yes to hide the account; Enter No to make the account active.

Table A-1: Headings and data requirements for importing the chart of accounts.

Account Type Keywords for Excel/CSV Files

The data in the Account Type column must match the text QuickBooks uses in the drop-down list. Use the following text for account types:

- Accounts payable
- Accounts receivable
- Bank

- Credit card account
- Cost of goods sold
- Equity
- Other expense
- Other income
- Expense
- Fixed asset
- Income
- Long term liability
- Other asset
- Other current asset
- Other current liability

QuickBooks also supports an account type of non-posting, but it's not in the drop-down list of the New Account dialog when you create an account manually, so you cannot import non-posting accounts with an Excel/CSV import file (you *can* import non-posting accounts with an IIF file).

Understanding Reimbursed Expenses Accounts

When you're posting expenses, either by entering vendor bills or direct disbursements, you can assign the expense to a customer:job, and invoice the customer for the expense. In addition, QuickBooks provides a feature that lets you post the income from those reimbursements to an income account, instead of "washing" the expense account. In order to implement the feature, you have to take the following steps:

- Enable the ability to track reimbursed expenses as income. This option is in the Company Preferences tab of the Time & Expenses section of the Preferences dialog.

- After the option is enabled, when you create or edit an expense account you see additional fields: a check box to track reimbursements to this expense account as income, and a drop-down list from which to select the income account that receives the postings for reimbursed expenses.

You must create an income account for each expense account you've marked as tracking reimbursements as income. That means a separate income account for each expense account so marked; you cannot post all reimbursed expenses to a single income account.

Tips for Importing the Chart of Accounts from Excel/ CSV Files

Data in your chart of accounts import files should follow certain protocols in order to ensure a successful import, and/or to make sure the data in the list is consistent and easy to work with.

Using Account Numbers

If you're planning to use account numbers, and have entered account number data in the appropriate column, QuickBooks imports the account numbers and saves them, even if account numbers aren't enabled in your company file.

By default, QuickBooks does not enable account numbers, and if you haven't changed the setting in the Accounting section of the Preferences dialog, you won't see your account numbers when you open the chart of accounts after you import the file. Don't panic, QuickBooks stored the account numbers you imported, and as soon as you enable account numbers, they'll show up.

Import the Chart of Accounts First

If you're planning to import the Item List, you must import the chart of accounts before you import the items. Some of the data connected to an item includes account numbers (income account, cost of goods sold for inventory items, and so on).

Importing Subaccounts

If you want to import subaccounts, you must list the parent account first, and then list the subaccount(s) in the following format (make sure there are no spaces before or after the colon):

ParentAccountName:SubaccountName

If any subaccounts are listed above the parent account, when you preview the import you won't see any errors. However, when you perform the import, any subaccounts listed above the parent account aren't imported. The error log indicates that the parent account didn't exist, so the subaccount wasn't imported.

Remember that the colon means "subaccount" to QuickBooks, so don't use colons in account names. It's a common writing technique to make text clear by using a colon, and you may find it logical to name an account Insurance:Automobile. However, because QuickBooks only uses a colon to indicate a subaccount, the account won't be imported if you didn't list a parent account named Insurance in a row above the listing for Insurance:Automobile. If you want to use text to clarify names, use a hyphen (Insurance-Automobile).

Retaining Leading Zeroes

Many users like to enter the account number in the Bank Acct.No/Card No./Note field of bank accounts, current liabilities (loans), and credit card accounts. If the account number begins with one or more zeroes, the leading zeroes are removed after you enter the number and move to the next cell. The reason is simple. The default format for cells is General, which is a numeric format that assumes that leading zeroes have no value and can be safely eliminated.

Before you begin entering data, select the entire column for this heading and change the format of the cells to Text. The data in Text cells is retained exactly as it's typed.

Customer:Job Headings for Excel/CSV Files

The QuickBooks headings that map to your column headings are represented in Table A-2, along with the data requirements.

Heading	Data
Job or Customer Name (Required)	The customer name, or the job name.
Opening Balance	Don't use this field; see the discussions in this book about the reasons to avoid entering opening balances in lists.
Opening Balance As Of	The As Of date for the opening balance you aren't going to enter.
Company Name	The company name.
Salutation	Mr., Mrs., etc.
First Name	Customer's first name.
Middle Initial	Customer's middle initial.
Last Name	Customer's last name.
Contact	Your contact name for the customer.
Phone	Phone number.
Fax	FAX number.
Alternate Phone	Alternate phone number.
Alternate Contact	Alternate contact name.
Email	Contact's e-mail address (used to e-mail transactions if you choose that Send Method).
Billing Address 1 Through Billing Address 5	Each line of the customer's billing address.
Shipping Address 1 Through Shipping Address 5	Each line of the customer's shipping address.
Customer Type	Customer type.
Terms	Terms for this customer.
Sales Rep	Sales rep assigned to this customer.
Preferred Send Method	Preferred send method for invoices, estimates, statements, etc.
Tax Code	Customer's Tax Code.
Tax Item	Tax item for this customer.

Resale Number	Resale number if the customer is not taxable.
Price Level	Price level for this customer.
Account Number	Your account number for this customer, if you use account numbers (can contain both letters and numbers).
Credit Limit	Credit limit for this customer.
Preferred Payment Method	Preferred payment method.
Credit Card Number	Customer's credit card number, appended with a single quotation mark (').
Credit Card Expiration Month	Expiration month with two digits (e.g. January is 01).
Credit Card Expiration Year	Expiration year with four digits.
Name On Card	Name on the credit card.
Credit Card Address	Address for the credit card.
Credit Card Zip Code	Zip code for the credit card.
Job Status	Job status (for jobs).
Job Start Date	Start date for the job.
Job Projected End	Expected completion date for the job.
Job End Date	Actual end date for the job (if completed).
Job Description	Description of the job.
Job Type	Job type.
Is Inactive	Enter Yes if inactive; enter No if active.
Note	Notes connected to the customer.

Table A-2: Columns (categories) that are used for importing customers and jobs.

Customer:Job Data Mappings for Excel/CSV Files

Customer and job records have quite a few keywords that are useful for defining customers, or for tracking information about customers so you can create transactions quickly. Unfortunately, the keywords aren't preconfigured in QuickBooks; instead, they are the data entries in other lists. The other lists cannot be imported with an Excel/CSV file; instead, you must enter everything manually (or import the list with an IIF file).

Your text must match the text of the entries in the lists described in Table A-3. The list entries must have been created before you import the customer list. Except for the Sales Tax items, all of the lists are in the Customer & Vendor Profile Lists submenu. The Sales Tax Code List is on the Lists menu, and Sales Tax Items must be predefined in the Item List (or included in an import file for Items).

QuickBooks prepopulates some of the lists (e.g. Terms and Payment Methods) with generic items you may or may not be able to use. If you use a predefined company file (available in some Premier editions), other lists, such as Customer Type, may also have some prepopulated data. However, you may have added entries to any of these lists, or renamed or removed pre-loaded entries. To have the correct text available when you create your import file, print each list's contents by opening the list window and pressing Ctrl-P.

Heading	List Name
Customer Type	Customer Type List
Preferred Payment Method	Payment Method List
Price Level	Price Level List
Sales Rep	Sales Rep List
Tax Code	Sales Tax Code List
Tax Item	Item List
Terms	Terms List

Table A-3: These lists must be populated before you import customer data that includes entries from the lists.

Job Keywords for Excel/CSV Files

Jobs have two data fields you can use to categorize the job record, and your data must match the text in the associated lists:

- Job Type, which is a list in the Customer & Vendor Profile Lists submenu.

- Job Status, which is a descriptive phrase that appears in the Jobs & Estimates Preferences dialog which you access by choosing Edit | Preferences.

Tips for Importing the Customer:Job List from Excel/ CSV Files

Your QuickBooks tasks will be easier if your customers and jobs are set up for efficiency, so you need to pay attention to some protocols as you create your import file.

Jobs are Like Subaccounts

Jobs don't stand alone; they're subordinate to customers. To import jobs, the data must be in the format CustomerName:JobName (no spaces around the colon). This is similar to the way subaccounts are managed in an import file for the chart of accounts. The customer must exist in order to import a job, so you must be sure to list the customer name before the job name in your import file.

Customer Financial Information

As described earlier, your import file contains columns for financial information about the customer. Here are some guidelines for entering this data:

- **Credit Limit**. Enter the amount without a dollar sign.
- **Credit Card Number**. Don't use this field, it's dangerous. In fact, it's probable that either your merchant account agreement, or state law (or both), makes it illegal to have this information stored in plain text. The laws and rules that govern computer storage of credit card numbers usually limit you to storing the last four digits only (either omitting the other digits or using XXXX to replace them).

Vendor Headings for Excel/CSV Files

Mappings represent the columns that QuickBooks will import, which in turn represent the fields available in the Vendor dialog you work in if you're entering vendors one-at-a-time in QuickBooks. QuickBooks will map your column headings to the QuickBooks field names, if your column headings don't match those in Table A-4.

Mapping	Data
Name (Required)	Vendor name (your vendor code).
Opening Balance	Don't use this field; see the discussions in this book about the reasons to avoid entering opening balances in lists.
Opening Balance (As Of)	The As Of date for the opening balance you aren't going to enter.
Company Name	Company name.
Salutation	Mr., Ms., etc.
First Name	Vendor's first name.
Middle Initial	Vendor's middle initial.
Last Name	Vendor's last name.
Address 1 Through Address 5	Each line of the vendor's address.
Contact	Your contact name for the vendor.
Phone	Phone number.
Fax	FAX number.
Alternate Phone	Alternate phone number.
Alternate Contact	Alternate contact name.
Email	E-mail address.
Print Name On Check As	Vendor's name as printed on a check.
Account Number	Your account number with this vendor.
Vendor Type	Vendor types.
Terms	Terms
Credit Limit	Your credit limit with the vendor.
Tax ID	Tax ID number.
Vendor Eligible For 1099	Yes or No.
Is Inactive	Yes to hide the vendor's listing; No to display the listing.
Note	Your notes about the vendor.

Table A-4: Columns (categories) for importing vendors.

Vendor Data Keywords for Excel/CSV Files

Some of the data referenced in Table A-4 (vendor categories) requires you to enter text that matches existing data in other existing lists, such as Vendor Type and Terms. Be sure to populate those lists before importing your vendor list.

Tips for Importing the Vendor List from Excel/CSV Files

To make sure it's easy to enter transactions and get the reports you need, you must be careful to import your vendor list accurately, using all the data you'll need. While you can always correct or add data by editing each vendor's record, that's a time consuming, annoying task.

Enabling 1099 Tracking

If a vendor receives a 1099, you must enter the vendor's Tax Identification Number in the Tax ID field. You must also enter the text Yes in the field labeled Vendor Eligible For 1099.

Don't forget to enable 1099 tracking in the Company Preferences tab of the Tax: 1099 category of the Preferences dialog. (You must also configure the expense accounts that are associated with Form 1099 tracking.)

Account Number Means Your Account Number

The Vendor Account Number is your account number (your customer number with the vendor). The text you enter in this field is automatically printed on the Memo line of checks (if you print checks), and this is the commonly accepted method of providing your account number to the vendor when you pay bills.

If you use online bill paying, the Account Number field must contain your customer account number with the vendor. The data is included in the online bill paying information, and it's the only way the vendor can identify your payment.

E-Mail Address is for Sending Purchase Orders

QuickBooks lets you send purchase orders to vendors via e-mail. The e-mail has message text, and the PO is attached as a PDF file. If you plan to use this feature, enter the e-mail address of the person who receives purchase orders from you in the Email field of your vendor import file.

Vendor Name as Printed on a Check

The vendor name you assign a vendor should be a code, and your protocols for entering vendor codes should be consistent. However, the name/code probably won't work for addressing mail, or for printing the payee name on checks. The field Print Name On Check As is a nifty solution.

When you're entering vendors directly in QuickBooks (using the New Vendor dialog), after you enter the text for the Company Name field QuickBooks automatically copies that text to the Print Name On Check As field. That's almost always appropriate. Therefore, to save a little time when you're creating your import file, use the Copy feature in Excel to copy the Company Name text to the Print Name On Check As field.

Item Headings for Excel/CSV Files

For importing items, the QuickBooks headings that map to your column headings are represented in Table A-5, along with the data requirements.

Mapping	Data	Data Requirements
Type (Required)	Item type.	Must match keywords (see the section "Item Type Keywords")
Name (Required)	Item name	
Is Reimbursable Charge	Yes or No	For services performed by others, use item type Service. For reimbursable expense, item type should be Other Charge
Description/ Description on sales transactions	Item description	
Tax Code	Three character tax code from the Sales Tax Code lists	Data must match existing Tax Code text in the Tax Code list

Account/ Income account (required)	Name of account linked to this item	Account name must match existing account
Expense/COGS Account	Name of expense account linked to this item	Account name must match existing account
Asset account	Name of asset account linked to this item	Account name must match existing account
Deposit To (Account)	Name of bank account for deposits	Account name must match existing account
Description On Purchase Transactions	Description.	For Inventory Part only
On Hand	Number on hand.	For Inventory Part only
Cost	Cost amount	For Inventory Part only
Preferred Vendor	Vendor's name.	Vendor name must match existing vendor
Tax Agency	Tax agency (vendor)	Name must match existing vendor
Price/Amount Or %/Rate	Price or percentage rate .	To enter a percentage, the Cost category must have data. For inventory items or reimbursable expenses, data must be a dollar amount.
Is Inactive	Yes or No	
Reorder Point	On hand number that kicks in the reorder reminder	
Total Value	The number representing the value of this item	Inventory parts only —You can manually enter a number, but it's better to let QuickBooks calculate this amount by multiplying the number on hand by the cost of each item
As Of (Date)	Effective date of Total Value	
Payment Method	Default payment method	Text must match existing entry in Payment Method List

Table A-5: Columns (categories) for importing items.

Item Type Keywords for Excel/CSV Files

For item type, the text in your file must match the keywords for item types. Following are the keywords for item types:

- Service
- Inventory Part
- Inventory Assembly
- Non-inventory Part
- Other Charge
- Subtotal
- Discount
- Payment
- Sales Tax Item

Tips for Importing the Item List from Excel/CSV Files

The Item List is rather complicated, especially if you want to import information over and above the required fields. If you have a product-based company, it might be less complicated to import only inventory parts, and enter other types of items manually.

Import or Create Other Lists First

Be sure you install (or import) the chart of accounts before you import the Item List. The accounts linked to items are required entries, and the account names in your Item List file must already exist in your company file. Otherwise, the import fails.

ProAdvisor CAUTION: *The data for the account names in your Item List import file must be exactly the same text as the account name in your already-installed chart of accounts.*

Refer back to Table A-5 to see the other lists that impact the Item List. You must either import those lists with an IIF file, enter the data manually in the Add/Edit Multiple List Entries feature, or enter the data manually in each item's record.

Importing Subitems

If you want to import subitems, you must list the parent item first, and then list the subitems(s) in the format ParentItemName:SubitemName. Be sure there are no spaces before or after the colon. QuickBooks recognizes the colon as the format for a subitem.

If any subitems are listed above the parent account, when you preview the import you won't see any errors. However, when you perform the import, any subitems listed above the parent account aren't imported. The error log indicates that the parent account didn't exist, so the subaccount wasn't imported.

Group Items Cannot be Imported

If you check the drop-down list for item types in the New Item dialog, you'll notice that when I listed the keywords for item types earlier in this section, I omitted two item types: Group, and Sales Tax Group. You cannot import a group item type with an Excel/CSV file. Import the items, and then manually create the group items you need.

Add/Edit Multiple List Entries

The Add/Edit Multiple List Entries feature is a utility you can use to add entries to lists in to your QuickBooks company file. You can also use this utility to add data to existing entries, and to change existing data. The following lists are supported:

- Customers
- Vendors

- Service Items (not a QuickBooks list—part of the Item List)

- Inventory Parts (not a QuickBooks list—part of the Item List)

- Non-Inventory Parts (not a QuickBooks list—part of the Item List)

The power of this utility is that you can add or change multiple list entries quickly, instead of making changes one record (and one dialog) at a time. For example, if you need to change the Terms for a group of customers, this tool makes it easy.

To open the Add/Edit Multiple List Entries window, choose Lists | Add/Edit Multiple List Entries. By default, the utility's window opens with the Customer list displayed (see Figure A-6).

Figure A-6: The spreadsheet-like window makes it easy to move among columns and rows.

Customizing the Window

Part of the power inherent in the Add/Edit Multiple List Entries utility is the ability to customize the window so it's easy to get your work done.

Change the Columns

You can add, remove, and change the order of columns in the window. If you add and remove columns to match the type of data you're entering, the window is easier to work with. For example, if you're entering customer data and you want to create customer types, add the Types column to the window. If you don't send faxes, remove the Fax column. If your customer/vendor addresses don't exceed 4 lines, remove the column for the 5th line of the address block.

The first time you open each list, it has a set of columns loaded by default. You can remove those you don't need and add those you do need. Click the Customize Columns button to display the Customize Columns dialog.

- To remove a column, select it in the Chosen Columns pane and click Remove to move the column title to the Available Columns pane (you cannot remove the Name column for any list).

- To add a column, select it in the Available Columns pane and click Add.

- To change the order of columns, select the column you want to move in the Chosen Columns Pane and click Move Up or Move Down until the column is where you need it. Moving a column up moves it to the left. Down moves it to the right.

> **ProAdvisor TIP**: *You can also drag the right edge of any column to the left in order to narrow the column width. This makes it possible to view more columns while you're working. QuickBooks remembers the column width the next time you open the list in the Add/Edit Multiple List Entries window.*

Sort By Column

Click a column heading to sort the list by that column's data. The data is sorted in ascending order; reverse the order by clicking the column heading again.

This is handy for ascertaining which list entries are missing data. For example, if you click the Terms column, any customers or vendors who haven't had their terms configured (the cell is blank) appear at the top of the list.

Find Data in Entries

You can use the Find field on the Add/Edit Multiple List Entries window to search for data within the entries of the list currently displayed. This feature works exactly like the Find feature in the Customer/Vendor Centers and in List windows.

Filter the List

You can filter the display in the Add/Edit Multiple List Entries window to make it easier to get to certain records (which is very handy if you're editing entries).

You can choose the following filters for the list:

- All entries.
- Active entries (the default filter).
- Inactive entries.

You can choose the following filters for the data displayed in the window:

- Unsaved entries (data you've added, removed, or changed but haven't yet saved).

- Entries with errors (something is wrong with the data you entered, and you haven't corrected it yet).

You can also design a custom filter to narrow the search to specific fields, instead of searching all fields. Table A-6 catalogs the filters available for each list supported by the Add/Edit Multiple List Entries utility.

List	Available Filters
Customers	Name Address Phone Customer:Job Name Company Name E-mail Account Number Custom fields
Vendors	Name Address Phone Vendor Name Company Name E-mail Account Number Custom fields
Service Items	Item Name Description (Sales) Purchase Description Preferred Vendor Custom fields
Inventory and Non-inventory Parts	Item Name Description (Sales) Purchase Description Preferred Vendor Man. Part Number Custom fields

Table A-6: Locate list entries by searching for text in certain fields.

Adding Entries to a List

You can use the Add/Edit Multiple List Entries utility to add lists to a new QuickBooks company file if you're just starting out in QuickBooks. You can also use this utility to add entries to existing lists.

Add Lists to a New Company File

When you create a company file, a large part of that task is adding your lists to the file. Whether you should use the Add/Edit Multiple List Entries for that task depends on the way you've been storing list information.

If your existing records are on paper, the Add/Edit Multiple List Entries utility might be an easy way to add list entries. However, you could also decide to enter your data in a spreadsheet and then import the data using the Import Excel/CSV utility, but that's two steps instead of the single step involved in using this utility.

The decision really depends on the type of data you've been storing. Many data fields that are available for importing from Excel/CSV files aren't available in the Add/Edit Multiple List Entries utility (specifics are covered later in this appendix).

If your data is already stored in a spreadsheet you could copy and paste the rows of data into the Add/Edit Multiple List Entries window. However, you have to spend time editing your spreadsheet to match the order of the data columns in the Add/Edit Multiple List Entries window (or re-order the columns in the window to match the data in your spreadsheet). You also have to add or remove columns in your spreadsheet as well as in the Add/Edit Multiple List Entries window to match the data in your spreadsheet. That's a time consuming task, and it's usually faster to import the data from Excel or a CSV file.

ProAdvisor NOTE: *In addition to supporting more fields in lists, an Excel/CSV import file includes the ability to import all QuickBooks lists and almost all types of items*

Add New Entries to Existing Lists

When you need to add new entries to existing lists, the Add/Edit Multiple List Entries window is fast, efficient, and accurate (assuming all the fields you need are those included in the utility).

As you're entering data for a new listing, when you get to a column that's linked to another list (for instance, Terms or Type), the Add/Edit Multiple List Entries window provides a drop-down list of the existing entries. You can select the appropriate data or click <Add New> to enter the data you need and automatically add it to the list.

If you ignore the drop down list and enter your own text, QuickBooks asks (when you try to move to the next field) if you want to add the new data. Say Yes to open a New <item name> dialog. If you click No and keep going, the cell in which you entered the wrong data displays your text in red, indicating an error. Errors are not saved when you save your changes.

Editing List Entries

The Add/Edit Multiple List Entries utility makes it easier to edit data in multiple existing entries. You don't have to open each listing, move to the correct tab or field, make your changes, save them, and then open the next listing to repeat that exercise.

Four tools exist to make your editing faster and more accurate:

- You can copy and paste among cells.
- You can copy down to fill all the rows below the cell you're in with the data in that cell.
- You always know which entry you're working on because the window displays the name in the field labeled Currently Editing. (In Excel, if the column you're using has forced you to scroll to the right, you have to lock the spreadsheet display at the appropriate column to see the Name column.)

- You can select existing entries for data that's from another list (e.g. Terms or Sales Tax Item) to avoid errors.

As an example of the power of Copy Down, suppose your list has twenty customers that lack Terms data and you want to add terms of Net30 to their records.

1. Customize the columns to include the Terms field.
2. Click the column heading for Terms to sort the list by the data in the Terms column. All the customers lacking Terms are at the top of the list.
3. Click the column heading for Terms again to reverse the sort order. All the customers lacking Terms are at the bottom of the list.
4. In the first row that is blank in the Terms column select the terms you want to assign to these customers (in this case Net30).
5. Right-click in that cell and choose Copy Down to add these terms to every customer.

Many data fields (such as Terms, Credit Limit, Tax Code, Tax Item) only exist in the Customer record and are not in the Jobs records. This creates two scenarios you need to understand:

- When you use the Copy Down feature, only the cells for Customers are filled in.
- You cannot enter or paste data for these fields into a row that contains a job.

ProAdvisor NOTE: *You cannot paste data into fields that have "fixed" values, such as the fields for "Inactive" and "Vendor eligible for 1099". Instead, you click in the field to toggle a check mark (a check mark is Yes, an empty field is No).*

Adding and Editing Custom Fields

You can use the Add/Edit Multiple List Entries utility to add or change data in custom fields, which is a real advantage. The names of your custom fields appear in the Available Columns pane of the Customize Columns dialog, so you can add them to the window.

Unlike Terms, Tax Items, and other fields that are parts of other lists, you can't control the way data is entered when you're adding or editing data for custom fields. You have to have a "company rule" established with your users for the way data is entered into these fields. When you create customized reports that are based on data from custom fields, you have to be very specific in your text to be sure you see all the list entries.

For example, if you have a custom field named "ContractRenewal-Month" and you want to create a report for all customers who need to renew their contract in November, you enter November in the Filter tab of the Customize Report window. However, if some of the customers have Nov instead of November entered in the custom field, they won't show up in the report.

The Add/Edit Multiple List Entries utility won't issue an error message that says "Hey, sometimes you have Nov and sometimes you have November, please pick one ". Enforcing these important data entry rules is your responsibility.

Using Third-Party Add-Ons

The import utilities included with QuickBooks are handy, but somewhat limited. If your import needs are more sophisticated, you might want to try one of the third-party utilities available for purchase. While there are several worthwhile programs on the market, we have found one to be particularly useful. It is called Transaction Pro Importer by Baystate Consulting (www.baystateconsulting.com).

It offers a wide range of import options, including the ability to import data from Excel files, Access database files, and a variety of text files (.csv, .tsv, .txt, and more). The type of data you can import is also impressive. In addition to list information, you can import transaction data, as well. As a matter of fact, you can import 12 different list types and 21 different transaction types, including invoices, bills, credits, item receipts, receive payments, and a lot more.

When you first open it, QuickBooks asks you to confirm that you want to allow the application to access the QuickBooks Company file. Provide the type of permission you want Transaction Pro Importer to have and click Continue to open the Transaction Pro Import Wizard (see Figure A-7).

Figure A-7: The wizard walks you through the steps to import your data.

The wizard offers a lot of import options that cover most concerns you might have when bringing new data into QuickBooks. For example, you can map incoming fields to match existing QuickBooks fields, you can tell the utility not to add new customers or vendors, etc. You can even enable custom fields created in QuickBooks.

APPENDIX B

Using IIF Files

- Understanding IIF file formats
- IIF file keywords documentation
- Updating lists with IIF Files

Y ou can import data into QuickBooks directly from a tab-delimited text file that has the filename extension IIF. However, the file must be configured properly for importing to QuickBooks.

In this appendix, we'll go over the steps for creating and importing IIF files for lists into a QuickBooks company file. We'll also provide the keywords and format information for the commonly imported lists. (This appendix does not cover the use of IIF files for importing transactions.)

About IIF Import Files

IIF import files are a bit complicated to create, but they are more powerful as an import tool than the Excel or CSV files discussed in Appendix A.

Unlike importing an Excel or CSV file, QuickBooks does not preview or error-check the contents of an IIF file, which is a tab-delimited text file. If the import fails at some point, it just fails. Therefore, you must be careful about the way you create the file.

On the other hand, using a tab-delimited file means you can import all the data you need to set up a company, instead of being restricted to the few lists provided in the Excel/CSV import feature, each of which is limited in the number of fields it accepts. An IIF file can contain data to populate every list in QuickBooks, including detailed information about each record in the list.

Sadly, starting with QuickBooks 2006, Intuit stopped updating IIF file data standards (keywords and required entries) for new fields introduced in the software. Any attempts to gain information about the missing data results in advice to use the Software Developer Kit (SDK) and develop programs to import files.

Few accountants or business owners have the time or desire to become programmers, and many have contacted us to express their displeasure over this attitude, as well as ask for advice and information. Unfortunately, we can't "invent" IIF data standards – that's up to Intuit – so we haven't been able to provide any assistance.

Luckily, the limitations imposed by this decision aren't enormous – only a few data fields are affected (so far) and we've found that they're fields that aren't commonly used, or aren't commonly imported. From the e-mail we receive, many accountants apparently share our hope that Intuit reverses their attitude about IIF files for lists. While, there's nothing wrong with encouraging users to turn to the SDK for importing transactions, it's not terribly practical for lists.

Accountants and IIF Files

An IIF file is a great way for accountants to provide all the data required for a client's company file. It's like creating a perfect company file from scratch in QuickBooks, and delivering the file to the client.

Entering data in a spreadsheet is faster and easier than going through all the work involved in creating a company file in QuickBooks. Entering data in rows and columns in an Excel worksheet is faster than opening one QuickBooks list window after another, and then opening one dialog after another within each list.

Most accountants are extremely comfortable working in a spreadsheet application, and after they've created a series of boilerplate import files for different types of companies, they can zip through the process of customizing a boilerplate for any particular client. Do your work in a regular spreadsheet file, saving it as an Excel file, so you can avoid all those reminders from Excel about text files not having all the features of a regular spreadsheet file. Then, when you're ready to create an import file for QuickBooks, save the file as a tab-delimited text file with the extension IIF.

Format of an IIF File

To work correctly as an import file, an IIF file has to follow a certain format. Figure B-1 is an Excel worksheet for the chart of accounts that displays the proper format.

	A	B	C	D	E	F
3	!ACCNT	NAME	ACCNTTYPE	DESC	ACCNUM	EXTRA
4	ACCNT	Checking	BANK	Cash	10100	
5	ACCNT	Savings	BANK	Savings	10300	
6	ACCNT	Petty Cash	BANK	Petty Cash	10400	
7	ACCNT	Accounts Receivable	AR	Accounts Receivable	11000	
8	ACCNT	Undeposited Funds	OCASSET	Undeposited Funds	12000	UNDEPO
9	ACCNT	Inventory Asset	OCASSET	Inventory Asset	12100	INVENT(
10	ACCNT	Employee Advances	OCASSET	Employee Advances	12800	
11	ACCNT	Employee Tips	OCASSET		12900	
12	ACCNT	Pre-paid Insurance	OCASSET	Pre-paid Insurance	13100	
13	ACCNT	Retainage Receivable	OCASSET	Retainage Receivable	13400	
14	ACCNT	Furniture and Equipment	FIXASSET	Furniture and Equipment	15000	
15	ACCNT	Vehicles	FIXASSET	Vehicles	15100	
16	ACCNT	Vehicles:Original Cost	FIXASSET		1510	
17	ACCNT	Vehicles:Depreciation	FIXASSET		1520	
18	ACCNT	Buildings and Improvements	FIXASSET	Buildings and Improvements	15200	
19	ACCNT	Construction Equipment	FIXASSET	Construction Equipment	15300	
20	ACCNT	Land	FIXASSET	Land	16900	
21	ACCNT	Accumulated Depreciation	FIXASSET	Accumulated Depreciation	17000	
22	ACCNT	Security Deposits	OASSET	Security Deposits	18700	

Figure B-1: This file is formatted properly for importing the chart of accounts.

Notice the following characteristics of this sample IIF file:

- The list being imported is identified by that list's keyword in Cell A-1 (the exclamation point is the identifier).
- Each record (row) indicates the list into which the data is being imported (keyword in Column A).
- Each category (column header) has the keyword for the field into which the data in that column is imported.

ProAdvisor NOTE: *As we discuss each list we'll present the Header Keywords and the other keywords for each. As a reference, a summary of Header Keywords for the lists we discuss is at the end of this appendix.*

To create an IIF file from scratch, make sure you've set up your columns properly, with the appropriate headings (using keywords). When you enter data, remember that some data requires special handling (keywords again). The documentation for those keywords is in this appendix.

Unlike the Excel/CVS column heading text covered in Appendix A, an IIF file doesn't use the field names you see when you're entering entries into a list in QuickBooks. Instead, the column headings (field names) are indicated by specific keywords that are internal to QuickBooks. The keywords for each list are documented in this appendix.

Exporting Data into an IIF File

You can export data from another application and specify a tab-delimited file for the exported file format. The application could be another accounting software application, or a spreadsheet in which you've been keeping customer information, inventory information, etc.

To open a tab-delimited file in your spreadsheet application, right-click the file's listing in My Computer or Windows Explorer and choose Open With. Then choose Microsoft Excel (or another spreadsheet application if you don't use Excel).

Creating Multiple Lists in One IIF File

You can actually create an entire company in one IIF file, by having all the entries for all the lists you want to import in one worksheet. If you're an accountant, this is a good way to deliver a "company in a worksheet" to your clients.

Each list must be in its own contiguous section of rows, with the appropriate keyword headings as the first row of each section. To make it easier to work with the file, insert a blank row between each section (list).

Many accountants who work in Excel save the file as a standard Excel (.xls) file while they're building import files. Then they create a separate worksheet for each list being created. This method is more efficient, and lets you build boilerplate worksheets for each QuickBooks list.

However, you can't save multiple worksheets when you save a document as a tab-delimited file. When you're ready to turn your Excel document into QuickBooks import files, you can either save each worksheet as a separate IIF file, or you can copy the contents of every worksheet into a single worksheet in a new Excel document. Then, save the new combined document as an IIF file.

Importing an IIF File

Importing an IIF file is an uncomplicated process, and takes only a few easy steps. It's even easier if you copy the file to the folder in which the QuickBooks company file is installed, so you don't have to navigate through the computer to find the file. Use the following steps to import an IIF file:

1. Open the QuickBooks company that needs the imported file.
2. Choose File | Utilities | Import | IIF Files.
3. Double-click the listing for the IIF file you want to import.

QuickBooks automatically imports the file and then displays a message indicating the data has been imported. Click OK.

IIF File Keywords for Lists

In the following sections, we'll provide the keywords and instructions for building IIF files for QuickBooks lists. For many lists, we'll provide only the keywords for fields that are commonly imported, instead of covering the full range of possible keywords.

For example, all lists accept data in a field (column) named HIDDEN, and you enter Y (meaning "yes it's hidden") or N (meaning "no, it's not hidden") for each entry (row) to indicate whether the entry is active (not hidden) or inactive (hidden). It's normal to omit that column in an import file. In the absence of information about the active status, QuickBooks assumes the entry is N (not hidden.)

For lists that permit custom fields in the names lists and the Item List, QuickBooks has keywords you can use to import that data. However, it would be unusual to take the trouble to create these in a worksheet.

It would also be unusual for a file imported from another application to contain this information. Custom fields are usually specific to a particular company and its company file.

Profile Lists Import Files

Profile lists are the lists that contain entries to help you categorize and sort major lists. The entries in profile lists are fields in major lists, such as Terms or Vendor Type fields. You can see the profile lists by choosing Lists | Customer & Vendor Profile Lists.

We're starting the discussion of importing lists with the profile lists, because if you import the profile lists, you can use their contents in other lists. For example, if you import your Customer Type List, you can enter data in the customer type category of your customer import list. However, we're not covering all the profile lists; instead, we'll discuss those that are commonly imported.

Customer Type List Import File

The Customer Type List has one keyword: Name. Your worksheet needs only two columns:

- Column A contains the list keyword !CTYPE in the top row, and the entry keyword CTYPE on each entry row.
- Column B contains the data keyword NAME on the top row, and the data (the name you've created for a customer type) is in each following row.

Vendor Type List Import File

The Vendor Type List is almost the same as the Customer Type List:

- The list keyword for the first row of Column A is !VTYPE and the entry keyword in Column A for each row of data is VTYPE.
- Column B contains the data keyword (NAME) on the top row, and the data in each following row is the name of the type.

Job Type List Import File

The Job Type List is also similar to the Customer Type List:

- The list keyword for the first row of Column A is !JOBTYPE and the entry keyword in Column A for each row of data is JOBTYPE.
- Column B contains the data keyword NAME on the top row, and the data in each following row is the name of the type.

Sales Rep List Import File

The Sales Rep List has the following format:

The list keyword for the first row of Column A is !SALESREP and the entry keyword in Column for each row of data is SALESREP.

- Column B contains the data keyword INITIALS on the top row, and the data (1-5 initials) is in each following row.
- Column C contains the data keyword ASSOCIATEDNAME on the top row, and the data (the name of the sales rep) is in each following row.
- Column D contains the data keyword NAMETYPE on the top row, and the data (a code representing the list the name listed under ASSOCIATEDNAME is a member of) is in each following row.

The NAMETYPE codes are:

- 2 if the rep is in the Vendor list
- 3 if the rep is in the Employee list
- 4 if the rep is in the Other Names List

Because the list references other lists, import the Vendor, Employee, and Other Names lists before importing the Sales Rep List.

Ship Via List Import File

The Ship Via List (which supplies data for the Ship Via field in transactions) is also similar to the Customer Type List:

- The list keyword for the first row of Column A is !SHIPMETH and the entry keyword in Column A for each row of data is SHIPMETH.
- Column B contains the data keyword NAME on the top row, and the data (UPS, FedEx, Truck, etc), is in each following row.

Terms List Import File

The Terms List import file must contain all the information for each named set of terms. The terms you include must cover the terms you need for both customers and vendors (QuickBooks doesn't provide separate Terms files for customers and vendors).

- The list keyword for the first row of Column A is !TERMS and the entry keyword in Column A for each row of data is TERMS.
- The remaining columns contain the data keywords on the top row, and the data is in each following row. The data keywords for columns are explained in Table B-1.

Keyword (Column Title)	Data
NAME	(Required) The name for the terms.
TERMSTYPE	The type of terms. **0** = standard terms (within a specific number of days). **1** = date driven terms (by a certain date of the month).
DUEDAYS	When TERMSTYPE = 0, the number of days in which payment is due. When TERMSTYPE = 1, the day of the month by which payment is due.
DISCPER	The discount percentage earned for early payment. The data is a number and the percent sign (e.g. 2.00%).
DISCDAYS	The number of days by which the discount specified by DISCPER is earned.

Table B-1: Terms List import file keywords.

Standard Lists Import Files

The information in the following sections covers the commonly imported lists that are displayed on the Lists menu. After your profile lists are imported, the data in some of the "regular" lists can be linked to the data in the profile lists.

Chart of Accounts Import File

The chart of accounts import file is not terribly complicated:

- The list keyword for the first row of Column A is !ACCNT and the entry keyword in Column A for each row of data is ACCNT.

- The rest of the columns on the first row contain the data keywords. The data is in each following row.

Table B-2 shows the important column headings for importing a chart of accounts.

Keyword (Column Title)	Text
NAME	(Required) The name of the account.
ACCNTTYPE	(Required) The type of account. The text must match keywords (See Table B-3).
DESC	Description of the account.
ACCNUM	The account number.

Table B-2: Keywords for the chart of accounts.

The ACCNTTYPE entry is required and your text in that column must match the keywords in Table B-3.

Section	Account Type	Keyword
Assets		
	Bank	BANK
	Accounts Receivable	AR
	Other Current Asset	OCASSET
	Fixed Asset	FIXASSET
	Other Asset	OASSET
Liabilities		
	Accounts Payable	AP
	Credit Card	CCARD
	Other Current Liability	OCLIAB
	Long-Term Liability	LTLIAB
Equity		EQUITY
Income		INC
Cost Of Goods Sold		COGS
Expense		EXP
Other Income		EXINC
Other Expense		EXEXP
Non-Posting Accounts		NONPOSTING

Table B-3: Keywords for account types.

Account Numbers in COA Import Files

If the company file into which the chart of accounts is imported has enabled account numbers, the numbers in the IIF file are displayed in the chart of accounts window and the drop-down lists in transaction windows.

If account numbers are not enabled in the company file, QuickBooks stores the account number data that was imported. When (or if) the user enables account numbers, the imported account numbers are available and are automatically assigned.

EXTRA Account Keywords

You can include a column named EXTRA to import accounts that QuickBooks automatically creates when such accounts are needed (when specific features are enabled).

For example, when a QuickBooks user enables the inventory feature, QuickBooks creates an account named Inventory Asset in the Assets section of the chart of accounts.

To use these accounts in an import file, the text you enter in the EXTRA column must match the required keywords. If the text doesn't match the required keyword, QuickBooks will create another account when the user enables the appropriate feature. Table B-4 contains the keywords required in the EXTRA column when you create these special accounts.

Account	EXTRA Column Keyword
Inventory Asset	INVENTORYASSET
Opening Balance Equity	OPENBAL
Retained Earnings	RETEARNINGS
Sales Tax Payable	SALESTAX
Undeposited Funds	UNDEPOSIT
Cost of Goods Sold	COGS
Purchase Orders	PURCHORDER
Estimates	ESTIMATE

Table B-4: Keywords for configuring the EXTRA column for special accounts.

Although QuickBooks adds these accounts automatically when needed, including them in the import file lets you control their account numbers. If you're an accountant, you can create boilerplate import files by client type, and include the appropriate EXTRA accounts. For example, product-based businesses need inventory and purchase order accounts, and some service-based businesses may need estimates.

Customer:Job List Import File

If you've been keeping a customer list in another software application, you can avoid one-customer-at-a-time data entry by importing the list into

QuickBooks. This is only possible if your current application is capable of exporting data to a tab-delimited text file.

Load the tab-delimited text file into a spreadsheet program (we're assuming you use Microsoft Excel), and use the instructions in this section to create an IIF file.

A QuickBooks customer import file can contain all the information you need to fill out all the fields in the customer dialog, such as customer type, sales tax status, and so on.

However, it's unlikely you've kept records in a manner that matches these fields. Therefore, we'll provide the keywords and instructions for basic customer information. We'll include some of the additional fields so you can fill them in manually if you wish (or skip the keyword column for any data you don't want to import).

Customer Import File Format

If you're dealing with data from another source, after you import the data to Excel, you need to format the worksheet using the following guidelines.

- To make room for the QuickBooks keywords you need, insert a column to the left of the first column, and insert a row above the first row.

- In cell A1, insert the text !CUST (the exclamation point is required). This is the code that tells QuickBooks the import file is a Customer:Job list.

- In the remaining cells in the first column, for every row that has data, insert the text CUST. This identifies the data in that row as data for a Customer:Job list.

- In the first row, starting with the second column (the first column contains !CUST), enter the QuickBooks keywords for customers.

Table B-5 describes the keywords and the text that belongs in the column under each keyword.

Keyword (Column)	Text
NAME	The customer name (the code you use for the customer).
COMPANYNAME	Name of the customer's company.
FIRSTNAME	Customer's first name.
MIDINIT	Customer's middle initial.
LASTNAME	Customer's last name.
BADDR1	First line of the customer's billing address, which is usually a name (customer's name or company name).
BADDR2	Second line of the customer's billing address, which is the street address.
BADDR3	Third line of the customer's billing address, which is either additional street address information, or the city, state, and zip.
BADDR4	Fourth line of the billing address, which is either additional street address information, or the city, state, and zip.
BADDR5	Fifth line of the billing address, which is either additional street address information, or the city, state, and zip.
SADDR1	First line of the default shipping address.
SADDR2	Second line of the default shipping address.
SADDR3	Third line of the default shipping address.
SADDR4	Fourth line of the default shipping address.
SADDR5	Fifth line of the default shipping address.
PHONE1	Phone number.
PHONE2	Second phone number.
FAXNUM	FAX number.
EMAIL	E-mail address of a contact.
CONT1	Name of the primary contact.
CONT2	Name of another contact.
CTYPE	Customer Type (must match text in the Customer Type import file).

TERMS	Terms (must match text in the Terms import file).
TAXABLE	Y or N
SALESTAXCODE	Tax code (must match text in the Tax Code import file)
LIMIT	Credit limit (e.g. 5000.00)
RESALENUM	Resale number for tax exempt customers

Table B-5: Keywords for a Customer:Job import file.

> **ProAdvisor TIP**: *The only required entry is the customer name, which is linked to the keyword NAME. If that's the only information you have, use it to import your customers—you can fill in the rest of the fields as you use each customer in a transaction.*

QuickBooks supports multiple shipping addresses for customers, and when you're creating customer records you can name each shipping address. The import file can only manage one shipping address. When you import the file, the shipping address data becomes the default shipping address. However, there is no keyword for the shipping address name.

Importing Jobs

A job is like a subaccount, it's linked to a parent, and the text must be in the format **customer:job**. Notice that no spaces exist before or after the colon.

To import jobs, you must make sure the customer is imported first; the text for the customer must appear in the Name column before the text for the job. For example, if you have a customer named LRAssocs with jobs named Consulting and Auditing, enter the following in the Name column:

LRAssocs

LRAssocs:Consulting

LRAssocs:Auditing

Most jobs have the same basic information (address, taxable status, and so on) as the customer, so you don't have to enter text in the other columns. However, if any specific information is different, such as the name of the primary contact, or the job type, enter the text in the appropriate column.

Vendor List Import File

If you're exporting your vendor list from another software application, follow the formatting rules described earlier for the customer file.

- The list keyword for the first row of Column A is !VEND and the entry keyword in Column A for each row of data is VEND.
- The remaining columns contain the data keywords on the top row and the data is in each following row.

The data keywords are explained in Table B-6.

Keyword	Data
NAME	The Vendor Name (the vendor code).
PRINTAS	The Payee name that prints on checks.
ADDR1	First line of the vendor's address.
ADDR2	Second line of the vendor's address.
ADDR3	Third line of the vendor's address.
ADDR4	Fourth line of the vendor's address.
ADDR5	Fifth line of the vendor's address.
VTYPE	Vendor Type (must match text in the Vendor Type import file).
CONT1	Your primary contact.
PHONE1	Phone number.
PHONE2	Second phone number.
FAXNUM	FAX number.
EMAIL	E-mail address of a contact.

NOTE	The text you want to print in the Memo field of checks (usually your account number with the vendor).
TERMS	Terms (must match a name in the Terms import file).
TAXID	Tax identification number for a 1099 recipient.
SALUTATION	Salutation or title.
COMPANYNAME	Vendor's company name.
FIRSTNAME	First name.
MIDINIT	Middle initial.
LASTNAME	Last name.
1099	Specifies whether this vendor receives a 1099-MISC form. Enter Y or N as the data.

Table B-6: Keywords for importing vendors into QuickBooks.

Item List Import File

If you've been keeping your items in a software application (usually this means inventory items only), you can import those items, saving yourself some manual work. Use the instructions earlier in this chapter to format the file.

The required keywords for items import files are the following:

- NAME-the item name
- INVITEMTYPE-the item type
- ACCNT-the account to which you post transactions for the item

Some QuickBooks item types don't have an account (such as prepayments or tax items).

The keyword for the Item List is !INVITEM on the heading row, and each record (row) must have INVITEM in the first column. Table B-7 describes the keywords for the rest of the columns on the first row of the import file. Table B-8 (referenced in Table B-7) has the keywords for the Item Type required in the import file.

Keyword	Data
NAME	Item Name or Number
INVITEMTYPE	Item type. The data must match the keywords in Table B-8.
DESC	The description that appears on sales forms
PURCHASEDESC	(Inventory part items only) The description that appears on purchase orders
ACCNT	The income account you use to track sales of the item
ASSETACCNT	(Inventory part items only) The inventory asset account
COGSACCNT	(Inventory part items only) The cost of goods account
PRICE	The percentage rate or price of the item (not for Group, Payment, or Subtotal type).
COST	(Inventory part items only) The unit cost of the item.
TAXABLE	Specifies whether the item is taxable—enter Y or N.
PREFVEND	(Inventory part items only) The vendor from whom you normally purchase the item.

Table B-7: Keywords and data information for an Item List import file.

Keyword	Item Type
ASSEMBLY	Inventory Assembly item
COMPTAX	Sales tax item
DISC	Discount item
GRP	Group item
INVENTORY	Inventory part item
OTHC	Other charge item
PART	Non-inventory part item
PMT	Payment item
SERV	Service item
STAX	Sales tax group item
SUBT	Subtotal item

Table B-8: Item Type keywords.

Several item types have additional options when you create them in the standard dialog while working in QuickBooks. When you select any of these options, the dialog changes, making the item a two sided item. It now includes fields for Cost, Expense Account, Purchase Description, and Preferred Vendor. Keep in mind that while the description may or may not match your use, the important thing is that new fields are available to you.

- A Non-Inventory Part item type has an option labeled This Item Is Used In Assemblies Or Is Purchased For A Specific Customer:Job.

- A Service item type has an option labeled This Service Is Used In Assemblies Or Is Performed By A Subcontractor Or Partner.

- An Other Charge item type has an option labeled This Item Is Used In Assemblies Or Is A Reimbursable Charge.

You can set these options in your import file by creating a column with the keyword ISPASSEDTHROUGH. The data for this column is either Y or N (for Yes or No). For any item that has a Y in this column, you can enter data that is marked Inventory part items only in Table B-7.

Employees List Import File

When you import the Employees list, you can only import basic data about the employee. Wage, tax, deductions, and other financial information have to be set up in the employee record in QuickBooks. There's no getting around it. However, importing the basic information still saves you quite a bit of work.

The keyword for the Employees list is !EMP on the heading row (Cell A1), and each record (row) must have EMP in the first column. Keywords for the remainder of the columns on the first row of the import file are described in Table B-9.

Keyword	Data
NAME	(Required) Employee's name.
ADDR1	First line of the address.
ADDR2	Second line of the address.
ADDR3	Third line of the address.
ADDR4	Fourth line of the address.
ADDR5	Fifth line of the address.
SSNO	Social Security number (XXX-YY-ZZZZ).
PHONE1	Phone number.
PHONE2	Alternate phone number.
FIRSTNAME	First name.
MIDINIT	Middle initial.
LASTNAME	Last name.
SALUTATION	Salutation (Mr., Ms., Mrs., etc.).

Table B-9: Keywords for Employees list import file.

The Mystery of Employee Initials

QuickBooks' documentation for IIF files says that the INIT data (employee initials) is a required entry for an employee list import file. It's not; we've imported many Employees lists without it. In fact, the field doesn't appear in the employee record dialog when you create an employee in QuickBooks, or view an existing employee's record. If you've consulted the QuickBooks documentation to build IIF files, you can ignore this requirement, and omit the column from your import file.

It's probable that the INIT data requirement dates back to earlier versions of QuickBooks when sales reps had to be employees, and sales reps are listed by initials in drop-down lists.

Other Names List Import File

Some companies never use the Other Names List, but this list is necessary for some company types, and handy for others. For proprietor-ships and partnerships, or any business in which a draw occurs, the owners should be in the Other Names List instead of the Vendors list.

Companies that occasionally issue non-payroll checks (such as loans or reimbursement of expenses) to employees must add the employees to the Other Names List. That entry is the payee for non-payroll disbursements.

The keyword for the Other Names List is !OTHERNAME on the heading row (Cell A1), and each record (row) must have OTHERNAME in the first column. Table B-10 describes the keywords for the rest of the columns on the first row of the import file.

Keyword	Data
NAME	(Required) The name.
BADDR1	First line of the address.
BADDR2	Second line of the address.
BADDR3	Third line of the address.
BADDR4	Fourth line of the address.
BADDR5	Fifth line of the address.
PHONE1	Phone number.
PHONE2	Alternate phone number.
FAXNUM	FAX number.
EMAIL	E-mail address.
CONT1	Primary contact (if a company).
SALUTATION	Salutation, or title (Mr., Ms., Mrs., etc.).
COMPANYNAME	Company Name (if a company).
FIRSTNAME	First name.
MIDINIT	Middle initial.
LASTNAME	Last name.

Table B-10: Keywords for the Other Names List import file.

Price Level List Import File

Price levels are assigned to customers and sales transactions, and the IIF file has the following format:

- The list keyword for the first row of Column A is !PRICELEVEL and the entry keyword in Column A for each row of data is PRICELEVEL.
- Columns B and C contain the data keywords NAME and VALUE.

The data is percentages, such as 10.00%, 5.50%, etc. A discounted price level has a minus sign.

Sales Tax Code List Import File

Sales tax codes are assigned to customers and items, and indicate whether sales tax should be imposed. These are not the sales tax items, which determine the rate (those are in the Item List).

Sales tax codes only need to be imported if you need more tax codes than QuickBooks provides automatically. QuickBooks preloads the entries Tax and Non, which suffice for many businesses. However, in states that require explanations for nontaxable sales, you need additional codes. Here are some examples of sales tax codes you can assign to customers:

- NPO for nontaxable nonprofit organizations.
- GOV for nontaxable government agencies.
- RES for customers who are nontaxable because they resell products (your customer record should include the resale tax number).

The list keyword for the first row of Column A is !SALESTAXCODE and the entry keyword in Column A for each row of data is SALESTAXCODE.

The following keywords are used in this import file:

- CODE is the name of the code (and is required data). Data entries cannot exceed three characters.

- DESC is an optional description of the code.
- TAXABLE specifies the taxable or nontaxable status (and is required data). The data is Y or N.

Class List Import File

Classes are assigned to transactions in order to track income and expenses by class. The list keyword for the first row of Column A is !CLASS and the entry keyword in Column A for each row of data is CLASS.

The column heading for Column B is NAME and the data in the rest of Column B is the class name.

Summary of List Headings

Table B-11 contains the HDR keywords for importing lists via IIF files. The data in the column labeled HDR must be in cell A1 of your IIF import file.

HDR	List
!ACCNT	Chart of Accounts.
!CUST	Customers & Jobs list
!VEND	Vendors list
!EMP	Employees list
!OTHERNAME	Other Name List.
!CLASS	Class List
!CTYPE	Customer Type List
!INVITEM	Item List
!INVMEMO	Customer Message List
!PAYMETH	Payment Method List
!SHIPMETH	Shipping Method List
!TERMS	Payment Terms List
!VTYPE	Vendor Type List

Table B-11: Header keywords that identify the list you're importing.

Updating Lists with Import Files

Do any of these scenarios seem familiar?

- A client needs to track certain information about customers, and you've suggested a custom field. You (or the client) created the custom field for the Customers & Jobs list, and added it to sales transaction windows by customizing the templates. The client has 500 customers to update with data for the new field.

- A client has created price levels and wants to assign a price level to many of the 400 customers in the system. Or, instead of price levels, it's sales reps (or both).

- A client tracks jobs and doesn't use the same rep on every job for the same customer. QuickBooks doesn't provide a Rep field for jobs; instead, the Rep for the customer is automatically the Rep for the job. The customer needs the right Rep assigned to all the jobs in the company file.

Tweaking and updating information in lists is a common practice as users become more familiar with QuickBooks. The additional data can be the solution for producing more sophisticated detailed reports.

Performing these tasks on a customer-by-customer, vendor-by- vendor, or item-by-item basis means opening each record, moving to the appropriate tab, entering the data, closing the record, opening the next record, and...you get the picture.

Not only is this time consuming, but the user is likely to be inconsistent about data entry in the custom field, making it hard to track the needed information. The fastest, most accurate method for upgrading data in lists is to import the information. You can provide this service to your client.

Any field in any list can be updated with an IIF file. For example, you may create a Customer Type that you want to use to sort customers in reports, or to prepare mailings. Or, you might create a custom field and have to enter data in that field for most (or all) of the entries in a list. Working in QuickBooks means opening the record for each entry in the list, moving to the right tab in the record's window, typing in the data, closing the record, selecting the next record, etc. etc. This could take a few days if the list is large.

For some lists, you can use an IIF file, an Excel file, a CSV file, or the Add/Edit Multiple List Entries feature. However, there are some serious drawbacks to all of the file types except IIF.

For one thing, only the following lists can accept Excel/CSV imports:

- Customer
- Vendor
- Items
- Chart of accounts

In addition, not all fields are available for import when you use an Excel import file, or the Add/Edit Multiple List Entries feature. For example, you cannot import data for custom fields, which is a severe limitation. As a result, IIF files are better for all of these tasks.

Creating Import Files to Update Existing Lists

Start by exporting the appropriate list from the company file. Choose File | Utilities | Export | Lists To IIF Files. Do not export multiple lists, even if you want to update more than one list; instead, update the lists one at a time.

Open the resulting IIF file in Excel and look for the first row of "real" data, which has the list name preceded by an exclamation point. Select all the rows above that row and choose Edit | Delete to remove those rows from the worksheet. This data isn't necessary in an import file, and removing it makes it easier to work with columns (because the column names for the rows you're deleting are not the same column names you'll work with as you add data). Figure B-2 displays a customer list where all the rows above !CUST (the list header) have been selected for deletion.

Now that you're ready to add data to fields (columns), you must be able to see the NAME column so you know which Name you're editing. Freeze the column that holds the names so that as you scroll through the columns the NAME field stays visible. To freeze the column, click the column heading of the column to the right of the NAME column to select it. Then, choose Window | Freeze Panes. (View tab | Freeze Panes in Excel 2007 or higher.)

	A	B	C	D	E	F
1	!HDR	PROD	VER	REL	IIFVER	DATE
2	HDR	QuickBooks Premier	Version 24.0D	Release R3P	1	12/15/2017
3	!CUSTNAMEDICT	INDEX	LABEL	CUSTOMER	VENDOR	EMPLOYEE
4	!ENDCUSTNAMEDICT					
5	CUSTNAMEDICT		0 Contract #	Y	N	N
6	CUSTNAMEDICT		1 Discount Availab	N	Y	N
7	CUSTNAMEDICT		2 B-Day	N	N	Y
8	CUSTNAMEDICT		3 Date of last raise	N	N	Y
9	CUSTNAMEDICT		4 Spouse's Name	N	N	Y
10	CUSTNAMEDICT		5 Favorite Wine	Y	Y	Y
11	ENDCUSTNAMEDICT					
12	!CUST	NAME	REFNUM	TIMESTAMP	BADDR1	BADDR2
13	CUST	Register1	223	1513372740		
14	CUST	Cash Customer	222	1513369551		
15	CUST	Smith9045551234	220	1513359081	J Smith Mfg	John Smith
16	CUST	Abercrombie, Kristy	21	933272658	Kristy Abercromb	5647 Cypress Hill Rd
17	CUST	Abercrombie, Kristy:Family	22	933272658	Kristy Abercromb	5647 Cypress Hill Rd
18	CUST	Abercrombie, Kristy:Kitche	23	933272658	Kristy Abercromb	5647 Cypress Hill Rd
19	CUST	Abercrombie, Kristy:Remo	24	933272658	Kristy Abercromb	5647 Cypress Hill Rd
20	CUST	Allard, Robert	208	1182061376	Robert Allard	92834 Chandler St.
21	CUST	Allard, Robert:Remodel	209	1182061396	Robert Allard	92834 Chandler St.

CarverHillsCustList

Figure B-2: Find the first row of real data, and eliminate every row above it.

Adding and Modifying Data

Except for data going into custom fields (covered in the next section), the data you enter in any column must match the data already in the QuickBooks file.

For example, if you're adding Customer Type data to your customer list, the data must match the Customer Type entries you created in the Customer Type List. If you created a Customer Type named Stmnt (to indicate customers who should receive statements), the text you enter must be Stmnt; you cannot enter Statement, Stamnt, or any other text. The same is true for Terms, Price Level, Rep, and all other data contained in QuickBooks lists.

ProAdvisor CAUTION: *If the data you're entering or changing is a QuickBooks Keyword you must use the keyword. See the documentation for IIF keywords earlier in this appendix.*

To make sure you enter data correctly, open QuickBooks, open the list you're working with, and press Ctrl-P to print the list. Then, with the entries in the Customer Type, Price Level, etc. list in front of you, you'll be able to enter the text correctly.

When you're working in Excel, you can take advantage of the Windows clipboard and the Excel data entry tools to enter data.

1. After you enter data in the first row (record) for which you're entering or modifying text, select the cell and press Ctrl-C (or right-click in the cell and choose Copy) to copy the text to the clipboard.

2. Find the next row that needs the same data, and press Ctrl-V to paste the text.

3. Move to the next row that needs the same data and press Ctrl-V to paste the text there. Continue to paste until you've pasted this text into all the records that should have it. (Once you have text in the Windows clipboard, you can continue to paste it endlessly, as long as you don't stop pasting to perform another task.)

4. Enter the next data text into the appropriate row, and follow the same pattern to paste that text into every row that's appropriate.

If you have a section of contiguous rows that require the same data (e.g. all the jobs listed below a customer), enter the data in the first row, and then select that cell. Position your mouse in the lower right corner of the cell, and when your pointer turns into vertical and horizontal intersecting lines drag down to fill all the cells with the same data.

Working With Custom Fields

The Custom Field columns do not have the name of the custom fields you created. The columns are labeled CUSTFLD1, CUSTFLD2, and so on. Open QuickBooks, and then open the custom field list in QuickBooks to see the names of the custom fields you created. The top custom field is CUSTFLD1, the next is CUSTFLD2, etc. Write down the names of the custom fields so you know the type of data you have to enter as you update the list.

- In the Item List, open any item, and click the Custom Fields button to see the custom fields.
- In a Names list, open any entry in the list and move to the Additional Info tab to see the custom fields.

When you enter data into custom fields, you must be consistent, or else it will be difficult to create reports on the contents of the fields. For example, if you have a custom field in your Customer & Jobs list named Backorder (to indicate which customers will accept backorders), devise a protocol for the data. For customers that do not accept backorders, if you use the text NoBO, don't also enter text No BO (note the space), or just No.

Saving the Import File

It's better to use the Save As command in Excel to save the file with a new name in order to retain the original exported data (in case you have to repair a mistake you made). You also might want to add a dash and a number to the original filename (such as custlist-2 if the original exported file was named custlist).

Save the file as a Text (Tab Delimited) file with the extension IIF. Excel issues warnings about text files not retaining formatting, etc. Just ignore the warnings. Then close Excel.

Importing Updated Data into QuickBooks

Before you import data in batches with an import file, back up the company file. If anything goes amiss, you can restore the backup and continue to work in the file. Then examine your import file to find any errors, and try again (backing up the file again first, if you've worked in the file).

To import the file, choose File | Utilities | Import | IIF files. Select the file you created and click Open. QuickBooks automatically imports the data. Open the list you tweaked and make sure everything is as you expected.

Index